FINE GAEL 1923 - 1987

A GENERAL HISTORY
WITH BIOGRAPHICAL SKETCHES
OF LEADING MEMBERS

BRIAN MAYE

BLACKWATER PRESS

Printed in Ireland at the press of the publishers 1993

© Blackwater Press 1993
Broomhill Business Park,
Broomhill Road,
Tallaght,
Dublin 24

ISBN: 0 86121 510 9

Editor
Anna O'Donovan

Contents

FOR MY WIFE, ANN

Acknowledgements

My late father, Pat Maye, had an abiding interest in history and politics and it was this which first directed my own attention to these subjects. My mother, Mary, greatly facilitated my growing concern with them in both secondary school and university. To them both I am deeply grateful.

It was my father-in-law, Conn Sheehan, who first drew my attention to the enormous contribution of Arthur Griffith to the creation of an independent Ireland. My research on Griffith led indirectly to this book and my father-in-law has helped me in ways too numerous to mention and for which I am eternally in his debt.

Almost three years ago, I approached Senator Maurice Manning with a proposal to do work on a related subject, and it is in consequence of his suggestion that this general study has emerged. He is currently researching and writing the life-story of James Dillon and kindly contributed the biographical sketch of Dillon contained in this book. For this and the many other ways in which he has aided me I am most grateful.

I am most appreciative of the assistance Mr Liam Cosgrave has afforded me. I thank Dr Garret FitzGerald and Mr John Bruton for contributing the Foreword and Afterword.

The staffs of the National Library, the University College Dublin Library and the various Dublin Corporation Libraries were at all times patient, courteous and helpful.

A special word of thanks goes to Angela Edghill, Fine Gael Administrator in the Oireachtas, who gave up so much of her working and leisure time to the painstaking process of drafting and redrafting the book.

Finally, this work would not have been possible without my wife, Ann. She has endured domestic disruption, not only for the three odd years this book has taken, but for the previous four years spent working on Griffith. No-one knows better than she the oscillating moods of euphoria (infrequent) and despair (far too regular) that have accompanied this process. I thank her for her limitless patience and unwavering support, and to her I dedicate the fruit of my labours.

I am responsible for any errors the book contains.

i

Preface

From the outset I have sought to present an independent and objective study of one of Ireland's major political parties. I have received every cooperation from many people in Fine Gael but at no time has any effort been made to influence my presentation or interpretation of events. I am grateful for the help and equally grateful for the respect accorded my independence.

For my material, I have relied largely on secondary sources, essentially the works of historians, political scientists, journalists, biographers and autobiographers. I much regret that I had neither the time nor the means to scrutinise all the relevant primary sources, which would have enabled me to write a comprehensive history of the party, an ambition devoutly to be realised.

While I hope that all adherents and erstwhile supporters of the party will read this book, I also hope that the readership will extend widely among all others who have an interest in the development of Ireland since independence. After all, the foundations of the state were established by the patriarchs of Fine Gael, operating from a bedrock of integrity, which continues to be the lodestar of a political organisation that has been - and is - an intrinsic part of independent Ireland.

Recently, there has been a profusion of baseless and sometimes malignant media forecasts of Fine Gael's impending demise. As this book notes, such gloomy predictions are not novel. The party, notwithstanding its lengthy record of valuable service to the Irish state, has on occasions been mocked with dismal estimates of its popularity, but has invariably confounded its Cassandras with a capacity for spectacular reinvigoration. At the very least, I trust that my current account of it affords reason for being confident that Fine Gael is destined to endure.

Brian Maye

Foreword

It is 28 years since I first joined Fine Gael - and 27 since I attended my first meeting - a commentary on the frequency of meetings in those days! I remember the earliest meetings I attended were of the students' branch in Dublin. They had to be held in hotels in the city centre, because party politics was banned from the UCD campus in Earlsfort Terrace.

Amongst the first meetings I was at were a series of historical retrospectives on the period 1916-66. We, students, were addressed by some of the great historic figures of the party - General Dick Mulcahy, John A. Costello, Paddy McGilligan, James Dillon, General Seán McEoin, Dan Morrissey and Professor Michael Hayes. I remember, too, the first ard-fheis I attended - 1966 - which was, I believe, Liam Cosgrave's first as President of Fine Gael.

There has been a huge change in the psychology of the party in the period since then. In 1966, Fine Gael seemed to me to have acquired the psychology of a permanent minority, destined for opposition like the Nationalist Party in the old Stormont. One had the sense that no matter how hard one tried, the legendary Fianna Fáil machine would pull some rabbit out of the hat at the last moment. Party speeches seemed to be constantly littered with references to successes that then seemed very remote to the ears of a twenty year old - the Shannon Scheme, the founding of the Gárda Síochána, the founding of the IDA. There was a pervasive sense of patronage in the country, nourished by protectionist economic policies. To get a licence you had to be a government supporter, and one party had by then been in uninterrupted power for ten years.

All this dramatically changed in 1966, with the first presidential campaign of Tom O'Higgins; he came within just 10,000 votes of winning. Suddenly, the government did not seem invincible any more. Fine Gael entered a turbulent period, with a vigorous, and sometimes noisy, debate over policy questions and philosophic direction - a debate culminating in the ard-fheis of 1968. Suddenly, Fine Gael seemed to matter. The direction it took was important. Because the party again had the sense that power was within its grasp. Reading through Brian Maye's book, I am struck by the fact that this renewal in 1966-68, was actually no new experience in the party's history.

The same pessimism I experienced as a new recruit after the 1965 general election was also felt by the party after the 1938 general election, in the late forties, and was again to be felt after 1977. Even the historic victory of 1981 was preceded by a by-election in Donegal in which the party was forced into third place. But Fine Gael has a unique ability to put that pessimism aside, and start again. I believe Fine Gael has this resilience because it has certain central values - which transcend and outline old-fashioned concepts like 'Left' and 'Right'.

Firstly, Fine Gael's philosophy centres on the dignity of each person - the idea that every person counts. In the 1920s, the Cumann na nGaedheal government established the Civil Service and Local Appointments Commissions to ensure that each applicant has an equal chance of appointment to public office. Secondly, it is a philosophy that opens Ireland outwards towards the wider world of Europe. In the 1930s the party, like parties of Christian Democratic inspiration elsewhere in Europe, drew explicitly on Papal encyclicals which sought to affirm the dignity of the individual producer, in free association with others, and opposed itself to the abstract rationalist doctrines of either the unfettered free market or of socialism.

This sense of the importance of giving individuals the chance to make their own decisions about their own future was summed up pithily in the slogan Cumann na nGaedheal used in 1933, to differentiate itself from Fianna Fáil: *Markets instead of Bounties, Work instead of Dole.*

I have no doubt that the most important political contribution to social thought in Ireland, for many years, was made by Fine Gael in its document *Towards a Just Society*, issued just before the general election of 1965.

This document was much more than a policy document advocating greater social justice, and favouring social spending. It set out certain basic philosophic principles, reconciling liberty and justice, in a way that remains entirely relevant to the Ireland of the 1990s. It said: *Freedom is much more than the absence of tyranny - it only becomes real when economic and social conditions permit the full development of the human personality.*

It went on: *Government action along the lines we suggest, far from curtailing personal freedom, will help extend it and make it meaningful for all our people.*

The *Just Society* was not a charter for meddlesome state intervention in every aspect of life - regulating and persuading, on every issue, in the manner of discredited socialism. In contrast, it emphasised the point that: *We accept the belief that individual human beings are the foundation, the cause and the end of every social institution, and the State has been created for man and not man for the State.* It stressed the principle of subsidiarity, saying that it was wrong for a higher association to arrogate to itself functions which can be performed efficiently by lower 'societies'.

The *Just Society* document stressed, in this context, that the state must depend, for the production of the great bulk of the wealth of the community, on the efforts of individual producers in the private sector.

It was on the basis of this thinking, that Fine Gael went on to advocate the idea of social planning - that population projections should be used to plan proper provision of schools, hospitals and infrastructure. Ireland's first ever comprehensive policy on mental handicap was put forward, and the party gave a commitment (yet to be fulfilled) to regional authorities, which would bring political power closer to the people. I believe that Fine Gael's advocacy of social justice and social investment in the *Just Society* document, led directly to the introduction of free secondary education two years later.

Apart from this commitment to enhancing the potential of each individual, the other recurrent theme in Fine Gael is the opening up of Ireland to the wider world. In this, Fine Gael carries forward the tradition of constitutional nationalism going back through Redmond and Butt to Daniel O'Connell. Daniel O'Connell always saw Irish nationhood, not as an anti-British phenomenon, but as a case of a distinct people taking up its own separate responsibilities in the wider world. The Treaty of 1921 itself was an expression of this wish to work in harmony with our neighbours rather than against them.

Fine Gael and its predecessors opposed the introduction of protective tariffs - during the first twenty years of the state, maintaining that Ireland should remain open, economically as well as politically, to outside influences. It opposed de Valera's economic war of the 1930s, because it dug a deep financial trench between the two parts of Ireland and between Ireland and Britain. In the 1950s, Fine Gael led the way in promoting the liberalisation of the Irish economy, seeking the repeal of the Control of Manufactures Act that inhibited foreign investment, introducing export tax relief, and setting up CTT - the Irish Export Board.

The party was the first to advocate Irish membership of the European Community - something that was especially stressed by James Dillon in his first Presidential address to the ard-fheis in 1960. Dillon saw Europe as the wider stage, on which Ireland could gradually reduce its overdependence on Britain, but without noisy confrontations of the kind beloved of his political opponents.

Fine Gael did not look at international institutions from the sole perspective of what these institutions could do to serve Irish interests alone. It sought to improve the institutions themselves for the benefit of all. This wider view differentiates the attitudes of Fine Gael and Fianna Fáil to the European Community, even to this present day.

Kevin O'Higgins and Paddy McGilligan were responsible for transforming the British Commonwealth, in the negotiations that led to the Statute of Westminster of 1931, from a body that subordinated all the members' interests to those of Britain, into a confederation of equals. Liam Cosgrave led Ireland into the United Nations in 1956, and, as Ireland's first EC President, he was responsible for direct elections to the European Parliament. This openness to wider concerns, is the reason why it was a government led by Garret FitzGerald which came closest, in 1986, to the UN target of 0.7% of GNP in aid to the Third World.

Just as Fine Gael was realistic in seeing the benefit of cooperation with other states, be they in the Commonwealth or the European Community, it was also realistic in its attitude to Northern Ireland.

In an article published in 1934, one year after the amalgamation of Cumann na nGaedheal and the Centre Party to form Fine Gael, the party said: 'There is only one method of bringing about unity; that is by producing a situation in which the people of the North will *choose* to join us' (my emphasis). This principle of unity by consent has been an enduring Fine Gael principle, one for which it has occasionally been prepared to pay a high political price.

For instance, the advocacy by Eoin O'Duffy of militant tactics on Northern Ireland contributed to his removal from the party leaderhsip, because it was inconsistent with the principle of 'consent'. It is no accident of history therefore that all the major initiatives to break the logjam in Northern Ireland have been undertaken when Fine Gael was in government - Sunningdale in 1973, and the Anglo-Irish Agreement in 1985.

Fine Gael is now undergoing a major process of renewal - in its organisation and in its presentation of policy in the Dáil, the European Parliament and at local authority level. We intend to use the most sophisticated methods, and the most modern policy ideas, to give expression to the enduring values of our party.

John Bruton, TD, Leader of Fine Gael. October, 1993

Chapter 1

Cumann na nGaedheal 1923 - 32

(i) Foundation

Fine Gael's parent party, Cumann na nGaedheal, was formally established on 27 April 1923 and evolved from the pro-Treaty section of Sinn Féin. The Articles of Agreement for an Anglo-Irish Treaty were negotiated with Britain on behalf of Sinn Féin mainly by Arthur Griffith and Michael Collins between 11 October and 6 December 1921. The 'Treaty', as the Agreement soon came to be called, deeply divided Sinn Féin and led to a bitter Dáil debate throughout December 1921 and early January 1922. Although a majority of TDs supported it, opposition to the measure continued both inside and outside the Dáil, culminating in the tragic Civil War which lasted from June 1922 to May 1923. This conflict claimed the lives of Griffith, the foremost philosopher of the Irish independence movement, and Collins, arguably its greatest activist.

The pro-Treaty group in the Dáil took responsibility for the formal transfer of power from the British authorities in mid-January 1922 and set about constructing the machinery of a native Irish government. In the general election of June 1922, the people voted by a majority of more than three to one in favour of the Treaty. Clearly, there was little opportunity for much foundation-laying while armed opposition to majority rule existed, and almost all pro-Treatyite efforts went into pursuing the Civil War to a successful conclusion.

On 7 December 1922, a year after the signing of the Treaty, about a hundred of its supporters, 38 of whom were TDs, attended a private meeting at which it was decided to set up a countrywide political organisation to be called Cumann na nGaedheal (the name was taken from that of the first nationalist organisation established by Griffith in 1900). A committee of 25 was appointed to prepare for the public launching of the new party. Around the middle of February 1923, possible supporters were written to and asked to form branches in their own areas. In early April, public meetings were held in Cavan, Kilkenny and Tuam, and at the end of the month the formal inauguration of the party occurred at a day-long gathering in Dublin's Mansion House. During the morning of the day of initiation, the delegates agreed to a programme and constitution and, in the evening, leading figures made speeches which were enthusiastically received.

Eoin MacNeill, founder-member of the Gaelic League, first president of the Irish Volunteers and Professor of Early and Medieval Irish History at University College, Dublin, told the party's first convention that for a government to operate, 'the age-old system of political organisation without definite policy or class interest' was necessary. In his inaugural address, William T. Cosgrave, who became leader of the pro-Treatyites following the deaths of Griffith and Collins in August 1922, and who was unanimously chosen as leader of the new party, stressed that an important task for the new organisation was to reconcile the many differences in the community:

> Cumann na nGaedheal ought to attract to itself the best elements of the nation and it ought to bring home to everyone the vital need for a sound national organisation, knowing neither creed nor class, but working for the best interests of the whole of the people and the whole of the nation.

Although Cumann na nGaedheal was a new party in 1923, its roots went back much further into Irish political history. Perhaps its most important begetter was Arthur Griffith and the non-violent Sinn Féin organisation, which he created to propound a philosophy for an independent, self-reliant Ireland. Many of the party's founding members had taken an active part in the Easter Rising of 1916. More immediately, Cumann na nGaedheal was closely related to the independence struggle of 1919-21, in which so many of its members acquired their first taste of politics, both peaceful and violent. The apprenticeship which several of its leaders served in the first Dáil was to benefit them in meeting the ministerial responsibilities they were soon to assume. The party, and its successor, Fine Gael, were to embrace elements from other Irish political traditions in the years to come, including the Irish Parliamentary Party of Parnell, Redmond and Dillon, the Centre Party and farming groups, and a certain number of ex-Unionists, but at its inauguration it was in essence pro-Treaty Sinn Féin, and perhaps most of all the party of Arthur Griffith and Michael Collins. It was set up to give permanence to the achievements of those men, and it saw itself always as the inheritor of their values and aspirations.

(ii) Cumann na nGaedheal in power

Cumann na nGaedheal's first electoral test came in the general election of August 1923. Its percentage of the vote (39%) was slightly higher than that secured by the pro-Treaty candidates in June 1922, and it won 63 seats, five more than in June 1922. It might have expected to do better - after all, the party was in government - but one likely reason why it did not was that an economic depression became widespread in 1923, farmers being especially badly hit as bad weather added to the blow of falling prices for their produce. The party performed particularly well in Dublin, however, with Kevin O'Higgins and Richard Mulcahy getting more than 20,000 first preferences each. In fact, Mulcahy's 22,005 is still the highest number of first-preference votes won by a candidate in a general election in Ireland.

Under the terms of the 1922 Free State Constitution, the government was known as the Executive Council and the leader of the government had the title of President of the Executive Council. William T. Cosgrave occupied this post and the other members of his cabinet were: Kevin O'Higgins, Vice-President of the Executive Council and Minister for Home Affairs (later to become Justice); Ernest Blythe, Minister for Finance; Richard Mulcahy, Minister for Defence; Desmond FitzGerald, Minister for External Affairs; Eoin MacNeill, Minister for Education; Joseph McGrath, Minister for Industry and Commerce; J.J. Walsh, Minister for Posts and Telegraphs; Patrick Hogan, Minister for Lands and Agriculture; Fionán Lynch, Minister for Fisheries; J.A. Burke, Minister for Local Government and Public Health. On the shoulders of this young team fell the onerous task of laying the foundations of the newly independent state. Even their harshest critics agree that their achievements were remarkable.

The earliest measures of the new government were mainly administrative, understandably enough, and were concerned with the civil service, the police, the law courts and local government. The Ministers and Secretaries Act 1924 established the structure of the government and the civil service. Eleven ministerial departments were set up under it and have survived, largely intact, to the present. The Civil Service Commission, the function of which was to oversee public appointments, has been described as one of the finest achievements in the history of the state: 'Given the scope for corruption permitted by the feeble sense of public morality, the imposition of a high degree of integrity in appointments to the central administration verged on the miraculous.'[1]

The same high standards were carried over into local government, the structures of which were regularised under the Local Government Act 1925. In view of the widespread corruption governing the appointments made by local bodies around the country, the Local Appointments Commission, set up by the Cosgrave government, was, according to one authority, 'something of a wonder in Irish political culture. . . .The idea that assessor boards might evaluate candidates on their professional merits, rather than on their foresight in being born with the right connections, or at least in cultivating the right connections, imposed intolerable strains on many an imagination.'[2]

In fact, integrity proved to be the hallmark of Cumann na nGaedheal in power. This was seen particularly in its attitude towards the use of patronage. An American political scientist, who visited Ireland in 1930 and who was one of the earliest students of post-independence Irish politics, observed that Cumann na nGaedheal in government indulged in little patronage, passing a law to this effect in 1924. Furthermore, he remarked that 'even opponents of Cumann na nGaedheal say that those who supported the party for private gain were filled with hopes rather than rewards'.[3] In 1932 W.T. Cosgrave extracted a promise from Eamon de Valera in the Dáil that ministers would hold no directorships or other remunerative posts while being part of his government - a practice established on Cosgrave's personal initiative in 1925.[4]

In the aftermath of the Civil War, the restoration of law and order was clearly a priority with the government. The decision by Kevin O'Higgins to replace the Royal Irish Constabulary with the unarmed Gárda Síochána was a courageous one in the circumstances of the time, but one that was to be vindicated totally as the new force won an acceptance it has never since forfeited. General Eoin O'Duffy, its first commissioner, supervised the installation of the Gárda Síochána all over the country, and it played a crucial role in establishing normality and stability.

The legal system was also reformed by the new government, under the guidance of the Attorney General, Hugh Kennedy, who possessed an alert and broad ranging intellect. A Judiciary Committee was set up in 1923 and the Courts of Justice Act of the following year restructured the courts system. The introduction of district and circuit courts, it has been remarked, 'went far to achieve the main object of government policy, which was by decentralising the administration of justice, to give the citizens quicker and less costly access to the law'.[5] In keeping with the general tenor of his government, 'Cosgrave would show continuing political courage in replacing the bulk of the judges, who retired under the Treaty, by successors appointed as far as possible on legal merit', it has been observed.[6]

As well as reforming the administration of education, the government took some steps in the direction of equality of educational opportunity. The Local Government Act allowed local authorities to levy a rate to finance secondary school scholarships. The Vocational Education Act 1930 gave some chance for poorer children to acquire technically oriented further education, but the era of 'free' second-level and subsidised third-level education was still far away.

(iii) Crises
The daunting challenge the Cumann na nGaedheal government

faced in setting up the institutions of an independent democratic state was further complicated by three crises which occurred during its first four years in office and which posed major problems: the so-called 'army mutiny', the Boundary Commission, and the murder of Kevin O'Higgins.

As a result of the Civil War, the army had swollen to way beyond the size permitted under the terms of the Treaty, and a process of reorganisation and demobilisation was set in train by the Minister for Defence, Richard Mulcahy. The internal details of the 1924 army crisis are not central to the history of Cumann na nGaedheal and have already been analysed elsewhere.[7] What is relevant here is the repercussions on the cabinet and party.

Although it was pro-Treaty, the party consisted of a wide spectrum of views. The military crisis has been seen as a power struggle between different groups within the party: an IRB faction whose main cabinet champion was Mulcahy, and an 'old IRA' faction whose main government spokesman was Joseph McGrath. Kevin O'Higgins dealt speedily with the two groups, branding their rivalry contemptuously as 'a faction fight between two letters of the alphabet'. O'Higgins's action established complete government control over the army and the two ministers resigned in March 1924. McGrath left Cumann na nGaedheal with eight other Dáil deputies, and they called themselves the National Party. They resigned from the Dáil at the end of October 1924, but only one sought re-election in the subsequent by-elections and he was unsuccessful. Patrick McGilligan succeeded McGrath as Minister for Industry and Commerce. Cosgrave, who had never relinquished control even when he was ill, himself acted as Minister for Defence for eight months before appointing Patrick Hughes; he succeeded in restoring calm to the situation during that time. Mulcahy was reinstated in cabinet as Minister for Local Government and Public Health after the June 1927 election.

The history of the Boundary Commission, which met in 1925, is, again, not germane to a history of Cumann na nGaedheal, but its consequences for both party and government are. Its outcome was a major disappointment for both the people and the administration of the Free State in that their expectation that large nationalist areas of Northern Ireland would be handed over to the Dublin jurisdiction was not realised. Perhaps the terms of reference of the Commission precluded this eventuality from the start. Certainly the fact that the statelet of Northern Ireland had been in existence for nearly five years by that time and the fact that the British-appointed chairman of the Commission was a lawyer with a deep, instinctive respect for existing institutions, made the task of Eoin MacNeill, the Free State representative on the Commission, a very difficult one. He has been criticised for not keeping his colleagues informed of the proceedings, but in his defence it must be stated that, man of principle and honour that he was, he felt himself debarred from doing so by the Commission's terms of reference, and in this he was in stark contrast to his Unionist counterpart.

In addition to losing MacNeill from the cabinet (he resigned in November 1925) Cumann na nGaedheal lost two TDs who resigned from the party and reconstituted themselves as Clann Éireann. They contested the 1927 general election under this banner, but secured a paltry vote. The army and the Boundary Commission crises showed the dangers inherent in Cosgrave's attempt to forge a broadly based party. The government's reaction to the Boundary Commission debacle was to face up squarely to the reality of partition and to seek to try to bring it to an end by developing a better understanding between the two parts of the island. W. T. Cosgrave, in particular, referred to the impossibility of forcing a million Protestants into a united Ireland against their will and held that the best approach for the Free State was to create within itself conditions of stability and prosperity which would appeal to the Unionists. It is impossible to assess the electoral damage done to Cumann na nGaedheal by the Boundary Commission; there must have been some, but it was probably not very much. It did allow de Valera to rationalise his return to constitutional politics and gave him the chance to try retrospectively to justify his stance on the Treaty as a protest against partition.

Probably the greatest blow Cumann na nGaedheal suffered,

the consequences of which could not be determined, except to contend that they were probably unfathomably deep, was the tragic loss of Kevin O'Higgins, murdered on his way to church by the IRA on 10 July 1927. His death was clear evidence that violence was an ever-present threat in the early years of the Free State, and that its public representatives performed their onerous duties in the shadow of the gun. The Electoral Amendment Act, which the government passed in response to the assassination of O'Higgins, compelled a Dáil candidate, upon nomination, to declare that he or she would take the oath prescribed by the Constitution and thereby assume his or her seat in the Dáil if elected. This measure has drawn extensive comment from historians and political scientists.

Even before the June 1922 election, where a clear majority of the people voted to accept the Treaty, Griffith had argued that the 'fight now being forced upon us. . . transcends the issue of "Treaty or no Treaty". It is the issue of whether the people have a right or have no right, to decide on the issues which affect them and the country.' Similarly, Kevin O'Higgins contended that

> if civil war occurs in Ireland it will not be for the Treaty. It will not be for the Free State versus anything else. It will be for a vital, fundamental, democratic principle - for the right of the people of Ireland to decide any issue, great or small, that arises in the politics of this country.

From this distance it is easy to forget or to be unaware of the uncertainty of democracy in the early years of the state. Soon after the Civil War, the Cumann na nGaedheal government began the long and arduous journey back to constitutionalism, despite the unfavourable circumstances of the time - a growing European economic depression, a bad harvest, wage-cuts, reductions in the public service and unrest in the army. Prisoners were released in 1924 and the following year all public servants and bodies were required to swear an oath of allegiance to the Free State. The opposition was being forced onto a democratic and pacific path.[8]

The government's decision, in the wake of the murder of Kevin O'Higgins, to force Fianna Fáil to take its seats in the Dáil if it wished to continue to contest elections, was a crucial event in the political history of the state. By deciding to enter the Dáil, 'Fianna Fáil signalled its rather belated public acceptance of constitutional politics', it has been remarked.[9] Historians are agreed that Cosgrave and his colleagues must have foreseen that one of the consequences of the Electoral Amendment Act would be to jeopardise Cumann na nGaedheal's supremacy and that the measure clearly had not been passed with a view to party advantage. The result of this statesmanship was the strengthening of parliamentary democracy and the emergence of a stable two-party system.

(iv) Economic, social and cultural policies

Cumann na nGaedheal's economic policy was never clearly defined and Cosgrave's cabinet contained both protectionists and free traders. But in so far as it had a coherent economic policy, it must be argued that it was one of *laissez-faire* rather than protection or active state intervention. When J.J. Walsh retired from political life in September 1927, the case was settled in favour of free trade. Indeed, it has been suggested that the reason Walsh left Cumann na nGaedheal was because of its commitment to free trade.[10] It was not until the end of 1931 that the government seemed to be rethinking its stand on the issue. The attitude of party members to economic policy is impossible to define. When Cumann na nGaedheal was set up, the issue was discussed. An amendment to the draft programme to be put to the convention at which the party was to be launched in late April 1923 proposed imposing tariffs on goods which could be manufactured in Ireland. Although this amendment was not accepted at the convention, Richard Mulcahy's impression was that the mood of the meeting favoured protection.[11]

Arthur Griffith was a strong advocate of protection and of the idea of developing Irish industries behind a wall of tariffs. It remains one of the curiosities of Cumann na nGaedheal's history that his political heirs did not follow his economic testament. Some tariffs were applied and Ernest Blythe, Minister for Finance, declared that the government was not committed rigidly to either free trade or protection. A Tariff Commission was set up in 1926, which, it has been remarked, 'discharged its duties, carefully, meticulously and - according to ardent protectionists - appallingly slowly'.[12] The large and well-established industries - brewing and distilling - did not want protection, and agricultural products were completely exempt from tariffs. In typically uncompromising manner, Kevin O'Higgins declared, countering the charge that the government was betraying a vital aspect of Griffith's legacy: 'The propagandist writings of any one man cannot be accepted simply as revealed truth, requiring no further investigations, something that must be accepted forever as beyond question, beyond doubt, beyond the need of examination.'

The first government was convinced that agriculture was the backbone of the Irish economy, and it is important to recall that at the time more than half the people worked in agriculture, with nearly two-thirds of the population living in the countryside. The government believed that if agriculture could be made to thrive, the benefits would filter through to other sections of the populace. With a small home market, the vital trade was in exports to Britain, which did not impose tariffs in any form, but in the British market the Irish farmer had to compete with suppliers of agricultural produce from all over the world. Accordingly, the government passed a series of Acts, aimed at ensuring the excellence of the Irish goods. These measures, considered to be totalitarian by some at the time, represented the first instance in Ireland of state intervention in such a way.

In order for farmers to produce as cheaply as possible, the cost of raw material had to be kept low. It was seen as cheaper to import maize or wheat than to sacrifice land for growing them at home. Correspondingly, tariffs on industrial products could be exacted only with great care, so that farmers would not have to pay more than necessary. Rates and taxes, too, had to be kept as low as possible in accord with the same strategy. Taxes could be kept low - and they were very low at the end of the 1920s - only by tightly controlling public expenditure, which in practice meant little social expenditure. This approach was unwelcome to many sections of society. However, it could be viewed as having been highly successful: employment in industry grew from 103,000 in 1926 to

111,000 in 1931; Irish agricultural produce regained its place on the British market; the export figure for 1929 was £47 million which was not approached again until 1948, and the volume of exports in 1929 was not surpassed until as late as 1960. Finally, the value of imports in 1929 was 77% of the value of exports - a percentage never since attained except during World War II, when few imports were available anyway.[13]

Circumstances changed immensely with the Great Depression at the end of the 1920s. For the first time since the 1850s, Britain introduced a general tariff. There was a worldwide revulsion against the old economic orthodoxies that had been so acceptable in the 1920s. The new mood favoured extensive protection and when Britain, whose 19th-century prosperity was based on free trade, turned to it, things had come to a serious pass. 'The full protectionist case advanced slowly as long as world prosperity lasted. It leaped ahead with the spread of the Great Depression', it has been observed. There is little point in asking which was the better policy: free trade or protection. Differing circumstances made comparison well nigh impossible. Some had no doubt that the policies pursued in the 1920s were those best suited to the circumstances of the time and that, had Patrick Hogan and his colleagues been returned to power in 1932, they would inevitably have revised these policies to some extent.[14]

On the other hand, it has been argued that there was a good case for industrial protection which dogmatic free traders succeeded in confusing at the time. O'Higgins's counter to the accusation that Cumann na nGaedheal abandoned Griffith's economic policy has been seen 'as illusory as it was courageous', and it has been maintained that no detailed analysis of the situation was carried out by the government. While Griffith's set of unproven assumptions made at least some attempt to wrestle with the evidence of economic history, this argument goes, the government substituted for them another set of unproven assumptions based on no historical evidence at all. The Fiscal Inquiry Committee of 1923 seemed to be a major investigation of industrial policy, but may have been arranged in such a way as to secure a safe majority for dogmatic free traders and may have provided little of the additional investigation O'Higgins proclaimed necessary. This was not to suggest that protection would necessarily have been better for the country at the time; simply that the case for it was never fully considered. Blythe, introducing some few 'experimental' tariffs in 1924, asserted that he was no dogmatic free trader, but his actions seemed to belie his words. In fact, experimental tariffs were relatively successful.[15]

The Cumann na nGaedheal government's social policy has been both strongly condemned and stoutly defended. Its harshest critic considered Blythe to have held little instinctive sympathy for the idea of social expenditure, and went so far as to declare that Cosgrave's cabinet 'waged a coherent campaign against the weaker elements in the community'. The Poor Law legislation of 1923 was little better than the pre-1922 system; the recommendations of the Commission on the Relief of the Sick and Destitute Poor of 1927 were ignored and little was done about the serious housing problem, according to this view. Blythe's cuts in expenditure in his 1924 budget were regarded as an attack on the old and the blind, and Cosgrave was seen as institutionalising the neglect of labour by demoting the Department of Labour, set up by the first Dáil, to a mere section of the Department of Industry and Commerce.[16]

But it has been widely maintained that such criticisms are anachronistic, because large-scale government involvement in the planning and running of society was simply not a feature of 1920's thinking, nor indeed for decades afterwards. It has been shown how Department of Finance officials impressed on the new government the need for extreme financial stringency in the matter of state expenditure and how this was unanimously accepted by the ministers. Old-age pensions were an inordinate drain on government finances because of the disproportionately large number of elderly people in Ireland. So, in a programme of cut-backs, old-age pensions inevitably were affected.[17] Budgets throughout the 1920s were balanced with what has been well described as 'an almost penitential zeal'.[18]

It should be recalled that income tax was kept very low, that duties on tea and coffee were abolished, and the duty on sugar lowered. Cumann na nGaedheal has often been portrayed as the party of the business classes, but 'these important reductions in the costs of the poor man's comforts have also to be remembered', it has been observed.[19] Given the major task of restoration and reconstruction the government faced after the Civil War, it is understandable that it set about creating the conditions in which future economic developments could occur and this it achieved. According to one opinion:

> The rule of law had been upheld, the Free State's international standing as a creditor nation had been maintained, budgets had been scrupulously balanced and taxation held firmly in check, administration had been frugal but competent, and if the economic ideas of ministers and their advisers savoured more of Adam Smith than of J.M. Keynes, no-one could deny that within the limits this implied, their policies had been remarkably effective.[20]

In the last analysis, Cosgrave and his colleagues could have defended their record on the grounds that, in a period of unprecedented upheaval, they had ensured simply the survival of the country.

Another who believed that it is unhistorical to condemn the first government in today's terms, pointed out that the economic benefits of political independence were very small between 1921 and 1958, described how particularly unfavourable circumstances were at the time of independence, and averred that indeed little or no improvements occurred in the 1930s, 40s or 50s.[21]

It should not be concluded from this brief survey that there was no active government intervention at all in the 1920s because this was far from being the case. A major preoccupation of the new government was to conclude the process of land purchase begun by the Land Acts of the previous century. The 1923 Land Act (and its amended form in 1925) completed the transfer of the land from the landlords to the tenants and empowered the Land Commission to acquire untenanted land both inside and outside the 'Congested Districts' for the relief of distress in these areas of the south and west. As well as this measure, Patrick Hogan pushed through a vigorous series of others between 1924 and 1930, aimed at improving marketing and breeding, insisting on improved standards of cleanliness, packaging, marking and an honest description of the quality of the produce. However, the most radical innovation in agriculture was the decision to make loans available to farmers on reasonable terms and to this end the Agricultural Credit Corporation was set up by the government in 1927.

The first sugar company was established at Carlow by the Cosgrave government and it was easily the best and most efficient of the sugar factories, as time has proved, but the government's most spectacular achievement was the Shannon Scheme begun in 1925, and the establishment of the Electricity Supply Board (ESB) in 1927. This enabled the government to provide the basis for the future economic development of the state and to show, both at home and abroad, that Irish independence had a definite economic content. (Its social impact must not be forgotten either.) Patrick McGilligan played a crucial role here, relentlessly driving ahead with this enormously ambitious project, against the best advice of financial officials, economists and banks and, against all predictions, having it completed on time.

The Shannon Scheme has been described as 'a gigantic undertaking for an impoverished country'. In his 1931 play, *The Moon in the Yellow River*, Denis Johnston considered the significance of such an enterprise. One of the characters, the German engineer Tausch, pronounced:

> As Schiller tells us, Freedom cannot exist save when united with Might. And what Might can equal electrical power at one farthing a unit? . . .Soon you will be a happy nation of free men - free not by the magic of empty formulae or by the coats you wear, but by the inspiration of Power - Power - Power.[22]

However, even these adventurous undertakings were not altogether contrary to the prevailing economic orthodoxies. As has been pointed out, McGilligan said in the Dáil at the time of the setting up of the ESB that it was essential to make any such state venture 'as independent as possible of government'. Likewise in the case of the Agricultural Credit Corporation (ACC), also a creation of that formative year 1927, 'the state was intended to be a mere shareholder in an ordinary company, taking up the shares the public did not want and having the right to appoint a minority of directors'. Because the public did not invest in this and similar ventures, the state was forced to become the sole owner and controller.[23]

Nevertheless, the ESB and the ACC were signs of things to come: increasing state intervention into those aspects of the economy where private capital was either unwilling or unable to participate. In fact, in this important economic sphere of the state corporation, the Irish Free State was almost from the start among the advanced countries of the world. The ESB, the ACC, the Fiscal Inquiry Committee of 1923 and some of Hogan's agricultural policies have been regarded as foreshadowing 'Whitakerism'.[24]

The government's attempt to revive and restore the Irish language dominated its cultural policy in the 1920s. Michael Collins proclaimed in the Dáil in mid-1921 that the biggest task facing an independent Irish government would be to restore Irish, and political and national self-respect became identified with this goal. Cumann na nGaedheal subscribed fully to this view, because it counteracted de Valera's and the anti-Treatyites' pretence to be the only true nationalists, and also because two key ministers, Blythe and MacNeill, were zealots in the cause of the Irish language, and Mulcahy always could be relied on to support them. The Gaeltacht Commission of 1925, of which Mulcahy was the chairman, declared it to be 'the national duty' to uphold and foster Irish. Blythe played the central role in the revival attempt, partly because he was so convinced of the rightness of the cause and partly because of the control he had over the public purse in the low-spending 1920s. Basically, a three-fold strategy was pursued by the government involving the educational system, and favouring Gaeltacht areas and the speaking of Irish in the public service.

Perhaps only MacNeill, Blythe and Mulcahy would have approved of so draconian a programme, but the other members of the government acquiesced in it up to a point. There were a number of reasons why they and the general populace did so: the crusades of the Gaelic League since its foundation in 1893 convinced a generation of Irish people that their nationality was somehow bound up with the language; the first Dáil had clearly stated its commitment to rapid and intensive Gaelicisation and its decisions had become holy writ, especially after the split over the Treaty. Blythe's schemes have been stigmatised as 'wildly ambitious'. [25] The chief responsibility was placed on three groups: teachers, children and the inhabitants of the Gaeltacht.

All teachers graduating from training colleges were expected to have a knowledge of Irish; boarding schools were set up to prepare young people to become teachers, with an emphasis on Irish; school inspectors had to study Irish and no more would be appointed without a knowledge of the language; it was made a compulsory subject for the Intermediate and Leaving Certificate scholarships, and various inducements were offered to both schools and individuals to speak Irish more often. But the main focus of the effort was the primary schools, initially under the auspices of Professor Eoin MacNeill. He well understood that it would be inadvisable to depend on the schools alone to revive the language (MacNeill was reputed to have said 'you might as well be putting wooden legs on hens as trying to restore Irish through the school system') but, ironically, because he was so busy with other government affairs, he presided over the legislation which created that dependence. A change in social conditions was needed, especially in the Gaeltachtaí, and without this 'the schools alone could not perform a linguistic miracle', it has been observed.[26]

The Irish National Teachers' Organisation, under the influence of the Jesuit Professor of Education in University College Dublin, Father Corcoran, recommended that all singing in primary schools should be in Irish; that history and geography should be taught through Irish from 3rd class onwards; that one hour per day be spent on the direct learning of the language and that all teaching in the two infant classes be in Irish. Professor Corcoran believed that because the non-English immigrants into the United States could be taught English in first-level schools even though it was not the language of their homes, so Irish children from English-speaking homes could be taught all subjects in Irish in primary schools. 'The obvious point that European immigrant children in the United States were being introduced to the language of the wider community, whilst in Ireland children certainly were not, apparently did not weigh with him', remarked one authority. Nor did he take much cognisance of the emotional and mental stress that the children might endure since 'his dismal creed' of educational experience left little room for the idea of joy in learning.[27]

Although the conference appointed by the government in 1926 expressed reservations about the basic features of this endeavour, it remained the major educational innovation of the 1920s. Professor Michael Tierney, Professor of Greek at University College Dublin, and a TD who had served on the government's 1925 commission to study the Gaeltacht, warned in 1927:

> The task of reviving a language. . . .with no large neighbouring population which speaks even a distantly related dialect, and with one of the great world-languages to contend against, is one that has never been accomplished anywhere. . . .Still less has it proved possible to impose a language on a people as its ordinary speech by means of the schools alone.[28]

The reasons why the school-centred approach failed are not germane to a history of Cumann na nGaedheal and have been dealt with elsewhere,[29] but they may be summed up as follows: Irish essentially became a written subject for examinations; the element of compulsion won it few friends, and it was little used outside the schools.

The other prong of the government's approach suffered a similar fate. The Gaeltacht areas were to receive economic and technical aid; people from these parts of the country were to spearhead the educational drive and were to be given preferential treatment in the civil service, Gárda Síochána, army and local government. A network of secondary schools and colleges was planned for the Gaeltacht, and the professionals who serviced it were intended to be Irish speakers. However, the figures from the 1926 Census and from the Gaeltacht Commission's report showed a continuing decline in the numbers of Irish speakers in the wholly or partly Irish-speaking areas of the country. Parents whose first language was Irish were bringing up their children solely through the medium of English in regions from which emigration continued unrelentingly.

Another aspect of the Cumann na nGaedheal government policy which has received much - and not always balanced - attention has been its censorship measures. Many governments in the early 20th century felt that the accelerating growth in publications, especially cheap newspapers and magazines, was something they could not ignore. According to one authority on the subject, 'A Committee of Enquiry on Evil Literature, set up by the Free State Minister for Justice in 1926, which prepared the way for the eventual Bill, found it could seek guidance from the example of 11 countries and states where statutes relating to obscene publications were in force.' The League of Nations had in fact held an international convention in 1923 to suppress the dissemination of such publications. 'A responsible government in the 1920s in almost any country would have felt that there was nothing unusual about the enactment of a Bill to censor certain publications and to protect populations from pornography', was the judgement of the authority just quoted.[30]

The report of the Committee and the debates in the Dáil and Senate showed that the legislators tried to differentiate between mere pornography and works that might be of literary worth. Indeed, the legislation was aimed mainly not at literary productions but at numerous imported magazines and newspapers considered unsavoury and also at material which gave information on and advised about birth control. The public demand for legislation came mainly from Irish vigilance societies rather than from members of political parties, from the Catholic Truth Society and from editors associated with the Irish-Ireland movement like D.P. Moran of *The Leader* and J.J. Kelly of the *Catholic Bulletin*.

When the Bill appeared, it was much less draconian than had

18

been anticipated. The Minister for Justice, James Fitzgerald-Kenny, was willing to amend it at the time of its presentation to the Dáil and it did not include the proposal of the Committee on Evil Literature that there should be recognised groups in the country, which would have responsibility for drawing the Censorship Board's attention to doubtful publications. The *Irish Statesman* of George William Russell (AE), which had carried out a long campaign against the Bill, expressed relief that it was better than expected, and the Irish correspondent of *The Round Table* probably articulated the general satisfaction of all those who were worried about the possible implications of the proposed enactment, when he opined that 'the debates on this measure in the Dáil have been more courageous than was to be expected.'

This piece of legislation, like the Censorship of Films Act 1923 and the Intoxicating Liquor Acts of 1924 and 1927, was undertaken following the appointment of a committee or the holding of a conference on or at which all the interests concerned were represented. In one view, the Censorship of Publications Act 1929 'appears to have hit fairly accurately the centre of gravity of Irish opinion at the time, being criticised by some for going too far, and by others for not going far enough.' Eamon de Valera promised to facilitate the Bill's passage and while some Fianna Fáil TDs were critical, it received more criticism from the government's own backbenchers.[31]

Looking back 20 years later, the writer and critic Arland Ussher, who had fought against the legislation in the 1920s, stated:

> We were wrong and over-impatient - unjust, also, to the men who were rebuilding amid the ruins. . . .We concentrated our indignation on their Acts for prohibiting divorce and for prohibiting the sale of 'evil literature' - measures which might have been expected from any Irish Catholic government, and which, considering the social atmosphere of Ireland, did little more than register prohibitions that in any case would have been effective in fact if not in form.[32]

19

(v) Foreign relations

During the Dáil debates on the Anglo-Irish Treaty, Griffith declared that the status it conferred on Ireland 'had no more finality than that we are the final generation on the face of the earth', and in his memorable stepping-stone argument, Collins avowed that the Treaty gave freedom, 'not the ultimate freedom that all nations aspire and develop to, but the freedom to achieve it.' Speaking during the same debate, Kevin O'Higgins expressed his belief that the countries within the Commonwealth were evolving towards equal status. This sentiment has been regarded as summing up the policy of the Free State towards the Commonwealth in the decade after the Treaty and O'Higgins himself has been seen as playing a leading role in this process.[33] Griffith, Collins and O'Higgins were all vindicated in their argument that the Treaty set no boundary to the onward march of the nation.

The Cosgrave government quickly set about seeking international acceptance as a full sovereign state. In 1923 the Free State became a member of the League of Nations and the following year appointed its own minister in Washington, something no other dominion had yet done. It sought to reshape the Commonwealth and bring it more into line with Irish interests and attitudes. The main theme of the 1926 Imperial Conference in London was status. Kevin O'Higgins was the Irish representative, as he had been at the 1923 Conference, and he was accompanied by Desmond FitzGerald and Patrick McGilligan. They worked closely with the Canadian and South African delegates, and the Balfour formula declared the dominions to be equal in status, autonomous, not subordinate in either domestic or external affairs, freely associated and united by a common allegiance to the Crown. Equality was declared to be the basis of British Commonwealth relations.

The first Irish ambassador to the United States was appointed in 1928 and in 1930 Ireland won a seat on the Council of the League of Nations. The Irish delegation again played a full role at the 1930 Imperial Conference and in the drafting of the Statute of Westminster which, in effect, acknowledged the right of the dominions to secede from the Commonwealth. McGilligan, the

Irish representative at the 1930 conference, declared in July 1931 that the Statute ended forever the system of empire 'which it took centuries to build'. It has been observed that the Statute of Westminster 'marked. . . .the climax of a decade of achievement in which Irishmen had taken an honourable share and for which, in a sense, Kevin O'Higgins might be said to have died.'[34]

This measure gave any dominion the power unilaterally to repeal British legislation which had been binding on its territory up to that time. So the Free State now could repudiate any clause in the Treaty it found unsatisfactory. Cumann na nGaedheal had sown the seeds of the crop de Valera was to harvest in the 1930s. It also laid the foundation for an independent foreign policy, which was neutral in approach and displayed the small states' concern for international order. But, as has been pointed out, international diplomatic success did not translate into domestic electoral gain. The ordinary people had little interest in such matters, while the government's desire to win ex-Unionist approval meant that it did not publicise its continuing dismantling of the ties with Britain.[35]

(vi) Elections and organisation

Cumann na nGaedheal emerged from the general election of August 1923 as the single biggest party, but was far short of an overall Dáil majority. However, the abstention of the anti-Treaty TDs meant that the party had a comfortable overall majority in the Dáil. In the June 1927 general election, however, the party lost 16 seats and 100,000 votes and was only three seats ahead of Fianna Fáil, but because the latter continued to abstain, W.T. Cosgrave again formed a government. The murder of Kevin O'Higgins was followed by a tough Public Safety Act and by the Electoral Amendment Act which forced Fianna Fáil into the Dáil. This removed Cumann na nGaedheal's Dáil majority and the government just survived a Labour-National League 'no confidence' motion in August. (The National League was a party founded in 1926 by Major William Redmond, son of the leader of the Irish Parliamentary Party from 1900 to 1918, which attracted support mainly from former adherents of that party and from ex-soldiers who had fought in the British army in World War I. It won eight seats in the June 1927 election.) Realising that there was little point in trying to survive in such circumstances, W.T. Cosgrave called an election for September 1927. As a result of this, Cumann na nGaedheal remained the single largest party with 62 seats and gained 135,000 votes on its June performance, but Fianna Fáil was only five seats and 40,000 votes behind. With the backing of the Farmers' Party and Independents, Cosgrave formed his final government. In fact, Cumann na nGaedheal gains in the September election (it increased its number of seats from 47 to 62) were made at the expense of potential allies, Farmers, Independents and Redmond's National League.

The 1927-32 government was an insecure administration with only a slender majority and evidence from by-election results confirmed that Fianna Fáil was making advances. Once in 1930, Cosgrave was defeated in the Dáil and resigned, but he resumed office when de Valera refused to form either a minority government or a coalition. This last Cumann na nGaedheal administration was one of consolidation and retrenchment, and popular support was lost during those years. Why was this the case?

Various reasons have been suggested. It has been supposed that the outcome of the Boundary Commission gave the government the image of being compliant towards Britain and must have cost it electoral endorsement. Its economic policy has been depicted as electorally unpopular. The security measures introduced by the government in response to the increase in IRA activity in the early 1930s were extremely stringent (military tribunals were given power to impose the death penalty) and proved very unpopular. Just before the 1932 general election, the Fianna Fáil newspaper, *The Irish Press*, was prosecuted by the government before the tribunal for seditious libel.

The global economic depression, which affected Ireland increasingly from 1930, was a misfortune for the Cosgrave government, but its response has been considered ineffectual. According to this view, the government showed no innovation, but clung desperately to the old approach of rigorously balancing the budget.[36] Teachers and civic guards' salaries were reduced in 1931 and an austere budget was introduced on the eve of the 1932 election.

The 'Red scare' tactics used by Cumann na nGaedheal against Fianna Fáil in the late 1920s and early 1930s did not benefit the party electorally. Its main rallying cries were law and order and the defence of religion, and its election programme of February 1932 effectively ignored the social and economic issues, in contrast to Fianna Fáil's which was largely concerned with them.

Cumann na nGaedheal, it has been maintained, was mainly responsible for its own electoral misfortune. It has been seen as making a strategic mistake by moving to the right, instead of consolidating the centre and especially trying to retain Labour support. Labour backed the Treaty in 1922, almost put Cumann na nGaedheal out of office in 1927, kept it in power in 1930 and finally put it out of office in 1932. It was unnecessary to consolidate the right, according to this view. The pact with the Farmers' Party before the September 1927 general election was not needed because, in a direct contest between Cumann na nGaedheal and Fianna Fáil, the large-farmer vote could have gone only to Cumann na nGaedheal.[37]

It is widely agreed that an inadequate organisation contributed to Cumann na nGaedheal's fall from power in 1932. The party began largely as a parliamentary party; the leadership structure existed before its foundation and the party developed around this national core of leaders. As a result, proper emphasis was never placed on the importance of local organisation. Because they were primarily concerned with winning the Civil War and building up an infrastructure for the new state, the leaders of the immature party paid little attention to party organisation. As one commentator has written: 'The party was in fact never much more than a parliamentary coalition of pro-Treaty deputies.'[38]

Cumann na nGaedheal built up whatever organisation it had by sending letters to influential people in various areas asking for financial assistance and support, often making use of existing social groups. So locally influential people and their social circles made up the party machine in towns and cities, while in the countryside, generally, there was no organisation. The extra-parliamentary origins and early years of Fianna Fáil were important because they convinced the leadership of that party of the need to maintain well-developed local structures, which made the party far superior in its organisation than its opponents. Cumann nGaedheal had constituency executives, a national executive and an annual policy - making convention, or ard-fheis, just like Fianna Fáil, but unlike its major rival, it was 'lamentably deficient in local associations and relied far too much on an elite in the large towns', it has been contended.[39]

Richard Mulcahy afterwards referred to a clique around the leadership, what he termed a 'Ballsbridge complex', which was against organising the party around the country because they viewed branches as inconvenient, annoying and wasteful of government energy, and in consequence, organisational affairs were neglected after 1924. The Irish correspondent of *The Round Table* had no doubt why Cumann na nGaedheal lost the 1932 and 1933 general elections:

> The reasons for Mr Cosgrave's defeat are obvious. His political organisation was far inferior to that of his opponents. The Fianna Fáil party had a network of effective branches all over the country. Whilst the Cosgrave government was in office they neglected their political machinery, and have not had the time to recondition it properly since they went into opposition.[40]

While Fianna Fáil realised the need of a strong organisation to win power, Cumann na nGaedheal felt no such need - it was, after all, in office - and it tended to lose touch with the electorate.

What were Cumann na nGaedheal's sources of electoral support? According to one view, it was regarded as a conservative party, because it restored law and order in a determined manner, protected property rights and pursued cautious economic and social policies. Although it had developed from the separatist Sinn Féin movement, it upheld co-operation with Britain in an active Commonwealth role. It was neither extreme nor exclusive in its nationalism and tried to attract the Protestant Unionist minority. It was acceptable to businessmen and farmers, especially big farmers, and it was strongest in the east and midlands and weakest in the south and west. *The Irish Independent, The Cork Examiner*, and later *The Irish Times* backed it. No doubt its pro-Treaty base transcended socio-economic divisions.[41]

Most commentators agree that the wealthier sections of society were sources of Cumann na nGaedheal backing, since these generally favoured the Treaty. Business people, medium-sized and large farmers, professionals and most of the clergy and hierarchy of all the churches voted for it.

Adherents of the old Home Rule Party and former Unionists also gave it their allegiance. Cosgrave was proud of his achievement in winning Unionist loyalty to the new state. Cumann na nGaedheal's method of organising - sending letters to local notabilities and enlisting the help of them and their friends - reinforced the nature of this support since it recruited the better-off in the community into the party.

Perhaps the hope Cosgrave expressed in 1923 that Cumann na nGaedheal would attract the best elements in society regardless of class or creed was realised more than is suspected and it was only at the end of the 1920s and the beginning of the 1930s that its following became more class-based. When minor party support collapsed between the two 1927 elections, Cumann na nGaedheal benefited in the richest and Fianna Fáil in the poorest areas.[42]

(vii) Achievements

The achievements of Cumann na nGaedheal in power were many and impressive. Among them were the restoration of law and order, the completion of land-purchase measures, improvements in agriculture, the careful management of the state's finances, the successful completion of the Shannon hydro-electric scheme, and the establishment of the Electricity Supply Board, the Agricultural Credit Corporation and the Carlow Sugar Factory.

It has been remarked that under the unobtrusive but firm leadership of W.T. Cosgrave, the state's administrative and financial systems were rebuilt out of the chaos left by the War of Independence and the Civil War, order was restored and the international status of the Irish Free State had been firmly established. 'When the moment of change came, though some were fearful for the future stability of the state, William T. Cosgrave made way, as a good parliamentarian and a good democrat', it has been averred.[43]

The measures enacted by the Cosgrave government 'laid the foundations for the firm and efficient government that rapidly became the hallmark of the Free State', according to one authority, who paid tribute to it as follows: 'By any standards this programme would have been a formidable achievement, but at a time when much of Ireland was still in the grip of the Civil War or its aftermath, it was an astonishing performance'.[44]

A stringent analyst of its performance agreed that the Cumann na nGaedheal record between 1923 and 1932 was 'a historic one'. Mulcahy, in his graveside oration for Michael Collins, revealed how fragile and uncertain his young survivors felt: 'We are all mariners on the deep, bound for a port still seen only through storm and spray, sailing on a sea full of dangers and hardships and bitter toil'. They 'steered the ship [of state] into quieter waters and navigated a safe subsequent course', according to this view.

This government of young men had responsibility thrust upon them before having the chance to mature or learn 'the arts of political manoeuvre'. They did not enjoy de Valera's ten-year apprenticeship which enabled him to broaden his political perspective. Looking back some 40 years later, both Seán Lemass and Gerry Boland admitted that Fianna Fáil was hardly ready for government in 1927 and this was what has rightly been termed 'a handsome, if oblique tribute to the calibre of the men who had proved themselves ready in even more trying circumstances'.[45]

Here is a list of these men, because they deserve to be remembered by future generations of their compatriots and only three of them - Mulcahy, McGilligan and Costello - had the opportunity to prove their mettle again in government: W. T.

26

Cosgrave, President of the Executive Council 1923-32 and Minister for Defence, March-November 1924; Kevin O'Higgins, Vice-President of the Executive Council and Minister for Justice, 1923-27; Ernest Blythe, Minister for Finance, 1923-32 and Minister for Posts and Telegraphs, 1927-32; Richard Mulcahy, Minister for Defence, 1923-24, and Minister for Local Government and Public Health, 1927-32; Patrick Hughes, Minister for Defence, 1924-27; Desmond FitzGerald, Minister for External Affairs, 1923-27 and Minister for Defence, 1927-32; Joseph McGrath, Minister for Industry and Commerce, 1923-24; Eoin MacNeill, Minister for Education, 1923-25; John Marcus O'Sullivan, Minister for Education, 1925-32; Patrick McGilligan, Minister for Industry and Commerce, 1924-32 and Minister for External Affairs, 1927-32; J. J. Walsh, Minister for Posts and Telegraphs, 1923-27; Patrick Hogan, Minister for Lands and Agriculture, 1923-27 and Minister for Agriculture 1927-32; Fionán Lynch, Minister for Fisheries, 1923-27 and Minister for Lands and Fisheries, 1927-32; J. A. Burke, Minister for Local Government and Public Health, 1923-27; James Fitzgerald-Kenny, Minister for Justice, 1927-32; Hugh Kennedy and J. A. Costello, Attorneys General.

It has been observed that it has never been easy to create successfully a democratic order because it depends on a number of complex circumstances such as the socio-economic condition of the country, but 'the values and beliefs of political elites may well be the crucial variable'. The following view from the same authority is given in full as a testimony to the dedicated democrats just listed:

> In Ireland, an extraordinary political elite established the infrastructure of a democratic state and successfully defended it in a civil war. For them the very establishment of Dáil Éireann as a popularly and freely elected parliament marked the triumph of the revolution. For several years thereafter they patiently tolerated a recalcitrant and unrepentant opposition which had to be coaxed (and finally pushed) back to constitutional politics, and then upon electoral defeat, they peacefully handed over power. This remarkable performance had little to do with Ireland's low

level of economic development or the authoritarian quality of Irish Catholicism. It sprang from the political elite's basic commitment to democratic values and institutions, a commitment it was prepared to translate into action.[46]

Chapter 2

Fine Gael and the Blueshirts 1932 - 37.

(i) Background to formation, February 1932 - August 1933

In the February 1932 general election, although Cumann na nGaedheal's share of the vote declined by only 3,000 on its September 1927 performance (down from 453,000 to 450,000), it suffered a reduction from 62 to 57 seats, whereas Fianna Fáil gained 155,000 votes and 15 seats. It seems that Cumann na nGaedheal managed to retain most of its established support and that Fianna Fáil gains were mainly afforded by people who had abstained from voting in 1927 and by erstwhile Labour and Farmer supporters. Before the subsequent Dáil met, the possibility of the army refusing to serve under its former enemies was debated in public and, on 26 February, *The Irish Press* referred to a rumour that two Cumann na nGaedheal Ministers and others would try to obstruct the transfer of power to Fianna Fáil. Cosgrave immediately rejected the charge as being 'grotesquely untrue', but it was afterwards repeated by a Fianna Fáil TD in the Dáil. It has been observed that, 'The coming of their Civil War enemies to power was a bitter pill for men like Cosgrave and Mulcahy, but for them there could be no question of interfering with the due process of parliamentary democracy'.[1] With the help of Labour's seven deputies, Fianna Fáil formed a government and for the first time since its foundation Cumann na nGaedheal was in opposition.

The new government so rapidly implemented an extensive list of policies and election promises that Cumann na nGaedheal at times feared that a new revolution was at hand. In the face of so radical and wide-ranging a programme, its role was that of an entrenched opposition, proposing nothing and attacking everything. It hoped that the new government would collapse through incompetence and when it did not, Cumann na nGaedheal seemed to lose all sense of direction, and its opposition throughout 1932 has been characterised as very negative.[2]

There is no doubt that the speed with which Fianna Fáil

fulfilled its election pledges and the type of policies it was pursuing made many in Cumann na nGaedheal uneasy and caused growing alarm in the organisation as 1932 progressed. The party's newspaper, the *United Irishman* (named after Griffith's pioneering journal of 1899 - 1906) interpreted the government's release of IRA prisoners as an effort to intimidate the opposition, as a threat to freedom of speech and as increasing the Communist threat. Fianna Fáil was accused of creating conditions that would facilitate armed reprisals. Cumann na nGaedheal opposed the abolition of the oath contained in the Treaty as a deliberate and uncalled for attack on the document. (The oath, which had been the cause of the Civil War but which Fianna Fáil afterwards regarded as an 'empty formula' in order to enter the Dáil, required that allegiance be sworn to the Constitution of the Free State and fidelity to the British Crown by virtue of Ireland's membership of the Commonwealth.)

The party was also against the government's withholding of the land annuities, because it regarded the agreement to pay them as being morally binding, and, in addition, because it perceived that engagement in an economic war would be a major threat to farmers' livelihoods. (The annuities were repayments by Irish farmers for loans given to them by the British government to purchase their land under the various British Land Acts. When the Fianna Fáil government refused to pay the half-yearly amount for 1932 at the beginning of July, the British retaliated by imposing swingeing tariffs on Irish imports to Britain. De Valera's response was to treat British goods coming into the Free State in like manner, which led to the so-called 'economic war'. Irish agricultural products were particularly badly hit.)

The history of the Blueshirts is a separate study from that of Fine Gael, and Maurice Manning's account is the standard work on the subject.[3] What is of concern here is how that movement became interwoven with and affected the fortunes of the Fine Gael party. The Army Comrades Association (ACA), founded in February 1932, was originally a benevolent organisation set up to look after the interests of ex-Free State army men. It declared itself to be non-political and non-sectarian. However, in August 1932 it was reorganised under the leadership of Dr T. F. O'Higgins, a brother of Kevin O'Higgins, and a Cumann na nGaedheal TD for Laois-Offaly. A member of Sinn Féin from 1917, Dr O'Higgins had been imprisoned in both Mountjoy and Ballykinlar. Joining the Free State army in 1922, he became director of medical services in May 1924. He resigned from the army in 1929 and was elected to the Dáil that year. His becoming leader of the ACA signalled a significant change in the policy and role of the Association.

Evidently, there were three main reasons why the ACA became a major political force. One was that Cumann na nGaedheal supporters were becoming convinced that, with the government's cooperation, the IRA and Fianna Fáil were determined to deprive Cumann na nGaedheal public representatives of the rights of free speech and assembly. The party and its supporters felt intimidated by the IRA with its ominous slogan 'No free speech for traitors'. A second was the belief that communist forces were making progress and would soon pose a real threat. Finally, ex-army members were no longer given preference in the awarding of public posts, as had been the practice during the years when Cumann na nGaedheal was in power, and there were growing fears that they were being victimised. From August 1932 onwards, the ACA began to protect Cumann na nGaedheal public meetings, and this led to an increasing number of clashes with Fianna Fáil and IRA elements.

In early 1932, Farmers' and Ratepayers' Associations sprung up in counties Roscommon, Cavan and Leitrim, seeking cutbacks in government spending and subsidies for farmers. J. F. O'Hanlon was elected for Cavan and Frank MacDermot for Roscommon in the February 1932 election on behalf of these Associations. James Dillon spoke at the first Roscommon meeting of the Association, but was elected for Donegal as an 'Independent Nationalist'. Each of the newly elected candidates was linked to the old Home Rule Party: Dillon was the son of its last leader; MacDermot, who had fought in the Great War, had stood for the Nationalist Party in West Belfast in the 1929 British general election; O'Hanlon had contested the East Cavan by-election for the Irish Parliamentary Party in June

1918 which Arthur Griffith won.

In September 1932, farmers' associations from all over the country held a meeting, at which MacDermot presided, and decided to set up a new national body, which came into existence on 6 October under the name National Farmers' and Ratepayers' League. Predominantly concerned with agricultural interests, it advocated an end to Civil War bitterness and a solution to the problem of partition by getting rid of the antagonisms between the two parts of Ireland. In early December, the League announced that it would soon form a Dáil party, to be called either 'The National Party' or 'The Centre Party' and declared that members of the League should not belong to Cumann na nGaedheal, Fianna Fáil or Labour.

At the beginning of 1933, the Independent Senator Vincent publicly urged Cosgrave and MacDermot to unite to counter Fianna Fáil, and Alfie Byrne, the popular Lord Mayor of Dublin and a Cumann na nGaedheal sympathiser, assembled a group of mainly businessmen, who called for a similar development. Cosgrave and his fellow TDs welcomed Byrne's proposal, but MacDermot was opposed because of Cumann na nGaedheal's links with the Civil War. The sudden election called by de Valera at the beginning of January 1933 (at least one of the reasons for de Valera's action was to forestall these moves towards uniting some of the anti-Fianna Fáil strands) prevented any further progress and forced the League onto the hustings before it was prepared.

On 4 January 1933, MacDermot and Dillon met to form the National Centre Party which would be independent of both Cumann na nGaedheal and Fianna Fáil. In a newspaper advertisement it outlined the ten principles to which it aimed to subscribe, among them being control of public spending, protection of property rights, more influence for farmers on government policy, and friendly relations with Britain and Northern Ireland. Although Dillon avowed that the new party was independent of both of the major parties, its policy was markedly different from Fianna Fáil's and almost identical with Cumann na nGaedheal's.

Basically, the Centre Party was a revival of the old Farmers' Party, with the support of a few nationally minded politicians like

Dillon and MacDermot. Of its 26 contestants, six of whom were outgoing TDs, in the January 1933 election, 21 were farmers and they appealed mainly to farming interests for support. The Centre Party won over 9% of the vote and 11 seats in the election, becoming the third-largest Dáil grouping. The bulk of its support came from these areas of the country where the Farmers' Party had been strong. It abstained from voting on de Valera's renomination as President of the Executive Council, but it could not long maintain a neutral Dáil stance. Its almost identical policies and the increasingly polarised nature of politics drove it closer to Cumann na nGaedheal. In fact the two parties had transferred extensively to each other at the polls. Despite MacDermot's doubts about the Blueshirts, by the summer of 1933 some sort of merger appeared inevitable.[4]

Cumann na nGaedheal's policy for the 1933 election was similar to that of the year before, except that it promised to end the economic war immediately, to halve the annuities and to suspend payment of them for two years, because of the economic crisis in agriculture. It also pledged not, without careful scrutiny first, to interfere with the tariffs Fianna Fáil had implemented. Eighty-five Cumann na nGaedheal candidates contested the 1933 election, 16 fewer than in February 1932, and 18 less than the number of Fianna Fáil candidates. It was a bitter and violent campaign, especially as far as Cumann na nGaedheal and the Centre Party were concerned. The ACA provided security at Cumann na nGaedheal and Centre Party public meetings. Both the *United Irishman* and Frank MacDermot declared after the election that, but for the ACA, there would have been no freedom of speech during the campaign.

The election result was a catastrophe for Cosgrave's party. Cumann na nGaedheal lost 40,000 votes and its number of seats dropped from 57 to 48. This was the party's second defeat within a year. For de Valera it was a triumph as his party was returned to power with an overall Dáil majority, the first time such control had been achieved since the foundation of the state. Prospects appeared bleak for the major opposition party: a total of 14 seats lost at the 1932 and 1933 elections; some important rural seats had been lost to the new Centre Party; the belief that Fianna Fáil could not last in power for more than a year because of inexperience and incompetence was shattered; Ernest Blythe, former Minister for Finance, had lost his seat in Monaghan. Its second electoral defeat, coming so closely on the heels of the first, caused much questioning within Cumann na nGaedheal. The party's journal, the *United Irishman*, believed that the failure was organisational rather than one of policy or leadership. Some, however, thought that a new leader was necessary to confront de Valera successfully.

In mid-February 1933, the national executive of the ACA decided to adopt a distinctive uniform for the movement, and the wearing of a blue shirt was decided upon near the end of March. From this time onwards the *United Irishman* began to devote more space to ACA activities. At the end of February, the de Valera government dismissed General Eoin O'Duffy from his position as Gárda Commissioner. There was much public controversy about this: Cumann na nGaedheal and the Centre Party championed O'Duffy's cause in the Dáil, and *The Irish Times*, *The Irish Independent* and the *United Irishman* also took it up. They all regarded the dismissal as a piece of blatant political victimisation and as indicative of the influence of the IRA and left-wing supporters of the Fianna Fáil government. Ernest Blythe and Professor Michael Tierney, men prominent in both Cumann na nGaedheal and the ACA, urged O'Duffy to become leader of the latter organisation as Dr T. F. O'Higgins wished to step down. When O'Duffy took over the leadership near the end of July, he renamed the association the National Guard and proclaimed that it would be strictly non-party while he was at the helm. The new constitution of the movement contained provisions for the creation of national organisations of employers and workers which, with the help of judicial tribunals, would work for harmonious industrial relations, and also the setting up of a national statutory organisation of farmers. These proposals have been seen as marking the 'first tentative introduction of corporate ideas into Irish politics and certainly the first espousal of these ideas by an Irish political movement'.[5] Under O'Duffy, the Blueshirt numbers increased greatly.

(ii) Formation

From June 1933 a series of meetings had been held with the aim of uniting Cumann na nGaedheal and the Centre Party into a single opposition party. Cosgrave and Hogan for Cumann na nGaedheal and Dillon and MacDermot for the Centre Party attended the first meeting, chaired by T.W. Westrop-Bennett, Chairman of the Senate. Little progress was made, but larger meetings of both parties took place in early August, and Blythe and O'Higgins, both of whom were also among the leaders of the National Guard, attended these. On 9 August *The Irish Times* predicted that the two parties would soon merge. Significantly, at this point O'Duffy declared that he had emphatically rejected any overtures made to him by the two organisations. But when on 12 August the government banned the annual commemorative parade to Leinster Lawn in honour of Griffith, Collins and O'Higgins, due to take place the next day, in which O'Duffy proposed to lead the National Guard, and followed this on 21 August by proclaiming the National Guard to be an illegal organisation, O'Duffy was in a very different position. Now the leader of an isolated movement which was outside the law, he needed new and strong allies.

In fact, it was the government's banning of the National Guard that gave the impetus to opposition unity. At the end of August and in early September representatives of Cumann na nGaedheal, the Centre Party and the National Guard held further meetings, the basis for discussion being the following proposals put forward by the Centre Party:

(a) The name of the new party was to be the United Ireland Party.
(b) General O'Duffy was to be the leader.
(c) W.T. Cosgrave was to be the party's Dáil leader.
(d) Twelve members, nominated by Cosgrave, MacDermot and O'Duffy, were to form the executive committee.

Following another series of separate and joint party meetings, merger proposals were agreed. Special conventions of Cumann na nGaedheal and the Centre Party were addressed by

O'Duffy on 8 September and the new political party, to be known as the United Ireland Party or Fine Gael, was formally launched on the same day.

Three of the organisation's vice-presidents, Cosgrave, Dillon and MacDermot, were predictable and expected choices, but the three others - Peter Nugent, nominated by MacDermot, Professor James Hogan, Professor of History at University College, Cork and a brother of Patrick Hogan, and Professor Michael Tierney, Professor of Greek at University College, Dublin and a former Cumann na nGaedheal TD were not. None of the three was a member of the Dáil. The title 'Fine Gael' was suggested by Professor Tierney. Its English equivalent would be the 'Family of the Irish'. The Centre Party would have preferred the name the 'United Ireland Party', but both Cumann na nGaedheal and the National Guard preferred the Irish appellation. (It originated at the Irish Race Convention in Paris in 1923.) As a compromise, the new party's full title was 'United Ireland Party - Fine Gael', but Fine Gael was so far less cumbersome that it soon became the widely used label of the new organisation.

The executive of Fine Gael had 18 members, six from each of its three constituent groups. O'Duffy nominated T.F. O'Higgins, Commandant Ned Cronin, Colonel Jerry Ryan, Captain Padraig Quinn, Seán Ruane and Charles Conroy. Cosgrave's nominees were Richard Mulcahy, Ernest Blythe, John Marcus O'Sullivan, Daniel Morrissey, James Fitzgerald-Kenny and John A. Costello. Representing the Centre Party were F.B. Barton, P. Baxter, E.J. Cussen, Robert Hogan, E. Curran and E.R. Richard-Orpen. Together with the president and the six vice-presidents, the new party had a national executive of 25, which made it an unwieldy body. Most of those nominated had no political experience and were not nationally known figures. Cosgrave was in a difficult position because he had to leave out from the list of nominees former cabinet ministers like McGilligan, Hogan and FitzGerald. The National Guard was reformed as a new organisation within Fine Gael under the title of the Young Ireland Association.

The attitude of Cumann na nGaedheal to the new party must

now be considered and especially that of its leader, W.T. Cosgrave. Having been a founder-member of Cumann na nGaedheal and having led it in government for ten years, he now had to contemplate union with two other groups, one of which was less than a year old and had far fewer Dáil representatives; whatever few publicly elected members the other had were also members of his own party. He was being asked to take a position secondary to a man who had until recently been his subordinate and who had almost no political experience. In fact, Cosgrave was not enthusiastic about the whole idea, nor were some of his front-bench colleagues, especially Patrick Hogan. Both Cumann na nGaedheal and the Centre Party held separate conventions at the Mansion House on 8 September to endorse their union. Cosgrave's speech to his party gathering made obvious his lack of enthusiasm for O'Duffy. He stated that at the August meetings 'a full appreciation of the services and public work of General O'Duffy was present in the minds of the Centre Party', and while he contended that it did not matter to Cumann na nGaedheal who the leader was, he did not make any recommendation in respect of O'Duffy.[6]

There seem to have been two main reasons why Cosgrave favoured the merging of his party with the other two organisations. The chief one was that opposition unity was essential, whatever the cost, because de Valera seemed bent on destroying his opponents and, unless they came together, they would all perish separately. But since neither the Centre Party nor the National Guard appeared anxious to have Cosgrave as leader, he would have to step down in order for unity to come about, and this he was prepared to do. A second factor was that it seems that some in Cumann na nGaedheal wanted to replace Cosgrave as leader, because the party had just lost two successive elections within a short period, and it was felt that a more charismatic man was needed to combat de Valera. It was in keeping with Cosgrave's character that he was ready to sacrifice his own position and accept a subordinate role. Whatever his reservations about O'Duffy, based in part on what he knew of his uneven performance as police commissioner, he gave him his full support and loyalty for the year during which he led Fine Gael.

Without Cosgrave's willingness to step down, unity would not have come about, and it was probably this realisation that weighed most with him.

The Centre Party drove a hard bargain. Despite its anxiety that the opposition come together, it was not willing to be subsumed by the much larger Cumann na nGaedheal. One way of preventing this was to have O'Duffy as leader and to include his organisation in the negotiations. A second was the procedure of each of the three leaders nominating six members to the party executive, which seemed to give the Centre Party equal status with Cumann na nGaedheal, and also to give it an influence out of proportion to its size. Its 8 September convention which decided on unity with Cumann na nGaedheal and the National Guard was held in private, and it is not known whether any opposition was expressed to the move. MacDermot, in his address, said that they were uniting on equal terms and were not being swallowed up. Almost 30 years later he expressed the opinion that his party had been mistaken to have merged with Cumann na nGaedheal. But most of the Centre Party's TDs settled easily into Fine Gael and James Dillon later became its leader. MacDermot was the only one who remained uneasy, resigning in October 1935 and afterwards being nominated to the Senate by de Valera.

(iii) O'Duffy's leadership and its aftermath

Fine Gael had a lively beginning under O'Duffy which seemed to augur well for its future. It brought a novel dimension to Irish politics in that it was the first party to have a youth organisation. Within a month of its inauguration it had issued a detailed and comprehensive policy document, had started to set up branches around the country, was holding a considerable number of meetings with a view to gaining recruits and its opposition to Fianna Fáil in the Dáil had reached a new pitch of intensity. The party's policy on Northern Ireland was that of Cumann na nGaedheal in the 1920s: Irish unity within the Commonwealth. It affirmed its loyalty to the parliamentary system and its absolute opposition to communism and to any 'self-declared army or dictatorship'. The abolition of proportional representation as it then existed and the reform of local government were also Fine Gael policy. To deal with the unemployment problem, reconstruction works for the able-bodied unemployed were advocated. But the party's most novel departure was its call for the establishment of industrial and agricultural corporations with full statutory powers. This, it has been noted, 'marks the first advocacy by an Irish political party of a nascent corporatism'.[7]

O'Duffy had acquired a reputation as an accomplished organiser, in consequence of his impressive part in the setting up of the Gárda Síochána and his supervision of the civic arrangements for the holding of the 1932 Eucharistic Congress in Dublin. He took the lead in establishing the branch structure of the party, claiming it had more than 700 such units by the end of November 1933 and 1,038 by the time of the first ard-fheis the following February. Whether these were new or simply old Cumann na nGaedheal or Centre Party branches is impossible to say, but it seems that Fine Gael was determined to construct a much more extensive grass-roots network than Cumann na nGaedheal had. The widespread series of meetings held by O'Duffy (who had spoken in 23 out of the 26 counties by March 1934) tended largely to be Blueshirt rallies, providing guards of honour for their leader, with the right-arm salute becoming more and more a feature of them.

W.T. Cosgrave was the Dáil leader of Fine Gael and his front bench of Dillon, MacDermot, Costello, McGilligan, Mulcahy, O'Higgins and J. M. O'Sullivan represented all three groups within the party. This meant that former Cumann na nGaedheal ministers Desmond FitzGerald, James Fitzgerald-Kenny, Patrick Hogan and Fionán Lynch had to be relegated to the back benches. Hogan was by general consent regarded as one of the most able of the Cumann na nGaedheal ministers. It seems that he retired to the back benches by personal choice, partly to build up his county Galway solicitor's practice, which he had had to neglect while in office, and partly also because he had made known his lack of faith in the new arrangement, especially the choice of leader. Between this time and his tragically premature death in a car accident in July 1936, he became more and more distant from public life. The presence of Mulcahy and O'Higgins on the front bench was more attributable to their membership of the National Guard than their having been in Cumann na nGaedheal. The first TD to appear in the Dáil in his blue shirt was Sidney Minch of Kildare on 27 September. The next day about a dozen Fine Gael TDs did so, among them T.F. O'Higgins and Desmond FitzGerald.

For most of the first year of its existence, Fine Gael operated in the shadow of the Blueshirt movement. When the police raided and closed down the premises of the National Guard at 5 Parnell Square on 15 September, a bitter Dáil debate followed in which the government contended that the aim of the organisation was to overthrow the democratic institutions of the state, while Fine Gael responded that it was not anti-democratic or fascist, and that it existed only because of the government's deliberate and provocative failure to protect its opponents from IRA gangsterism. In late November the police raided the houses of some prominent members of Fine Gael around the country, searching for arms, and on 8 December the Young Ireland Association was declared an illegal organisation and banned. Fine Gael's official statement described this as a 'monstrous and illegal act of political persecution without any shadow of moral justification'. On 14 December the national executive of Fine Gael decided to dissolve the Young Ireland Association and to form a new organisation called the League of Youth.

Late 1933 and much of 1934 was a violent time in Irish politics. Fine Gael public meetings were held amid scenes of much unrest; two Blueshirts were murdered and exchanges in the Dáil during this time were of unprecedented bitterness. Farmers suffering the effects of the economic war were refusing to pay their rates and many Blueshirts supported them in this. The Fine Gael February 1934 ard-fheis saw a striking display of Blueshirt strength, and morale was high. In late February, the government introduced the Uniforms Bill to outlaw the wearing of the blue shirt. The arguments from both sides were recitals of the debates at the time of the closing of the National Guard's Parnell Square premises five months before. The Minister for Justice, P.J. Ruttledge, compared the Blueshirts to contemporary continental movements. In reply, John A. Costello stated:

> The Minister gave extracts from various laws on the Continent but he carefully refrained from drawing attention to the fact that the Blackshirts were victorious in Italy and that the Hitler shirts were victorious in Germany, as assuredly, in spite of this Bill, and in spite of the Public Safety Act, the Blueshirts will be victorious in the Irish Free State.

Costello's political opponents did not allow him forget this statement.

Although the Bill was passed by the Dáil, the Senate rejected it and, in so doing, signed its own death warrant, because on the day after it had thrown out the uniforms measure, de Valera introduced a Bill into the Dáil proposing the abolition of the upper house. Naturally, the Senate rejected the move to bring about its demise, but it delayed legislation for only 18 months, and already its days had been numbered.

Certainly there was a marked contrast in the way the government treated the IRA and the Blueshirts at the time. There are instances of sentenced IRA men being released on the intervention of the Minister for Justice. A number of Blueshirts were murdered but no one was brought to justice for the crimes. De Valera stated in the Dáil that, while the IRA had roots in the past and a national objective, the Blueshirts had none and, although no attempt was made to disarm the IRA, ex-Cumann na nGaedheal ministers had to give up their legally held arms.

A special armed auxiliary unit of the Gárda Síochána was established, consisting of ex-IRA men, which became known as the 'Broy Harriers'. A particularly bad incident occurred at Marsh's Yard in Cork in August 1934 when a number of Broy Harriers shot dead a youth. Their action was afterwards defended by the Minister for Justice. But Mr Justice Hanna of the High Court, in his judgment of the case taken by the youth's father against three of the Harriers for damages, described that force as ill-trained, undisciplined IRA men.   He found that the men involved had used excessive force and had shot to kill.   He awarded damages to the youth's father and called on the Attorney General to prosecute the three Harriers for manslaughter.   This did not occur.[8]

The local elections of late June 1934 provided Fine Gael with its first electoral test and represented a break with the Cumann na nGaedheal practice of not directly contesting such elections on the grounds that party politics should be divorced from local authorities.   Fianna Fáil had taken part in them from its foundation, viewing them as valuable platforms for potential politicians and as a way of strengthening local support.   Fine Gael saw the June 1934 contest as an ideal chance to show how much support the new party had attracted and how unpopular the government's policies were. The preparations were frenetic with many violent clashes at Fine Gael meetings between Blueshirts and Fianna Fáil and IRA supporters.   However, by this time most Blueshirt activity was in the anti-rates campaign.   The cattle farmers of the midlands and south were suffering as a result of British tariffs on Irish agricultural exports and these were the areas where the strongest opposition to the payment of rates was made manifest.   Large forces of police were being used to protect the bailiffs who were seizing cattle and goods from the farms of those who refused to pay.

It was because of this that the 1934 local elections took on an unusual significance.   They were O'Duffy's first electoral test. As the campaign drew to a close he became convinced that his party was going to be spectacularly successful.   Perhaps it was the euphoria generated by the large crowds that attended his meetings which encouraged him to predict on the eve of polling that Fine Gael would win control of 20 of the 23 councils being contested. The elections would also show whether Fine Gael had won any new support or had merely managed to hold on to what Cumann na nGaedheal and the Centre Party had already won.

O'Duffy's prediction - made, it seems, against the advice of some of the other Fine Gael leaders - turned out to be very wrong. Fianna Fáil emerged as the biggest party in 14 counties, in contrast to Fine Gael, which was biggest in only six; the parties were equal on three councils; overall, the Fianna Fáil-Labour alliance gave Fianna Fáil control of 15 councils, while Fine Gael controlled seven. It was a decisive defeat for Fine Gael under O'Duffy in the first direct contest with Fianna Fáil.

After the local elections there was a marked intensification in the anti-rates unrest and some of O'Duffy's speeches revealed a new note of extremism. While the more moderate Fine Gael leaders probably felt uneasy about the rural violence and the part being played by the Blueshirts, it is likely that many within the party felt that unity must be maintained in the face of Fianna Fáil-IRA opposition. It is also probable that most people in Fine Gael felt that the cause the Blueshirts were defending was a just one, since a hostile government seemed to them to be pursuing a vindictive course against farmers confronting financial ruin as a result of the government's own policy which destroyed the only market the farmers had for their produce.

The Blueshirt movement held its own separate congress in Dublin on 18 and 19 August. Part of the central resolution, introduced by O'Duffy himself and unanimously passed by the congress, called on farmers not to pay the land annuities if the government insisted on collecting them during the current agricultural depression and unless the government set up an independent tribunal to examine the farmers' case generally. Although this amounted to an open call for people to engage in unconstitutional and illegal activities, it did not arouse any public interest. At least part of the reason for this was the strike of Dublin newspapers throughout July, August and September 1934. Then, in a speech at Cavan at the end of August, O'Duffy asserted that British outposts in Northern Ireland were being fortified and that if this led to war, he would lead the Blueshirts in it. A native of county Monaghan, O'Duffy had strong feelings on partition, had many close friends who were prominent nationalists in the North, and seldom spoke in public without making some reference to the need to work for Irish unification.[9]

On 30 August the Fine Gael national executive held its regular meeting at the party's headquarters in Merrion Square,

Dublin. As well as discussing routine matters, the land annuities motion passed at the Blueshirt congress and O'Duffy's recent statement on partition were considered. For a party with a proud constitutional and democratic record, the land annuities motion was fraught with dangers for Fine Gael. It has been acutely observed that 'to adopt the Blueshirt motion would be to opt for a course of action blatantly unconstitutional, potentially violent and alien to the principles which had activated both the Cumann na nGaedheal Party and the Parliamentary Party tradition of Dillon and MacDermot.'[10] Following a long, confused and sometimes acrimonious debate, O'Duffy withdrew his motion which sought to have the Blueshirt congress resolution made official Fine Gael policy. Professor James Hogan, one of the party's vice-presidents, resigned on the grounds that it was the strongest personal protest he could make against what he termed O'Duffy's 'generally destructive and hysterical leadership'.

Although Fine Gael publicly denied that there was any split in the organisation, Hogan's resignation brought to a head the unhappiness with O'Duffy's leadership which existed in the upper levels of the party. This, indeed, may have been what Hogan had intended to accomplish by resigning. Soon afterwards a series of meetings took place involving O'Duffy, Cosgrave and Dillon, among others. These councils were held in secret and the details of what occurred are not clear.   A period of apparent calm followed and there was no sign that things were other than as usual in Fine Gael, as party gatherings continued to be held throughout the country. This quiescence came to an abrupt end at the next national executive meeting on 21 September when O'Duffy, without warning, resigned from the leadership. The ordinary party members had no inkling that this was going to take place. The brief statement issued by the national executive after its meeting clarified nothing. It announced the resignation, regretted it and paid a warm tribute to O'Duffy for his work on behalf of Fine Gael, but it gave no reasons for his decision.

There were important policy differences between the Cosgrave and O'Duffy wings of Fine Gael. O'Duffy was much more favourable to corporate ideas than were Cosgrave and his colleagues. The O'Duffy faction was prepared to go much further in resisting the government over the land annuities issue than was the Cosgrave group, whose basic position was that a constitutional political movement must use only constitutional methods. There was also a difference between the two sides on the question of partition. The official Fine Gael policy was unity within the Commonwealth. Cosgrave and McGilligan, as a result of their experience in the 1920s, appreciated the role Ireland could play in the Commonwealth; because of their Parliamentary Party background, Dillon and MacDermot were in favour of Ireland's continuing membership. On the other hand, O'Duffy probably had little enthusiasm for the idea. But despite these disagreements, it is most likely that O'Duffy's personality and style of leadership precipitated the crisis in Fine Gael.

One cause of dissatisfaction was the lack of consultation between O'Duffy and his vice-presidents. The leader was thought to be autocratic and his unpredictable statements sometimes caught the other national executive members unawares. Probably the most important source of discontent was with O'Duffy's speeches. These have been variously described as 'imprudent and contradictory', 'irresponsible and exuberant', 'injudicious and not in accordance with party policy'. It has been averred that 'his statements on Ulster reveal an exuberance and a belligerency, his references to the economic war situation were often inflammatory, his attitude to corporatism ambiguous, and his attitude to European fascism unpredictable'.[11] Some of O'Duffy's impromptu statements proved very embarrassing to his colleagues. A final point of dissatisfaction was the question of finance. O'Duffy's insistence on bringing bus loads of supporters into areas where Fine Gael was weak to attend his meetings, and the engagement of full-time and part-time officials in various parts of the country, proved financially draining to the party.

In retrospect, it must be adjudged that the choice of O'Duffy to lead Fine Gael was a mistake. Whatever vigour he brought to the leadership was at a great cost. He lacked judgment, parliamentary experience, subtlety, diplomacy, and the intellectual ability to distinguish between the corporatist ideas of Professors Hogan and Tierney, which were based on Pius XI's 1931 encyclical *Quadragesimo Anno*, and the extreme fascist regimes in European countries. As an authority on the subject has affirmed: 'He was too impetuous, too naive, too forthright, and too muddle-headed to be a serious politician'.[12]   The compromises which are a basic ingredient of political life were foreign to him.

The unexpected and obscure nature of O'Duffy's resignation plunged the Fine Gael-Blueshirt movement into great discomposure which stimulated a process of decline. A particularly deep and bitter rift occurred within the League of Youth, with O'Duffy asserting that he was still its director, while the Fine Gael national executive had appointed Commandant Cronin to succeed him in the post. On 4 October, Fine Gael TDs and Senators met, unanimously accepted O'Duffy's resignation and decided that Cosgrave, Dillon, MacDermot and Cronin would lead the party until the next ard-fheis. Patrick Belton TD, a member of Fianna Fáil until 1927, then an Independent TD and afterwards in the Centre Party before the merger, tried to reach a compromise between Cronin and O'Duffy on the basis of the reinstatement of the latter as leader, but failed and was expelled from the Fine Gael party on 30 October. The leadership dispute then subsided because O'Duffy became increasingly involved in international affairs, attending the International Fascist Congress in Montreux, Switzerland and being appointed to its Labour Committee, and because Fine Gael and the Blueshirts decided to close ranks because only Fianna Fáil would gain from their further internecine quarrels.   The agrarian unrest and violence continued unabated during September and October 1934 and at the end of October Cosgrave condemned incidents such as blocking roads and railway lines, felling trees and cutting wires (with which Blueshirts had been associated), as 'deplorable breaches of the law'.

The disarray in the Blueshirt movement caused by the leadership struggle and the lack of any clear support from the Fine Gael leaders for the tactics it had been using contributed to the abatement in rural unrest which occurred in the final months of 1934. The Coal-Corn Pact, negotiated by the Irish government with Britain in January 1935, which increased the quota of Irish cattle to be exported to Britain, contributed to a return of calm in rural Ireland. These factors meant that from the beginning of 1935 the Blueshirts played a new and very subdued role. According to their historian:

> While the split was largely instrumental in bringing about this situation, with its demoralisation and confusion, there was also the fact that the Fine Gael leaders such as Cosgrave, MacDermot and Dillon, whose authority had been asserted after O'Duffy's departure, were now anxious to play down the importance of the Blueshirts and to direct the energies of the movement into different channels.[13]

The 1935 ard-fheis was held in March and was the first assembly of the party since the split, although it was not discussed or debated at the gathering. The Fine Gael leaders had had their fill of controversy by this time and made sure that the dispute with O'Duffy was given as little prominence as possible. At the ard-fheis, Cosgrave was unanimously elected president of the party; the vice-presidents chosen were Dillon, MacDermot, Cronin and O'Higgins. This convention lacked the spectacle and excitement of its predecessor. It was decided to continue the League of Youth as a permanent part of the Fine Gael organisation as a means of 'providing the youth of Ireland with opportunities of discipline, voluntary, national and social service'.

Fine Gael lost one of its most colourful figures when Frank MacDermot resigned from the party late in 1935. It is likely that he had never been altogether at ease in the organisation. Entering politics as an Independent in 1932, his co-founding of the Centre Party represented for him an attempt to rid Irish political life of what he saw as the burden of the Treaty and the Civil War. But his agreement to merge with Cumann na nGaedheal in 1933 brought him into the mainstream of Civil War politics (Fine Gael to most people was merely Cumann na nGaedheal by another name). MacDermot was unenthusiastic about the Blueshirts and never managed to establish a good relationship with General O'Duffy. It has been said of him: 'He was perhaps too cosmopolitan for the insularity of Irish politics in the 1930s and too much of a dilettante to remain for long in an atmosphere obviously so uncongenial'.[14]

But the issue over which MacDermot resigned concerned foreign affairs. In a speech at the League of Nations, de Valera condemned the Italian invasion of Abyssinia and declared that Ireland stood by its obligations under the Covenant of the League. Both Cosgrave and O'Higgins attacked de Valera's stand as a missed opportunity to highlight Ireland's grievance over partition and as a mistake to pledge Irish assistance without a prior settlement of the country's quarrel with Britain. MacDermot wrote to Cosgrave to complain that he regarded this approach as far too negative and carping and shortly afterwards he resigned. Thereafter, he sat as an Independent TD until 1937 and was nominated to the Senate by de Valera in 1938. His resignation coincided with the virtual disappearance of the Blueshirts from the political scene.

The Fine Gael ard-fheis of March 1936 was a quiet affair. The address of its re-elected president was concerned mainly with economic and agricultural problems. He did not refer to the corporate state and no mention of the subject appeared on the programme. A small number of Blueshirts were in attendance, but the movement took no special part in the proceedings. *United Ireland* (the *United Irishman* was so renamed following the formation of Fine Gael) stressed the changed situation of the Blueshirt organisation and the alteration of its functions consequent upon that (which the paper regarded as educational, cultural and propagandistic), especially now that the Fianna Fáil government was finally coming to grips with the IRA.

The summer of 1936 saw yet another blow administered to Fine Gael, a party now much weakened by internal troubles. In July, Patrick Hogan was the fatal victim of a car crash in his native county of Galway. He was possibly the most successful of the Cumann na nGaedheal ministers in the 1923-32 period, and although he had retired from the front bench, he still had the reputation of being one of the liveliest and most practical members of Fine Gael. His death, following a chain of misfortunes - the murder of Kevin O'Higgins, Ernest Blythe's comfortless 1932 budget, major reversals in two successive elections, the Blueshirt debacle, and the resignation of Frank MacDermot - increased the sense of dejection with which Fine Gael had become afflicted.

A further dent in party morale was sustained with the closing down of its newspaper, *United Ireland*, in late July 1936. Almost every issue of the paper called for financial aid and it had been urging Fine Gael members for some time to give it more support. It seems to have fallen victim to the diminution of enthusiasm and activity during these years. The reason given for winding up the publication was to enable all resources and energies to be devoted to the contesting of by-elections in East Galway and Wexford, but the newspaper did not reappear after the elections, and its sacrifice could not prevent Fianna Fáil from winning both seats comfortably. James Hogan was the defeated Fine Gael candidate in East Galway.

The final internal upheaval of the turbulent thirties occurred over the question of what the role of the League of Youth should be in the new political circumstances. Ned Cronin was anxious to retain as independent an existence as possible for it, but the other Fine Gael leaders, especially Cosgrave and O'Higgins, maintained that the Blueshirt movement had fulfilled the function for which it had been founded - the defence of the rights of free speech and free assembly - and now with the IRA proclaimed an illegal organisation, this was no longer necessary. The issue of finance was also at stake, because the Blueshirts had proved to be extremely costly and by the time of O'Duffy's resignation the Fine Gael coffers were in a serious state. It was felt that two organisations and two separate headquarters catering for more or less the same group of people was unnecessary duplication and that Fine Gael headquarters could deal adequately with Blueshirt administrative work.

Cronin resisted any attempt at change and in September 1936 the party's national executive decided to reorganise the League of Youth. In early October, Dr O'Higgins put a series of proposals to this end before the party's standing committee, mainly to abolish the League of Youth's headquarters and to give Fine Gael's standing committee control of that organisation by means of the power to appoint its officers. His scheme was accepted and O'Higgins was authorised to administer the League on behalf of the standing committee pending its submission of a new plan of organisation to the party's national executive. Cronin refused to accept this decision and was expelled from Fine Gael. Dr T.F. O'Higgins was the prime mover in the evolution of the Blueshirts, and fate decided that he was to arrange for its peaceful demise and to preside over the obsequies. Fine Gael had become Cumann na nGaedheal reincarnated.[15]

In contrast to the general election of 1933 and the local elections of the following year, which took place in a bitter, tense and violent atmosphere, the general election of 1937 and the referendum on the Constitution which accompanied it were the most peaceful since the founding of the Free State. W. T. Cosgrave described it as the 'most good-humoured' campaign he had fought, a sentiment echoed by the newspapers of the time. Some of those who had entered public life through the Blueshirt movement were Fine Gael candidates. Colonel Jerry Ryan in Tipperary and Captain P. Giles in Meath-Westmeath were both elected, but Captain John L. O'Sullivan in Cork West and Gerard Sweetman in Carlow-Kildare were unsuccessful. Commandant Cronin came bottom of the poll in North Cork, where he stood as an Independent. Patrick Belton, continuing on his maverick way, lost his seat in Dublin County (where he ran as an Independent), but was re-elected as a Fine Gael candidate in 1938. By the 1943 general election he was again an Independent and lost his seat. Ernest Blythe, elected to the Senate in 1934, did not contest a Dáil seat.

In the 1937 election Fine Gael won 48 seats, 11 less than the combined Cumann na nGaedheal and Centre Party total gained in 1933, and its percentage of the vote was down from 39.6 to 34.8. Fianna Fáil lost seven seats, but its complement was equal to the aggregate of all the rest, and Labour's support enabled it to continue in office.

(iv) Fine Gael, fascism and the Blueshirt legacy

Some historians believe that the National Guard, before it decided to merge with Cumann na nGaedheal and the Centre Party, was developing many of the features of a fascist movement: the uniform, drilling and a characteristic salute; the distrust of and impatience with traditional parliamentary institutions and political parties; its support for some type of corporatist state; its obsessive anti-communism; its membership comprising in the main ex-army men, and the fact that it attracted the backing of a section of the middle class which felt that its livelihood was under threat. But its merger with Fine Gael brought about significant changes. It was no longer independent and dismissive of political parties, but part of a constitutional party, and one of the conditions of O'Duffy's becoming leader was that he would forgo whatever fascist tendencies he had been cultivating and agree to work strictly within the constitutional framework.

Following the inauguration of Fine Gael, there was considerable interest in the development of corporate ideas and how to apply them to Irish politics and this was reflected in the party's newspaper. Professors Michael Tierney and James Hogan were the main exponents of these doctrines. This is not the place to explore their theories, which have been examined by Maurice Manning in the penultimate chapter of his study of the Blueshirts, but his conclusions certainly merit consideration. He pointed out that the movement he was chronicling predated the emergence of such ideas, that they contributed little or nothing to the influence of the Blueshirts around the country or the nature of their activity, and that both Hogan and Tierney hoped to use it as a means of putting into practice their ideas on politically and socially restructuring Irish society. He had no doubt that the dominant influence on their thinking was Pope Pius XI's encyclical *Quadragesimo Anno*, but added that they were aware of and influenced by some of the European fascist leaders and movements, especially the Catholic ones of Austria and Spain. How did these ideas affect the Fine Gael leaders and the party rank and file?

O'Duffy took them seriously and wished to bring about a

corporate state in Ireland, calling the political party he set up in 1935 the National Corporate Party. He regarded the Blueshirts as similar to other contemporary European movements, and was quick to identify himself as leader. Willingly calling himself a fascist, he became very active in international fascism, backing Mussolini's invasion of Abyssinia and fighting for Franco in Spain. Although 'his fascism may have been emotional and instinctive rather than intellectual he certainly took it seriously' it has been observed.[16] Convinced that it was the Christian answer to the communist threat, he seemed unaware of the less palatable aspects of the movements he praised and sought to imitate, 'and his natural muddle-headedness may have made it unclear what exactly he wanted', it has been further avowed.[17] After his resignation and the split in the Blueshirts, none of the leaders and few of the ordinary members followed him.

It is not easy to be certain about how seriously the Fine Gael leaders entertained corporate ideas. A few, such as Blythe, O'Higgins and FitzGerald, gave them much attention and may have considered them important, but many others, especially Cosgrave, Dillon and MacDermot, regarded them simply as a policy detail, not of basic significance and not as an end in themselves. After the Blueshirt rift, corporate ideas quickly disappeared from Fine Gael policy, and the fact that the old Cumann na nGaedheal patterns reasserted themselves so easily suggests that the party was never deeply committed to such concepts. For the vast majority, both of leaders and ordinary members and supporters, the question of a corporate state was largely academic. The following judgment from the leading authority on the subject has been accepted by all subsequent commentators:

> The issues which gave Blueshirtism its impetus, which concerned the minds and activities of its members, which determined the manner in which it developed, were far from academic. Blueshirtism was essentially the product of Civil War memories, fear and distrust, and the threat of economic collapse. Beside these, the promise of a new corporate state counted for very little. [18]

A distinctive feature which all European fascist movements shared was an openly proclaimed opposition to democracy and the intention to establish a dictatorship. Fine Gael and Blueshirt leaders emphasised their adherence to democracy and contended that the Blueshirts had arisen in response to the threat to democratic freedom presented by the IRA and Fianna Fáil. Time and again, they declared their antipathy to all dictatorships, denied that they had intentions in that direction, challenged their critics to come up with any proof to substantiate their allegations to the contrary, and claimed that the corporate policy they advocated would complement rather than replace parliament.

In the early 1930s, being fascist was not perceived as especially reprehensible; it was a new and fashionable phenomenon which had an aura of respectability because of its anti-communism, alleged efficiency and supposed affinity with Catholicism. It has been said that fascist movements were proud to call themselves fascists - indeed, most gloried in the title but the Blueshirts were never officially described as fascist and most of the leaders consistently denied any connection between the movement and fascism.

The view has been expressed that the fascist trappings associated with the Blueshirt movement were never taken seriously by the Fine Gael leaders, that corporate ideas meant little to most people in Fine Gael - that the marches, salutes and suchlike activities provided a physical outlet for energetic young men in a violent age. It has been further pointed out that Mussolini was perceived in Ireland as a friend of the Catholic Church and as an effective administrator, that his government was respected in Europe and had not yet identified itself with the nascent Hitler regime in Germany: 'Parliamentary democracy was certainly in no danger from Mr Cosgrave, who went on patiently speaking of constitutional and economic issues, half the time as if neither corporatism nor Blueshirts had ever existed', and little evidence was found that more than one or two of the parliamentary leaders took corporate notions seriously. Having lost two elections in a row, they were determined to oust de Valera: 'They chanced a bet on the charismatic personality of the General and they lost'.[19]

The Blueshirts capitalised on farmer discontent during the economic war and supported the withholding of land annuities and rates, but this afforded no electoral advantage to Fine Gael since it did not help to attract new supporters to the party to overcome Fianna Fáil's majority. The illegal actions of farmers and their Blueshirt supporters in not paying rates and in blocking roads and railways could not be condoned by the Dáil leaders of Fine Gael. The best response to the question of whether the Blueshirt episode was a flirtation with fascism is that, whatever about a small number, it was patently evident that the vast majority of the Fine Gael party was solidly dedicated to parliamentary democracy.

It has been argued that while some Fine Gael intellectuals were obsessed with the threat of communism and although both Professors Hogan and Tierney admired the corporate state in Italy and saw all states evolving socially and politically to this particular form, the ideas they put forward in *United Ireland,* and which even appeared in the Cumann na nGaedheal party programme in 1933, owed far more to Pius XI than to Mussolini. The papal emphasis on vocational organisation was much more likely to have appeal in Catholic Ireland, influenced all parties and found expression in the de Valera 1937 Constitution.[20]

When Fine Gael chose O'Duffy as their leader, 'had the arch-constitutionalists taken aboard an embryo dictator?' it has been wondered. De Valera's policy in July 1933 of setting up an armed police force and seizing firearms had certainly intensified the suspicions of many as to his intentions and, in fear for their defencelessness, they had turned to O'Duffy. However, when he sought their endorsement for unconstitutional and illegal activities, they removed him from the leadership. Fine Gael's innate constitutionalism ensured against any significant recourse to lawlessness. De Valera could not have achieved what he did between 1932 and 1936 without what have been described as the 'responsive selflessness and democracy' of his political opponents, and it is abundantly clear that there were very few, if indeed any, fascists in the full continental sense of that term in the Blueshirts.[21]

There can be little dispute with the view that its liaison with the Blueshirts harmed Fine Gael in a number of ways. Because it was involved in a movement that had obvious parallels with Hitler's and Mussolini's organisations, it was harder for it afterwards to present itself as other than a right-wing, indeed an extreme right-wing, party. Its claims to be the guardian of the law and of the democratic institutions of the state were also weakened. Some of the attitudes expressed during the 1932-34 period suggested a conditional loyalty to democracy. O'Duffy's advice to the farmers in August 1934 to break the law by withholding annuities and rates sounded strange coming from the head of a party committed to defending the rule of law.

'In addition, the Blueshirt alliance reinforced Fine Gael's image (and its self-image) as a party of losers,' it has been maintained.[22] It made it seem that even when the party struck out in a new direction, it failed. This resulted in feelings of defensiveness and pessimism, an inferiority complex which, it has been argued, did not begin to go until the 1980s.

On the other hand, the Blueshirt demise may have strengthened unity within the party, causing members to be loyal in the same way that Civil War defeat contributed to Fianna Fáil solidarity. But Fine Gael never managed to do what Fianna Fáil did - that is to convince the electorate that it was on the right side. In fact, its reluctance to admit that it had made a mistake may have contributed to its failure to attract the uncommitted vote. There was the incident at the May 1971 ard-fheis, when Senator Michael O'Higgins, who was chairing the policy committee, announced that he had been a Blueshirt and would be proud to be one again.[23] The author of *The Blueshirts* has pointed out that the association with fascism, in however diluted a form, proved an embarrassment for Fine Gael in later years, especially after World War II, and an unlimited source of opposition taunts.[24]

Chapter 3

A Period of Prolonged Decline: 1937-48

(i) General elections: 1937, 1938, 1943 and 1944

In the 1937 general election the Fine Gael share of the vote had declined by almost 5% from its 1933 level and it won 11 fewer seats. Not only did the party poll worse than Cumann na nGaedheal and the Centre Party had done in 1933, but its percentage of the vote was actually lower than Cumann na nGaedheal's had been in 1932.

Following nearly five years of controversial Fianna Fáil rule it might have been expected to do better, and its performance must have been a great blow to members' morale, because both Labour and Independents made significant gains at Fianna Fáil's expense. One of the Fine Gael casualties of this election was Desmond FitzGerald, Cumann na nGaedheal Minister for External Affairs 1923-27 and Minister for Defence 1927-32. This election marked the end of his Dáil career. His son, Garret, the party's leader in more propitious times, was to prove the most successful in leading Fine Gael at the polls. Patrick J. Lindsay, a future minister and one of Fine Gael's more colourful characters, contested North Mayo unsuccessfully for the first time at the 1937 election.

It has been remarked that the 1937 defeat and the return to power of Fianna Fáil for the third successive occasion ushered in for Fine Gael 'the 11 most dismal and disastrous years in the history of the party'.[1] The view has also been expressed that with the Treaty dismembered, and since it was unable to stop de Valera doing what Cosgrave claimed could not be done, Fine Gael had no alternative to offer.[2] One different policy its 1937 manifesto did put forward was the idea of vocationalism. The influence was the Pius XI encyclical of 1931, *Quadragesimo Anno*, as mediated through the writings of Professors Tierney and Hogan, and the manifesto called for a national vocational council to advise parliament. The election result suggests that the idea seems to have had little appeal for the electorate. It has been contended somewhat unsympathetically, that while out of office at this time and having no idea how the party might assume it, Fine Gael flirted with the notion of vocationalism. However, at the same time it has been perceived that the advancement of so radical a doctrine by Fine Gael was evidence of Fianna Fáil growing more conservative in the late 1930s.[3]

The art of revising constituency boundaries with the aim of maximising party political advantage, which was practised in Ireland with great skill until the end of the 1970s was initiated by Fianna Fáil. Article 26 of the Free State Constitution called for such revisions to take place periodically to take account of changes in the distribution of the population. As soon as Fianna Fáil got into office in 1932, the Minister for Local Government Seán T. O'Kelly was asked to examine the matter, and after the 1933 election, a cabinet committee comprising de Valera, O'Kelly, Seán Lemass and James Ryan 'performed the operation with surgical skill', it has been observed.[4] The number of Dáil seats was reduced from 153 to 138 and the six university seats - four of which happened to be held by Fine Gael - were abolished. In 1937, Fine Gael won no more seats than they were entitled to on strict proportionality, while Fianna Fáil won six; the figures for 1938 were: Fine Gael, one seat less, Fianna Fáil, four seats more; for 1943: Fine Gael, its exact share, Fianna Fáil, nine seats more; for 1944: Fine Gael, two seats more, Fianna Fáil, seven more. The 1933 cabinet committee had helped enormously to consolidate Fianna Fáil in power for ten years.

But whatever the ramifications of proportionality, it does not account for Fine Gael's continuing electoral decline in these years. The Anglo-Irish agreement of April 1938, which ended the economic war, settled the annuities question greatly in Ireland's favour and returned the Treaty ports to Irish control, represented a diplomatic triumph for de Valera, and his success in negotiating it further damaged Fine Gael's electoral prospects. He called a snap general election in June 1938 and easily recovered his overall majority. The Fianna Fáil share of the vote was up from the 45.2% of the previous year to 51.9%, the only time in de Valera's career that it exceeded 50%. It has been concluded that this was the first occasion on which Fianna Fáil enticed a significant number of voters away from Fine Gael and gained the support of some ex-Unionists.[5]

In 1938, only 76 Fine Gael candidates contested the election, as opposed to 95 the previous year, and almost all of them would have had to be elected if the party were to have formed a government of its own. The successful end of the economic war had a bad effect on Fine Gael morale and its opposition to the trade agreement seemed inconsistent with its former stand. In the event, its share of the vote dropped to 33.3%, down 1.5%, and its number of seats to 45, down three on its performance of the previous year.

Concerning the Anglo-Irish trade agreement of 1938, a feature of which was the elimination of British tariffs on Irish agricultural imports into Britain, it has been considered no surprise that the opposition quickly claimed that Fianna Fáil was really stealing policies long-advocated by Fine Gael - free trade with Britain and a cautious approach to industrial protection. The agreement did appear to contribute to a narrowing of the gap between Fine Gael and Fianna Fáil economic policies, and in retrospect that may be its most noteworthy aspect.[6]

Under the 1937 Constitution, the country was to have a President for the first time and the parties decided to try to agree to a candidate rather than have a contest. The first names proposed by Fianna Fáil were Frank Fahey, Seán T. O'Kelly and Conor Maguire, President of the High Court. Fine Gael put forward Dr Richard Hayes, Judge Caher Davitt and Chief Justice Tim O'Sullivan. Since there was no agreement between the parties on these men, Fine Gael presented a second list, on which was Dr Douglas Hyde, a founder-member of the Gaelic League and its president from 1893 to 1915. Fianna Fáil accepted Hyde and, as a result, some ex-Unionist support was transferred to that party.

The advent of World War II placed Fine Gael in an acute dilemma. It did not have a coherent policy on the difficult question of neutrality and of Ireland's relations with Britain and the Commonwealth in the event of a world conflict. There were many and varied views on neutrality in Fine Gael, 'differences which, perhaps, reflect the composite origins of the party and the conflicting views on the moral obligation arising from Ireland's association with the British Commonwealth', according to one view.[7]

John A. Costello, in July 1938, maintained that while in theory Ireland could remain neutral, it would be very difficult to do so if she were to hold on to her trade with Britain. In February 1939, well in advance of the outbreak of hostilities in Europe, James Dillon advocated giving Britain and the United States any port facilities they required in time of war (this was in keeping with his later position). On the other hand, General Seán MacEoin, veteran of the Anglo-Irish war and a TD since 1929, in March 1939, proved a strong proponent of neutrality, seeing it as both possible and desirable, and thought it better to forgo Irish exports to Britain rather than abandon neutrality.

It has been suggested that Fine Gael's failure to adopt a clear pro-Commonwealth stance at this time was extremely significant for the party, because from then on it became more difficult to distinguish its policies from those of Fianna Fáil. While there is some substance in this view, there are those who believe that it must be weighed against the fact that, in the circumstances of the time, it was very difficult for parties to take any approach other than one of 'watchful neutrality'. No one Irish party or its faithful had a monopoly of hostility towards partition and suspicion of British claims and intentions at that time.[8] It should also be remembered that the official Dáil policy of neutrality was by no means unconditionally accepted. Especially after the fall of France, opposition TDs, principally Dillon, McGilligan and O'Higgins, did not think it could possibly be maintained, and there were some who did not morally approve. Even among the government's own front bench, which was subject to tight control, there was not total unanimity.[9]

Concerning Irish defence policy, in the Dáil in early February 1939, seven months before war was declared, Fine Gael moved that a select committee be set up to report on the government's failure to provide protection against the possibility of an air attack. Party spokesmen maintained that the army could not provide a defence plan, because the government had no defence policy. Generally, Fine Gael argued that money should be spent developing an air force rather than a ground army. Doubts were expressed about Ireland remaining neutral if Britain was at war and Ireland exported foodstuffs to her. Dillon believed that Ireland should declare for 'decency, tolerance and freedom' and against 'the medieval barbarism of the dictators'.

Patrick McGilligan posed the government some searching questions. If the country was going to counter a continental attack with joint Irish-British troop operations, was there to be a unity of command? What would Northern Ireland's part be in such a scheme? 'Would it not be better to admit that we could not ourselves exploit the strategic value of Berehaven, Cork harbour and Lough Swilly, and that indeed - although in the matter of defence our road was parallel with the British road - we had no wish to do so; would it not be better to admit that and to make a new arrangement with the British for the defence of the ports?' W.T. Cosgrave bluntly stated that if Ireland was going to be neutral, it would have to be 'armed against all sides'. Fine Gael spokesmen advocated defence cooperation between Ireland and Britain and it is interesting to note that British cabinet papers for that period show that de Valera's government was more anxious for it at the time than he or his ministers would admit in the Dáil the following year.[10]

Fine Gael found itself in a dilemma when the war began. According to one authority, 'It realised that to support neutrality was virtually to abandon its Commonwealth position and to lose its remaining distinguishing mark, while to oppose neutrality would have been both futile and highly unpopular'.[11] As it turned out, it adhered with fidelity to the neutrality policy, even going so far as to expel its deputy leader, James Dillon, in 1942 for his public declaration of opposition to that course. It seems that there continued to be doubts about the party's real attitude, however, and Richard Mulcahy's call for an Anglo-Irish military alliance in 1944 as part of Fine Gael's future programme, may to some extent have confirmed such suspicions.

The onset of war inevitably led to a lessening of party political competition. Some form of party truce was demanded by the exigencies of national defence. But opposition demands for an emergency coalition or national government were dismissed out of hand by de Valera. To quote an eminent authority on the history of the period, 'Fine Gael and Labour, despite their staunch parliamentary support for neutrality, were treated as virtual pariahs'.[12] The most de Valera would agree to was to give the opposition seats on a National Defence Conference, a purely advisory body which he more or less ignored. Nevertheless, it was a forum for cooperation and members of all parties also appeared together on recruiting platforms. The championing of neutrality must have contributed to a diminution in party antagonisms. Involvement in the Red Cross or in local defence forces meant less time for party organisations, and the wartime restrictions on travel and newsprint limited party publicity at election times. But, unfortunately for Fine Gael and Labour, the reduction in political activity had perforce to be least damaging to Fianna Fáil, the party in power.

The policy of neutrality had all-party endorsement, but for declaring and upholding it, the bulk of the credit was given to Fianna Fáil, which exploited the attribution to utmost effect in the wartime elections. The theory was put forward that only de Valera's achievements had made neutrality possible, and only with him at the helm could the country be seen safely through the war. Hence the Fianna Fáil election slogan of 1943, 'Don't change horses when crossing the stream', which implied a questioning of Fine Gael's sincerity and competence regarding neutrality. It benefited Fianna Fáil that 'emergency' exigencies so limited opposition activity, and indeed it has been surmised, 'opposition beyond a certain limit could always be branded as a danger to national solidarity'.[13]

The general population rallied behind the government at the outbreak of war, but soon became disenchanted with Fianna Fáil's performance. Wages were controlled but prices rose. The government had failed to deliver on its rather lavish promises to the farmers and in 1938/39 a new party, Clann na Talmhan, appeared which appealed mainly to small and medium-sized farmers, mostly in the west of Ireland, formerly Fianna Fáil's heartland. Labour was also making headway and the fact that de Valera, contrary to his usual practice, postponed the general election until the last possible moment, June 1943, revealed how worried he was.

Not without reason, as it turned out, because Fianna Fáil lost 10% of the popular vote and ten seats. (It actually won nine seats more than it was entitled to on strict proportionality.) Clann na Talmhan won 13 seats, most of them in the west of Ireland, and Labour almost doubled its Dáil representation. The only reason Fianna Fáil continued in government was because of the failure of the opposition to coalesce.

For Fine Gael, the June 1943 election was calamitous. While all the other opposition to Fianna Fáil made ground, it lost heavily. Its share of the vote had declined by 10% since 1938 and it lost a staggering 13 seats. With 32, it had less than half the number of Fianna Fáil seats for the first time ever. Two former ministers, Richard Mulcahy and John Marcus O'Sullivan, and the former Attorney General and future Taoiseach, John A. Costello, were casualties of this electoral debacle. Oliver J. Flanagan, elected as a member of the Monetary Reform Party, began his long association with Laois-Offaly at this election. The most notable addition to the Fine Gael parliamentary fold in June 1943 was Liam Cosgrave, son of the leader of Cumann na nGaedheal and Fine Gael, himself a future leader of the party and a future Taoiseach. He won a seat in Dublin County, and was practically the only newcomer to Fine Gael's Dáil benches during the 1940s.

Fine Gael fell into disarray after the 1943 election. It had failed to take advantage of Fianna Fáil's unpopularity and appeared to be heading for extinction. W.T. Cosgrave, who has been described as 'much more a man of government than of opposition',[14] resigned as leader in the spring of 1944. T.F. O'Higgins became the parliamentary party leader and Richard

Mulcahy was chosen unanimously at the Fine Gael ard-fheis, shortly afterwards, to become party president.

After the disastrous loss of 13 seats, a stoic and gloomy acceptance of minority party status seemed to set in and with it the disappearance of any will to strive for power. Cosgrave's retirement was a further blow, and it has been written of him, 'Like some of his colleagues, he seemed to regard the party's historical task as having been already accomplished in the 1922-32 period.'[15] Following the crushing defeat of 1943, tired and unwell, Cosgrave seemed to have doubts about the future of the party and felt he could be of no further help to it as leader. His departure ended the interest of those who had stayed active in public life because of their affection and respect for Cosgrave. That the new leader, Richard Mulcahy, did not have a Dáil seat at the time, endorsed the feeling of the party's lassitude.

Labour appeared to be on the point of a significant electoral breakthrough after the 1943 election, but the party succumbed to bitter internal rivalry which seriously damaged it in the eyes of its followers. With the Labour party in disarray and Fine Gael dispirited, de Valera decided to take advantage of the credit he had won for resisting Allied demands for the expulsion of Axis diplomats from Dublin by calling a snap general election for May 1944. His gamble paid off in the sense that he had recovered his overall Dáil majority but, with turnout at its lowest since 1923, Fianna Fáil regained less than half the votes it had lost in 1943. It has been acutely observed that, 'victory in 1944 reflected despair in the opposition more than confidence in the government'.[16]

In 1944, Fine Gael lost a further two seats and slumped to an all-time low, returning only 30 TDs to the 138-member Dáil. (Fianna Fáil's 76 was over two-and-a-half times the Fine Gael total.) It had not attracted new members. Only one of its TDs was a newcomer to the Dáil in 1944, and even W.T. Cosgrave's Cork seat was lost. It has been remarked how 'candidates minimised their party affiliation in their election literature as if it was an albatross around their necks, and the internal solidarities of Fine Gael transfers declined to a record low'.[17]

In fact, the party put up only 57 candidates, not even enough to win a majority. A possible reason for this was that some former Fine Gael TDs and candidates now contested as Independents. Even *The Irish Independent*, a faithful supporter of Fine Gael over the years, was forced to concede that the 1944 election was a conclusive verdict in favour of Fianna Fáil. The return of Mulcahy and Costello to the Dáil was some consolation, but the decline seemed set on an irreversible course. The party lost a seat in a by-election in South Kerry in November 1944, and in 1945 did not contest three out of four by-elections. It had not won a by-election in ten years and in some places its imminent extinction was being forecast.

(ii) Electoral support and organisational defects in the 1930s and 1940s

It has been argued that Cumann na nGaedheal, afterwards Fine Gael, was originally the party of the status quo introduced by the Treaty and had the backing of business (especially the larger and longer-established businesses) and of middle and big farming interests, that it was, essentially, a middle-class party. It behaved and appeared like a conservative party in the 1920s and won the allegiance of those who wanted a peaceful situation and stability of government. Former Irish Parliamentary Party members and former Unionists gave their allegiance because, in their view, there was no better alternative and this helped integrate these into the new Ireland. It was probably also the party of the clergy, apart from some radical young curates of rural background. It got most support in the major cities, Dublin and Cork, and least in the agrarian west. Since Fianna Fáil proved that it could govern responsibly, it inevitably attracted away some of Fine Gael's Dublin support. It has also been held that, 'Although the party continued to behave like a party that might resume office again after the next election, its image as both conservative and pro-Commonwealth was hardly calculated to attract majority backing and it went into decline.'[18]

It is evident that Fine Gael began with a lot of fidelity from three strands which merged at its formation: business and commercial interests, substantial farmers, shopkeepers, many Protestants and, of course, those who opted for the Treaty. It was mainly, though not exclusively, a middle-class party from its inception. Where did it lose support during its period of decline from 1933 to 1948? Some of the business classes obviously transferred their allegiance to Fianna Fáil once they were convinced of its respectability and also because they benefited from its protectionism. Clann na Talmhan apparently garnered some farming sympathy from Fine Gael, while during the war the party must have lost people who felt that only a strong party, capable of forming a government, could provide stability in those uncertain times. The Blueshirt chapter must have disheartened some, while the lacklustre performance of the 1940s clearly disillusioned others, especially the young. Perhaps it lost some of its ex-Unionist, Protestant support with the departure of Dillon over the neutrality issue in 1942.

Its anti-republican, pro-Commonwealth image, inherited from Cumann na nGaedheal, harmed the party particularly in the border counties and in the west; its middle-class and big-farming representation, also in part passed on from Cumann na nGaedheal, damaged it among the working class. The involvement of the Centre Party, the mouthpiece of the larger farmers, did it little good in the eyes of the western smallholders; Clann na Talmhan did well in the west in the 1940s instead of Fine Gael. The Blueshirt episode undermined both its image and morale, and the problem of being an effective opposition during World War II weakened the party further.

At every general election between 1933 and 1948 Fine Gael's share of the vote fell, from 35% in 1937 to less than 20% in 1948. It was short of finance and took part in only six out of ten by-elections between 1944 and 1948, failing to win any of them. Indeed, it found difficulty in getting candidates to go forward. When W. T. Cosgrave retired in 1944, the party had the chance to adopt a fresh approach, but instead chose as his successor a man who was unpopular with many because of his role as Minister for

Defence during the Civil War and his involvement with the Blueshirts. Of this juncture, there was a comment made to the effect that 'not only observers, but even some leaders of the party seem to have felt that Fine Gael was nearing the end of its life.'[19]

The party seemed to have nothing in particular to offer any stratum of society: commerce and farming had accepted Fianna Fáil and workers supported either the latter or Labour. Farmers, unhappy with Fianna Fáil's performance, were able to express their discontent through Clann na Talmhan. A commentator has recorded: 'By 1948, then, Fine Gael was firmly rooted in the past, lacklustre, moribund and, as far as policies were concerned, little more than a pale shadow of Fianna Fáil.'[20] In the 1937 and 1938 elections, Fine Gael got least endorsement from the less well off and from Irish speakers, and most from employers, managers and bigger farmers. This support held even in the period of the greatest decline, between 1938 and 1943, when its electoral approval diminished by 10%. Its heavy losses in this period were most marked in agricultural Ireland, when it lost out greatly to Clann na Talmhan. The advent of Clann na Poblachta, led by Seán MacBride and offering a radical social, republican programme, made little difference to its electoral fortunes.

Fine Gael's local organisation trailed way behind Fianna Fáil's. It relied mainly on individuals of influence in cities and towns and during elections depended on ad hoc committees of stalwarts and sympathisers. This sufficed when Cumann na nGaedheal was in government, but was totally inadequate when, in opposition, the party needed to bring in young disciples and voluntary workers. It also failed to develop a worthwhile method of fund-raising until the end of the 1940s. It displayed a dearth of realism by failing to act with vigour in local politics and it further manifested weakness by refusing to attempt matching Fianna Fáil's forceful and effective electioneering skills. This diffidence in Fine Gael was in strange contrast to Cumann na nGaedheal during its 1927-32 campaigning when it used advertisements widely in the provincial press and introduced ingenious and imaginative cartoon propaganda.

Weak organisation and lack of funds resulted in the selection of prosperous farmers, professionals and businessmen as candidates. So there were too many amateur and part-time politicians, a factor which simply added to the organisational inadequacies. Fine Gael representatives had educational advantages, but this did not make up for the insufficiency of professional, energetic and enthusiastic politicians, especially in comparison with Fianna Fáil. It has been remarked that: 'The aura of middle-class respectability which clung to Fine Gael, especially in the country towns, militated against popular support at a period when, ironically, it was already losing middle-class votes to Fianna Fáil'.[21]

As already mentioned, the parliamentary party provided Fine Gael's initial structure and it never at this stage grasped the importance of strong local organisation; it made little attempt to attract new members, or to create the type of framework which would sustain it through periods of difficultly and electoral setback.

(iii) After World War II and the 1948 election

The appointment of Douglas Hyde as Ireland's first president in 1938 had been on a non-party basis but de Valera departed from this principle seven years later because he was confident of victory. There were three contestants in the 1945 presidential election: Seán MacEoin of Fine Gael, Seán T. O'Kelly of Fianna Fáil, and Patrick McCartan, a republican candidate. All three were veterans of the days of the Anglo-Irish war and the first Dáil. Considering at how low an ebb Fine Gael fortunes were at the time, it would have been a major surprise had MacEoin won. O'Kelly was duly elected, but not only did he not win an overall majority, but to Fianna Fáil's consternation 118,000 of the republican McCartan's transfers went to MacEoin, as opposed to only 27,000 to O'Kelly. This shock for the government produced another revision of the constituency boundaries. The newly formed Clann na Poblachta's success in by-elections, and gains in the 1947 local elections, mainly at the expense of Fianna Fáil, gave added urgency to the process. The result was a Dáil enlarged from 138 to 147 members, the maximum permitted under the Constitution, and this despite the decline in population since the revision in 1935, which had reduced the number of members from 152 to 138. The number of three-seat constituencies was raised from 15 to 22, which as *The Irish Independent* remarked, 'inevitably loads the electoral dice in favour of the big party'.

The years after the war were a time of social unrest and discontent in Ireland. In addition to the continuation of wartime shortages and rationing, the summer of 1946 was one of the wettest on record and the following winter was one of the hardest of the century. Inevitably, there was widespread dissatisfaction with the Fianna Fáil government, but it was Clann na Poblachta rather than Fine Gael that seized the initiative. With an attractive blend of radical republicanism and social and economic reform, it looked for endorsement from the electorate reminiscent of the way in which Fianna Fáil had done in 1932. De Valera called a general election for February 1948 with the obvious purpose of preventing Clann na Poblachta from consolidating its by-election gains.

Richard Mulcahy inherited the leadership at the darkest hour in Fine Gael's history, but he brought to his task an unshakeable faith in the ability of the party to survive, and a firm belief in its distinctive role in Irish politics. His style of leadership was austere and disciplined, leading by personal example, and displaying a commitment to bringing new people into the party. Under him there were significant developments in policy, especially in agriculture and economics.

Because of the weakness of its organisation and because it was unable to get candidates, Fine Gael contested only one of the five by-elections held in December 1945 but after that the party made a determined effort to reactivate itself. Eighty-two candidates contested the 1948 election for Fine Gael, 25 more than in 1944, but their campaign was subdued and they did not go to the polls with any great optimism. The party had continued to lose support: one midland TD had resigned in 1947 for unclear reasons and sat as an Independent, rejoining Fine Gael in 1952; another sitting TD contested the 1948 election as an Independent, and three TDs died during the campaign. Therefore, only 22 outgoing deputies took part in the 1948 contest - less than half the number elected in 1938.

In retrospect, the 1948 election can be viewed as having determined Fine Gael's survival. Most observers had expected it to slump even further. If this had happened and Fianna Fáil had come to power again, the party of the men who had established the state may well have disappeared. Its share of the vote was actually lower than in 1944 - for the first and only time in its history it fell below 20% - but it gained a seat. Seemingly there had been a belief that Fine Gael was facing near extinction as evidenced after the election by comments like 'The remarkably firm stand by Fine Gael', and 'Fine Gael polled well' in Dublin newspaper leading articles. Few, if any, could have realised it at the time, but Fine Gael was on the verge of what has been humorously described as 'the greatest come-back since Lazarus'.[22]

Chapter 4

Two Periods in Government: 1948-57

(i) First inter-party government 1948-51

As a result of the February 1948 general election, Fianna Fáil had 68 seats, Fine Gael 31 seats, Labour and National Labour 19, Clann na Poblachta 10, Clann na Talmhan 7, and Independents 12. Although Fianna Fáil had lost its overall majority, de Valera, with the support of National Labour and some Independents, confidently expected to form a government once again. However, 16 years of Fianna Fáil hegemony were about to end and, against all odds, the country was on the threshold of experiencing its first ever inter-party government.

It was the Fine Gael leader, Richard Mulcahy, who took the initiative after the election results were announced by immediately starting talks among the parties with a view to forming a coalition government alternative to Fianna Fáil. There were obvious difficulties. One was the incompatibility between Fine Gael and Clann na Poblachta, the former being, according to one authority, 'widely regarded as the Commonwealth, conservative, strong farmer party', while the latter was a radical, republican party.[1] A second obstacle was the traditional antipathy between Fine Gael and Labour. A third was the fact that Labour itself was divided. But these barriers were overcome.

'Problems of personality compounded problems of policy', it has been observed.[2] Although Mulcahy was the obvious alternative prime minister, he was unacceptable to Seán MacBride and Clann an Poblachta because of his association with the Civil War. MacBride, the son of Maud Gonne and Major John MacBride who was executed for his part in the 1916 Rising, fought on the anti-Treaty side during the Civil War and was afterwards chief-of-staff of the IRA. But Mulcahy himself removed this final obstacle by means of the selfless gesture of proposing John A. Costello for Taoiseach. The years 1937 to 1948 had been disastrous for Fine Gael but now, almost unexpectedly, the party was given an opportunity to arrest what looked like an inevitable and irreversible decline.

Seven of the ministers in the 1948-51 government belonged to Fine Gael. (This is to include James Dillon who was, strictly speaking, an Independent. But it seems right that he should be numbered among Fine Gael ministers because he had remained on very friendly terms with the party since his departure in 1942; it did not challenge him in his Monaghan constituency, and he was soon to return to its fold.) Seán MacEoin was Minister for Justice; Patrick McGilligan, Minister for Finance; T.F. O'Higgins, Minister for Defence; Daniel Morrissey, Minister for Industry and Commerce; Richard Mulcahy, Minister for Education, and James Dillon, Minister for Agriculture. The other portfolios were held by Labour's William Norton (Tánaiste and Minister for Social Welfare) and T.J. Murphy (Minister for Local Government); Clann na Poblachta's Seán MacBride (External Affairs) and Dr Noel Browne (Health); National Labour's James Everett (Posts and Telegraphs) and Clann na Talmhan's Joseph Blowick (Lands and Fisheries). T.J. Murphy died suddenly in 1949 and was replaced by his party colleague, M.J. Keyes.

Costello's position of Taoiseach at the outset of the 1948 government was unique in Irish terms, and the contrast with de Valera could hardly have been more marked. The division of ministries among the parties had already been decided before he agreed to be leader and the choice of the individual ministers was up to the various party leaders and not to Costello. MacBride urged him to appoint McGilligan to Finance (Mulcahy seems to have been the initial choice for that portfolio) and was successful. It was also at first intended to give External Affairs to Mulcahy but because MacBride coveted that position for himself, Mulcahy accepted Education. The Fine Gael leader seldom intervened in cabinet discussions except when the affairs of his own Department were being discussed. These factors bear, it has been rightly remarked 'further tribute to his remarkable selflessness'.[3]

MacBride was intensely suspicious of the higher civil servants and caused Maurice Moynihan, the Secretary to the

Government, to be excluded from cabinet meetings, so that the task of recording decisions and keeping the minutes was entrusted to Liam Cosgrave, who by that time had been almost five years in the Dáil and had been chairman of the Committee of Public Accounts for three years. Moynihan remained Secretary to the Government and did his best to keep the machinery of the state running smoothly, but he was working in the dark and the view has been expressed that this departure from established procedure weakened both Taoiseach and cabinet. The practice did not recur in Costello's second government.[4]

The first inter-party government was the beginning of a new departure in Irish politics. The large number of parties involved, the wide diversity of their policies, the uncertainty of the administration's majority and the size and homogeneity of the opposition, all seemed to presage a brief term in office. But an avoidance of potentially divisive legislation, the introduction of measures likely to make ministers more popular, especially more government spending, ensured survival. Obviously there was not the same sense of collective responsibility as in a single-party government, and although some ministers from different parties often appeared on the same platform to show their solidarity, it is clear that many of them (especially the leaders of the parties) conducted their responsibility as it suited them and often spoke in public about matters which fell within the brief of other ministers. Despite these difficulties, Costello has been universally described as a sensitive, diplomatic, skilful, patient and impartial chairman of the cabinet.

(ii) The Republic of Ireland Act

It has been remarked that the 1948-51 government displayed more reforming initiative than posterity has given it credit for, but that, ironically, it is not its domestic successes that are remembered but its one domestic failure and the dramatic change it affected in Ireland's relationship with the Commonwealth.[5]

De Valera himself admitted that his 1937 Constitution made Ireland a republic in everything but name. His External Relations

Act of 1936 allowed the British monarch a very limited and conditional role in Ireland's foreign relations. Costello greatly disliked this measure and had been its most outspoken Fine Gael critic when it was introduced into the Dáil. Although some other members of the party were unhappy with its ambiguities, Fine Gael was generally seen as favouring the link with the Commonwealth. The 1948 election speeches of its leaders had, like those of all other parties, many condemnations of partition, but they did not go so far as to demand a republic (which was much more likely than not to strengthen partition). However, despite the basic incompatibility between becoming a republic and getting rid of the border, the government decided to declare Ireland a republic.

No doubt the presence of MacBride, who was pledged to work for a republic, was a factor in the decision to do so. Another, as Costello explained himself, was that because the parties were so finely balanced in the Dáil, the government was vulnerable to some member taking the initiative and seeking to introduce such a motion to embarrass and possibly even to destroy the government. A third factor was Costello's own attitude. His primary interest on becoming Taoiseach was economic reform, but he disliked the External Relations Act and was deeply aware of the way in which the idea of a republic had so divided Irishmen since the Civil War. Although the move would be a painful departure from his own party's history, it would be worth it if it took the gun out of Irish politics.

The dramatic and apparently sudden nature of the way the intention was announced on Costello's visit to Canada in September 1948 has led to much speculation about why this particular forum was chosen. The most extreme example was that either he or his wife had been insulted by the Governor General of Canada, Earl Alexander, who was of Ulster Unionist stock, and that in a fury he stormed off to a press conference where he announced the dissolution of the final link with the Commonwealth. Not only would this have been out of the question constitutionally, it is completely untrue.

The cabinet had decided to repeal the Act before Costello

went to Canada. The cabinet papers from the time reveal no advance preparations to Costello's dramatic public announcement. 'Indeed there is nothing in the government or cabinet minutes to indicate that *any* decision respecting the External Relations Act was taken before Costello went to Canada', it has been pointed out,[6] but this may have been the result of the procedure which excluded officials from the Taoiseach's department from government meetings. It may have been agreed in principle to get rid of the Act, but when it was to be announced and what it would actually mean had perhaps not been considered. On the other hand, although there is some confusion about the exact date, both Costello and MacBride have stated that it was decided that summer, probably in August, and both MacBride and Norton had made it clear in the Dáil that the Act would be repealed and had gathered from Fianna Fáil that there would be no opposition on its part.

Costello was invited to address the Canadian Bar Association in early September. His speech, 'Ireland in international affairs', had been approved by the cabinet before he left Dublin. It was, mainly, a capable and detached account of how Ireland's relations with the Commonwealth had changed since the Treaty, but he criticised the shortcomings he saw in the way the External Relations Act dealt with the Crown. At the Bar Association dinner the toast was 'The King', and when asked by the Canadian Minister for External Affairs if that did not cover Ireland, Costello had to argue that it did not because Ireland was not a real member of the Commonwealth.

At an official dinner in Ottawa, as a guest of the Canadian government, Costello had two unpleasant experiences. On the Governor General's table was a replica of 'Roaring Meg', the cannon used at the siege of Derry in 1689 and a hallowed symbol to Unionists. It was not a very tactful gesture on the part of Earl Alexander, but it was hardly the reason why Ireland left the Commonwealth. More serious was that the Irish High Commissioner had arranged with the Canadian government that as well as a toast to 'The King' there would also be one to 'The President of Ireland'. However, the Irish toast was omitted. In retrospect, Costello believed this to be simply a slip in protocol. He had had a similar experience a few months before in London. Both incidents denied the existence of Ireland as a republic and showed the shortcomings of the External Relations Act.

However, Costello's reaction was caused, not by these irritations, but by the headline in the 5 September *Sunday Independent* which read 'External Relations Act to go'. While it is difficult to say whether or not the article was deliberately published at that time, it is worth remarking that the *Independent* newspaper chain was usually seen as close to Fine Gael. Costello, who learned of the article by telephone that afternoon, was due to give a press conference on 7 September and so had one-and-a-half days to consider his response to the inevitable questions. It was impossible to consult with his colleagues in Dublin in any depth and he seems to have come to his decision on his own, but with what the cabinet had decided before his departure from Dublin very much in his mind. He has written that if that decision had not been taken, it would have been very wrong for him to have acted as he did and that he could very easily have dealt with the *Sunday Independent* article. He felt that he should be frank and make known his government's decision to repeal the Act.

The announcement caused quite a reaction in Ireland, even among members of the cabinet who were probably as surprised as anyone else by the timing of it. The justness of the observation that 'the Irish people had a reasonable right to expect that an announcement of such momentous import might most appropriately have been made on their own soil'[7] must be conceded. The real significance of what Costello said at the 7 September press conference lay in the fact that he made it clear that it was not just a question of repealing the External Relations Act but that it meant Ireland leaving the Commonwealth.

It has been contended that the amendments Costello made to MacBride's draft of a Bill show that his dissatisfaction with the ambiguities of the Act and his determination to put an end to these were most responsible for the form and substance of the Bill put before the Dáil in November 1948.[8] Similarly, Costello decided that it should be he, and not MacBride, who would present it to the Dáil. The result of the measure, according to Costello, was finally 'to place the question of Irish sovereignty and status beyond dispute or suspicion or guesswork', and afterwards he regarded it as his government's greatest achievement.

The Republic of Ireland Act repealed the External Relations Act, renamed the state and enabled the President to exercise the state's foreign relations functions. During the Dáil debates on the measure, Costello said that his government had two purposes in enacting the legislation: to end old enmities within Ireland and to put Anglo-Irish relations on a better, because more unambiguous, footing. In reply to the argument that the move would make partition even more difficult to end than before, he stated that not making it in the past had done nothing to remove the border and asked what was the point in continuing with it, that being the case. The validity of such an argument may be doubted on the grounds that, although it might not make things any worse, the measure would make it harder to make them better. It did seem to worsen matters in the short term because, as part of their official response, the British gave the Unionists a guarantee that Northern Ireland would remain part of the United Kingdom unless the Northern Irish government decided otherwise.

Was the measure 'unnecessary, precipitate and fruitless - entrenching the Northern Unionists in their position, destroying a possible bridge to unity, leaving the gun in politics and involving a futile and frustrating anti-partition campaign?' it has been asked.[9] The decision to adopt republican status in Ireland was closely related to the abstract factor of national honour and self-respect: Ireland's geographical proximity to Britain and the long, troubled history of Anglo-Irish relations made the Irish feel that any sort of a constitutional link, however insubstantial, implied inferior status and made it vital to take on formal sovereign status, regardless of the results.[10]

Since 1932, Fianna Fáil continually had been able to trump its pro-Treaty opponents with the green card and label them 'pro-British' or 'anti-national'. After 1949 this no longer applied. The

76

Republic of Ireland Act ended the era begun by the Treaty split, during which the chasm between the political parties centred on the link with Britain and how that could and should be altered. 'Henceforth independence was no longer a cause of contention', it has been affirmed.[11] Post-1951 politics changed significantly from what had gone before. Economic issues - prices, wages, inflation - mattered much more, and the old Civil War questions receded into the mists of time. So, Costello's defence of the Republic of Ireland Act was justified, his argument having been that it aimed

> to take away from Irish internal politics all the dissensions between classes because we will have complete sovereignty, independence and freedom. The removal of these internal political differences will enable the people to centre their energies on the economic problems which have to be met.

The declaration of a republic may have been out of line with Fine Gael's traditional approach, but it did not alienate any significant section of its support. During the 1951 election campaign there was only the odd comment about Fine Gael betraying its former Commonwealth support. It has been remarked that the Republic of Ireland Act did not damage Fine Gael among the electorate and 'perhaps washed away some of the anti-national mud its opponents had thrown at it over the years'.[12]

The other major foreign policy item with which this first inter-party government was concerned was the establishment of the North Atlantic Treaty Organisation. When NATO was set up in 1949, Ireland declined the invitation to join. It is probably true that if it had been in a position to decide independently, Fine Gael's history and inclinations probably would have been in favour of Irish membership of NATO. But, because Britain was in the organisation and because of the partition issue, the other coalition parties could not appear to be less intransigent on the subject of the border than Fianna Fáil.

In 1949 and 1950, direct contact with ministers in Northern Ireland was made by Daniel Morrissey, Minister for Industry and Commerce, who met his opposite number in Belfast. Later, owing to illness, Morrissey was unable to travel and Liam Cosgrave went to Belfast twice and met McCreery and Maynard Sinclair, Minister for Finance, concerning the Great Northern Railway and the Erne hydroelectric and drainage scheme. This scheme was a combined effort between the Irish ESB and the Northern authorities. The two Northern ministers travelled to Dublin to continue discussions on these matters with Cosgrave. Such encounters were years before the Lemass-O'Neill meetings but received far less publicity because this was the pre-television era of reporting.

(iii) Economic planning

It deserves emphasising that the beginnings of economic planning in Ireland belonged to the 1948-51 period, predating by seven years Dr T.K. Whitaker's famous memorandum to the Department of Finance in 1956, which is still popularly believed to be the point of departure for government economic programming. *Ireland's Long-Term Recovery Programme* was a government white paper published as early as January 1949, setting out a coherent series of economic aims and policies for the 1949-53 period. It was the first exercise in economic planning by an Irish government.

The economic reforms initiated by the inter-party government were to have a far greater influence than could have been predicted at the time. It would be to oversimplify matters grossly to suggest that this variegated coalition had anything like a common economic policy but the ideas the cabinet developed and implemented did prove that the administration was distinctly different from Fianna Fáil in outlook. As Patrick Lynch, then Costello's private secretary and afterwards a distinguished economist succinctly put it: 'State spending was to become the conspicuous feature of inter-party economic policies'.[13]

To make the most of government investment, two organisations were set up to provide expert advice; these contributed greatly to economic planning in Ireland. The Industrial Development Authority, the establishment of which Fianna Fáil strongly opposed, assembled a corpus of experienced financiers and industrialists who were to plan industrial growth for the country and to consider the protectionism that lay behind the existing industrial structure. Córas Tráchtála or the Export Board was set up to improve the market for Irish exports to America and Canada; it was so successful that it became an enduring aspect of Irish export marketing, not only across the Atlantic but all over the world.

The historian of the Department of Finance has argued that 'after 1948, ministers and government officials alike became increasingly concerned with framing a longer-term financial and economic policy than had previously been contemplated. The days of ad hoc, year-to-year financial management were clearly numbered.'[14] By the end of the 1940s, old issues like the Treaty, the Civil War and partition no longer had the same relevance. Sovereignty had been achieved and exercised and the Republic of Ireland Act was its final proof. Economic issues henceforth became predominant electorally. Because the new government was formed from four parties rather than from one, consensus concerning financial policy could no longer be taken for granted.

All MacBride's conditions for agreeing to coalesce (afforestation, hospital building, increases in pensions and health benefits, the repatriation of foreign investments for development in Ireland) had major implications for the government's financial policy. (MacBride has been commended for his commitment to afforestation, but there seems to be an unawareness that it was a basic plank in Arthur Griffith's Sinn Féin programme as far back as 1905. That it should not have become a serious government issue until almost 30 years after Griffith's death is an eloquent comment on at least one glaring oversight in the policies of the various governments of Ireland since independence.)

MacBride, as Minister for External Affairs, was in charge of Ireland's participation in the European Recovery Programme (ERP) or Marshall Plan and he made many valuable contacts (his fluent French was a great help) in the Organisation for European Economic Cooperation (OEEC). Both these factors gave him an influence on economic policy far beyond that possessed by any previous Minister for External Affairs. Without the knowledge of the Department of Finance, MacBride was able to draw up an Irish recovery programme and to earmark ERP funds for it. Dillon, who as Minister for Agriculture planned land reclamation and drainage schemes and who was to garner ERP funding for these, often supported MacBride and urged Costello to help break Finance's stranglehold on government spending. The main significance that has been seen in these developments was that the philosophic consensus between elected representatives and public servants about economic policy in Ireland since the foundation of the state was finally breaking down. A new generation of ministers were no longer inhibited by the traditional wisdom of the Department of Finance.[15]

It was MacBride's view that funds from the ERP should be used for economic development, especially land reclamation and reafforestation, a view which Department of Finance officials strongly opposed. He was careful to discuss his proposals with both the Taoiseach and McGilligan before making them known and before the Department of Finance became aware of them, using the Shannon Scheme from the 1920s as an example of the type of state intervention which he believed was now required. Pleas by his officials that Finance rather than External Affairs control the ERP funds that Ireland received made no impression on McGilligan - 'their minutes on the subject are scarred by his queries and exclamations in red crayon'.[16]

McGilligan's budget of May 1950 was the country's first capital budget and has been described by Patrick Lynch as 'the first explicit expression of Keynes in an Irish budget'. Its origin lay in a speech Costello made on economic and financial policy to the Institute of Bankers in Ireland in November 1949. This in turn evolved from conversations Costello had been having with Dillon, his economic adviser Patrick Lynch and his son-in-law Alexis Fitzgerald. Lynch's role was particularly crucial. He had been transferred from Finance to the Department of the Taoiseach when Costello requested J. J. McElligott (Secretary of the Department of Finance) to find him an official to advise him on economic affairs. His was an unprecedented appointment and further proof that economic policy henceforth would be uppermost in the legislators' minds. It also showed that Costello viewed his own role to be spokesman on important issues which might divide the coalition; he followed a similar approach in his government's foreign policy.

The importance of Costello's November speech cannot be exaggerated, in the opinion of one authority. He was not an economist and had little deep knowledge of the Department of Finance, but 'never before in the history of the state had the head of government delivered a major speech devoted *exclusively* to the principles underlying his government's economic policy'.[17] Lynch and Alexis Fitzgerald drafted the speech; for the former, it was an ideal chance to implant Keynesian principles at the forefront of government economic policy. Finance officials opposed him, but McGilligan gave him his support.

So, whatever his officials thought, McGilligan strongly supported the new government approach to economic planning. His own economic ideas were ambiguous. On the one hand he often expressed the view that the state should not intervene in the entrepreneur's domain, yet he was the person who had undertaken the Shannon scheme many years before which was, according to Lynch, 'one of the first and the most successful of the more ambitious experiments in public enterprise in Great Britain or Ireland'. There is no doubt that McGilligan was one of the first Irish politicians to embrace Keynes's ideas, and his personal papers show how interested he was in the debate in Britain on the need for greater state involvement in the economy after 1945. 'He was thus an obvious choice for the sensitive Finance portfolio in the inter-party government, as MacBride's prior knowledge and approval of his appointment shows', it has been averred.[18]

McGilligan's departmental officials regarded him as the most intelligent of the ministers under whom they had served until that time, but they knew that the nature of the coalition government imposed limitations on his penetrating, open-minded approach. His bad health was another disadvantage and he frequently missed government meetings because of it. When present, he was a most effective contributor and Lynch, the secretary to the economic committee of the cabinet, has recalled how, although ill at home, McGilligan, over the phone, could change decisions taken on very important issues.

The economic committee of the cabinet, set up to survey the state's economy and to make suggestions, initiated the first consistent debate on economic policy in government since 1922. McGilligan made effective use of this committee to achieve agreement on issues that might have divided the parties in the inter-party government. There can be little doubt that his long 16-year sojourn in the wilderness of political opposition since 1932 had made him aware of the need for compromise. The fact that the coalition consisted of five parties complicated financial policy because rivalries and ideological discrepancies could exacerbate disagreements over the financial control of departmental budgets. When McGilligan was Minister for Industry and Commerce during the Cumann na nGaedheal period, he had often collided with and been defeated by the Department of Finance; this made him aware of the necessity for compromise in an administration where the ministers responsible for the main spending departments were not of his own party (Daniel Morrissey of Industry and Commerce, although then in Fine Gael, began political life in Labour). The unity of the coalition could be endangered if McGilligan had turned down the spending demands of a member of a party not his own. Because he played such a significant role in holding together the coalition, he was slow to put forward in their undiluted form the policies his senior officials would have liked him to propound.

Finance officials' counsels of an austere and conservative approach often fell on barren ground as far as McGilligan was concerned. He did indeed differ from MacBride on some important issues, but did not pursue the orthodox Finance line. 'If less radical than MacBride and others might have wished, he was at the same time less ready to imbibe the conventional wisdom of the Department of Finance than any of the former political heads of the Department,' it has been maintained.[19]

There were differences over financial policy between Fine Gael and Clann na Poblachta ministers. When, in September 1949, the Department of Finance was informed by the British government that the pound sterling was to be devalued vis a vis the dollar, the government met in emergency session, with Finance officials and Patrick Lynch, the Taoiseach's economic adviser, also present for the long and difficult discussions. MacBride and Browne strongly opposed an Irish devaluation equivalent to that of the British, but McGilligan and Dillon were very much against their Clann na Poblachta colleagues. Finance officials felt that the same devaluation must take place and when William Norton of Labour agreed with their advice, it was decided to devalue on a par with the British.

An undoubted result of the devaluation was MacBride's firm opposition to the reappointment of Joseph Brennan as Governor of the Central Bank in 1950. He argued that such an appointment should be made by agreement in a coalition government. But he objected in vain, and Brennan's redesignation, on McGilligan's recommendation, was confirmed. McGilligan, as Minister for Finance, had to face the difficulties of being 'caught between the conflicting pressures of advice proffered by his departmental officials and the contrary financial policies of his ministerial colleagues.'[20]

(iv) Agriculture and Social Welfare

James Dillon proved a creative Minister for Agriculture and was one of the inter-party government's major successes. He was fond of quoting a slogan, invented by Patrick Hogan many years before, to summarise his objectives in office: 'One more cow, one more sow, and one more acre under the plough.' Two achievements in particular were associated with Dillon. One was the 1948 Anglo-Irish trade agreement which secured improved terms for Irish produce, especially by linking the prices for Irish cattle and sheep with the guaranteed price received by British farmers. As a result, the cattle and sheep sectors expanded significantly during Dillon's tenure.

His major venture was the 1949 Land Rehabilitation Scheme which sought to bring back into full use land made idle because of lack of capital or other reasons. It was intended to extend the scheme to some four million acres over ten years and the state was to spend £40 million, part of which would be paid for by United States loans through the European Recovery Programme. Whatever about its economic value, there is no doubt about the scheme's psychological impact in bringing hope to very poor districts, especially in the west of Ireland. As Patrick Lynch remarked: 'Removing the rocks from Connemara may have been bad economics for Irish adherents of the Manchester School, but to many people emotionally involved in the West of Ireland and its people, it was the best news since the activities of the Congested Districts Board.'[21] Dillon's energy found many other outlets, such as promoting agricultural education at parish level and cooperating with the government of Northern Ireland in developing the Foyle fisheries which straddled the border.

Dillon has been described as 'a resounding political success, the star electoral act of the inter-party government.'[22] Certainly his Land Rehabilitation Scheme recovered some of the political territory lost to Fianna Fáil which Clann na Talmhan had shown would still richly reward the effort ploughed into it.

Dillon was the first person to raise the question of family allowances as a political issue in 1939 and his land scheme too had an undoubted social dimension. Two other measures showed a very clear concern on the part of this government for welfare . The number of houses built, especially in rural areas, was remarkable. The credit for the housing drive belongs to the Labour Minister for Local Government, T.J. Murphy, and to his successor, M.J. Keyes. Costello supported Murphy by pressing the unwilling banks strongly for finance for the building programme, arguing that social stability was threatened by the housing situation. The rate of building undertaken far exceeded anything attempted before the war and greatly improved the condition of life in the countryside. The almost complete wiping out of the scourge of tuberculosis was an even more impressive feat, the credit for the speed with which it was achieved going to Dr Noel Browne.

Both the devaluation of sterling in 1948 and the Korean War added to the problem of inflation, which in turn provoked demands for wage increases to match the rising prices. The inter-party government inherited its Fianna Fáil predecessor's dispute with the national teachers, and discontent among white-collar workers climaxed in a bank strike in 1950. Both the increasing cost of living and the lack of adequate social services were affecting all sections of the community, even those in secure employment. The government did what it could, McGilligan, in his first budget, reducing spending in the defence and other areas in order to improve the pensions and allowances of widows, orphans and the old. Eventually the government evolved a wide-ranging social welfare scheme. It introduced it in the Dáil in early 1951 but the administration did not survive to enact it.

(v) The Irish Language

Cumann na nGaedheal had left little unattempted in the crusade to revive and restore the Irish language. Fianna Fáil had proclaimed this as one of the party's twin national aims (together with the unification of the country) on its foundation in 1926.

Thomas Derrig was Fianna Fáil Minister for Education from 1932 to 1948 and, under him, more pressure was brought to bear upon the schools to Gaelicise the young. Any complaints from teachers were met by what has been described as an 'almost hysterical' refusal of any sort of impartial enquiry from Derrig and his Department.[23]

In the Dáil, the ebullient Dillon was the most articulate and persistent critic of the policy of teaching through Irish. He argued that the method was removing detached support for the language, causing parents and children to become anti-Irish and doing further serious harm to the general standard of education. John Marcus O'Sullivan, Minister for Education from 1925 to 1932, had sponsored the language policy during that period. Following the publication of the Irish National Teachers' Organisation Report on the subject in 1941, O'Sullivan, while still defending the general policy, expressed his belief that the INTO's case for investigation was an unanswerable one and contended that in any event it would be unwise for Derrig 'to flout the opinion of those on whose cooperation in the schools he depended'.

Some feared that the inter-party government would attempt dramatic changes in relation to the position of Irish in the schools. As a result, many Fianna Fáil speakers, including Seán Lemass and Jack Lynch, welcomed Mulcahy's appointment to Education, since he was 'a dedicated revivalist'. Mulcahy accepted some of the criticisms of the educational system current at the time and introduced some reforms. The system of rating teachers was abolished in 1949 and the following year a Council of Education was set up to advise the Minister on the use of the primary school, its curriculum and the teaching of Irish.[24]

(vi) The Mother and Child controversy

The complex background to, and indeed the details of, what became known as the 'Mother and Child' controversy are not integral to this study. What is of concern here is the part played by Fine Gael in that dispute.

Fine Gael strongly opposed the Public Health Bill introduced by the Fianna Fáil government in 1945. A large number of Fine Gael deputies spoke against it and a record number of amendments was put down, mostly by Fine Gael. At one stage Fine Gael members left the Dáil in protest at what they considered to be the government's attempt to rush through the Bill. Fine Gael opposed it mainly on the grounds that it was contrary to Catholic social teaching. They criticised its bureaucratic nature, especially its provisions for compulsory inspection and detention. Mulcahy thought it 'an unprecedented series of attacks on public liberty'. Costello considered it unconstitutional, and McGilligan stated that he was defending the 'Christian tradition that there are individual rights which no State can take away'. Fine Gael speakers wondered if the bishops had been consulted and predicted a clash with the Church.

However, by 1947, although the Health Bill of that year was essentially the same as its 1945 predecessor (the latter had not been pursued because the Fianna Fáil Parliamentary Secretary for Local Government and Public Health, Dr F.C. Ward, resigned when a public enquiry showed that he had made incomplete tax returns on the profits of his bacon factory in Monaghan), Fine Gael gave it a much friendlier reception. Perhaps the reason was the conciliatory approach of the new Minister for Health, Dr James Ryan, which was in sharp contrast to that of Dr Ward. O'Higgins thought it uncontroversial, while Morrissey welcomed it on behalf of Fine Gael. The only real opposition came over the compulsory inspection of schoolchildren, the main opponent being Dillon. He saw it as going against parents' rights, parents having first responsibility for their children's welfare. Dillon decided to test the constitutionality of the Bill in the courts; his counsel consisted of three prominent Fine Gaelers - Costello, Lavery and McGilligan. Before the courts had a chance to rule, the government had fallen and the problem had been passed on to its successor.[25]

The new government at first did not know that the Mother and Child section of the 1947 Health Bill had prompted the bishops to a protest to de Valera. Speaking during the Dáil debate on Browne's resignation in April 1951, Costello stated that he had learned of it sometime after assuming office, but he could not say exactly when.

Dillon withdrew his court action as Dr Noel Browne agreed straightaway to amend the clauses relating to the compulsory inspection of schoolchildren. The government considered at an early stage whether to include a means test in their Bill (the Fianna Fáil measure did not), and decided against it. Browne himself did not feel strongly on the matter at that time (in fact, he suggested that including it might placate the Irish Medical Association (IMA) whose opposition to Browne's Bill was hardening) but, as Costello afterwards explained, they were inexperienced in government and thought that they would not be able to get such a change through the Dáil.

As well as getting into trouble with the bishops, Browne also crossed swords with the IMA, many of his fellow ministers and with his party leader, MacBride. The crux of his difficulties with the IMA was the means test. By 1950 Browne had become adamant that there was to be none. 'Dr Browne appears to have become very bitter against the IMA at this time', it has been observed.[26] One of his fellow ministers recorded that he seemed to develop a 'pathological hatred' of the profession. This brought him into conflict with his cabinet colleagues, who were uneasy about the way he was handling relations with the doctors.

Most perturbed of all were the Fine Gael ministers, many of whom were in the professions themselves and would not accept his hostile view of the doctors. Costello, for example, was 'shocked' at Browne's attitude. As he afterwards declared in the Dáil: 'They acted the part which you would expect a noble profession to act in regard to this matter and the only thanks they have got is vilification.' Dr T. F. O'Higgins, the Minister for Defence, was in a particular quandary since he was a medical doctor who had cordial relations with the IMA. Even the Labour members of the government were unhappy with the way Browne handled the situation. At various times Costello, Norton, Dillon and O'Higgins tried unsuccessfully to act as intermediaries between him and the IMA.

When Browne decided abruptly in March 1951 to proceed with the scheme, his relations with his colleagues deteriorated greatly. The decision seems to have been taken without consultation and understandably angered the members of the government. The newspapers reported that on 6 March Costello, Norton, Mulcahy, McGilligan, Dillon and MacBride met to discuss the Mother and Child scheme and were dissatisfied with how it had developed. When Browne resigned from the government in April 1951, he declared (and this was one of the few things he said which was not contradicted by other ministers) that in early March Costello and many of the ministers expressed their unease about the burgeoning dispute with the IMA and suggested that a means test should be included after all. He defied them to sack him by saying that if they reversed their decision taken as a cabinet in 1948, he would have to consider his position. They did not do so, he added. The reason they did not was because they probably still hoped to resolve the situation amicably. Browne was playing with fire by defying his colleagues in this way because it meant that if he faced opposition from elsewhere he would be less likely to have their support.[27]

In October 1950, the Catholic bishops sent a letter to the Taoiseach expressing their reservations about certain aspects of the proposed legislation. Before sending it, their representatives met Dr Browne to tell him of their protest in advance of raising it with Costello. There are some very different accounts of what happened at this meeting. One is Costello's, given in the Dáil the following April, and is based on what he remembered Archbishop McQuaid telling him of it just after the meeting had taken place. According to this, Browne brushed aside any objection concerning the means test and would consider only the question of education, on which he believed the bishops had a point and which he promised to consider; he then ended the meeting and walked out. In the Dáil on the same occasion, Browne gave a contrary account to the effect that he understood that he had assuaged the hierarchy's reservations.

As well as the recollections of the meeting, those of what happened afterwards are also at odds. According to Browne, Costello told him the day after his meeting with McQuaid that Archbishop McQuaid had informed him that the bishops were satisfied with their interview with Browne. In mid-November, Costello gave Browne a copy of the hierarchy's October letter. Browne maintains that since the letter was dated the day before his encounter with the bishops, he presumed that he had been given it simply as a record and he prepared a reply for Costello to send to them for the same purpose. As Browne's version had it, because he heard nothing from either Costello or the hierarchy for some months, he presumed that all was well.

Costello's memories are very different. He said that after the October meeting he asked Browne and McQuaid to give him time to consider the matter and told them that he would send a formal reply to the bishops' 10 October letter; he remembered telling Browne twice since Christmas 1950 that he had not yet replied to that missive. Costello's recollections are endorsed by MacBride's. It has been believed that Costello delayed a month before giving the bishops' letter to Browne and then did not send them the latter's detailed rebuttal because he hoped 'to avert the growing possibility of a confrontation'.[28]

It might seem hard to believe that ministers can have been at cross purposes on so serious a matter for so long. But it is important to emphasise that the main issue between October 1950 and March 1951 was the differences between Browne and the IMA, and the bishops had agreed to await its resolution before their own objections were to be considered. As Costello explained, he was in close touch with McQuaid throughout the period, kept him informed of the efforts to solve the impasse, and McQuaid approved of those attempts.

But in March 1951, when Browne ended talks with the IMA and published details of the scheme, the clash with the bishops came to the fore. He sent a copy of his brochure, outlining the details of the scheme, to all the bishops. McQuaid's reply reiterated their objections and the Archbishop also sent a copy of this letter, as he told Browne, to Costello. Browne seems to have dismissed the letter and, according to Costello, neither replied to nor acknowledged it. Costello showed it to his cabinet colleagues and when Norton asked Browne what he proposed to do about it, Browne replied 'Nothing'. Costello then asked Browne about it, to be told that there was nothing in the letter to worry about.

The next day Costello tried to convince Browne of the gravity of the situation and sent him a formal letter telling him that he would have to meet the bishops' objections as expressed in their letters. In his reply, Browne denied that the hierarchy was opposed to his scheme, claimed that he had satisfied the bishops at their 11 October meeting, that McQuaid was the only objector now and that another bishop had assured him that, as far as he knew, the hierarchy did not object to the scheme. Browne's attitude can be explained in terms of his main preoccupation being with the IMA. Costello recalled Browne requesting from him on 14 March an immediate cabinet meeting to authorise the spending of another £30,000 on the Mother and Child scheme, believing that this would administer the coup de grace to the IMA. This, if true, probably explains Browne's decision to leave McQuaid aside for the interim.

Not until 22 March did Browne finally decide that he would

have to deal with the bishops (Costello believed that it was Norton who had finally managed to persuade him). The Minister met McQuaid and the only account of this encounter is from Costello, who was told of it by the Archbishop later the same day. According to Costello, Browne made the case that he had satisfied the hierarchy; McQuaid persuaded him his recollection was wrong; Browne then asked McQuaid if he believed the scheme contravened Catholic social teaching, and on being told yes, he said that would mean his resigning from the government and requested a decision from the entire hierarchy.

Browne telephoned Costello to tell him that he had agreed with McQuaid to have the bishops adjudicate on the faith and moral aspects of the scheme, that he had promised to accept their decision and had asked McQuaid to put the matter before the hierarchy as soon as possible. Browne then sent Costello a memorandum which the Taoiseach in turn sent to their lordships. Their decision, conveyed to Costello on 5 April, following consideration of Browne's memorandum, was that his scheme was contrary to Catholic social teaching. It has been felt that they did not give Browne's detailed and able memorandum adequate scrutiny; one of the reasons for this may have been that they knew he did not have united government backing for his scheme. The newspapers had already reported some ministers' dissatisfaction and Costello, when he sent Browne's memorandum to the bishops, did not add anything in support of it. The point was not lost on the hierarchy because in their reply, they expressed satisfaction that Costello's accompanying letter contained no evidence that Browne's scheme was backed by the government.

When the cabinet met on 6 April, Browne argued that the bishops had not responded to his query as to whether or not his scheme was against Catholic moral teaching, merely asserting that it was contrary to Catholic social teaching, but the rest of the cabinet did not consider the distinction important. Each of Browne's colleagues told him that they would not support the scheme. He then left saying that he would have to consider his position, and the rest of the government decided to abandon his scheme and replace it with a less controversial one. Costello wrote to McQuaid to this effect, and received a grateful reply.

When reports began to circulate that the scheme might be abandoned, and that Browne might resign, the national executive of the Irish Trades Union Congress sent a deputation to him requesting him to stay on in office and to introduce a compromise scheme. He agreed to consider the possibility and allowed the newspapers to report that he was reconsidering his resignation at the ITUC's request. This served only to further anger his colleagues. Costello remarked, with indignation: 'I do not suppose that in the history of cabinet government any such thing has happened as that a minister who was considering his position, whose colleagues had treated him as we had treated him, proceeded to tell the press what he was doing at the instance of the Trade Union Congress and did not discuss matters in private with his colleagues'. MacBride decided that Browne had gone too far and requested him to send his resignation to the Taoiseach. Costello fully supported MacBride and said that he would have called for Browne's resignation if MacBride had not done so.

Browne could have conciliated his four opponents - the IMA, the bishops, most of his fellow ministers and his party leader - but instead chose to fight them. Why? Some of his colleagues believed that by temperament he was not able to cope with the problems he faced. Costello's indictment was formidable:

> Deputy Dr Browne was not competent or capable to fulfil the duties of the Department of Health. He was incapable of negotiation; he was obstinate at times and vacillating at other times. He was quite incapable of knowing what his decision would be today or, if he made a decision today, [whether] it would remain until tomorrow.

It has been concluded that Browne must have been a very difficult colleague.[29]

In his speech during the debate over Browne's resignation, Costello articulated the widespread feeling that it did not look well to have the Church's role subject to public scrutiny. Browne had made public all that had occurred and Costello showed that he was shocked: 'All this matter was intended to be private and to be adjusted behind closed doors and was never intended to be the subject of public controversy, as it has been made by the former Minister for Health now, and it would have been dealt with in that way had there been any reasonable person, other than the former Minister for Health, engaged in the negotiations at that time.' To the present generation, Costello's view that such 'a matter of great public importance' should have been hushed up may itself seem shocking, but the fact that he could so unselfconsciously express this view in 1951 showed that he was sure that public opinion would be at one with him.

Politicians readily expressed their willingness to accept the hierarchy's authority in matters relating to social teaching. Costello made this clear in his letter to McQuaid telling him of the government's decision to withdraw the scheme. In the Dáil afterwards he restated this attitude: 'I, as a Catholic, obey my Church authorities and will continue to do so, in spite of *The Irish Times* or anything else' (*The Irish Times*, the day after Browne's resignation, declared that the most serious aspect of the affair was that it showed the Roman Catholic Church to be the real government of Ireland and some Ulster Unionists took this up). Other ministers, Norton and MacBride for example, adopted a similar standpoint.

Some Fine Gael ministers have been referred to as 'almost truculent in their defence of what happened.'[30] McGilligan told a Fine Gael meeting that he would not transgress the moral law and if he was not sure what the moral law was, he would consult the bishops. He declared that they were proud of what had occurred. MacEoin afterwards remarked that the cabinet had been attacked for accepting advice in the spiritual domain from those with authority to give that advice, and no government could reject it. Even Browne himself declared his unequivocal acceptance of the bishops' authority and did not criticise them in any way in his resignation speech.

One of Browne's cabinet colleagues, James Dillon, felt uneasy enough about the hierarchy's decision to do something about it. He had been very opposed to the Mother and Child provisions of the 1947 Health Bill and had even resorted to testing them in the courts. But he had objected to the element of compulsion in them and this had been removed from Browne's 1950 measure. Part of the hierarchy's objection to the latter was that it had no means test provision, but Dillon did not share this objection and had actually defended it. He felt strongly enough about this to write to the Pope asking him to rule on whether it was opposed to Catholic social teaching to have a health scheme without a means test. But, as has been rightly pointed out, this was only further proof of the unanimous acceptance of the bishops' authority. Although he adjudged it unwise in this instance, Dillon did not feel able to ignore it and thought that the correct way to query it was by appealing to the only authority in canon law which could overcome the bishops.

One should not conclude from what happened that whenever the hierarchy made a pronouncement, the politicians obeyed without demur. It suited Browne's cabinet colleagues well to follow this particular Church ruling, it has been maintained.[31] Some of them did not like the scheme, Costello, for one - and he later confirmed that he agreed with the bishops' denunciation of it. It is likely that some of the other Fine Gael ministers agreed with him because, as in opposition, the party had been against the way health policy was developing. T.F. O'Higgins must have been in a particular dilemma because, as a medical doctor, he would have been torn between loyalty to his colleague in government and loyalty to his profession.

What of the theory that the politicians used the bishops as a means of getting rid of Browne? The following comment on the Taoiseach is absolutely clear: 'It certainly would not have been in character for Mr Costello, who was a kindly and straightforward person, to have indulged in such a manoeuvre'.[32]

A little-known aspect of the sequel to the controversy, and a surprising one in view of the later reputation of the politician in question, is that Oliver J. Flanagan, on the brink of being admitted to the Fine Gael party at that time, sympathised with Dr Browne in his contribution to the Dáil debate on his resignation.

(vii) Opposition 1951-54.

The government collapsed soon after Browne's departure but even before the problem with the hierarchy, it was displaying signs of division. The so-called 'Battle of Baltinglass', where the Minister for Posts and Telegraphs, James Everett of National Labour, was forced to withdraw his nominee for postmaster in the village as a result of local opposition, brought ridicule upon the government. Clann na Poblachta was riven with dissension. Inflation proved an intractable foe, so much so that in 1951 the government froze prices at their level of the previous December. When two Independent Farmer deputies withdrew their support from the government in May 1951 because of its refusal to raise the price of milk, it lost its majority and Costello called an election.

Perhaps the greatest achievement of the first inter-party government was to show that there was a viable alternative to Fianna Fáil. The benefits to Fine Gael of participating in such an experiment were many. Its image and morale were greatly boosted and it had the added prestige of a Fine Gael Taoiseach. It had had its first taste of power for 16 years and this restored its self-confidence. Having finally been in government after so many years in opposition clearly benefitted the party electorally. The factor that has been considered to be perhaps the most important 'was the simple fact that Fine Gael was in government and doing things, rather than an ageing party of sterile opposition living on its memories'.[33] Its self-esteem was greatly enhanced; it had reasserted itself as Fianna Fáil's main contender (which Clann na Poblachta had recently challenged) and had jettisoned its image as a constant loser.

Fine Gael's performance in the 1951 election was impressive. Its share of the vote rose by 6% and it gained nine seats. This increase in the vote was the first in nearly 25 years and most of its progress was made outside Leinster. It benefited from a growing tendency among inter-party voters to distribute their preferences in an organised anti-Fianna Fáil manner. So the party won nine extra seats from a gain of 81,000 votes, while Fianna Fáil won only one extra seat despite gaining 61,000 votes. The Fine

Gael gain in first preferences partly reflected the political impact of James Dillon, it has been maintained, as witnessed by the fact that while its overall vote went up by 6%, in agricultural constituencies it increased by 9%. Ominously for Fianna Fáil, Fine Gael was making inroads into its heartland - the west of Ireland.[34]

The increased Fine Gael vote in 1951 was an acknowledgement that it had once again become recognised as a party capable of governing. Despite its long period of decline, there was evidently a repository of potential support for the party. Once it had displayed its mettle in government, supporters returned to it in large numbers.

There could have been another coalition government formed as a result of the 1951 election if the parties had been able to agree among themselves, but the balance of power lay with the 14 Independents, most of whom supported the return of Fianna Fáil to office. An interesting sideline of the Fianna Fáil resumption of power, according to one historian, was that J. J. McElligott, Secretary of the Department of Finance, welcomed back Seán MacEntee as Minister because it meant that he would no longer have to deal with 'the intellectual audacity of McGilligan'.[35]

In opposition in the 1951-54 period, with a larger number of deputies in the Dáil and with the experience of government behind it, Fine Gael behaved with much greater self-confidence and spirit than it had shown in the 1940s. Although de Valera clearly disliked being in a minority government position, he could not resort to the old tactic, practised so often in the 1930s and 40s, of calling a sudden election because now there was manifestly an alternative government in existence. This was clearly demonstrated by Costello, the ex-Taoiseach, assuming the role of Leader of the Opposition - and not Mulcahy, who remained leader of the Fine Gael party. James Dillon rejoined the party in 1952 and Oliver J. Flanagan was admitted to it the same year.

The noteworthy revival in the party's electoral fortunes that occurred in 1951 continued unabated, the party winning five of nine by-elections between 1951 and 1954, in contrast to none such victories at all in the 1935-49 period. Consistent transferring of votes among its opponents was the new challenge to Fianna Fáil and this usually benefited Fine Gael most at by-elections. The party won two by-elections in 1954 (the two victorious Fine Gael candidates were Stephen Barrett in Cork and George Coburn in Louth) and, although no change resulted in the balance of parties in the Dáil, since these contests occurred because of the deaths of two Fine Gael TDs, a remarkable increase in the Fine Gael vote share prompted de Valera to go to the country in May 1954.

Campaigning on an inter-party ticket, Fine Gael emerged from the 1954 general election stronger than at any time since its foundation. The party made conspicuous gains. Its popular vote increased from 343,000 to 427,000; its percentage of the poll rose from 25.7% to 32%; the number of seats it won went up from 40 to 50. In the Dáil, it was now just 15 seats short of Fianna Fáil; ten years earlier it had been 46 behind. Richard Mulcahy had presided over what has been described as 'the near miracle of Fine Gael rehabilitation'.[36]

(viii) Second inter-party government: 1954-57

The signs seemed favourable for Fine Gael as it began its second period in coalition. This government was less fragmented than its 1948 predecessor, consisting of just three parties - Fine Gael, Labour and Clann na Talmhan. Clann na Poblachta, now reduced to three TDs, supported but did not join this second inter-party administration. Fine Gael was in a much more dominant position than it had been from 1948 to 1951 and, in addition, this coalition had an overall majority in the Dáil. John A. Costello was once again elected Taoiseach and was probably in a stronger position this time around. Seán MacEoin, who had been Minister for Justice from 1948 to March 1951, when he became Minister for Defence, retained the latter portfolio. Richard Mulcahy and James Dillon took up their former responsibilities of Education and Agriculture respectively. Tom O'Higgins, son of Dr T.F., and elected to the Dáil for Laois-Offaly for the first time in 1948, became Minister for Health.

The new inter-party government, it has been remarked, was 'far from being a replica of the old, either in composition or in energy', and Patrick McGilligan has been referred to as being 'conspicuous by his absence'.[37]   Now 65 and in ill health, McGilligan chose to become Attorney General rather than Minister for Finance again.   Gerard Sweetman was given the important Finance portfolio.   First elected to the Dáil for Kildare in 1948, Gerard Sweetman had been Chief Whip of the Fine Gael party during the first inter-party government.   Liam Cosgrave, who had been Parliamentary Secretary to the Taoiseach from 1948 to 1951, became Minister for External Affairs and made an admirable debut. When a special department to look after the interests of the Gaeltacht was established in October 1956, Patrick Lindsay became its first Minister.

This second coalition has received some unfavourable comments from historians.   Because of the absence of MacBride and Browne, it lacked 'much of the colour and initiative' of its predecessor, is one example.[38]   It is said that it was a less talented government than its 1948-51 precursor, but in fairness it must be pointed out that it faced greater difficulties.   The 1950s was a bleak decade in Ireland and the government had to cope with serious economic problems.   Worried about what it regarded as a very high balance of payments deficit (£35 million in 1955, exacerbated by a capital outflow which added to the decline in external reserves), the government introduced import levies and public expenditure cuts, and the inevitable consequences were high unemployment and increased emigration.   In justice, it should be pointed out that the government went some way towards closing the trade gap by reducing the deficit in the balance of payments from £35 million in 1955 to £14 million in 1956, but it had to resort to such extreme measures to do so that it seemed to be making the economic situation worse without giving any hope for the future.   Its response to the continuing inflation - reduced government spending and increased taxation - made it as unpopular as the previous Fianna Fáil administration had been.

Ironically, the process which led to a period of unprecedented economic prosperity for Ireland, over which Fianna Fáil presided and from which it benefited electorally, was set in train by the second inter-party government. As a result of its desire to work out the best way to obtain and use capital, the government set up a Capital Investment Advisory Committee which urged the drawing up of a programme for economic development. The inter-party government fell before a report could be completed but, by a curious chance, it bestowed on its successors the man most capable of preparing such a document. At the young age of 40, T.K. Whitaker had been chosen by Gerard Sweetman to occupy the vital position of Secretary of the Department of Finance.

Sweetman's promotion of Whitaker 'contravened the hitherto sacrosanct principle of seniority', it has been remarked.[39] Although the formal responsibility for Whitaker's appointment was Sweetman's (it has been suggested that he was the one senior official in the Department whose views were most akin to Sweetman's; Whitaker himself has recorded that since he and Sweetman were contemporaries, they found it easier to get on with each other), the view has been put forward that it was largely through the efforts of the former Minister for Finance, McGilligan, that Whitaker was elevated.[40]

The grim background against which this momentous appointment was made has been well depicted:

> a period of unprecedented gloom and depression. No longer could the state of the economy be attributed to colonial misgovernment or wartime restriction. Economic growth was non-existent, inflation was apparently insoluble, unemployment rife, living standards low and emigration approaching 50,000 a year, a figure not far below the birth rate. Even some who were securely employed threw up their jobs to seek a new life in countries which held out brighter prospects for the future of their families.[41]

In a speech to an inter-party meeting in October 1956, Costello outlined the government's long-term plan for dealing with the economic crisis. A significant aspect of this was the proposal to set up a Capital Investment Advisory Committee of experts to carry out research and advise the government on economic policy. Sweetman endorsed Costello's speech and initiated the moves to have it implemented in so far as his Department would be involved. He also took the initiative in setting up the Committee, nominating six of its nine members.

The Committee first met on 14 December 1956 and Sweetman asked it to deal with what he expected to be the deficit in the government's capital budget for the following year. The inter-party government had fallen from power before it got the chance to put the Committee's report into effect but the new Fianna Fáil government accepted it and kept the Committee in existence. Ireland was not admitted into the International Monetary Fund and the World Bank until 1957, but Sweetman had initiated the process of application. Whitaker has remarked that Sweetman was 'a singularly unfortunate Minister for Finance' because he had to leave office before the seeds he had sown came to fruition.[42]

'Even though the 1950s were years of economic and psychological gloom, the first diffident step away from claustrophobic insularity was taken in 1955 when Ireland became a member of the United Nations', it has been observed.[43] Liam Cosgrave who, as Minister for External Affairs, oversaw the formal admission, was responsible for enunciating the Irish policy principles: (a) strict adherence to the requirements of the UN Charter; (b) to pursue as independent a line as possible, and (c) to uphold Christian civilisation and to support as far as possible countries defending democracy against communism. Cosgrave asserted in the Dáil: 'We belong to the great community of states made up of the United States, Canada and Western Europe.'

In 1955, the IRA renewed its cross-border campaign with a series of daring raids. The government tried to play these down, but when members of the Royal Ulster Constabulary (RUC) and IRA raiders were killed at the end of 1956 it could no longer do so. On New Year's Day 1957, two IRA men, Seán South and Fergal O'Hanlon, were killed during a raid on Brookeborough Barracks in County Fermanagh. The IRA campaign eventually died out, but for its duration there was intense pressure on Costello. He promised in January 1957 that 'the full resources of the state would be used to prevent further raids'. As a result of the measures taken by the government to deal with the problem, the three Clann na Poblachta TDs withdrew their support and MacBride moved a motion of no confidence in the Dáil. This condemned the administration's failure to unify the country or to improve the economic situation. But in retrospect Costello was certain that his government's attitude to the IRA was as significant in provoking the response that it did from MacBride as any failure on the economic front.

Costello decided to call an election rather than face the no confidence motion in the Dáil. Why the government decided to do this, when it had a fair chance of defeating it, and the discussions between Fine Gael and Fianna Fáil during the election campaign on possible cooperation to cope with the economic crisis have never been fully explained.[44]

In the general election of March 1957, Fine Gael lost ten seats and its popular vote dropped by 100,000 or almost 5.5% on its 1954 performance. It did not emerge unscathed from the difficulties of its second term in office, unlike its first. The deteriorating economic situation, rising unemployment and emigration, and Fianna Fáil's capitalising to the utmost on the government's problems, proved harmful to Fine Gael not only in the 1957 election but during those of the 1960s when the country was experiencing an economic boom.

However, the party could console itself a little. It still retained 40 seats, well above its lowest point in the mid-1940s. Because it had held on to this number despite the economic doom and gloom, it could, it was argued, only do better in the future. It had fared much worse in Dublin and the east than in the west. Labour transfers still tended to go to Fine Gael rather than to Fianna Fáil, but only as a last resort, preferring Clann na Poblachta or the Independents. So, at least the coalition idea as a creditable alternative to Fianna Fáil remained as a cause of hope. 'Nevertheless, the few genuinely professional politicians in Fine Gael had cause to be bitterly disappointed at the blighting of the bright hopes of 1954', it has been contended.[45] Then their party was within 15 seats of Fianna Fáil but now it was 38 behind. Unlike 1951, after its first period in coalition, when it had emerged as the clear winner compared with the other coalition government parties, it was now the loser.

It has been further maintained that 1957 was a self-engendered defeat, on the grounds that but for Sweetman's fiscal rectitude, Fianna Fáil probably would not have recovered. To support this contention it was claimed that by-elections in mid-1955 displayed no swing back to Fianna Fáil. Had the party been more adept or more fortunate, Fine Gael might have undermined its main opponent even further. The mid-1950s witnessed the most fluid party political situation since 1927 but, whether through lack of perception or ill-luck, Fine Gael missed the opportunity to overtake its principal rival.[46] The 1957 general election ushered in another long period of Fianna Fáil dominance, and Fine Gael began its second stretch of 16 years in opposition.

(ix) Party organisation

It has been pointed out that Fine Gael's parent party, Cumann na nGaedheal, paid little attention to party organisation or, as it has been more colourfully expressed, its leaders 'remained indifferent to the very notion that they should soil their hands in cultivating anything as soil-encrusted as grass roots'![47] Apart from the brief interlude of the Blueshirts, this neglect of organisation persisted throughout the long spell in opposition and it was not until after the nadir of 1945 that some effort was made to organise locally and attract new, and especially young, people to the party ranks.

Its accession to office in 1948 gave Fine Gael a new lease of life. It made up for its former lethargy by employing a full-time organiser and by establishing active local associations, designed especially to appeal to the young, something which had been hitherto neglected, except during the Blueshirt era.

The party also set about putting its finances in order. Only at that late stage in its existence - in 1949 - did Fine Gael begin holding a national collection. This revitalisation, it has been rightly suggested,[48] came at a crucial time because it is debatable whether or not the party could have survived so long a period in opposition again.

Chapter 5

Prolonged Opposition Once More: 1957-73

(i) Change of leadership; 1959 PR Referendum

One commentator has asserted that after the 1957 general election Fine Gael seemed to lose direction again.[1] Public statements from some of its Dáil deputies on the alleged communist threat and the need for private enterprise to have primacy seemed to place it to the right of Fianna Fáil. A liberal wing, focused on the party's central branch and on its monthly organ, the *National Observer*, and led by Declan Costello, son of the former Taoiseach, showed tentative signs of growth, but was making little impact at this stage.

Richard Mulcahy continued to be president of Fine Gael while John A. Costello was still the leader of the opposition in the Dáil. 'The dual leadership was not a success, with Mulcahy little more than a figurehead and Costello devoting as much time to his legal work as to politics', it has been maintained.[2] As a result, when Mulcahy, who had presided over a remarkable resurgence in the party's fortunes, decided to relinquish command in October 1959, it was felt that a full-time leader was required and Costello was persuaded to give up his leadership of the parliamentary party, doing so only because he would, otherwise, have had to put an end to his legal career. James Dillon defeated Liam Cosgrave in the contest which followed, by what margin is not known because, as has always been the practice in Fine Gael, the details of the ballot were not made public.

The most important electoral issue for Fine Gael in the late 1950s was the referendum on the country's voting system in 1959. The Proportional Representation Society had been very active in the United Kingdom in the early part of this century and, as a result, the single transferable vote electoral system was widely discussed. Arthur Griffith was a founder member of the Proportional Representation Society of Ireland, established in April 1911, and argued strongly in his newspapers in favour of this means of voting. As a result, it was adopted as a political objective by Sinn Féin in order to ensure that the Unionist minority would be properly represented. This was the electoral form that was embodied in the 1922 Free State Constitution.

The first strong condemnation of the Irish PR system appeared in the Cumann na nGaedheal weekly, *An Réalt*, in May 1930. The author of the article believed it retarded 'normal political development' in the Free State, having been thrust on Ireland by the British, and that it was non-democratic. It has been asserted that this attack sprang from the experience of the 1923 and 1927 elections.[3] The government was urged to change the voting system and, at that stage, it could have abolished PR because the Constitution could have been changed by government legislation during the first eight years after its enactment. Ernest Blythe was one minister who was certain after 1927 that PR would never produce stable government in Ireland, but no one else in the cabinet seems to have supported him. In any event, the government's uncertain majority may have deterred it from any such daring constitutional innovation.

Eamon de Valera's 1937 Constitution differed from its 1922 antecedent in that it specified the single transferrable vote where the older Constitution simply prescribed 'the principles' of PR. During the Dáil debate on the de Valera document, John A. Costello expressed the view that the change should not have been made, arguing that the electoral system should be more flexible and ought to be amenable to alteration by government legislation as in the 1922 Constitution. He was not faulting the system, but suggesting that the country should not be tied to a measure that would be more difficult to change once it became a basic part of the Constitution. At the first ard fheis of the reorganised Fine Gael party in 1935, the abolition of PR was proposed, but the national executive did not support the motion and it was dropped. However, in February 1935 the party organ, *United Ireland*, renewed the attack on it made by *An Réalt* five years before, claiming that it was a British imposition.[4]

Although some of the more prominent members of Fine Gael came to dislike the fissiparous consequences of PR, they never managed to swing the party as a whole against it. However, up to the end of 1937 there was no question that Cumann na nGaedheal or Fine Gael were dedicated to maintaining it. But when, during the 1938 election campaign in a speech at Kilrush, de Valera implied favouring an electoral system that would enable the party that had polled the highest number of votes to form the government, Fine Gael forgot its 'former doubts and misgivings' and vigorously defended the system as a protection against dictatorship, which it asserted was what de Valera really wanted.[5]

The Irish Independent, at the end of August 1958, referred to a possible move against PR, and de Valera, at a press conference in early September, stated that Fianna Fáil had as yet taken no decision but Fine Gael was slow to react. This was to be expected in view of its ambiguous attitude to PR over the years, according to the most detailed analyst of the 1959 referendum.[6] Some members must have entertained the idea that reform of the system eventually might help the party to become the only alternative government to Fianna Fáil, instead of the senior partner in coalition arrangements. The *Independent* article had suggested that it was not only Fianna Fáil members who were opposed to PR. It is reasonable to assume that it was referring to the ranks of Fine Gael because the smaller parties had hardly anything to gain from its abolition.

Fine Gael has been perceived as having three choices when the Fianna Fáil ard-fheis in late October 1958 disclosed that an attempt was to be made to change the electoral system: (a) to accept the Bill in principle (or offer a token resistance); (b) to try to reach a compromise on the single-transferable vote in single-member constituencies; (c) to offer all-out opposition together with Labour, the smaller parties and the Independents. If the party had cooperated with Fianna Fáil in allowing the Bill through, or had not hindered it, and left it up to the public to decide, it could not have been accused of failure in its duty. It could have allowed the Bill through and then have campaigned, quite consistently, among the people against it. The second option was never seriously considered and Fine Gael decided to meet the attempt with opposition at all stages, as Costello made clear in a speech at the beginning of

October. All the party's front bench members became actively involved in the campaign, except for Liam Cosgrave, who did not speak at all on the issue either inside or outside the Dáil, and it was known that he was opposed to PR.[7]

It has been thought that the main reason for the Fine Gael decision may have been the fear that the first election following a change would have led to large losses for the party, as had occurred between 1932 and 1948, which would have damaged morale, even though from a longer perspective it could emerge as the only viable choice to Fianna Fáil. Its monthly organ, the *National Observer*, strongly advanced this point of view in May 1959, when it suggested that 'a long sojourn in the wilderness had implanted some of the. . . "small party". . . mentality in Fine Gael'. John A. Costello and his son, Declan, Tom O'Higgins and Patrick McGilligan have been seen as contributing the speeches of most value made by Fine Gael deputies in the Dáil debate on the issue.

The party's stance on the Bill was summed up in an amendment tabled by Mulcahy and Costello on 26 November, which gave the following reasons for not doing away with PR and setting forth the likely results if it were jettisoned: (a) it would infringe the rights of minorities; (b) it would go against Irish democratic traditions; (c) it would lead to unrepresentative and arrogant government; (d) it would make Irish unification more difficult; (e) it had not been sought by the people; (f) given international and economic conditions, it would make the solution of Irish problems more, rather than less, difficult. The amendment called for no second reading for the Bill and the establishment of a commission of experts to scrutinise and report on the existing system.

Fine Gael speakers tended to concentrate on foretelling the future, emphasising that the long-term consequences for the parties of the course the government was embarking on could not be predicted although an immediate advantage might accrue to Fianna Fáil. Costello took it for granted that, with the passing of the Treaty politicians, the party structures would undergo a redrawing:

We are coming to the end of an era. We do not know how

the parties will split up. There may very well be what I might describe, with not any overemphasis, as a Radical Party. Certainly, in a few years there will be a break-up of the present political parties. God alone knows what will be the result.

This was the opposition's strongest argument: in a period of transition, when those of the Treaty era were about to leave politics, de Valera was endeavouring to force the parties into his own chosen form, rather than allowing them to realign rationally. (It has been pointed out that when Fianna Fáil had fared badly in general elections, such as in 1938 and 1943, de Valera had considered changing the electoral system, but the decision to try to do so in 1959 occurred after a sweeping victory. The purpose was to ensure his party's survival following his own departure.)[8] It was also argued that it would be harder to coax Unionists into a united Ireland if proportional representation was discarded; that subversives, who had returned four TDs to the Dáil in 1957, would be driven underground, and that there would be less chance for Protestants to get elected.

Opposition speakers seemed to take it for granted that Ireland possessed unique conditions; Dillon, in a typically rhetorical style, may have given voice to this consensus:

This is not the United States of America. This is not Great Britain. Harold Macmillan has not fought Hugh Gaitskell in a civil war. Nobody looks across the floor of an English Parliament to recall that his father may have fallen at the hands of another member's father. I know that, happily, the bitternesses of the past are receding behind us but I shall obey no injunction to forget the past or those who have gone before. I think we should remember all of them but forget the injuries in so far as we can. But make no demand upon us to act like Englishmen or to act like the polyglot people of the United States of America, for we are neither one nor the other. We are a cohesive, perhaps too intimate, people, knowing the history of our father and our father's father. We are as God made us and as history has destined us to be.

Debating societies all over the country held meetings to discuss the merits of the case, the more articulate politicians being invited to address them. Declan Costello was among those most often requested. When de Valera announced his intention to contest the presidential election, the opposition made the most of the opportunity thus presented them. Their reaction has been succinctly expressed as follows: 'They were able to claim that Fianna Fáil was throwing the personality of the leader into the scales against PR, that an emotional appeal would be made to the people not to refuse "Dev's last request", and they furiously denounced any suggestion to hold both elections on the same day as an attempt to defraud the people.'[9]

When the Minister for Local Government, Neil Blaney, introduced, in early January 1959, a technical bill to provide a suitable ballot paper for the referendum, Fine Gael scored heavily against him. Party speakers were able to cite the existing law, which specified that the ballot paper would have to have an understandable summary of the question for the benefit of the voter, while Blaney simply provided for the short title, *The Third Amendment to the Constitution Bill, 1959*. Although his Bill got through the Dáil, Blaney could give no adequate response to the opposition case that the original requirement would give valuable information to the voters, which his Bill denied them.

Another technical wrangle over the form in which the Referendum Bill was drawn up saw the government conceding to the opposition the right to have all its aspects discussed again. When the part abolishing the multi-seat constituencies had been passed, Dillon urged the retention of the single transferable vote and stated that Fine Gael would accept that arrangement as a 'second worst'. This got no cooperation from Fianna Fáil, but no one in his own party spoke on behalf of the offer. The last section dealing with a constituency commission was derided by Fine Gael as impracticable and aimed at giving 'a thin veneer of respectability to an unscrupulous political manoeuvre'.[10]

The Senate rejected Blaney's Bill by a margin of one (two government supporters were absent through illness). The government then introduced a motion in the Dáil to pass the Bill unchanged, despite the Senate veto. The debate lasted for five days with a rehash of the speeches of the previous December and January. Few would dispute that the decision to hold the presidential election and the referendum on the same day was designed to use de Valera's standing to ensure the success of the attempt to alter the voting system. The former Cumann na nGaedheal Minister, Ernest Blythe, was a vigorous supporter of Fianna Fáil on this issue and did not conceal his preference for stable government at the cost of broader representation.

The attempt to mobilise public opinion against the government greatly encouraged Fine Gael - its monthly organ, the *National Observer*, had predicted in March that the Senate rejection of the Bill and the vigorous academic opposition would overwhelm the government's case. But since Seán MacEoin was contesting the presidential election, the party had to run his campaign, where it hardly expected to succeed, and Fine Gael speakers divided their energies between praising their candidate and the system of election that then existed. MacEoin polled better than he had done in 1945 (he did not contest the presidency in 1952), but de Valera won by an ample, yet by no means crushing, majority. However, Fianna Fáil lost the referendum.

(ii) 1961 general election

Relations between Fine Gael and Labour remained good in the late 1950s and the accession of James Dillon to the leadership of his party did nothing to harm these relations because he had served successfully and enthusiastically in the two inter-party governments and was a strong advocate of coalition. But William Norton's successor as Labour leader in 1961, Brendan Corish, although a member of both the 1948-51 and 1954-57 governments, was doubtful about the benefits of such an arrangement.

The 1961 election has been described by one commentator as 'the dullest on record' Independent campaigns were pursued by Fine Gael and Labour and there appeared to be no alternative government to Fianna Fáil. Indeed, this absence of any sort of

109

agreement between those parties has been regarded as the most significant feature of this particular general election.[12] However, the view that Fine Gael was not interested in another coalition and devoted its energies to forming a majority government on its own, must be questioned since the party maintained an open mind as regards coalescing, and it was Labour which wished to go it alone.

Dillon's proposal to abolish compulsory Irish as a prerequisite for the Leaving Certificate and employment in the public service won support among the electorate. Fianna Fáil strongly opposed the suggestion and it proved to be the most contentious issue at the 1961 election. In its manifesto, Fine Gael appealed to the people for a mandate to form a government on its own, but its argument that, with an application to be made to join the European Economic Community, it could be relied upon to keep up its good record in all previous negotiations, has been considered 'implausible' on the grounds that the last time it had conducted such talks was in 1931. [13] Surely this was to ignore the experience of Fine Gael ministers in the two inter-party governments since that time? The party's final rally in Dublin was interrupted by Irish-language enthusiasts, infuriated by its promise to abolish compulsory Irish.

Fine Gael performed well in the October 1961 election. Its losses of 1957 were wiped out; its percentage of the vote was up nearly 5.5 and it gained seven seats. However, the reduced incidence of vote transference cost both Fine Gael and Labour dearly. Although the two parties together got roughly the same share of the first-preference vote as Fianna Fáil, their combined seat total was actually less. Indeed, the number of Fianna Fáil's bonus seats was at its highest since the 1943 election.

Fianna Fáil lost eight seats, although it was presiding over an unprecedented economic upsurge at the time. Fine Gael's seven-seat gain provoked the following comment in the personal memoir of an author who termed the 1960s the 'best of decades': 'This was all the more surprising when one recalls how threadbare Fine Gael were for policies: only the promise to abolish compulsory Irish distinguished them sharply from Fianna Fáil on a major issue.'[14]

The party did not do well in Dublin, but its good performance in rural Ireland (and Fianna Fáil's losses there) was due to its relentlessly putting agriculture to the fore.

(iii) The search for an identity

Fine Gael's new leader, James Dillon, has been perceived as serving the same function for his party as that fulfilled for Fianna Fáil by Seán Lemass: bridging the gap between the present and the past. But whereas Lemass's ascendancy over his colleagues was undoubted, Dillon had a much more difficult task in trying to hold together a party which, while retaining its middle-class, conservative bias, was under pressure from some of its younger supporters to change with the times.

In Dillon's first address as leader to his party's ard-fheis in February 1960, he outlined a series of aims broadly similar to Lemass's: (a) since protection had run its course, Ireland must now make sure not to become isolated from the two large European free-trade blocs; (b) the Control of Manufactures Act should be repealed; (c) private enterprise should be the stimulus for industrial expansion; (d) balanced budgets must be adhered to, regardless of how much taxation this would entail. Dillon's attitude to agriculture, however, differed markedly from Lemass's. He doubted that there was much of a future for small farms and he wanted the activities of the Land Commission reviewed with this in mind. A commentator with a nostalgic affection for the 1960s has remarked that no Fianna Fáil politician would have made such a suggestion given that party's dependence on the small-farmer vote, but Fine Gael, with its traditional big-farmer support, could afford to contemplate the disappearance of the 35-acre farm.[15]

The same author has contended that another aspect of the policy laid down by Dillon was to benefit his party little over the decade. The new Fine Gael leader saw it as a basic policy principle that the country should rely on its main resource: the 12 million acres of arable land. This commentator regarded it as clear that the circumstances whereby agriculture could lead to widespread economic prosperity in the Ireland of the 1960s were not present.

But Fine Gael, perhaps out of a natural desire to woo the farming vote at a time when farmers resented their exclusion from the country's increasing prosperity, hammered at the point so hard that they allowed Fianna Fáil to become the 'industry party' almost by default.[16]   So, Fine Gael has been seen as continuing to give the impression, whether intended or not, over the succeeding years that it was not very enthusiastic about the newer industrial development, either belittling its achievements or ignoring them.

This line of reasoning must be regarded as open to question. Fine Gael's contribution to the industrial development which flowered in the 1960s has already been explored in previous chapters and the significance of the two inter-party governments in that regard should not be underestimated. Indeed, in response to his own question as to what extent the momentum which informed the sixties was due to Lemass, one historian has expressed his belief that it may well have been the '1948 change of government which shifted economic horizons'.[17]   And even the critic of Fine Gael's performance in the 1960s just quoted, acknowledged that its dilemma was obvious since it cannot have been easy to oppose the party presiding over the most successful economic boom in the history of the state.[18]

As a result of this predicament, Fine Gael had a negative image in that it tended to react to Fianna Fáil policy moves rather than develop its own positive contributions. 'The personal attacks made by party leaders on Lemass - that he was an irresponsible gambler and a nepotist, the latter charge arising out of his promotion of Charles Haughey, his son-in-law, to junior office - impressed nobody', it has been asserted.[19]   Fine Gael has also been arraigned for accusing the government of not carrying out actions which it actually was and thus appearing less credible as a result. Two examples were given of Gerard Sweetman declaring, first in March 1961, that Fianna Fáil was failing to take advantage of the unprecedented international economic growth, and secondly in July, before a party meeting, indicting the government for not adequately explaining to the people what Ireland's joining the European Economic Community would mean for the country.

This latter criticism has been dismissed as nonsense on the grounds that, almost every week, senior members of the cabinet, and often the Taoiseach himself, spoke on the subject, and in July the Committee on Industrial Organisation was set up by the government to study the Irish manufacturing industry. This criticism of Fine Gael's performance in the 1960s referred to Lemass's opinion that no constructive evaluation emanated from within the Dáil, Fine Gael merely belittling the government, and agreed completely with his remark at the November 1960 Fianna Fáil ard-fheis that while Lemass's party was 'dynamic and positive', Fine Gael was 'fundamentally conservative and negative'. This stringent commentator on the position of Dillon's party at the beginning of the 1960s concluded damningly that :

> Fine Gael remained a deeply conservative collection of comfortable, part-time politicians, attached to the notion that an expanding agriculture was the motor which would most efficiently drive the engine of Irish prosperity. They started the 1960s as they intended to go on: a party condemned to second place in Irish politics for want of dynamic leadership and national organisation, and a clear, coherent philosophy which distinguished them from Fianna Fáil.[20]

There can be little doubt that Fine Gael found itself in a quandary during this period of its history. It was unable to benefit from the increased prosperity of the time; indeed, Fianna Fáil, as the party in power, could represent it as a threat to this newly experienced affluence. Moreover, with the increasing emphasis in the 1960s on social and economic issues and a decreasing interest in old nationalistic and constitutional questions, Fine Gael found it difficult to discover distinctive subjects around which it could mobilise support against the government. There was a bipartisan approach on both Northern Ireland and EEC membership and it seemed as if the policies and attitudes of both the major parties were becoming more and more indistinguishable, the important difference being that Fianna Fáil was the party in power and enjoying its fruits. The 1960s was a decade of uncertainty for Fine Gael and this was reflected in the internal debates and differences within the party.

It has been contended that discontent within Fine Gael grew in expression over the next few years after the 1961 election, reaching a climax early in 1964 when Fianna Fáil won two by-elections in February in Dublin and Kildare. The parliamentary party postmortem exculpated Dillon, who was seen to be doing his best, and his offers to resign were turned down. It was mainly frontbenchers who were criticised, some of them in politics since the 1920s, because they were seen as giving too much time to their occupations and too little to their political careers, and as ineffective in their opposition to Lemass's businesslike team. The party's liberal wing saw this as their opportunity and seized it.

From the late 1950s onwards, there was pressure inside Fine Gael to move away from its traditional, conservative position. A young TD, Declan Costello, son of the former Taoiseach, argued in 1959 that the party should take a frank and definite leap to the left:

> . . . we should not be afraid to use techniques traditionally associated with the parties of the left . . . we should be prepared to jettison motives and concepts which belong to the heyday of nineteenth-century liberalism . . . we [should] try to bring about conditions where there is genuine equality for all, irrespective of the level of society in which they have been born . . . I believe that Fine Gael should move openly and firmly to the left.

It has been observed that this stance was in stark contrast to the terms in which the leadership still thought and which was typified by the '13 principles' of Fine Gael policy laid down by Declan's father, John A. Costello, in 1954. These emphasised as little state interference as possible, as can be seen clearly from the following extracts from those 13 principles:

> That all classes in the community be equally treated and that no-one goes in want or suffers from disease which can be alleviated through defects in organisation. That where possible, any assistance be stimulated or supported by state activity but not supplanted or coerced . . . . That a careful watch be kept on the development of the Central

Government and the expenditure in its hands to administer, and that the electorate be encouraged to a recognition that any promises or benefits are, in effect, promises by politicians to take more money from the people and spend it for them . . . .That the financial policy of the Government be primarily concerned to foster incomes instead of merely providing relief schemes for those for whom deficient prosperity has failed to provide. That this policy of increased incomes can be done less well by direct Government activity than by the stimulation of the activity of private enterprise . . . .That in all directions, whether in the fields of culture, industry or agriculture, a positive approach of encouragement replaces a negative policy of control.

The combination of internal party pressure from a younger generation of members and external economic and political circumstances served to alter fundamentally these tenets by the mid-1960s. Almost exactly ten years after John A. Costello had enunciated the main articles of Fine Gael faith, the parliamentary party unanimously accepted a resolution which declared

> . . . there is an urgent need for economic and social reform in order to produce a more just social order . . . [and] that such reform can best be brought about by a more effective management of our economy and a more equitable distribution of the nation's wealth . . . . sufficient economic progress cannot be achieved by economic 'programming'. Full-scale economic planning is necessary. [This would] involve not only detailed targets for the public sector, but for the private sector as well. . .the Government must undertake direct investment in the industrial field where desirable and in the public interest.

This resolution led to the *Just Society* manifesto of the 1965 general election and pushed Fine Gael in a social democratic direction. It has rightly been remarked that this document marked 'a major watershed in the general political approach' of the party.[21]

So significant was this development in Fine Gael that it has

115

been asserted that 'an ideological realignment'[22] occurred in Irish politics in the 1960s. Fine Gael and Labour discovered common ground in their shared social democratic appeal. As the country underwent an unprecedented economic boom in that decade, both parties redefined the position from which they would oppose Fianna Fáil. They both stressed social justice and a more equitable distribution of the country's wealth. While Fianna Fáil contended that the increasing prosperity would eventually benefit all ('a rising tide lifts all boats', as Lemass memorably phrased it), Fine Gael and Labour held that a more immediate redivision of resources was called for.

With this move to the left, Fine Gael consciously sought to broaden its appeal beyond its traditionally conservative and largely middle-class constituency. But its approach, like that of Fianna Fáil and unlike that of Labour, was a 'catch-all' one in that, as well as appealing to the working class and the trade unions, it tried to maintain its support among the better-off sections of society. However, while Fianna Fáil emphasised benefits for all, Fine Gael stressed relative benefits for the less well-off portion of the electorate.

(iv) 1965 general election and change of leadership

Many authors have maintained that senior Fine Gael party figures were either lukewarm about or opposed to the radical eight-point draft programme put forward by Declan Costello in May 1964.[23] In his address to the ard-fheis a few days afterwards, Dillon condemned 'young men in a hurry', and Gerard Sweetman was against the Costello programme. However, Liam Cosgrave favoured it and made the decisive contribution at the ard-fheis. Agreement was reached on a nine-point plan, involving all the proposals advanced by Costello (with the tax and price control suggestions somewhat diluted) together with a pledge to improve living standards for farmers.

The party has been seen as now embarking on a 'schizophrenic' existence in that no sooner had the *Just Society* agenda been declared official than conservative spokesmen made clear their opposition to it. In June, for example, Sweetman carefully stressed that Fine Gael was 'a middle-of-the-road party, suitable for the changing times in which we live', while Dillon portrayed it as the party of private enterprise, lest anyone should consider it otherwise.[24]

A committee was set up to work out a thorough policy document based on the nine points agreed after the ard-fheis. Meanwhile, Fine Gael won two by-elections in the second half of 1964 in traditional Fianna Fáil areas. In each case it probably secured a substantial non-partisan sympathy vote because one of the victorious candidates was the widow, and the other the son, of sitting TDs who had died. One of the contests was for the seat of Michael Donnellan, Clann na Talmhan TD for Galway from 1943 until his death in 1964 while attending the All-Ireland football final at which his son, John, captained the victorious Galway team. John subsequently won the seat for Fine Gael.

When a general election was called for March 1965, Fine Gael was unprepared. The committee charged with providing a complete policy document had not finished its deliberations as yet. There was clearly division and, some have claimed, deep disagreement within the party over the Costello initiative. Yet a manifesto appeared within a week of the election being called. Entitled *Towards a Just Society*, it reflected a victory for the liberals in the parliamentary party. It contained most of Costello's original programme and particularly emphasised 'freedom and equality', stressing that a thorough social policy was needed, giving an equal chance to everybody. This probed a Fianna Fáil sore point and Lemass had to resurrect a 1963 promise on social policy to counteract it. This move on Fianna Fáil's part has been dismissed by one author with the comment: 'But, as in 1963, it was just talk.'[25]

Lemass's belief was that if enough wealth were generated, social equality would be the automatic consequence. Although the *Just Society* directly confronted such an assumption, Dillon has been criticised for feeling it necessary, when presenting the document to the press, to emphasise that Fine Gael was a party which supported the entrepreneur and that it would rely on such species. The *Irish Times* political correspondent commented:

> The tragedy of the Costello plan is that it was launched by Fine Gael. Its whole purpose was destroyed when James Dillon declared that the party was still 'a party of private enterprise'. All who understand economic or political language know that there is no intention by Fine Gael of taking over the plan.

Garret FitzGerald, on the point of beginning his meteoric career in politics, regarded *Towards a Just Society* at the time as improving Fine Gael's chances of future coalition with Labour. He saw the earlier inter-party governments as weak because of the wide differences in policy between Fine Gael and the other parties which made those administrations vulnerable to various and divergent pressures. But his hope was premature because during the campaign Brendan Corish firmly declared his party's opposition to coalition. This decision has been caustically referred to as Labour's only contribution to the 1965 contest, because it 'effectively handed the election to Fianna Fáil'.[26]

Labour's election manifesto did not seem very different from Fine Gael's. If anything, it appeared the more conservative. The *Irish Independent* editorial for 24 March 1965 bore the title 'Has Declan Costello made off with the Labour Party's clothes?' Many Fianna Fáil spokesmen questioned how committed some conservative senior Fine Gael figures were to their party's leftward turn.

Although Fine Gael's share of the vote increased by 2.1%, its number of seats remained at 47. The party's vote was up in 31 constituencies and down in 17, but it won much of the support previously given to Clann na Talmhan, since it gained most in the two Mayo constituencies. Patrick McGilligan, the only remaining member of the Dáil from the Cumann na nGaedheal governments, lost his seat in Dublin North-Central. This contest was the first in Ireland to be given extensive television coverage, and one man in the panel of experts who made a particular impact was Garret FitzGerald who, in the Senate elections a few weeks afterwards, embarked on his own political odyssey.

James Dillon resigned as party leader after the 1965 election, not under pressure, but to give his successor adequate time to prepare for the next electoral contest. Gerard Sweetman nominated Liam Cosgrave to succeed Dillon and this was unanimously accepted. It has been suggested that this was 'a pre-planned manoeuvre to ensure that the leadership remained in safe hands'[27] but this view must be regarded as doubtful because 'Cosgrave was considered a cautious liberal in 1965, at least by Fine Gael standards'.[28] It was he who persuaded his party's annual conference to support the Costello proposals and he was chairman of the committee which eventually produced *Towards a Just Society*. So it was believed that the country's second major party had now acquired the leader the times demanded who would set about a fundamental and long overdue reform of its organisation.

(v) 1966 presidential election

It is arguable that the 1966 and the 1990 contests for the presidency have been the two elections for that office which have aroused most interest among the electorate since the position was created under the 1937 Constitution and it has been described as 'the most intriguing election of the decade'[29]. De Valera, contesting the presidency again at the age of 84, faced a Fine Gael lawyer from the *Just Society* side of the party, Tom O'Higgins. It has been well remarked that there has always been an element in Fianna Fáil which looks upon opposition to its desires as well-nigh an act of treason and on this occasion it numbered more than usual: 'Opposing the patriarchal Chief on the golden anniversary of the Rising: sacrilege rather than treason, perhaps, in some minds!'[30]

O'Higgins conducted an excellent campaign, projecting the image of the new generation's representative, more appropriate for the changed times. Garret FitzGerald believes that a lot of the credit must go to O'Higgins's policy adviser and speech-writer, Michael Sweetman, a cousin of Gerard, because of the emphasis he placed on the concept of a pluralist society.[31] Although the office did not lend itself to political promises, O'Higgins travelled the country proclaiming his intention to make Áras an Uachtaráin less remote and formal. (In this he set a precedent which was followed by Erskine Childers in 1973 and Mary Robinson in 1990.) 'For once in the decade, Fine Gael managed to look a younger, livelier party than Fianna Fáil', it has been observed.[32]

O'Higgins was making such headway in the campaign that Fianna Fáil had to resort to what has been descried as 'some old-style mud-slinging'.[33] Micheál Ó Móráin, Minister for Lands and the Gaeltacht, publicly stated that although it seemed for a while that there would be no opposition to de Valera, *The Irish Times* had insisted on Fine Gael doing so, it being the mistress of that party and, like all mistresses, it could be 'vicious and demanding'. Speaking in Ó Móráin's Mayo West constituency, O'Higgins replied that he knew nothing about the vicious demands of mistresses and bowed to Ó Móráin's superior knowledge on the subject! The *Irish Independent's* comment, 'To judge from ministerial speeches, [it] looks upon the presidency as a kind of honorary doctorate', best sums up the Fianna Fáil attitude.

The result of the election made it clear that Fianna Fáil was right to be anxious. From a total ballot of 1,100,000, de Valera won by a mere 10,500 votes as against 120,000 in 1959. Its candidate's winning of 49.5% of the vote was described as a moral victory for Fine Gael. A student of the contest has observed:

> O'Higgins's performance had been a revelation, suggesting to Fine Gael that under its new leadership it was poised to make the breakthrough that would enable it to offer a serious challenge to Fianna Fáil in the next general election.[34]

Another consequence has been suggested by Garret FitzGerald: that it strengthened the liberal wing within the party, because it showed that more adventurous policies could indeed prove popular with the electorate, despite what the conservative element thought.

1966 also witnessed a further significant development in Fine Gael policy. An organisation called the Language Freedom Movement (LFM) had been founded in 1965 to campaign to have

120

the element of compulsion removed regarding the speaking and learning of Irish. It had a quiet first year but was catapulted into the limelight by the Fine Gael policy on the language in 1966. Before the 1961 general election, the party had stated its opposition to compulsory Irish and in March 1966 its presidential candidate told a Cork meeting that many young people were questioning the idea of restoring Gaelic Ireland in the traditional sense and its relevance to modern times and he urged that the whole idea of language revival be re-examined.

This was followed by a party policy document promising to abolish the compulsory pass in Irish in public examinations and also as a test for entry into the public and civil service. The party carefully stressed that it still adhered to the policy of reviving Irish, but argued that government policy had to have the support of the populace and expressed the belief that support was being lost by the element of compulsion. It repeated its adherence to affording all Irish people the opportunity to learn the language and to allowing them access to effective teaching. But Fine Gael was wrong if it believed that this would soothe the susceptibilities of the Irish language enthusiasts. It has been pointed out that, 'Every Irish language body in the country united in opposition to their proposals.'[35] On the other hand, the LFM welcomed them.

What happened in 1966 changed nothing in the sense that the decline of the Irish language was neither speeded up nor stopped, but the debate about Ireland's culture, growing more intense as a result of the cosmopolitan influences which quickly stemmed from the material prosperity, was given a new direction. 'In particular, all those who dissented from the traditional orthodoxies concerning the Irish language now had a focus for their views and a voice within the political system', it has been well remarked.[36]

(vi) 1968 PR referendum

Immediately after the 1965 general election, in which Fianna Fáil had secured an overall majority of one, Lemass hinted at a reassessment of the Irish electoral system. In two articles in *The*

121

Irish Times soon afterwards, Garret FitzGerald agreed that the existing party system was unlikely to lead to either significantly strong majority governments or adequate oppositions. He argued strongly for the single transferable vote in single-member constituencies as Fine Gael had proposed in 1959, holding that, since this procedure was used in by-elections, the electorate was familiar with it. This suggested that there might be enough Fine Gael support for a change to enable agreement to be reached with Fianna Fáil; especially since the party's new leader, Liam Cosgrave, was known to have reservations about proportional representation.

It was not until February 1968 that the government was in a position to introduce a bill which proposed to abolish the single transferable vote and replace it with the first-past-the-post system. Because the attempt to do so had been defeated only nine years before, it appeared incredible to one commentator that Fianna Fáil had made another effort to alter the Irish system of voting in 1968: 'The country was cynical, for the proposal was a piece of gross opportunism aimed at securing Fianna Fáil in power forever, despite all the party's pious rhetoric about the instability created by PR and the need for strong government', was his unequivocal opinion.[37] That the issue was revived less than ten years after its defeat showed the overweening pride and lack of proportion that seemed to seize Fianna Fáil following Lemass's departure, he further believed.[38]

Liam Cosgrave, who had been silent during the previous referendum on the issue, now made the Fine Gael position abundantly clear: 'The people had already expressed their support for the existing system and there was no point in asking them again; there were far more urgent matters to attend to than changing the method of voting, or "rigging" the constituencies in favour of particular areas'.

There followed a long Dáil debate (although not quite as extended as that of 1959). Labour's Patrick Norton, son of the former leader, introduced an amendment identical to what Dillon had proposed in 1959 - the single transferable vote in single-seat constituencies - but Fianna Fáil was unreceptive. Majority opinion in the media was in favour of retaining the existing position. 'Fears of permanent Fianna Fáil domination reinforced by gerrymandering were continually and skilfully exploited,' it has been observed.[39]   In October 1968, the referendum proposal for change was rejected by a majority of more than 20%; the 'no' vote was particularly high in Dublin and Cork.

When the government introduced a bill for constituency revision in November 1968, both Fine Gael and Labour opposed it. The measure proposed greatly to reduce the number of five-seat constituencies and increase the number of three-seaters. In Dublin, where Fianna Fáil had seldom got more than 40% of the vote, there were to be mainly four-seaters, while in Munster, Connacht and Ulster, where it usually won around 50% of the vote, there were to be predominantly three-seaters. It has been remarked that, 'The opposition were not slow to draw the appropriate inference - that Fianna Fáil were introducing three-seaters where they were strong and four-seaters where they were weak.'[40]

To delay the second stage of the Bill, T.J. Fitzpatrick, Fine Gael's Local Government spokesman, introduced a private member's bill proposing that a commission of three TDs from each of the major parties in the Dáil, under a Supreme or High Court judge as chairman, should revise the constituencies.   Labour supported this, but Kevin Boland, Minister for Local Government, accused Fine Gael of inconsistency and quoted from a Tom O'Higgins speech during the 1959 referendum campaign where he rejected such a proposal. Fitzpatrick angrily replied that in the recent campaign Boland himself had backed the idea. He was not granted leave to introduce his Bill and, as a result, the government met more hostile opposition to its measure than had ever before faced a proposal for constituency revision.

Although Fianna Fáil had been accused of gerrymandering at several revisions (it has already been pointed out that in most elections since 1933 the party secured more seats than it was entitled to on the basis of strict proportionality), one political scientist has expressed the belief that 'only the 1969 revision seems to have been designed in this spirit'.[41]   This was also the first redrawing to have been undertaken before it was due under the Constitution. The opposition accused the 'Boland Gerrymander' of 'butchering' county boundaries. Fine Gael suggested two alternative schemes in the course of the debate on the second reading of the government's Bill. One of these came from Senator Garret FitzGerald, in a *Sunday Independent* article, and would have affected only 40,000 people, in contrast to Boland's scheme, which affected 100,000. The government Bill passed the second stage narrowly by 60 votes to 58 and became law in late March 1969.

(vii) 1969-1973

There seems to be something of a consensus among commentators that the course of Fine Gael in the late 1960s changed little under Liam Cosgrave. He has been accused of not realising the potential generated by the *Just Society* period, of not identifying with Declan Costello and the liberals, as appeared likely when he became leader, but adhering instead to Gerard Sweetman and the conservative wing of the party. Costello retired from politics early in 1967 and, although he returned briefly in the 1970s, it has been lamented that 'this gifted and energetic man never held high cabinet office'.[42] Despite Costello's loss, the liberal wing, which now tended to be represented mainly by the new Senator, Garret FitzGerald, tried unsuccessfully to assert itself. A motion at the 1968 ard-fheis to change the party's name to 'Fine Gael - Social Democratic Party' was supported by the liberal element. Some of the delegates who were present claimed that this proposal was put to a vote and accepted, but Sweetman, who chaired that particular session, paid no attention and persuaded the delegates to allow a postal ballot of the branches to decide. The latter overwhelmingly opposed the suggestion. On the same occasion some liberals tried to have the United States policy in Vietnam criticised, but the leadership refused outright to countenance such a move.

With this background in mind, it has been asserted that although the defeat of Fianna Fáil in the 1968 referendum and the extraordinary performance of Tom O' Higgins in the presidential election were good for Fine Gael morale, 'it was clear that the momentum gained by the commitment to the *Just Society* had been spent' by the time the party came to face the 1969 general election.[43]

Labour was in a supremely confident mood as the 1969 contest beckoned. A somewhat sceptical reviewer has summed up that party's position as follows:

> They were going it alone, all the way for socialism. The Fine Gael party, which they now professed to despise even more than Fianna Fáil, had made a few tentative enquiries about the possibility of a coalition arrangement, but Labour was in no mood to entertain suitors, and Fine Gael was sent packing.[44]

Labour was making a mistake but no one within the party seemed to realise it. To make a significant advance under PR not only requires great swings 'but the disciplined transfers of lower preferences', it has been accurately observed.[45] Without an agreement with Fine Gael, Labour would not be able to get sufficient anti-Fianna Fáil transfers and its opting for a unilateral approach in the two previous elections in effect had handed victory to Fianna Fáil.

It greatly annoyed Fine Gael spokesmen that their former Labour colleagues regarded them as no different from Fianna Fáil. Labour did not have the monopoly on academic talent in this election, despite the presence in its ranks of Dr Conor Cruise O'Brien, Dr David Thornley (who had contemplated joining Fine Gael), Justin Keating, Dr Noel Browne and Dr John O'Donovan (formerly of Fine Gael). Dr Garret FitzGerald and Professor John Kelly were standing for the first time as Fine Gael candidates for the Dáil. But the party seemed to be fighting on two fronts. It attacked Fianna Fáil for the shortcomings in its social policy, especially in the field of public housing which had sustained a sharp decline since 1957. But it also hit out at Labour for what Cosgrave called its 'absurd pretensions'. (For the first time in its history, Labour was contesting all the constituencies - it had 99 candidates - and Corish proclaimed that it was aiming to form a government on its own.)

Garret FitzGerald contended that Fine Gael was the only alternative government to Fianna Fáil and John Kelly argued that, while Fine Gael wanted power at that particular time, Labour seemed to be content to remain in opposition until the 1980s. 'Relations between the two opposition parties were at their lowest ebb since 1948', it has been maintained. [46]

During this campaign Fine Gael tried to project itself as the party of the centre, because Labour had moved so far to the left and Fianna Fáil was associated with what has been termed 'the more unsavoury faces of capitalism'.[47] However, it has been asserted that the Fine Gael programme lacked inspiration: although it called for some minor improvements (an ombudsman, for example) and repeated its 1961 promise to get rid of compulsory Irish, 'there was little to enthuse the voters'.[48] Fianna Fáil's campaign, orchestrated by Charles Haughey, concentrated on Labour as the main target and dismissed Fine Gael as 'dead', much to Fine Gael's chagrin. As usual *The Irish Press* supported Fianna Fáil, *The Irish Independent* opposed it, while *The Irish Times* found it increasingly difficult to discover differences between the two main parties.

In the election, Fine Gael held its 1965 share of the vote (34.1%) and gained three seats, going up to 50. Labour's vote increased substantially in Dublin and in six out of the ten constituencies there it was ahead of Fine Gael but, after all the euphoria, it lost four seats. Both Fine Gael and Labour suffered because of the low incidence of cross-party voting transfers, and may have lost as many as seven seats because of it. Fianna Fáil's share of the vote dropped 2%, but it actually gained three seats. The lack of Fine Gael-Labour cooperation, as well as Boland's surgical constituency 'revision' - nine seats hinged on 6,000 votes - gave Jack Lynch, the former Cork hurling star and Lemass's successor as leader of Fianna Fáil, an overall majority, with 75 seats.

Having made only a slight gain in the June 1969 election, Fine Gael accepted that if it was to come to power in the near future, coalition was the only means of doing so. The same realisation dawned even more dramatically on Labour after its chastening experience at the polls. In 1970 informal negotiations began between the two parties; they moved slowly at first because of Labour's opposition to Irish entry into the EEC. It has been argued that the two wings within Fine Gael became clearly marked in the late 1960s and early 70s. Gerard Sweetman's tragic death in a car crash in January 1970 has been seen as a blow to the conservative side (it was, of course, a severe loss to the party as a whole), while Garret FitzGerald's election to the Dáil in 1969 has been regarded as a boost to the liberal section, because he 'rapidly established himself as the party's most able spokesman on practically every subject'.[49]

In his autobiography, FitzGerald referred to tensions between Fine Gael's more liberal wing and its leader during this period, which culminated in Cosgrave's much publicised address to his party's ard-fheis in May 1972.[50] Departing from his prepared script, Cosgrave referred to people who had joined Fine Gael 'after it had been built up, and had then begun their attack' on it. Using a hunting image which came naturally to a keen horseman, he described these parvenus as 'mongrel foxes' who, he declared, would be 'unearthed, and then I will let the rank and file of the party, the pack, tear them apart'. This has been interpreted as providing evidence that Cosgrave was uncertain of his position as leader and that he realised that there were those in the parliamentary party who would have preferred someone with a less conservative image when the idea of coalition with Labour was being mooted.[51]

On the other hand, in his memoirs, Patrick Lindsay, a member of the front bench in the late 1960s, expressed his belief that three or four of his colleagues were plotting to replace Cosgrave as leader. Specifically, he named Declan Costello, Tom O'Higgins and Garret FitzGerald. They got nowhere, according to Lindsay, because they had no other support on the front bench and because Mark Clinton's opposition to them proved particularly cogent.[52]

The Northern Ireland crisis which erupted with such intensity in the late 1960s left Fine Gael unscathed at first while causing major upheaval within Fianna Fáil. Two government ministers,

Blaney and Haughey, were dismissed by Lynch in May 1970, an event to which Liam Cosgrave made a significant contribution. It seems that Lynch was forced into action by a threat from Cosgrave to publicly reveal information he had received that ministers were involved in supplying arms out of public funds to the IRA.

But the Northern crisis was not to leave Fine Gael unscarred. In November 1972 the government introduced an amendment to the 1940 Offences against the State Act which would enable a person to be convicted of IRA membership on the uncorroborated evidence of a Gárda chief superintendent. Fine Gael's front bench was deeply divided in its reaction to the Bill and it decided to refer the matter to the parliamentary party without a recommendation. Although Cosgrave wished to support the measure, the majority of TDs and Senators decided to oppose it. The leader accepted his party's decision, but his strong reluctance to vote against the Bill in the Dáil led to an approach being made to Fianna Fáil in an effort to secure a number of amendments which would have satisfied Fine Gael reservations and allowed it to back the legislation. Fianna Fáil, having perceived the disagreement among its chief opponents, rejected any changes, relishing the prospect of an election on a law and order issue with Fine Gael divided and possibly leaderless. On receiving Fianna Fáil's response, Cosgrave again tried to persuade his colleagues to change their minds but, in the end, only Patrick Donegan, shadow Minister for Defence, and Cosgrave himself were prepared to support the government. However, on 1 December, the day of the division on the Bill's second reading, two explosions in Dublin city centre killed two people and left 127 injured. This tragedy caused his party to rally behind Cosgrave and to support the Fianna Fáil measure.

The Offences against the State (Amendment) Act might have cost Cosgrave the leadership. However, Garret FitzGerald, who strongly opposed his leader's stand at the time, believed in retrospect that Cosgrave's response was the right one and that it was subsequently vindicated. Had there been a post-Christmas election on this law and order issue, Fine Gael would have lost badly, FitzGerald averred. He explained why the majority of his colleagues were opposed to the Fianna Fáil measure: their prolonged period in opposition had made them almost instinctively anti-authoritarian and they believed that ambiguity within the government concerning the IRA prevented existing laws being sufficiently enforced against that organisation.[53]

It has already been noted how, on the eve of the 1948 general election, the imminent disappearance of Fine Gael was being predicted. Studies of Irish politics published in the early 1970s similarly diagnosed the party as in a none too healthy condition. The following is a view of Fine Gael put forward by an eminent political scientist at the time: 'What is important for the political system as a whole is that it still behaves to a great extent as though it might win a majority, though after so long a Fianna Fáil hegemony, it usually has a somewhat tired air of resignation.'[54] Such an opinion appears completely dated in view of Fine Gael's sustained participation in government throughout the 1970s and 80s. In fact, those two decades have been the most successful in the party's history to date.

Jack Lynch called a general election for February 1973, 15 months before his government's term would have expired. He had planned to have it in December 1972 when Fine Gael was divided over the amendment to the Offences against the State Act, but, for various reasons, he waited a further six weeks. Unofficial talks between the two main opposition parties on the possibility of coalition had started in 1970, being spearheaded on the Fine Gael side by Tom O'Higgins and Garret FitzGerald. After May 1972 progress in these consultations was more pronounced and the unexpected dissolution of the Dáil on 5 February 1973 acted as a catalyst.

Two days later Fine Gael and Labour published what amounted to a joint election manifesto, a 'Statement of Intent'. It was an historic moment because this was the first time the two parties had agreed on coalition *before* fighting a general election campaign. The 14 points of the document they published have been seen as echoing the *Just Society*:

. . . higher welfare benefits, reduction of the pensionable

age, progressive abolition of rates, abolition of death duties, stabilisation of prices and also 'protection of the liberty and safety of the individual and the democratic institutions of the State' and 'the promotion of a peaceful solution in the North'.[55]

Fianna Fáil tried to make the North an election issue by asserting that only it could deal with the fragile situation there, but the coalition parties countered this by concentrating on economic and social issues. They attacked Fianna Fáil's assertion of the success of its policy on Northern Ireland by pointing to a lack of internecine strife within their parties and contending that, despite the expulsions from Fianna Fáil, it still had more extreme republicans in the party than it was willing to acknowledge. The publication of a 14-point plan by the coalition partners has been described as 'a masterstroke'.[56] It enabled them to seize the initiative and get the voters to concentrate on their programme. It placed Fianna Fáil spokesmen in a dilemma: if they attacked it, they gave it more publicity, but if they disregarded it, they risked ignoring issues vital to the electorate. And if they came up with their own similar alternative, they could be accused of borrowing and of imitation.

Fine Gael and Labour argued that their social programme would get its finance from expected grants from the EEC Regional Fund of around £30 million, so that no increases in taxes need occur. Fianna Fáil rejected this and declared that taxes would have to be extended to yield an extra £70 million. Lynch's announcement, contrary to all previous Fianna Fáil claims, on 21 February that it was indeed possible to abolish rates and that his party would do so and would use all the money available from EEC entry on social welfare spending, represented what has been called 'a turning point in the campaign'.[57] On television a few days later Garret FitzGerald produced before a bemused George Colley, the Minister for Finance, a *Limerick Leader* advertisement where local Fianna Fáil candidates dismissed the Fine Gael-Labour promise to abolish rates (this advertisement appeared *after* Lynch's about-turn!).

Declan Costello was again a Fine Gael candidate for Dublin

South-West but Tom O'Higgins, the party's deputy leader, made it known that he would not take part in the election, but would concentrate on the presidential contest due in June. Much more so than ever before, Fine Gael and Labour candidates worked as a team, and in newspaper advertisements they strongly advised their supporters to vote solidly for coalition candidates.

The result of the February 1973 election marked a triumph for the strategy of coalition. Fine Gael increased its share of the vote by only 1% on its 1969 performance but gained four seats, in contrast to Fianna Fáil, which lost six seats despite increasing slightly its share of the vote. With 54 seats, Fine Gael had its highest number since its inception. The election marked a significant victory for Liam Cosgrave himself as he secured the largest first preference vote in the country, more than either Lynch or Haughey. Declan Costello had an easy return to the Dáil. Concerning the outcome of this election it has been further remarked that:

> The high level of solidarity among the Fine Gael and Labour voters neutralised the traditional advantage Fianna Fáil had enjoyed in the rural areas, especially the three-seaters. Fine Gael also won seats from Labour in three Dublin constituencies and easily re-established itself as the second largest party in the Dublin area, being ahead of Labour in eight out of ten constituencies.[58]

After its second period of 16 years in the opposition wilderness, Fine Gael was again in government.

(viii) Electoral support and organisation

In the 1951, 1954, 1957 and 1961 elections, Fine Gael got its main support from employers, managers and larger farmers. One significant difference in 1961 was that it won more backing from non-Catholics than ever before. (This was probably because of its policy on compulsory Irish.) 1965 saw a major change in the pattern of Fine Gael support, which was highest in agricultural constituencies and in areas with high emigration rates, and weakest in constituencies with a high proportion of employers and managers and wealthier people generally. Its share of the vote went up from 19.8% in 1948 to 34.1% in 1965, but this growth was not evenly distributed around the country.

'Between 1961 and 1965 a remarkable change in Fine Gael support occurred', an authority on the subject of electoral support for Irish political parties has observed.[59] Its support declined slightly in the richest constituencies, hardly altered at all in the middle-range ones, but increased significantly in the poorer agricultural ones. Why did Fine Gael gain so dramatically in the most agrarian areas? Between 1957 and 1965, votes for the smaller parties and Independents dropped by more than 20% and Fine Gael seems to have garnered most of these. This was no doubt due in part to the change in Fianna Fáil's image as, under Lemass, the party became more closely identified with the industrial sector, but the significance of the changes taking place within Fine Gael itself should not be underestimated.

One of these was the change in leadership in 1959. James Dillon was a farmer; he sat for Monaghan and had been a dynamic and successful Minister for Agriculture in the two inter-party governments. His Land Rehabilitation Project gave hope to the long depressed areas of the west and it was in these that Fine Gael made its biggest gains in 1965. Secondly, the party's 1965 election programme differed sharply from past manifestos. The *Just Society* put forward a more progressive social strategy for the party, advocating greater state planning to bring about more social justice, attacking Fianna Fáil for its emphasis on capital expenditure, and calling for more government social spending on houses, for example. No doubt conscious of its image as the large-farmer party, it appealed directly to the poorest farmers by promising to abolish rates on land and buildings below a certain value.

This was a major policy change for Fine Gael and it has been argued that its impact on the voters has been played down: 'The small change in Fine Gael's overall strength has, however, obscured the very pronounced change in its strength in the poorest regions of the country, as a result of which it was fully 9% stronger there than in the least agricultural constituencies.'[60]

In 1969 and 1973 the Fine Gael share of the vote remained steady at around 35%, although it won three extra seats in 1969 and four more in 1973. Support in constituencies changed little over the 1965, 1969 and 1973 elections. It was almost 6% stronger in 1973 in the most agricultural areas than in the least agricultural ones. The change of leadership from Dillon to Cosgrave, who sat for the country's richest constituency, had little impact upon the nature of party support. Since the new pattern of Fine Gael support which emerged in 1965 persisted in 1969 and 1973, it has been maintained that the 1965 election can be seen as 'a realigning election' for the party.[61]

There is evidence from the 1960s which suggests that elements within Fine Gael were apprehensive that the new social democratic thrust of the party might lose it middle-class support. Following the 1965 election, when Fine Gael campaigned for the first time for the *Just Society* programme, an internal party report articulated fears concerning the possible divisiveness of the new direction:

> It is clear from the results in Dublin and in Cork that we are to some extent losing the support of a group which has consistently provided our staunchest supporters, the urban middle class . . . . For too many years we have taken it for granted that the middle-class voter should vote for Fine Gael without being offered anything in return. The voting figures - and the abstention figures - show that that day is passing. The complaint has been made that the published Fine Gael policy does not offer any reason whatever why any middle-class voter should vote for Fine Gael and that there is no place in Fine Gael's *Just Society* for the middle-class man except as a beast of burden for the rest of the community.

The move to the left occasioned by the Costello programme possibly cost the party some of its traditional middle-class support but it succeeded in retaining most of the backing it had always received from that social class. The findings of the Gallup survey in 1969, which was the first survey of electoral support to be carried out in Ireland, revealed that Fine Gael had 37% middle-class and 16% working-class endorsement.

How is one to explain this achievement of retaining traditional support while arguing the case for a redistribution of the nation's wealth? The main reason, it has been suggested, is that Fine Gael presented its case for reallocation 'in the context of *overall* growth and expansion'. So, although more social spending would be of more relative benefit to the less well-off, in the context of economic expansion, the better-off were gaining anyway, so that the cost to them would be less in absolute terms:

> Since the national pie was growing, any proposal to slice it in a new fashion did not appear overtly costly. In a context of growth, even the more privileged could afford to be altruistic.[62]

The growth in the economy was crucial to the party's new electoral approach. Continued economic expansion enabled it to stress social spending and the need for a reallocation of resources. In this way the party was able to make a play for more working-class support without gambling too much on its orthodox middle-class base.

The organisational shortcomings of previous decades do not seem to have been remedied in the 1960s. A report of the party's 1965 general election campaign strongly criticised the inadequacies of the local organisations, berating the 'long delays in getting the election machine started in some constituencies because of poor organisation and slothful, negligent officials'. Concerning the organisation in Dublin, it was reported in 1968 that almost no structures existed in two of the seven constituencies, each having only two branches and no constituency executive, while in another constituency the executive had not met for nine months because of internal disagreements. The same report added that before some effort was made to reorganise in 1968, 'clinics' existed in only two of the Dublin constituencies. However, Dublin North-East, North-West and South-East were sources of Fine Gael strength in the city. In the first there were 14 branches with a nominal membership of 300 and an active membership of roughly half that number; in the second there were nine branches and 125 members, while in the third there were ten branches and 200 members. On the other hand, Dublin North-Central had only one branch with ten members, its constituency executive not having affiliated to the party since 1961. Nevertheless, this constituency returned a Fine Gael TD in both 1961 and 1965, so that poor organisation did not necessarily signify no support among the voters.

The reaction to the publication of the *Just Society* manifesto in 1965 also revealed structural weaknesses. Although this document has been seen as a significant turning-point in the development of Fine Gael's electoral appeal, its impact at local party level seems to have been minimal. One local activist was quoted as explaining that:

> . . . there was not always a clear Fine Gael position on some issues so in writing speeches we would simply try to hammer out our own policy. When the belatedly issued copies of the *Just Society* reached us, we sometimes found that statements in it were in contradiction to positions our candidate, or other party candidates had taken.[63]

The rather precarious state of the Fine Gael organisational structure has been summed up thus:

> The general conclusion to be drawn is of the long-term persistence of a poorly organised, cadre-style, continuing to lay organisational emphasis on key notables or individuals, while eschewing mass involvement and tolerating a lax and sometimes non-existent branch network.[64]

A study of Donegal politics in the early 1970s found that the nucleus of the party in the county consisted of key individuals without branch organisations. Furthermore, these usually belonged to the most well-off of the local community - teachers and businessmen such as builders, shop-owners and publicans.[65]

Fine Gael has had the public image of being a party of the upper echelons of society - the professionals, the wealthy, well-educated and well-bred sectors. It has also seemed to be controlled by specific families, who pass on power and a sense of serving the country from father to son and even to grandson. Prominent examples are Desmond and Garret FitzGerald, John A. and Declan

Costello, W.T. and Liam Cosgrave. A high percentage of Fine Gael ministers have been educated at private, fee-paying schools. The net result of this has been described as a 'lack of involvement in mass politics'.[66] Notabilities may have been prepared to serve in government but, like many of those who went before them, they displayed what has been termed 'a positive contempt for the whole business of grass-roots organisation'. A Fine Gael organiser in 1967 complained that it was difficult to discover suitable candidates because 'most of the business and professional people would not bother'.[67]

There has been a marked organisational contrast between Fine Gael and Fianna Fáil in the matter of fund-raising. The national collection was an intrinsic aspect of Fianna Fáil from its inception, provided most of the party's income, and was regarded as a means of integrating branches into their local communities. The money collected was forwarded to head office, which made an effort formally to thank all the contributors regardless of the amount they had donated. As has been already pointed out, Fine Gael had been in existence almost 20 years before its national collection was initiated and in its case the money gathered was retained by local organisations, while head office had its own two national organisers who were responsible for fund-raising activities and who operated independently of local structures. This meant that there were two distinct, autonomous institutional arrangements.

This duality inevitably led to clashes, mainly because local organisations regarded money collected in their areas by the head office organisers as rightfully theirs. From 1968, there is an example of a TD complaining to head office about the organiser collecting money in his constituency for the referendum campaign of that year and insisting that whatever was collected be returned to the local organisation. The upshot of this was that the organiser was admonished by the General Secretary for having been in touch with the local TD at all. A similar incident later in the same year caused the General Secretary to expostulate as follows with the same organiser:

I must emphasise to you that any collections you carry out

on behalf of Headquarters are to be regarded as *strictly private and confidential*, and that you are not to discuss the amount with anybody, or to reveal names of subscribers. You have now put us in the same position as you did in . . . . , namely that the local organisation feel that monies collected by you should be offset against money due from their constituency.

It was a curious system of fund-raising, and the justness of the criticism that it gave the impression 'of an essentially secretive organisation, as much in conflict with itself as with its opponents' must be conceded.[68]

Chapter 6

Coalition Government 1973-77

(i) Cabinet formation

Cosgrave and Corish faced an embarrassment of riches in picking their cabinet colleagues and when they had completed their work, the result was described by the media at the time as the 'team of all the talents'. Cosgrave's generous offer of five cabinet posts to Labour did much to ensure harmony between the two parties throughout this government's term of office and has led to the coalition being described as 'a more formidable combination than its predecessors'.[1]

The Fine Gael leader had no say in which Labour men were to get portfolios, but he did have the right to turn Corish's nominations down. Fine Gael claimed Finance, Defence and Education in advance, Labour secured the Social Welfare and Labour Portfolios, and the rest were divided up evenly. Much subsequent discussion has centred on Cosgrave's decision not to make Garret FitzGerald Minister for Finance, since he had been shadow spokesman on Finance since 1971. The most likely reason for the new Taoiseach's decision was that he feared FitzGerald might prove too radical a Minister for Finance for some of his party colleagues and traditional Fine Gael supporters.[2]

FitzGerald's success over George Colley in a television debate during the election campaign was perceived as significantly affecting the election result. It has recently been maintained that Cosgrave felt FitzGerald had ambitions to become leader and had little time for his colleague's liberal social attitudes. In the first inter-party government, Cosgrave had been Parliamentary Secretary to John A. Costello and knew well how matters developed in that administration. Perhaps, it has been suggested, he hoped that Foreign Affairs would do for FitzGerald what it had done for MacBride during that period: 'FitzGerald might lose touch with the party, as MacBride had lost touch with his party'.[3]

In his autobiography, Garret FitzGerald rejected this theory as cynical, on the grounds that up until 1973 only the autumn session of the United Nations caused a Minister for Foreign Affairs to be absent for any significant length of time, and the extent of the same minister's involvement in EEC affairs had not become apparent by that time. FitzGerald accepted to some extent the view that reservations his leader may have had about his possible impact on the Department of Finance may have been instrumental in Cosgrave's decision not to allocate to him that portfolio, but he went on to suggest other, more positive, reasons.

One was that since Ireland had become a member of the EEC only ten weeks before and because the development of her interaction with that organisation was clearly going to be a priority of government policy, FitzGerald's knowledge of and interest in the European connection (a topic on which he had been lecturing at University College, Dublin for 14 years) must have counted for something in his leader's calculations. Another reason FitzGerald put forward was that Cosgrave may have been influenced by memories of his father's 1920s administration in which FitzGerald's own father, Desmond, had been Minister for External Affairs until 1927. This may also have been why Declan Costello was appointed Attorney General to the 1973-77 government, as his father had held that post under W.T. Cosgrave in the Cumann na nGaedheal period.[4]

Richie Ryan, who had been front bench spokesman on Foreign Affairs and who had no experience of Finance, was made Minister for Finance. Soon attacked from all sides, he had the unenviable experience of dealing with the problems cast up by the unprecedented economic recession caused by the oil crisis. However, even an unsympathetic commentator on Fine Gael has described him as 'a tough and brave Minister for Finance' in hard times.[5] From November 1973 Richie Ryan also became Ireland's first Minister for the Public Service.

It has been suggested that Patrick Donegan was appointed Minister for Defence because he was at one with Cosgrave over the Offences against the State Amendment Bill,[6] but it should be remembered that he had been a long-standing member of the Fine

Gael front bench. The capture of the arms ship, the Claudia, was a triumph for him. Patrick Cooney, who has been described as 'the placid, able and well-spoken solicitor from Athlone', became Minister for Justice.[7] On the liberal wing of Fine Gael, Cooney had been a stout defender of civil liberties and favoured family law reform but the serious security situation during his tenure of office occupied much of his attention. His firm handling of the Herrema kidnapping won the country international acclaim.

Tom Fitzpatrick was appointed Minister for Lands. As the party's national organiser and executive chairman, he was a very senior figure in Fine Gael. A skilled negotiator, he had been responsible for keeping harmony between the liberals and the conservatives within the party and has been well described as 'a healer of divisions in a time of difficulty'.[8] Fitzpatrick played a vital role for the government in by-elections, orchestrating a crucial success in Monaghan in November 1973 which made the coalition position secure in the Dáil and ensured that it would run a full term, barring a catastrophe.

Tom O'Donnell had been front bench spokesman on Transport and Power, but was now made Minister for the Gaeltacht. He immersed himself in the problems of the Irish-speaking areas and that he succeeded in improving conditions there during a period of deep economic crisis was a real achievement. 'The personality of the man fitted the job - homely, compassionate, good-humoured and kind', it has been written about him.[9] Thanks to his achievements, Fine Gael made significant electoral headway in the west, a traditional area of Fianna Fáil support.

Richard Burke was given responsibility for Education. He proved very popular with the media, announcing many proposed reforms, and 'his command of vocabulary and undoubted intellectual brilliance ensured that they made maximum impact'.[10] But lack of money meant that some of the reforms had to be abandoned. Unfortunately, Burke encountered problems with the teachers' unions, and his espousal of denominational education provoked the opposition of liberals and moderates.

The new Minister for Agriculture was Mark Clinton. He

proved a doughty fighter at the Community Council of Ministers meetings and his gains on their behalf made him immensely popular with the farmers. The Department of Agriculture took on an increased importance as Ireland's membership of the EEC became effective. Under the Common Agricultural Policy, Agriculture ministers from all the member states regularly reviewed the prices for agricultural products, especially beef, other meats, milk and dairy products. Ireland was to be well served by its Minister for Agriculture whose negotiating skills and tenacity were sufficient to ensure that on most issues Clinton had his way.

Peter Barry, as Minister for Transport and Power, completed the ten man Fine Gael portion of the coalition cabinet. His affable personality made him well-liked and he presided over the pleasant task of bringing ashore the offshore oil and gas in his native Cork.

There were six Fine Gael junior ministers. John Bruton, who was only in his mid-twenties, was the youngest TD in the 19th and 20th Dáil and 'had been one of the bright stars of the party in the last years of opposition'.[11] Regarded as a potential Minister for Agriculture, on which he had been front bench spokesman since 1972, he became instead Parliamentary Secretary to the Minister for Education; his day had not yet come. John Kelly, a distinguished university law professor, was appointed Parliamentary Secretary to the Taoiseach and the Minister for Defence and Government Chief Whip. Soon to be widely regarded as the finest orator in the Dáil, he could never have been accused of not speaking his mind.

The veteran midlands TD, Oliver J. Flanagan, was appointed Parliamentary Secretary to the Minister for Local Government in 1975 and became Minister for Defence in 1977. The junior team was completed by Michael Begley from Kerry South, Henry Kenny from Mayo West and Richard Barry from Cork North-East. Begley had been shadow spokesman on the Gaeltacht from 1970 to 1973, and on Fisheries 1972-73. He became Parliamentary Secretary to the Minister for Local Government in 1973 and two years later was transferred to fulfil the same role to the Ministers for Finance and Defence. Kenny was Parliamentary Secretary to the Minister for Finance until his death in 1975. Barry was the Junior Minister in the Department of Health.

The Labour ministers were Brendan Corish, Tánaiste and Minister for Health and Social Welfare; James Tully, Minister for Local Government; Michael O'Leary, Minister for Labour; Justin Keating, Minister for Industry and Commerce and Conor Cruise O'Brien, Minister for Posts and Telegraphs. O'Brien's views on Northern Ireland caused much controversy and at times the Taoiseach had to dissuade him from speaking on sensitive issues. Labour had two Parliamentary Secretaries: Frank Cluskey, who assisted Corish, and Michael Pat Murphy at Agriculture and Fisheries.

One of the first policies implemented by the new government was to fulfil the old Fine Gael promise to do away with Irish as a compulsory subject for gaining the Leaving Certificate and as an entry requirement for the civil service. But this was not the full extent of its Irish language policy. It will be remembered that it was a Fine Gael-led government which first established a separate Department of the Gaeltacht, and in Tom O'Donnell it had a most diligent Minister running its affairs. Gaeltarra Éireann, a semi-state body set up in 1958 to help the language revival, was restructured in 1975 as Bord na Gaeilge and has since been the main agent of government language policy.

(ii) 1973 presidential election

The 1973 presidential election took place in May. Tom O'Higgins, who had contested the office so impressively in 1966, was expected to win. But the Fianna Fáil nominee, Erskine Childers, defeated him by 48,000 votes. A number of reasons have been suggested for the Fine Gael man's defeat.

One argument has been that, although the Labour ministers in the coalition campaigned strongly on O'Higgins's behalf, Labour branch members were less than enthusiastic because 'O'Higgins seemed to some to project an urban bourgeois image which many did not enthuse over'.[12] Another contention which has been put forward is that the religious element of the campaign was important. Childers, a Protestant, probably won almost the entire Protestant vote as well as a large Catholic vote because to support him was an ecumenical gesture, made all the sweeter by being harmless.[13]

The coalition campaign on behalf of O'Higgins has been described as ineffective. 'It tried to fight the issue on the budget, which was a popular one, but the electorate were not impressed by this diversionary tactic',[14] it has been maintained. O'Higgins's own retrospective view was different. He believed that the Fine Gael-Labour success in the February general election harmed his own prospects because he found that he was being blamed at meetings for the taxation increases in Richie Ryan's first budget.[15]

Some of the speeches on his behalf at the Fine Gael ard-fheis perhaps went a bit too far. One speaker spoke of the need to banish Fianna Fáil from every public office in the land. Richie Ryan urged the election of a man 'of Irish stock'. This mixture of implied racism and single party dominance did less than justice to the calibre of the government candidate. He has been rightly described as having 'done much to fight for a more liberal Irish society'.[16] But his own performance was not as vigorous or impressive as it had been seven years before and his campaign lacked the energy and enthusiasm of the previous contest. He later regretted the effect created by publicising an opinion poll which showed him to be a clear winner over his opponent, and he admitted that he and his activists underrated the Erskine Childers campaign. In fact, Childers took a leaf out of O'Higgins's own book in 1966 by promising a more relevant and accessible presidency.

As the Fine Gael candidate recalled, 'The Civil War background to a contest between an O'Higgins and a Childers reared up only once in Monaghan, where a man shouted at him about Kevin O'Higgins being "the murderer of Childers".'[17] On his election, Erskine Childers paid tribute to his defeated opponent for refraining from any reference to the Civil War. In fairness, the same tribute should be paid to Childers himself, whose tenure of his new office was to be regrettably short. Now out of politics after a career that went back to 1948, Tom O'Higgins was appointed a High Court judge and, 18 months later, Chief Justice.

(iii) Constituency revision ('Tullymander')

It became necessary to revise the constituency boundaries because the old ones had become outdated as a result of population shifts. James Tully, the Minister for Local Government, undertook the task. As a recent historian phrased it, 'he laboured lovingly to reverse Kevin Boland's previous gerrymander',[18] and his handiwork was described as the 'Tullymander'.

The map was so arranged as to create three-seaters in constituencies where the coalition might expect to win two seats; four-seaters where they might win two, and five-seaters when they had a chance of winning three. Based on an exact repetition of the 1973 general election results, the outcome of a new contest would be Fianna Fáil 63, Fine Gael 64, Labour 19 and Independents 2. It would have taken an unparalleled swing in Irish electoral history for Fianna Fáil to return an overall majority in such circumstances.

The comment that, 'the coalition's 1974 Electoral Act appears to mark an attempt to maximise its own parliamentary strength at the next election' has been rightly described as 'judicious'.[19] In fact, politicians on both sides found themselves in reverse roles from those they had played in 1969.

(iv) Northern Ireland

Fine Gael was not subject to the same divisions over Northern Ireland as Fianna Fáil and Labour in that it had no so-called 'republican' wing. The party had long advocated good relations with Britain and Northern Ireland. 'Some of the new liberals who joined the party in the 1960s saw Unionist allegations that the South was intolerant and too wedded to Catholic concepts of morality as an additional strong reason for liberalisation in the South', it has been well remarked.[20]

Fine Gael reassessed its approach to Northern Ireland at an emergency meeting in September 1969. The policy which the liberal wing had been advocating (the main proponents were Paddy Harte, TD for Donegal North-East and Garret FitzGerald) was accepted: the use of force was ruled out; civil rights in the North were to be worked for rather than Irish unity; the emphasis was on the need to

144

change the Constitution and laws of the Republic to create a pluralist society which would entice Unionists. A policy committee was set up to develop these ideas and FitzGerald was their most persistent front-bench presenter.

In March 1973, the British issued a set of proposals for the creation of an 80-seat assembly in Northern Ireland to be elected by proportional representation which would form a power-sharing executive in which there would be Catholic ministers. The election was held in June 1973 and both Dublin and London hoped that a majority would be elected which would favour the formation of a power-sharing executive. Two speeches by Liam Cosgrave, to a party meeting in Blackrock, Co. Dublin, on 21 June and to British Conservative MPs in London on 2 July, were designed to show that Dublin would play its part in bringing about this devoutly-to-be-wished-for outcome. He emphasised the new direction Fine Gael policy had taken since 1969. There were none of the traditional references to the injustice of partition or to the Irish nation's inalienable right to be united. The idea was put forth of striving for broad agreement between the opposing sides in Northern Ireland:

> No one tradition, and no one community in Ireland can now determine the political future of our island. We must not therefore let an abstract approach deter us from beginning now to get the very necessary process of reconciliation underway. Let us not try to impose on each other rigid concepts of the kind of future Ireland we want and the kind of political structures we want to emerge. Let us trust to the process itself to determine the outcome.

In September 1973 the British Prime Minister, Edward Heath, travelled to Dublin to discuss a Council of Ireland. In November a power-sharing executive was formed in Northern Ireland. Representatives of the British and Irish governments and of the Northern Irish executive met at Sunningdale in Berkshire on 6 December 1973, exactly 52 years after the signing of the Anglo-Irish Treaty, to try to improve on the arrangement which Griffith and Collins hardly had expected to last for that length of time. Following almost a week of exhaustive discussions, an agreement was reached which provided for: (i) a Council of Ireland, with representatives from North and South; (ii) the existing position in Northern Ireland to be respected; (iii) extradition procedures to be worked out, and (iv) British support for Irish unity if a majority in Northern Ireland desired it. The Sunningdale agreement gave rise to great hopes on both sides of the border, although Fianna Fáil condemned it as a betrayal of Irish nationalism and Unionist extremists denounced British treachery.

The new Northern government began work in January 1974, but in the British general election in late February 1974 anti-Sunningdale Unionists had a sweeping victory and Labour, which had not been involved in the Sunningdale process, replaced the Conservatives in Britain. Despite these setbacks and the continuing violence, the executive carried on, but a widespread strike organised by the Ulster Workers' Council in May was to bring about its collapse.

One of the victims of the violence engendered by the Northern problem was the Fine Gael Senator, Billy Fox. He had been active in the Fine Gael youth group in the 1960s, belonged to the liberal wing of the party and was sympathetic to Irish republicanism. He had been a TD for Monaghan from 1969 to 1973 when, for the only occasion in its history, Fine Gael secured the election of two members for the constituency. (Billy Fox had contested the 1965 general election and had polled very well: Fine Gael won a majority of the votes, but Fianna Fáil won two out of the three seats because 246 of the other Fine Gael candidate's transfers either went to Fianna Fáil or were non-transferable and the Fianna Fáil candidate won the seat from Fox by 235 votes.) Billy Fox was murdered on 11 March 1974 at a farmhouse near the border by Provisional IRA men when he was on a visit to his fiancée. He had been elected to the Senate shortly before this tragic incident took away his young life.

On 17 May 1974, loyalist terrorist bombs in Dublin and Monaghan claimed 31 innocent lives. This tragedy gave rise to doubt in the Republic about pressing the Sunningdale agreement on the Protestant community in Northern Ireland, which clearly did not want it. As the general strike in the North intensified, the Council of Ireland was postponed for three years on 23 May. Moderate Unionists began to resign from the Northern Ireland Executive, the British government showed a reluctance to stand by it and on 28 May the rest of the members resigned.

This collapse was a deep disappointment for the Irish government. Sunningdale was a radical initiative well before its time; most Unionists were not prepared to go so far so quickly. The reaction to Sunningdale of working-class Protestants had been underestimated. The elections to the emasculated Convention, which the British put in place instead of the power-sharing Assembly, gave the anti-power sharers a significant majority. After that the Irish government seemed to do nothing in public on Northern Ireland 'but behind the scenes, through the quiet and persistent diplomacy of the Foreign Minister, Garret FitzGerald, they managed to place Anglo-Irish relations on a better footing than for many years', it has been pointed out.[21]

The IRA staged some daring and spectacular prison escapes during this time. In November 1973 a hijacked helicopter landed in Mountjoy prison and carried away three leading IRA men; in August 1974, 19 Provisional IRA prisoners dynamited the prison walls in Portlaoise and escaped. In July 1976 there was another dynamite break-out, this time from the Special Criminal Court in the centre of Dublin. Along with these went many bank raids, two kidnappings and a major art robbery.

The government's main response was to enlarge the police and armed forces. Legislation to try people for cross-border offences had a slow passage through the Dáil due to relentless Fianna Fáil opposition and Labour uncertainty. The murder of Sir Christopher Ewart-Biggs, the British Ambassador, on 21 July 1976, prompted a serious review of security policy. Two Bills were introduced increasing sentences for recruitment by banned organisations and extending the period of detention without trial to seven days. Fianna Fáil opposed them, some Labour TDs were undecided and the progress of the legislation was slow in the Dáil and later in the Supreme Court.

The Taoiseach, the Minister for Justice and the Minister for Posts and Telegraphs were among the most passionate defenders of these measures. The government's strong reaction to the kidnapping of Dutch businessman, Dr Tiede Herrema, in October 1975 led it to claim that it was taking 'a much firmer attitude towards subversives than Fianna Fáil had done' but some Labour members were uneasy. It has been observed that 'some indiscreet utterances by Ministers in 1976 about the necessity for "responsible" reporting were widely interpreted by the anti-government papers, *The Irish Press* and *Hibernia*, as the prelude to press censorship.'[22] The government also came in for criticism for its tough security policy but this hardly caused many qualms among Fine Gael followers because of the amount of violence at the time, and especially after the brutal murder of Billy Fox.

Nationalist orthodoxies definitely underwent revision in these years, Conor Cruise O'Brien being their greatest iconoclast. Clear evidence of this was provided in the West Mayo by-election in November 1975. Fianna Fáil fought it on the basis of an early British withdrawal from Northern Ireland and was overwhelmingly defeated. The victorious Fine Gael candidate was Enda Kenny whose father, Henry, had been a Fine Gael TD since 1954, a front-bench spokesman 1969-72 and Parliamentary Secretary to the Minister for Finance from 1973 until his death in 1975. Enda himself has gone on to play a prominent role in Fine Gael.

It has been acutely observed that the continuing violence 'began to produce a more general reaction against any type of involvement with the problems of the North, let alone Irish unity'.[23] This in turn caused the need to change social legislation in the Republic, which was strongly advocated by the liberals in Fine Gael, to seem less pressing. It had become customary for proponents of change to argue that if unity were desired, laws in the South would have to be changed to take account of Unionist fears. But with the loss of interest in unity, this contention lost much of its thrust. The defeat of the Contraception Bill in July 1974 showed the strength of the resistance to change.

(v) Social policy

Following the Supreme Court ruling in the McGee case, the houses of the Oireachtas had to consider the 1935 legislation which banned the importation, sale and manufacture of contraceptives. There was widespread disagreement in Leinster House and among the public on this question. The Fine Gael Leader of the Senate, Michael O'Higgins, son of Dr T.F., brother of Tom and long-serving public representative, had such strong convictions on the issue that another Senator had to present the Contraception Bill when it came up on the agenda in late 1973. In the Dáil, John Kelly argued that the 1935 Act was 'an unwarranted intrusion on privacy and should never have been enacted'.

The problem of dealing with the situation fell to Patrick Cooney as Minister for Justice. He introduced a Bill allowing contraceptives to be imported and sold under strict conditions: importers and sellers had to get a licence from the Minister; the contraceptives were to be sold through pharmacies; advertising was strictly controlled; abortifacients were banned; unmarried people were not allowed to buy contraceptives, although Cooney admitted that this provision would be hard to enforce.

It has been perceptively remarked that the Contraception Bill of 1974 was about much more than mere contraception: 'it was the symbolic battleground where the matter of the moral and social future of the country was fought out'.[24] If this modest measure were to be defeated, reformers knew that it would be an end to any more wide-ranging social changes. For conservatives, it was an attempt to shelter Ireland from what they saw as the permissive values of the rest of Europe and the United States. Oliver J. Flanagan spoke for the opponents of change when he declared in the Dáil in July 1974:

> We are living in a sick Irish society, and we should realise that this sickness has been brought along by the failure of the people in high places - Church and State - to speak up and act. The result was that pressure groups sponsored by the materialistic and atheistic theme of modern journalism, which gave prominence to these evilly disposed pressure

groups, has [*sic*] brought our society to the deplorable condition it is in today.

By permitting a free vote, the coalition government allowed for the marked division in opinion. Fianna Fáil's response was if the government did not do its best to ensure the Bill's passage, it was shirking its duty. 'This tactic cleverly papered over the divisions which equally existed on the Fianna Fáil side', it has been pointed out.[25] It was hardly surprising, then, that the Cooney measure was defeated because it faced a united Fianna Fáil opposition and a divided government. It *was* surprising, however, how big the vote against it was: it was defeated by 75 votes to 61. Seven Fine Gael TDs voted against the measure, including the Taoiseach and Richard Burke, the Minister for Education. Cosgrave's action surprised his colleagues because they had no prior warning of it. It has been maintained that he 'was criticised in private by other Fine Gael TDs for failing to indicate in advance that he would vote against the Bill, but his dominance in the party was such that no one dared take public issue with him'.[26]

In fairness to Cosgrave, it must be pointed out that his silence in cabinet was due to his desire not to influence his colleagues. He wished on the day of the Dáil vote not to enter the 'no' lobby until the coalition TDs had voted, but was persuaded by the Chief Whip that it was his duty as leader to vote first. Here, again, his desire not to influence Fine Gael ministers or TDs may be seen.

While Fine Gael was certainly divided on the issue, Fianna Fáil was even more so. It consisted of a group opposed in principle to legalising contraceptives and a section which felt that they should be available but which condemned the government Bill as inoperable. If Fianna Fáil hoped that this issue would destroy the coalition, as the Mother and Child case had undermined the 1948-51 inter-party government, it was to be disappointed. It was never clear whether the party was opposing the Bill on moral or on practical grounds. One commentator has remarked, curiously: 'Fianna Fáil won, though their victory was eclipsed by the action of Mr Cosgrave, Mr Burke and others, which was perhaps what was intended.'[27]

John Kelly, never a man to mince his words, berated the Fianna Fáil attitude in terms that were hard-hitting, if less than charitable:

Fianna Fáil, having themselves shirked the whole problem while in office, having produced no alternative scheme now which would stand up to a moment's scrutiny, pretended under the cover of alleged unworkability to find fault with the whole Bill, though their own leader had publicly declared that the old law needed amendment. Gun republicans and guff republicans, shadow-Ministers and backbench Nanky Poohs, they all crossed into the No lobby, not under the pricks of a free conscience but under the ignominious lash of opportunism and simple hatred of the people who put them out of office. The Legion of the Rearguard conducted themselves like slaves.

The defeat of the Contraception Bill was a bitter blow to the Fine Gael liberals. According to one authority, when Garret FitzGerald suggested two years later that there was a need to look again at such questions as divorce, contraception and multi-denominational education, 'a word from Cosgrave was enough to stop discussion of the matter'.[28] Richard Burke, supported the existing Church control of schools and sometimes cited papal encyclicals to reinforce his stand.

Although the Catholic authorities were not enthusiastic about it, the main obstacle to the attempt by parents in Dublin to have two multi-denominational primary schools set up in 1975 was the Minister for Education. He has been described as 'a conservative Catholic who had already gone out of his way to praise the existing denominational basis of primary education, and had promised to safeguard it, whether by legislation or otherwise.'[29] It seems that Burke put administrative difficulties in the way of the two Dublin schools, Dalkey and Marley Grange. In the case of the latter, he did not have a site picked out for the new multi-denominational school, and, for Dalkey, he denied that there was any need for more school places. But his attitude appears to have been a personal one. When he became a European Commissioner at the end of 1976, his successor at Education, Peter Barry, was more sympathetic.

(vi) Foreign Affairs

Ireland's membership of the EEC meant an enhanced role for the Department of Foreign Affairs, hitherto one of the less important departments of government with a small staff and a low budget. In Europe, Garret FitzGerald rapidly won respect for his hard work and dedication. He was a devoted European and very active in the Irish Council for the European Movement. When he presented his departmental estimates to the Dáil on 17 May 1973, his marathon 30-page speech was a stunning performance and displayed the extent of his knowledge of international affairs. It also signalled his intention significantly to expand his department. He followed this up with a series of meetings all over the world. As a recent historian has remarked: 'His ability, affability, appetite for hard work and genuine idealism, reinforced by his fluency in French, made a startling impact on Europe for ministers and officials unaccustomed to Irish performers of this calibre'.[30] He contributed significantly to improving his country's image and dispelling the begging-bowl stereotype of the Irish minister overseas.

Ireland was president of the EEC from January to June 1975. FitzGerald flew to Lomé in Togo, West Africa to sign a EEC-Third World agreement. He then travelled to Lisbon to establish good relations between Portugal and the Community. This was a task requiring great skill because Portuguese politics were in a state of disarray at the time. FitzGerald organised European aid for Portugal's unsound economy and established the possibility of that country's membership of the EEC as a real prospect.

A significant new departure of the coalition's foreign policy was to increase Irish representation abroad and develop a policy towards the Third World. Many new embassies were opened, principally in the Middle East and Africa and always with a view to developing trade as well. The decision which caused most controversy was to establish diplomatic relations with the Soviet Union in 1974. Despite the warnings of espionage and ideological incompatibility, the plan was carried out and the objections died down. It was a move that was to be of immense commercial benefit to Ireland.

But the greatest development in foreign policy in this period was to increase aid to the Third World. FitzGerald stated that the objective was

> to contribute to the Third World in a manner and to an extent that will meet our obligations, satisfy the desire of the Irish people to play a constructive role in this sphere, and add to our moral authority in seeking to influence constructively the policies of other developed countries towards the Third World.

This approach was based on a growing awareness of the crushing problems that Third World countries were facing. Irish help was immediately doubled and later quadrupled. FitzGerald's idealism was the main impetus here and it has been well remarked that, 'This probably reflected a personal interest by the Minister in the matter more than anything else: there were no votes in Third World aid; taxpayers' contributions were being sent abroad, and many pressures were operating in the other direction'.[31] At the United Nations Committee for Trade and Development meeting in Nairobi in the summer of 1976, Ireland and the smaller European countries argued for more stable prices for Third World goods, while larger countries, such as Britain, were reluctant to see any move in such a direction.

FitzGerald frequently expressed his opposition to the South African apartheid regime and the government also strongly opposed the white rulers of Rhodesia. The Anti-Apartheid Movement had much contact with Fine Gael and Labour intellectuals while those parties were in opposition and probably exerted no small influence on the coalition government's foreign policy. The military dictatorship which forcefully replaced Salvador Allende's government in Chile in September 1973 was anathema to Dr FitzGerald, and the Chile Solidarity Campaign was facilitated in looking after Chilean refugees who came to Ireland.

When the Franco regime in Spain executed a number of its

opponents in September 1975, Ireland was the only European country not to withdraw its ambassador from Madrid. The government was criticised for not doing so, but Foreign Affairs maintained that it would have been a pointless exercise because the withdrawn diplomats would be back within a week, which was what happened. 'However, for one aspect only to come under fire in a foreign policy which had expanded out of all recognition over a space of three years was generally considered to have been a reasonable record'[32] is an assessment with which few would take issue.

(vii) The economy

The coalition election manifesto of February 1973 promised significant changes in the economy. Although its main preoccupation became crisis-management, its action on farmer and capital taxation, natural resources and equal pay was to be remembered. True to its manifesto, the new government quickly removed Value Added Tax (VAT) from food, health charges from the rates, reduced the pensionable age and improved social welfare. But coalition economic policy was the result of compromise between the two partners. Increased social welfare spending, a wealth tax and expanded public ownership had long been planks in the Labour platform. Fine Gael favoured the first, but was doubtful about the other two.

Economic policy was mainly decided by Richie Ryan, Garret FitzGerald and Justin Keating, because they knew most about economics. All three Ministers were to the left of centre in their political outlooks. Ryan, never claiming to be an economic expert, acquired a genuine concern for the poor from his education in a working-class area of Dublin. He abhorred the excessive consumption of alcohol, cigarettes, petrol and the obsession with television and was more willing to tax those items than previous Ministers for Finance had been. FitzGerald, a much more expert and experienced economist, favoured a fair distribution of resources with no inordinate poverty or wealth. His was a very open mind as far as economic theory went and he supported agreements with the trade unions. Keating was also well versed in economics. When Gross National Product (GNP) rose by a remarkable 7% in 1973, there was little opposition within the cabinet to increased social spending.

The government proposals on capital taxation, published in late February 1974, came as a bombshell to Irish farmers and business interests. In the place of death duties a capital gains tax of 35%, a wealth tax of 1.5% to 2% on estates over £40,000 and a capital acquisition tax of from 6% to 55% were proposed. The reaction was intense. The government was accused of annihilating industry and investment; poverty, unemployment, closures and general economic decline were direly predicted. By May, Ryan had halved the effects of the wealth tax and had lowered the capital gains tax to 26%. The proposals slowly went through the Dáil and became law, with richer farmers also now liable to pay income tax.

Why did the government persist despite the furore? It was vital that death duties, worth £14 million annually to the exchequer, be replaced. Ryan argued that the new legislation would stimulate a more productive use of wealth; people would invest it rather than let it build up and be taxed. Another reason was that Liam Cosgrave was committed to honouring to the letter his agreement with Labour. Furthermore, the trade unions could not be persuaded to restrain their pay demands unless capital too could be seen to be carrying its share. Actually, capital taxes brought little practical gain to the government, but they had an important symbolic significance in that 'the principle that the limitless accumulation of personal wealth was no longer socially acceptable'[33] had been introduced.

A second prong to the government's income and taxation reforms was a commitment to equal pay. Progress was slow and difficult, making more headway in the public service than in the private sector. The world economic crisis militated against this, as against other government proposals, and the Federated Union of Employers exerted intense pressure to have equal pay and anti-discrimination legislation postponed.

The quest for natural resources was pursued diligently because these were seen as presenting potentially substantial revenue possibilities. Government policy in this field underwent a significant change. The mining companies were no longer exempt from taxation. This move was generally welcomed because it was felt that the state had the right to a share of the proceeds from the country's mineral wealth. A new Gas Board was established to give public control of the natural gas distribution which was coming ashore in Cork. It has been observed that 'The government was thus able to steer between the twin extremes of outright nationalisation (the view of the Labour left) and Fianna Fáil's hands-off policy.'[34]

Ireland joined the EEC in January 1973, and before long the electorate became familiar with conferences of ministers in Brussels and other European cities. These were scenes of what has been well described as 'hard-bargaining, in-fighting, seemingly intractable problems and some successes'.[35] The Common Agricultural Policy (CAP) and the Regional and Social Funds all benefited Ireland. Garret FitzGerald estimated that the CAP profited the country to the tune of £100 million a year, mainly through increased farm prices; the Regional Fund gave Ireland £35 million over three years - far less than expected - while the much more modest Social Fund helped finance schemes to fight poverty. The country depended less on the British market and a vast new arena was now accessible to Irish exporters. On the negative side, fisheries and some protected industries, such as textiles, footwear and the motor industry, suffered. But Ireland was gaining more from EEC membership than any other member state. 'For the government, and Garret FitzGerald and Mark Clinton who pressed home the Irish demands in Brussels, such material gains were to blunt the worst effects of the recession which hit the economy late in 1973', it has been noted.[36]

The impact of the Arab countries' decision to raise substantially the price they charged for their oil in October 1973 was crippling on the western economies. By 1975 fuel in Ireland cost almost three times as much as it had done ten years before. For most people the oil crisis meant long queues at petrol stations for scarce supplies and a cutting down on central heating. Yet the problem of inflation predated the economic problems unloosed by the oil price rises. In the decade 1965 to 1974 Irish prices had doubled and the inflation difficulty unleashed a series of others: 'rising prices, dearer goods, falling standards of living, union pressure to keep pace, wage inflation, less competitive exports, worsening balance of payments, fewer goods sold, declining employment'.[37] The coalition's election manifesto had pledged to arrest inflation and increase employment.

The coalition government was committed to maintaining public spending, because it regarded this as vital to protect the poor from inflation and to combat unemployment. Some economists criticised this approach as adding to inflation and it is believed that the Taoiseach himself was less than happy at the level of government expenditure.

A second aspect of the government's policy in this area was closer ties with the trade unions. In a 1974 White Paper, this relationship was referred to as a 'national partnership'. Pro-labour laws were passed and union agreement was sought to curb wage demands and prevent strikes in return for control of tax increases. This did not prevent some damaging strikes, especially those in the banks and in CIE.

The coalition was committed to increased social spending and did not allow the recession to divert it from this course. In its first budget (May 1973), social welfare expenditure was increased by £68 million, VAT was removed from food and higher taxes were imposed on luxury items. This strategy was termed by the media 'the most progressive budget in the history of the state'. This approach was repeated in the government's second budget in April 1974, although by then the oil crisis was underway. Social welfare spending went up by 18% (just keeping pace with inflation), taxes were increased and farmers paid income tax for the first time. The government believed that the depression would not last and that public spending would help the economy through it. This approach was pursued by many other countries in western Europe. To this end the amount the Irish government had to borrow rose gradually.

By mid-1975 it became evident that this strategy was not meeting with success. Unemployment, stable at around 60,000 in 1974, began to increase in 1975 and was over 100,000 by 1976. The inflation level, too, continued to climb and was around 20% by the middle of 1975. The government responded by introducing a supplementary budget in June, involving food subsidies and an employment premium. The January 1976 budget sought to raise revenue to pay for the subsidies by levying new tax increases: ten pence on petrol, five pence on the pint, higher VAT and motor tax. Social welfare allowances were increased by 10%.

By mid-1976, Richie Ryan had to announce that the government borrowing limit had been reached. The twin evils of inflation and unemployment had proved intractable and unamenable to increased public spending. The only bright star in the firmament was the marked improvement in the balance of payments deficit, which had occurred in 1975.

The government's response to the economic crisis in the autumn and winter of 1976 seemed to lack direction. Discussions were held with unions and employers but made little progress. The government's main proposal was to concentrate on capital expenditure, but the effects of this on the economy would take some time to become manifest. By the time it published a Green Paper in 1976, the administration was being widely assailed - from the business sector which felt itself hard-pressed, from the unemployed who felt abandoned, and from social welfare dependents suffering because of the rising prices. Fianna Fáil was quick to appreciate the coalition's unpopularity and began to produce what have been described as 'attractive, bright and "spending spree" policies of its own'.[38] It performed a complete turn-around on its opposition to borrowing, relying instead on a policy of spending which would get the economy moving again. Although the January 1977 budget was popular and contained something for everyone, it was a case of too little too late and the newspapers denounced it as nothing more than an election ploy.

(viii) Setbacks

When President Childers died suddenly in November 1974, the government did not seem to want an election and did not nominate a candidate. The Fianna Fáil nominee, Cearbhall Ó Dálaigh, was returned unopposed, but a bizarre incident terminated his tenure of office in 1976. He referred the Emergency Powers Bill, which was the government's response to the murder of the British Ambassador and which gave the police greater powers, especially by lengthening the permitted period of detention without trial from two to seven days, to the Supreme Court, and when the latter confirmed its constitutionality, he signed it and it became law on 16 October.

That should have been the end of the matter, but two days later the Minister for Defence, Patrick Donegan, in a speech at an army barracks, described President Ó Dálaigh as a 'thundering disgrace'. When questioned in the Dáil, the Taoiseach stated that Donegan had offered to apologise, but he did not rebuke his Minister for Defence publicly or issue a governmental apology. The President resigned on 22 October and sent to the newspapers his corrosive reply to what he regarded as Donegan's 'qualified apology'. It was only after Ó Dálaigh's resignation that Cosgrave made known that Donegan too had been willing to resign. 'The resignation of President Ó Dálaigh was followed by a storm of protest in the newspapers, most correspondents denouncing both Cosgrave and Donegan for a violation of common constitutional practice in parliamentary democracies,'[39] it has been observed. Lynch and Cosgrave agreed that Patrick Hillery, who was coming to the end of his term as a EEC Commissioner (he was to be replaced by Richard Burke) should succeed Ó Dálaigh.

The episode could be viewed in one way as a masterly political manoeuvre by the Fine Gael leader, according to a recent historian, who argued as follows:

> Donegan, a publican by trade, was not renowned for a fastidious sense of language. He may not have deliberately insulted the President to provoke the resignation of a man known for his fastidious sense of integrity.

Whatever his reasons, Cosgrave responded in purely party political terms. He regarded Hillery as 'the most dangerous potential leader of Fianna Fáil'. Since that party was expected to lose the coming election and because Lynch then would come under strong pressure to step down from the leadership, Cosgrave probably hoped that the ensuing power struggle would seriously damage Fianna Fáil, 'given the personal animosities known to exist between leading contenders for the succession'. Hillery was the obvious agreed successor, but with him out of the way in Áras an Uachtaráin, Cosgrave expected to stand by while his opponents tore their party apart.

Ó Dálaigh had been an unsuccessful Fianna Fáil candidate for the Dáil on two occasions and twice had been Attorney General to Fianna Fáil governments. As a result, Cosgrave treated him more as a Fianna Fáil politician rather than as President. But Ó Dálaigh had been a reputable Chief Justice, a distinguished judge of the European Court, and 'was widely respected as a scholar and a gentleman'. He took the only course open to him by resigning, in this historian's view, who contended that although Cosgrave may not have lost many votes as a result of the affair, he hardly gained any either. While there can be little doubt that Donegan should have resigned, and should have been asked to do so, the already - quoted historian's final assertion that the 'main casualty was the proud name of [Cosgrave's] own family as defenders of constitutional propriety', is excessively harsh.[40]

Perhaps Cosgrave's attitude on the matter may be construed as follows. It is likely that he felt that his Minister for Defence had allowed himself to be carried away by the circumstances in which he found himself, and his instinct was to stand by his old colleague, loyalty being a hallmark of the man. Donegan sincerely regretted his ill-judged remark and Cosgrave must have believed that he had conveyed this in his letter of apology to President Ó Dálaigh.

A general election was widely expected in 1977, the two most likely months being June or October. But, according to one commentator, Cosgrave 'kept his own counsel' and did not reveal how close an election was until his 'vehement' address to the Fine Gael ard-fheis in May.[41] He berated 'irresponsible commentators' as 'blow-ins' and condemned those who were attacking the Minister for Justice and the Gárdaí in the name of civil rights. The 'blow-in' has generally been taken to be Bruce Arnold, the English-born political correspondent of *The Irish Independent*. It has been maintained that senior party figures such as Garret FitzGerald, Eddie Collins and Tom Fitzpatrick subsequently apologised to Arnold about the reference.[42] Three days after the ard-fheis the Dáil was dissolved. Cosgrave was reported by the newspapers as being in a 'relaxed and smiling' mood.

In fact the cabinet was divided on whether to opt for a summer or an autumn election. A number of factors favoured an earlier rather than a later contest. One of these was what has been described as 'the evidence of continuing coalition voting solidarity in seven by-elections, and solidarity had been an important factor in the coalition's success in 1973'.[43] Secondly, the government believed that its February budget had been popular, and Fianna Fáil had not done well in opposition. But most decisive in coalition thinking was the belief that Tully's redrawing of the constituency boundaries guaranteed victory.

The factors advising against a June election were never as seriously considered as those in favour. Two of these put forward by analysts of Irish politics at the time have been the harm done to the image of the government by the Taoiseach's unprecedented vote against his own cabinet's Family Planning Bill in 1974 (made worse by the lack of advance warning to his colleagues) and the attack on the President by the Minister for Defence in 1976 which led to much government embarrassment. But, in retrospect, the effect of these occurrences must be seen as limited. The chief factor was clearly that prices had almost doubled over the previous five years. 'While the government could credibly blame this on external causes and the general world situation, there was ample poll evidence to suggest a generalised lack of confidence in the government's ability to handle the economy,' it has been maintained.[44] Some ministers who realised that the coalition position was weaker thought that the economic situation would be more favourable in the autumn; they opposed a June election and tried to curb the media speculation that was growing.

The matter was discussed on a number of occasions in cabinet. Some ministers, Ryan and FitzGerald for instance, were known to want to wait until the autumn on the grounds that the economy would look more promising then. This may have been the Taoiseach's view too. But others, aware that farming support was ebbing, and also worried about employment for young school leavers, held that there should be a summer election.

That the government did not commission opinion polls to try to gauge the public attitude has been considered strange. Quarterly television polls had shown Fianna Fáil consistently ahead of Fine Gael/Labour since the middle of 1976. But it must be remembered that at that time opinion polls did not have the widespread credibility they have since acquired. The results of the quarterly surveys were dismissed by the coalition because of the high percentage of 'don't knows' and because Fine Gael's strength had always been undervalued in opinion polls. Moreover, there was the difficulty of estimating the numbers of seats from opinion polls because of the constituency revision. What lay behind government confidence was the belief that this revision would prevent Fianna Fáil winning unless there were a huge swing to it, which had not been the case in the past.

The story of Fine Gael from 1973 to 1977 has been seen as largely, although not only, one of missed chances. That it was the main partner in government, following a protracted period in opposition, definitely boosted its supporters' morale. Some ministers, most notably Garret FitzGerald, emerged from their period of office with significantly heightened reputations. The party could refer to a record of commendable achievement and a number of important reforms. 'Moreover, through four years of international economic crisis and domestic violence stemming from the troubles in Northern Ireland, it had provided stable government and had greatly improved relations with Britain and Northern Ireland', it has been observed.[45]

Taking part in coalition brought to the surface what has been seen as Fine Gael's 'central dilemma'. As an essentially middle-class party, it had to (or it would be more accurate to say its supporters believed it had to) make compromises with Labour which some of its traditional followers could not accept. It had to broaden its support without alienating traditional backers or being seen to poach Labour followers. On an even more basic level, it faced the question, was it a credible party with working-class as well as middle-class support?

(ix) The 1977 general election

Fianna Fáil was completely prepared for whenever the election would be called; it had to be in the summer or autumn of 1977 or spring 1978 and the party was ready for the first of these three options. New, talented young men had been appointed to strategic positions in the party organisation; Lynch had formed a campaign committee in June 1976 and it was especially active from spring 1977 onwards. By contrast, the government parties were unprepared.

Garret and Alexis FitzGerald, Richie Ryan and James Dooge, a Fine Gael Senator since 1961 and an adviser to Cosgrave, served on the coalition election committee with O'Leary, O'Brien and Brendan Halligan of Labour. They were presented with a stunning Market Research Bureau of Ireland (MRBI) opinion poll ten days after the election had been called (they had commissioned it just *after* the dissolution was announced) which showed Fianna Fáil 20% ahead of the coalition. They decided not to reveal the finding because it would have demoralised their election workers.

Fine Gael has been seen by one commentator as being unprepared for the contest. Cosgrave requested Ryan to be the director of elections although Ryan had told him that he was so busy with his Department that he hardly knew what was happening in his own constituency. The party had no press officer and Cosgrave asked a young UCD economist, Moore McDowell, to fill the role, despite his total lack of experience at that particular task. 'Fine Gael's poky headquarters in Hume Street was an organisational disaster area', it has been observed.[46] The economist Brendan Dowling, who took holidays to try to combat Fianna Fáil's giveaway manifesto, found that Fine Gael ministers could not be communicated with, so that agreed statements could be issued; he also discovered that headquarters had no photocopying facility! Ministers Ryan and FitzGerald did not want to use government equipment for party purposes, but when a Finance official told them that had it been Fianna Fáil in government, not only equipment but staff would have been used, Dowling was permitted to use the facilities of the Department. Fianna Fáil ran an American-style campaign which included tour-buses, T-shirts, badges, hats and a special party song, while Fine Gael headquarters gave almost no back-up to its candidates and even rationed election posters!

What weakened both Fine Gael and Labour was that their parliamentary leaders were too busy with the business of their ministries to give enough attention to campaign preparation. This was clear immediately from the contrast between the manifestos offered by the two sides in the election. Fianna Fáil's, presented to the press on the day the Dáil dissolved, comprised 47 pages. It aimed at the widest possible range of electoral support with pledges to abolish domestic rates and road tax on smaller cars and motorcycles, to give a grant of £1,000 to first-time house-buyers, to tackle unemployment by creating 20,000 new jobs in a year by means of cash incentives (this concentration on the young was based on opinion polls which viewed poor job prospects for them as the greatest problem facing the country), and to curb inflation by cutting taxes to the tune of £160 million. It contended that the cost of these measures would be £250 million a year, which would be financed by increased government borrowing, by a 'buy Irish' campaign to reduce imports and by predicting a growing economy which would produce more revenue. The appeal of the manifesto was immediately recognised by the press and the public, but its estimated costs and economic viability were questioned.

The coalition document, appearing the next day, showed signs of haste in preparation and of being more a response to the Fianna Fáil declaration than a distinct choice. That some senior ministers were its main compilers was shown in the extent to which it dwelt on the government's record and achievements. All that was really new was the promise to speed up the phasing out of rates (which had been part of its original programme) and to set up a not very well defined National Development Corporation. It held that the government's policies were the right ones and had kept the economy stable through a period of unprecedented turmoil. Instead of making promises, it claimed that the economy was already over the worst and that government policies were creating employment and boosting exports. It cast serious doubts on the cost of the Fianna Fáil programme, but did not cost its own. It had to do so later and this initial failure to act in due time was to prove damaging.

Fianna Fáil was in the ascendant during the election campaign debate, presenting employment and economic management as the main issues and, what has been called 'an attractive and positive plan to deal with these'.[47] The coalition was forced to try to explain why its 1973 pledges had not been fulfilled, and although it could and did cite international and external problems, it was forced onto the defensive from the outset. This was a replica of the 1973 situation, but in reverse. The coalition also tried to make the campaign personal around Cosgrave, but not very successfully. The 'You can have confidence in Cosgrave' slogan did not distract from the Fianna Fáil-defined issues and, in any event, the chances of a successful personality campaign were very much weakened from the start by Cosgrave's refusal of Lynch's invitation to a television debate.

In addition to its success on the issues front, Fianna Fáil managed to nominate candidates quickly and with little bitterness. Although it started late, Fine Gael had little trouble choosing its runners. There were some exceptions. John Kelly let it be known that he was being moved unwillingly from Dublin Mid-County, where most of his organisation was, to Dublin South County where there was a safe Fine Gael seat (that of Richard Burke, who had become a EEC Commissioner); Cosgrave himself annoyed some Dún Laoghaire supporters by insisting on an all-male, elderly list of candidates in what was an uncertain constituency with a considerable feminist and young vote (this was the first general election at which the voting age was reduced to 18); in Dublin-Clontarf neither local party workers nor the other two candidates were enamoured of headquarters following its decision to run Ted Nealon, head of the Government Information Service, as the main candidate. Kildare and North Tipperary also threw up some difficulties. But even where the choice of runners caused no problems, it was soon evident that not nearly enough time had been given to getting used to the new constituency divisions. This could have been avoided by earlier nomination conventions.

So the contrast with 1973 was very marked from the start and a series of television debates between Garret FitzGerald and George Colley strengthened it. These men had taken part in two televised confrontations in 1973 which had drawn a lot of publicity. On the central issues of jobs and prices, government speakers were constantly defending their record, while Fianna Fáil could insist that it could do better and could point to an attractive, detailed programme for the voters. Although both sides agreed that the economic outlook was improving, the coalition claimed that its policies, together with the better international factors, had got the country through the worst, while Fianna Fáil argued that the improvement had occurred despite the government's bad decisions, but that more effort was needed to combat the serious unemployment problem and only a united, experienced party could do that. Cosgrave and other speakers on behalf of the coalition declared that they would not take part in 'a Dutch auction' with Fianna Fáil and dismissed its programme as poorly worked out and underestimated, so that costings and credibility dominated the opening part of the campaign.

It has been observed that the coalition did not seem to have a campaign plan. The first Fine Gael advertisements called for votes for itself, but had no reference to support for the coalition. The details of Lynch's very astutely planned tour of the country were well known, but Cosgrave's movements were not general knowledge. He appeared unexpectedly in Sligo and Mayo, then in Dublin and afterwards Offaly.

Opinion polls in *The Irish Times* showed Fianna Fáil well ahead and identified the central issues as economic ones - prices, jobs, taxation. Family planning and the Donegan affair carried little weight. Government spokesmen continued to denounce the Fianna Fáil programme as unrealistic, undercosted and necessitating far too much government borrowing; they insisted that their own solution was more practical and realistic. But Richie Ryan's argument that 'any attempt to put a cost on this programme would be unrealistic' sounded hollow in view of the coalition's sustained assault on the Fianna Fáil costings. As the second week of the campaign began, two issues were dominant: the cost of the Fianna Fáil programme and whether loans necessary to fund it would be available.

FitzGerald worked out a detailed breakdown of what the Fianna Fáil manifesto would cost and put forward a figure of £369 million. But this only gave it more publicity and the polls were showing a public preference for it over the coalition's. Conor Cruise O'Brien's attempt to raise a different issue by referring in a BBC interview to Haughey's involvement in the arms crisis of the early 1970s got nowhere and the opinion polls showed that the public was indifferent to the Northern Ireland question.

By the time the campaign reached its halfway point, some basic trends were clear. There was an obvious lack of coordination between Fine Gael and Labour. It was evident that organisationally the coalition was no match for Fianna Fáil. By now it could also be seen that the coalition would find it difficult to repeat its successful 1973 television campaign. Although no one was as yet predicting a Fianna Fáil victory, reports of anti-Labour feeling among Fine Gael's traditional farming support and of anti-Fine Gael discontent among the working class, who perceived it as dominating the coalition, were being taken seriously. It has been acutely remarked that although the coalition speakers

> . . . had tried hard to focus attention on their achievements in bringing real benefits to social welfare beneficiaries and in house building, as well as claiming credit for the increases in farm prices which followed Ireland's entry into the EEC, they were not able to shift the central emphasis from the focus on jobs and economic management in the Fianna Fáil manifesto.[48]

The security issue proved a peripheral one, so much so that the one television current affairs programme set aside to discuss it was dropped and replaced by a discussion on the coalition's special Dublin package which was designed to win it support there.

Cosgrave was confined to bed with laryngitis over the bank holiday weekend so his son, Liam T., stood in for him. However, some experienced commentators pointed out how in the past Fine Gael had conducted low-key and seemingly lacklustre campaigns but nevertheless had done well on election day. Whether and how much campaigns actually affected the allegiance of the electorate may also have been in many people's minds. The slow start by the coalition caused the thought to occur to some that it was designed to provoke an early surge and premature peak by Fianna Fáil and that Fine Gael and Labour would come with a late flourish. So much was seen in the cautious mid-term predictions which saw both sides fairly finely balanced. Above all it was thought that the constituency revision would provide an insurmountable barrier to Fianna Fáil success.

In the third week of the campaign, the dispute over the cost of the Fianna Fáil manifesto proposals erupted into a row. It had already been worsened by the comment of a EEC official that extra Irish borrowing would be possible, Colley now accusing FitzGerald of trying to draw the EEC Commission into the election by persuading the Economics and Finance Commissioner to state that Brussels would not be in favour of increasing the level of Irish government borrowing. Colley put it down to coalition 'dirty tricks', while FitzGerald replied that this EEC view revealed Fianna Fáil's programme as 'an illusion and a confidence trick'. However, an *Irish Times* poll showed that the Fianna Fáil promises were better known and more popular than the coalition's, which now needed to stage an effective counter-offensive.

The European Community again provided the fuel. Referring to an official EEC survey of a sample of the Irish labour force, the government repeated the assertion that unemployment was decreasing and that many on the register were not actually available for work, giving the actual number of unemployed as 107,000. Meanwhile, FitzGerald contended that the coalition's policies would create 47,000 new jobs for young school-leavers. The coalition also raised the point of Ireland's link with sterling, which had been a topic of debate for some years, some holding that Ireland could get out of the British inflationary spiral only by breaking it. Fine Gael sources suggested that the increased borrowing needed for the Fianna Fáil plan would endanger Ireland's ability to break if sterling came under pressure in foreign exchange markets in the autumn. They also suggested that a break in the autumn might be possible because the domestic economy was recovering well.

A third prong of the coalition attack consisted of two press conferences. In Cork the Minister for Education, Peter Barry (he had been transferred from Transport and Power in the cabinet reshuffle of 1 December 1976) and the Junior Ministers from Munster gave details of the benefits to that province of the Cosgrave coalition. In the Dáil, at a larger press conference, both Fine Gael and Labour ministers explained how their special Dublin measures would benefit the capital: a Dublin Transport Authority, a 'flat-dwellers' charter', flexible hours for civil servants, planned new hospitals, more teachers in city schools and better facilities for recreation. They also promised new industrial projects in city-centre areas and new job opportunities.

Back on his national tour, Cosgrave preferred to concentrate on law and order and leave economic arguments to others. This might have appeared a clear distraction but for two local newspaper initiatives which gave it an added relevance. In *The Sligo Champion*, James Gallagher, a former Fianna Fáil TD and now a candidate, put in an advertisement calling for the Offences against the State Act to be abolished. Quickly repudiated and denounced by Jack Lynch, this was nevertheless embarrassing for Fianna Fáil and substantiated coalition claims that the party was unsafe on security. Lynch's leadership was attacked in *The Longford Leader* by a local Fianna Fáil TD who had not been renominated and who claimed that the reason he had not been was because of his efforts to make his party pursue a tougher security policy. He praised Cosgrave and Fine Gael and declared that Fianna Fáil had not been doing enough to deal with the violence.

As the coalition campaign gathered pace, there were rumours of more good news to be announced in the closing days. The visit of the Minister for Industry and Commerce, Justin Keating, to an oil rig, created anticipation of the announcement of a major oil find; the planned meeting of the Taoiseach with Henry Ford II created speculation that the Cork Ford motor plant would be extended. So it seemed that Fine Gael and Labour had overtaken Fianna Fáil; the polls suggested otherwise, but they were known to few and dismissed by most.

Three government ministers made speeches during the final days of the campaign in what has been seen as 'a determined effort to make security and policy on Northern Ireland an issue and to rock public confidence in Lynch's control of his party'.[49] Conor Cruise O'Brien repeated the belief that there was a Fianna Fáil faction sympathetic to the IRA and that Haughey's presence on the front bench was merely 'the tip of the iceberg'. Tom Fitzpatrick, the Minister for Transport and Power (he had been transferred to this portfolio in the cabinet reshuffle), referred to the local newspaper episodes as evidence that Lynch would not be able to control the extremists in his party. Garret FitzGerald emphasised doubts about Lynch's leadership and what he called his ambiguous stance, outlining real policy differences between the two sides on Northern Ireland and suggesting that to call for the British to withdraw could lead the way to possible violence. But these public utterances probably had little effect on the eventual outcome because the polls showed people little concerned with security and Northern Ireland, and they could well have reflected what has been construed as a note of desperation on the coalition's part.[50]

The early indications from the count centres were that Fianna Fáil was doing well and the coalition transfers were not holding up as well as in 1973. But the first results surprised everyone. Cosgrave conceded defeat around 9.00pm from his Dún Laoghaire constituency, but it was some time before the magnitude of the swing to Fianna Fáil sank in. Its percentage of the vote was 50.6, up from 46.2 in 1973, and it won 84 seats out of 148, the biggest majority ever in the history of the state. Fine Gael suffered the largest loss of votes in this election, a loss which put an end to a series of slight gains in its first preference vote which began in 1961. It dropped from 35.1 to 30.5% of the vote, its worst performance since 1957, declining from 53 to 43 seats. Cosgrave headed the poll in Dún Laoghaire, but his share of the vote was down and his party lost its second seat here (long held by Percy Dockrell, brother of long-serving Fine Gael TD and front bencher, Maurice, and son of Cumann na nGaedheal and Fine Gael TD Henry) to Fianna Fáil. Patrick Cooney was one of three ministers to lose his seat (the others were Labour's O'Brien and Keating); 18 outgoing Fine Gael TDs lost their seats and only four of these went to party colleagues. The party did not have a single deputy in four constituencies. Brigid Hogan-O'Higgins lost her seat in Galway East (having served in the Dáil since 1957), which meant that for the first time since the setting up of the state the Hogan or O'Higgins dynasties were not represented in Dáil Éireann.

What caused such an unexpected and huge change in party support? Suggestions ex post facto were (a) that the organisation and professionalism of Fianna Fáil had contrasted sharply with the ineptitude of the government parties; (b) that Jack Lynch had great personal appeal in contrast to Liam Cosgrave's indifferent performance; (c) that many ministers had become aloof, distant from their supporters and unaware of popular feelings; (d) that farmers were discontented with the government's tax proposals; (e) that the young people wanted a change, and (f) that a government which had been in power throughout a period of inflation and economic crisis never before experienced inevitably would be unpopular.

Larger farmers had been very much the backbone of Fine Gael support since the Civil War and as EEC membership greatly boosted their incomes this inherent core should have been strengthened. Mark Clinton, the Minister for Agriculture, acquired a reputation as a champion of their interests in negotiations in Brussels and within the government. But suspicion of Labour and resentment at the coalition's proposals to tax farmers lost for Fine Gael whatever benefits participation in the EEC had brought. Regional analyses showed that while the party's vote held up in Connacht/Ulster, where small farmers predominate, it declined greatly in the rich farming areas of Leinster and Munster. It also fared poorly in Dublin but did well in border areas, which was probably an endorsement of its firm performance on security. A significant element in the defeat of the coalition parties was what happened to their transfers to each other. An analysis of transfer patterns between Fine Gael and Labour and vice versa for elections from 1961 to 1977 inclusive concluded as follows:

> Plainly, the highest level of mutual support between Fine Gael and Labour coincided with the poorest performance of Fianna Fáil (1973); while in 1977 Labour voters' support for Fine Gael candidates significantly declined, although Fine Gael support for Labour candidates remained stable - and more Labour transfers went to Fianna Fáil than in 1973.[51]

(x) Organisation

By this time it had become traditional to regard Fine Gael as the least professional of the main political parties and as the one that was most at home in opposition. It was frequently remarked of the party during the 1960s that its approach was part-time and that it preferred moral victories to real ones. It was the case that its organisation was haphazard and its long history of decline and defeat had bred in it a fatalistic acceptance of always finishing in second place to its major opponent. This attitude had changed somewhat in the 1960s, but its approach never came near to Fianna Fáil's, except perhaps in the 1966 presidential election in which it had been only narrowly defeated.

So the 1973 success and the great morale uplift it gave the party might have been expected to have resulted in significant changes in party organisation. What might have been expected to strengthen this was Liam Cosgrave's ambition to make Fine Gael a party capable of forming a government on its own and of winning a greater number of seats than Fianna Fáil.

Amazingly, little was done in this period to improve and modernise the organisation, even though the traditional pretext for doing little - shortage of money - no longer applied. The Hume Street headquarters, redolent of decay, was retained, but its communication facilities were well short of what a national party required. It was understaffed, especially as regards press relations and policy research. Overworked secretaries typed away on old-fashioned machines and the place was strewn with bundles of stationery and printed matter. Fianna Fáil's campaign to attract young members was not seriously imitated; little effort was made to bring in new members, nor was the party opened up to its own activists to any significant extent. In fact, most features of the party's organisation seemed shrouded in secrecy: membership numbers and finance were unknown details, and even mild criticism from within the party tended to provoke a crushing response from the leadership. This approach could be seen especially at the annual ard-fheis, which was usually the worst organised of the major parties and displayed Fine Gael at what has been described as 'its most amateurish and authoritarian'.[52]

After the 1977 defeat it became obvious how careless the party had been in not professionalising its organisation and one of the first undertakings of the new leader was to recruit a new national organiser and a new press officer. But it had taken an overwhelming electoral defeat for Fine Gael to get this particular message. A number of reasons for the lack of proper organisation have been suggested, but mainly (a) 'the traditional organisational conservatism', and (b) the failure of the front-bench to make it a priority (which did not apply only to this period).[53]

Lack of money was only part of the reason why Fine Gael had not developed its organisation, because it did not seem that the party ever made very much effort to gather revenue, and whatever money it had, it tended to spend sparingly. The lack of a strong, central body also reflected in part the wish of Fine Gael TDs to be independent in their own constituencies. It was customary for retired army officers to be appointed as party general secretaries, and these have been seen as 'invariably conscientious men, but rarely innovators, generally suspicious of the media and more concerned with maintaining the status quo and party discipline than with opening up or extending the party'.[54] These men were generally regarded within the party as having primary loyalty to the leader, keeping an eye on his party for him, as it were.

173

There is not much evidence of front-bench efforts to develop the party organisation in the 1973-77 period, or for that matter before. Indeed, after the 1977 election, some Fine Gael ministers admitted that their view of their roles was too lofty and that they had grown away from their own party and followers. Garret FitzGerald, in particular, made this point after the election.

The only new development during the period of government was that the party ran a series of regional and interest group conferences. On the initiative of Fergus O'Brien, TD for Dublin South-Central, Fine Gael held its first trade union conference in January 1976, but 'lack of wide enthusiasm prevented this from becoming an all-out drive to enlist working-class support', it has been lamented. [55] An attempt to start a party newspaper was not received with enthusiasm by the party hierarchy.

Fine Gael had been at its most unprepared when the election was called and it, whose leader best knew the date of the contest, began the campaign worst prepared. It had money, but did not know how to spend it. The director of elections was the Minister for Finance who had to run his department, contest a difficult constituency and guide the national election effort at the same time. The press officer, an academic economist, was not chosen until four days into the campaign, had no experience of journalism and had to construct an office out of nothing. This all reflected Fine Gael at its most organisationally inept.

Chapter 7

The FitzGerald Years : 1977-87

(i) Change of leadership

In his autobiography, Garret FitzGerald referred to the speculation following the 1977 general election that the leaders of the defeated Fine Gael and Labour parties would step down from their positions. He declared that no one in his party expected Liam Cosgrave to go at the young age of 57.[1] But the Fine Gael leader had by now been 34 years in politics and, it has been maintained, had long ago decided to leave at 60.[2] He had seen too many colleagues linger beyond their time and was not going to do so himself. Believing that Fianna Fáil would have a full term in government, he wanted to give his successor a good chance to prepare for the next election. An extremely private man, Cosgrave decided to retire without consulting anyone. On the morning of the first parliamentary party meeting after the election, before leaving home he told his wife Vera of his intention, and she was the only person who knew.

The 23 June meeting at first spent over an hour considering Senate nominations, the official reason why it was called. When the discussion was finished, Cosgrave suddenly stood up and calmly announced his intention to resign. His colleagues were stunned. He gave his reasons and forecast that the Fianna Fáil promises, which had won that party the election, would be catastrophic for the country. No one in the cabinet had had any idea that he was going to stand down. Patrick Donegan quickly stood up, protested at the decision, and called for a unanimous show of confidence in the leader. Although only about a sixth of those present failed to raise their hands, even a show of unanimity would not have changed his decision. As Garret FitzGerald has remarked: 'almost everyone knew that Liam Cosgrave was not the man to use a resignation offer as a ploy to get himself drafted back into the leadership'.[3]

A number of TDs expressed their regret at his going. When FitzGerald spoke, he said that relations between them had been strained in the past but that their time in government together had witnessed no difficulties. In reply, Cosgrave thanked his colleagues, referred to what FitzGerald had said and agreed with him, but he singled out no one as his preferred successor. He agreed to the call of some TDs for him to delay his resignation for a week to give the party time to consider who should follow him. The media saw Richie Ryan, Mark Clinton, Tom Fitzpatrick, Peter Barry and Garret FitzGerald as the contenders for the leadership. John Kelly, who had succeeded Declan Costello as Attorney General when the latter was appointed a High Court judge, said that he was available if his colleagues wanted him, but that he would not canvass.

Both Clinton and Fitzpatrick soon dropped out. Clinton had been a very popular and diligent Minister for Agriculture who was most unhappy with what he considered to be the electorate's unfair treatment of the Cosgrave government. The farmers on whose behalf he had striven had turned against Fine Gael because income tax had been extended to them. But his main reason for not running was that, at 62 years of age, he felt that a younger man was needed. Similarly Fitzpatrick, very well liked in the party and chairman of the national executive, felt that he was too old at 60. Peter Barry's second ministry had been Education, but most of his time had been spent in the fairly low-ranking Department of Transport and Power. However, he was popular, the leading Fine Gael TD in Cork, and would be supported by non-Dublin TDs who were usually more conservative in their outlooks, it has been argued.[4]

Ryan and FitzGerald were seen by the public as the main contenders. However, while FitzGerald had a popular public profile, Ryan did not, because he had been what has been well described as a 'tough and brave Minister for Finance' in hard times.[5] A doughty debater, he also carried the burden of having been director of elections in the recent contest in which his party had lost heavily. On the other hand, FitzGerald was almost unbesmirched. In the opinion polls, he was the second most popular politician after Jack Lynch and had built up a substantial reputation as Minister for Foreign Affairs. He was immediately regarded as the favourite to succeed Cosgrave. After the 23 June meeting, although he was meant to go to Paris for an OECD meeting, he remained at home

176

to prepare for the coming contest. The following day, in a leader, *The Irish Times* summarised how the public viewed him:

> In popularity with the public, in successful tenure of office, in possession (unlike so many others in the party) of a coherent philosophy, and in that invaluable physical attribute, the capacity for sustained hard work - in all these ways, Dr FitzGerald is ahead of any other rival.

Richie Ryan was abroad at a meeting in Washington, was then due to travel to Luxembourg and was not expected to return to Ireland for almost a week. It was agreed that there should be no formal canvassing until his return. In fact, Ryan had reluctantly decided not to seek the leadership. He accepted that the time was wrong because he was being held responsible for the wealth and farmer taxes which many of the party faithful would see as 'too great a handicap'.[6] So it was a straight contest between Peter Barry and Garret FitzGerald.

There was no ill-feeling between them and indeed in the days before the meeting at which the new leader was to be elected they compared tallies. Barry accepted that he would lose but he expected to do respectably, predicting that he would get around 25 votes out of the 62 TDs and Senators eligible to ballot. FitzGerald calculated that he had 43 supporters and he recorded that Barry was a bit upset that their numbers did not tally: 'I told him that if only half a dozen members of the party - less than ten per cent - had allowed *both* of us to believe they were supporters, that showed a very high level of political honesty!'[7] Barry realised that Fine Gael supporters around the country favoured a new type of leader and wanted FitzGerald, so he therefore withdrew.

At the short parliamentary party meeting on 1 July, 'the recollection of Fine Gael's humiliation in the general election was raw and vivid', it has been asserted.[8] Although there may have been a significant group who distrusted or did not know FitzGerald, they were desperate. He was already popular with the media, had an international standing and really wanted the job. An energetic, skilful and charismatic leader was needed. FitzGerald had intelligence and charm, was a well-known economic commentator, and was extremely skilful on television. He was proposed by Peter Barry, seconded by Kieran Crotty and was elected unanimously.

(ii) Organisational changes

The first job FitzGerald set about was bringing new life to the organisation and removing it from the control of the TDs. It has been suggested that Cosgrave had also been aware of 'this terrible, paralysing grip by the TDs'.[9] FitzGerald's 4 July 'Message to the Fine Gael Organisation' declared his intention of visiting every constituency during the winter and holding public meetings to recruit new members. It urged better communication between the leader and the organisation and repeated his invitation for personal contact from anyone who wished to join.

It has been argued that the party FitzGerald took over was under the control of businessmen, the professions and big farmers.[10] In 33 of the 42 constituencies, Fine Gael had only one TD and these individuals were very suspicious of any interference which threatened their hegemony. Its core support was 25% of the electorate, ranging from 15% support from the unskilled working class to 46% of bigger farmers, with 25% middle-class support. FitzGerald quickly commissioned a comprehensive MRBI survey of the result of the 1977 general election to discover who had and had not voted for Fine Gael. This revealed that the party's support came mainly from older people and more from men than from women. It also showed 23% of men and 22% of women had voted Fine Gael in comparison to 47% and 49% respectively for Fianna Fáil.

As many of his colleagues set off on their summer break, FitzGerald was active by getting his reorganisation move under way. The general secretary, Jim Sanfey, an ex-army officer, had held the post for ten years. The new leader made a redundancy agreement with him, but wished his replacement to be a national organiser as well as general secretary. As he has recorded in his autobiography:

> From 1966 to his tragic death in a car accident in February 1970, Gerry Sweetman, a man of exceptional energy, had combined his parliamentary duties with the role of national

organiser. Thereafter, the post had, in effect, been vacant, and the party had suffered accordingly. I was convinced that we needed a national organiser from outside the parliamentary party, as well as a full-time press and public relations officer; and with the approval of the ad hoc front bench I advertised these two posts.[11]

It has been maintained that, although there was an interview board consisting of Peter Barry, Richie Ryan and Tom Fitzpatrick, as well as FitzGerald himself, his was the real choice because whoever was appointed had to get on with the leader. He selected Peter Prendergast, a 38-year-old marketing consultant, as general secretary. Prendergast had been a member of Fine Gael since 1969, and had been involved in Tom O'Higgins's very successful campaign for the presidency three years before. He had also already worked with FitzGerald in 1973. In fact, he had unexpectedly been his running mate in Dublin South-East in the election of that year. He got 1,300 votes in the poll and helped to elect Fergus O'Brien. He ran most of FitzGerald's constituency clinics between 1973 and 1977, contested the 1977 election again but again failed to be elected, securing almost exactly the same number of votes as before. Since Prendergast had served on the national executive and the national council, he knew the shortcomings in the organisation.

In August, FitzGerald persuaded Ted Nealon to become Fine Gael Director of Press and Information Services. He was 48, Sligo born, a household television name following 12 years in current affairs on RTE, and had been head of the Government Information service (GIS) from 1975 to 1977. He had been imposed on the Dublin Clontarf constituency by the national executive in the 1977 election, and this had resulted in open fighting between his supporters and those of local councillor Michael Joe Cosgrave. The latter won the seat, but Nealon polled well and lasted until the ninth count. He returned to the GIS in the last days of the coalition, but lost his post when Fianna Fáil took office. He turned down a Senate nomination from Liam Cosgrave because he intended to go back to journalism, but FitzGerald persuaded him to stay on in Fine Gael.

FitzGerald, Prendergast and Nealon began a national tour of

the constituencies in Cork on 19 September 1977. They followed the same routine everywhere: they met the local Fine Gael representatives and constituency officers, the local media, visited institutions and held public meetings. These latter followed a deliberate question and answer pattern and FitzGerald's 'openness, dynamism and charisma' made a great impact, it has been contended.[12] From September 1977 to March 1978 he spoke at 45 meetings and met 20,000 people. He spoke of getting into government within eight years, the aim being to make Fine Gael the biggest political party; the young were encouraged to involve themselves, to stand up and say what was wrong; the central purpose was to broaden the party's appeal as much as possible and to achieve power.

On the long journeys FitzGerald was evolving a new constitution for the party. In mid-Cork a young vocational teacher, Finbarr Fitzpatrick, asked him how to get rid of long-serving office-holders. He had recently become local district executive secretary, taking over from someone who had been in the post for 29 years. He had also proposed motions at ard-fheiseanna that public representatives should not hold constituency offices and that all party officers should change every three years. Fitzpatrick succeeded Prendergast as general secretary in 1982.

Up to this time each Fine Gael constituency organisation was under the sway of the local TD; his friends had the main posts, he selected his director of elections and, indeed, his running mates. FitzGerald and Prendergast aimed to work out a constitution for the party which would change this situation.

Their document was sent to all branches in the spring of 1978 and was considered formally at the May ard-fheis. FitzGerald had become convinced that a party run by TDs would never make progress. He wanted to see rank-and-file members, not seeking public office, aspiring to senior party posts. Some of the parliamentary party members were against his ideas, but the advantage was on his side because he had travelled the country and knew that the ordinary members supported the proposed changes. Although he altered some things slightly in order to get them passed by the parliamentary party, he stuck to his main aims of taking the organisation out of the control of the local TDs and moving that control to party headquarters and independent local structures.

He depended on his friend, 'the lucid and concise'[13] Senator James Dooge, to get the draft constitution through the ard-fheis. The most dramatic indication of the transfer of power to the ordinary party loyalists was the suggestion that the ard-fheis elect eight members of the national executive, the party's ruling body, but the delegates decided that the number was not high enough and amended it to 12! They turned down the proposal that the parliamentary party elect 12 to the national executive and cut the number to nine. There was also a provision in the draft that at least one of the party's four vice-presidents and one of its two honorary secretaries would not be from the parliamentary party. All these posts had by tradition been held by TDs and Senators.

Most innovative of all was the new voting system to select Dáil candidates and constituency executives. Under it, the general election convention delegates vote only once, on a PR basis, for all candidates. This ended the old system of the TD or local officers being chosen by acclamation, or outgoing TDs using their blocks of votes in succeeding counts to make sure that they got the running mates they wanted. Also totally revised was the branch structure. Before this, each branch had sent three delegates to selection conventions, whether they represented a big town or a little village, which resulted in total Fine Gael weakness in larger towns and a predominance of rural candidates. The new structure has been explained as follows:

> From now on, branches would be reorganised so that their functional area would reflect precise blocks of voters on the electoral register, and would have proportionate delegate status. Each branch with up to 500 electors could send three delegates to a constituency or annual general meeting; each additional 250 electors in the branch's functional area entitled it to an extra delegate. Thus some larger urban branches could have 25 or more delegates, as against a rural branch having five or six.[14]

The process of branches registering with headquarters was made   stricter and more costly, but not until 1986 and the computerisation of registered members of the party did this system become almost foolproof.

One of the most controversial changes was also ratified by the new constitution: two new positions were created in every constituency, a constituency organiser or officer (CO) and a public relations officer (PRO). The CO had to be approved by the general secretary and to keep headquarters in touch with what was happening in the constituency. Some TDs saw the CO as a spy, reporting to Dublin and being used by headquarters to diminish their positions. The COs could also be serious rivals for local TDs and councillors and FitzGerald would not have got the parliamentary party to accept this innovation had he not agreed that they could not be candidates for upcoming elections (local, Dáil or European). The national executive acquired the power to change the list of candidates for local or Dáil elections. The change of party officers after three years was not introduced until 1982.

It has been rightly remarked that 'FitzGerald demonstrated commendable prescience in the case of two other innovations in the 1978 constitution'.[15] One of these was that the party leader would be subject to an automatic secret vote of confidence concerning his leadership within two months of a general election, unless the party was going into government. This led to the avoidance of a lot of potential bitterness and division. The second was that any TD or Senator who broke the party pledge was automatically expelled from the parliamentary party. Each candidate took this pledge *before* a selection convention and was bound by it to vote with the party. This also insured against potentially divisive and acrimonious party meetings where a motion calling for the expulsion of a member would be debated.

The new constitution gave official recognition to the party's trade-union group and new youth movement, Young Fine Gael. FitzGerald had promoted the latter idea on his national tour, calling for each district executive in the country to have at least one branch and each constituency in Dublin to have the same. In April 1978,

Michael Collins

Arthur Griffith

W.T. Cosgrave, President of the Executive Council 1922-32, Leader of Fine Gael 1933-44

Kevin O' Higgins, Minister for Home Affairs. Seated is General Eoin O'Duffy, later first Leader of Fine Gael

Richard Mulcahy, Leader of Fine Gael 1944-59

*Patrick McGilligan, T.D., Minister of External Affairs,
Industry and Commerce, Finance, and Attorney General*

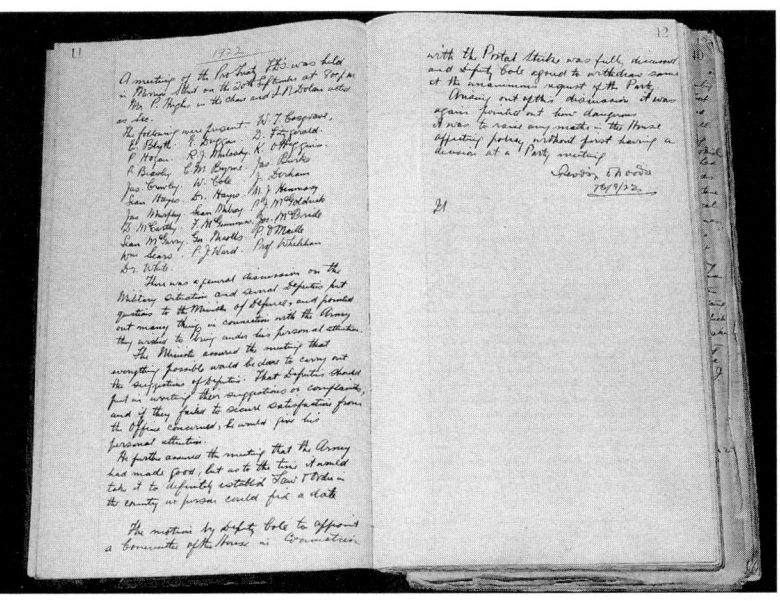

Minutes of meeting of 'Pro-Treaty T.D.s', September 20 1922

Eoin MacNeill, T.D., Minister for Education

Patrick Hogan, T.D., Minister for Agriculture 1922-32

*Desmond Fitzgerald, T.D., Minister for Defence in the
W.T. Cosgrave governments*

*Fionan Lynch, T.D., Minister for Fisheries in the
W.T. Cosgrave governments*

Liam T. Cosgrave, Taoiseach 1973-77, Leader of Fine Gael 1965-77

Garret Fitzgerald, T.D.

Peter Barry, T.D., at the sixtieth anniversary celebrations of Fine Gael, 1983

Mark Clinton, Minister for Agriculture 1973-77, M.E.P. 1979-89

The four most recent Fine Gael Leaders. Left to right, Alan Dukes, Garret Fitzgerald, John Bruton and Liam Cosgrave

John Bruton, T.D.

Alan Dukes, T.D.

Garret Fitzgerald – Offaly by-election 1984 with Tom Enright, T.D.

John and Finola Bruton

Tom O'Donnell, Garret Fitzgerald, John Blair, Alan Dukes – European elections 1979, Munster constituency

Some members of Fine Gael front bench 1993

Dan Egan, a 28-year-old former RTE reporter from Mayo, was appointed Assistant Organiser (Youth). By the time of the next ard-fheis, nearly 100 branches of Young Fine Gael already existed. It had the power to send delegates to selection conventions and senior party meetings. It annoyed the parliamentary party on occasions over various issues.

Its new constitution greatly changed and restructured Fine Gael. The local TD now respected his local organisation. He or she had to present themselves for reselection like any other aspirant. The new arrangement gave good candidates a real chance to succeed at selection conventions and ordinary followers a chance to become party vice-president.

After only 11 months as leader, FitzGerald could report great progress to the delegates attending the 1978 ard-fheis. The party had a new headquarters in Mount Street, directly opposite Fianna Fáil's. It was officially opened on 5 May by the vice-president of the European People's Party, to which Fine Gael was affiliated in the European Parliament. The purchase and renovation came to £140,000 which, even with the money realised by the sale of the old headquarters in Hume Street, left a substantial deficit. Prendergast showed his marketing skill with his scheme for party members to 'buy a brick' in the new headquarters by donating £5. At the ard-fheis, FitzGerald had urged the organisation to contribute more money because the party was already costing three times as much to run as in 1976, but it had never had a really efficient organisation before.

While making it clear that the immediate tasks were the June 1979 European and local elections, FitzGerald promised the delegates that within three years they would be able to take on Fianna Fáil face to face and defeat the old enemy. He called for more ordinary member involvement and spoke at length on the role of women and the young in Irish society. But despite the impressive nature of the ard-fheis, the organisation of the party was still very deficient, as the report of the joint secretaries, Gerry L'Estrange and Eddie Collins, showed: in some constituencies there were either no executives or, if there were, they had not met for years; only two-thirds of the branches had affiliated for the ard-fheis; only one-third of constituency executives responded to the request for information on their branches and finances and only one-quarter of the district executives did the same.

FitzGerald responded to requests from all over the country for a specifically Fine Gael journal by establishing the *National Democrat*, edited by Ted Nealon and first appearing in April 1978. FitzGerald and Prendergast used it as a vehicle for educating party members, and its early editions especially were concerned with basic organisational information.

FitzGerald's busy first year as leader was totally taken up with reorganising. The full shadow cabinet was appointed in the autumn of 1977. FitzGerald kept Northern Ireland as part of his own brief, but shared it with Paddy Harte, who also spoke on Security. The rest of the shadow front bench was Peter Barry (Economic Affairs and the Public Service), Michael Begley (Gaeltacht), John Boland (Health and Social Welfare), John Bruton (Agriculture), Eddie Collins (Education), Austin Deasy (Fisheries), Tom Fitzpatrick (Environment), John Kelly (Industry and Commerce), Jim Mitchell (Labour), Tom O'Donnell (Transport and Communications), Jim O'Keeffe (Law Reform and Human Rights), Richie Ryan (Foreign Affairs), Jim White (Defence), Dónal Creed (Chief Whip), Patrick Cooney (Leader of the Senate), Alexis Fitzgerald (Deputy Leader of the Senate) and Joe McCartin (Deputy Speaker of the Senate). Non-front-bench appointments were Michael D'Arcy (Agricultural Structures), John Donnellan (Public Works), Tom Enright (Tourism), Michael Keating (Urban Affairs), Enda Kenny (Youth Affairs and Sport) and Paddy O'Toole (Consumer Affairs). Four members of the shadow cabinet were new TDs: Boland, Deasy, Mitchell and O'Keeffe. Its average age was 44.

(iii) Elections and developments 1978-81
The European and local elections, to be held in June 1979, were the first electoral test for the new regime running Fine Gael. FitzGerald and Prendergast spent the year beforehand preparing. They were going to use the local elections especially to attract new talent to the

party, primarily young people and women. In the *National Democrat* in June 1978, a full year before polling, FitzGerald made it clear that inactive councillors must make way, or be forced to do so, for able and energetic replacements. He and Prendergast also used research and opinion polls to help them conduct their European campaign, which they were to employ even more in the next general election. Prendergast commissioned research based on guided discussion groups to discover what traits the people felt their European representatives should possess. This revealed a preference for experience and for the ability and expertise to fight for national interests in the European Community. It also disclosed that voters thought that their European candidates should be more intelligent and expert than the average TD. This information was used by FitzGerald in his search for appropriate candidates.

In the autumn of 1978, during a visit to Brussels, he looked up one of his former UCD economics students, Alan Dukes, who had gone on to be the Irish Farmers' Association's chief economist in the early 1970s and head of its lobby in Brussels. He was now a part of Commissioner Burke's cabinet. FitzGerald urged Dukes to put himself forward for the Munster constituency selection convention, an important farming region. After thinking it over, Dukes agreed. At a convention on 4 February he was chosen together with Tom O'Donnell, former Minister for the Gaeltacht, Jim O'Keeffe of Cork South-West and an alderman from Cork city, John Blair. Dukes was to be presented to the electorate as an expert in the economics of farming.

In Leinster, Mark Clinton and Senator Charles McDonald of Laois-Offaly became automatic candidates when Councillor Patsy Lawlor of Naas withdrew because of the national executive ruling that no European candidate could contest the local elections. The problem for the leadership now was that there was no Fine Gael runner with a specific women or urban appeal. FitzGerald turned to Monica Barnes, a notable campaigner for women's rights and administrator of the Council for the Status of Women, who was prominent in the non-party lobby group, the Women's Political Association. Long a member of Fine Gael, Barnes had challenged unsuccessfully for a nomination in her Dún Laoghaire constituency in 1977. The national executive ratified her addition to the Leinster ticket.

This gave added impetus to the search for an appropriate women's candidate in Dublin, and Prendergast had the ideal person in Nuala Fennell, foremost of all the campaigners for women's causes. She had set up a number of crucial support groups like Action, Information, Motivation or AIM (1972), ADAPT (1973) for single and deserted parents, and the Women's Aid hostel for battered women (1975). Fennell was well-known for her journalism. She had contested Dublin South County as an Independent in 1977 and had done well to poll nearly 3,500 votes. She consented to run for Fine Gael in the European contest. The other Dublin Fine Gael contenders were Richie Ryan and Maurice Manning; the latter had been a member of the party since the mid-1960s, but had not emerged as a political contestant until now.

Three Senators ran for Fine Gael in Connacht-Ulster: Joe McCartin of Leitrim, Myles Staunton of Mayo and, the best-known, Patrick Cooney of Longford-Westmeath, the former Justice Minister and a shock loser in the 1977 election.

The imposition of non-party people was not popular. The Dublin organisation was not happy with the arrival of Manning and Fennell, Fine Gael's more conservative followers seeing the latter especially as being much too radical. But when the first poll showed that Fine Gael was unlikely to win even one of the four Dublin seats, the party got down to active campaigning, led by the constituency director of elections, Enda Marren, who recruited the team in which he had been involved and which had run Nealon's attempt to be elected for Dublin-Clontarf in 1977. Three of these - Joe Jennings, Bill O'Herlihy and Pat Heneghan, - were professional public relations people and Shane Molloy of Unilever, a marketing expert, joined them. They identified lack of public interest and the lack of an electoral 'presence' as the main problems, and set about attracting publicity, seeking which aspect of the candidates was best to present to the public. Hence the slogan 'Richie was Right' to recall Ryan's criticism of the giveaway 1977 Fianna Fáil manifesto.

Fennell was promoted as a fighter for women's rights under the catchwords 'Back Your Woman', and Manning was portrayed as a Euro-expert. A Euro-bus, T-shirts and stickers were used to arouse public awareness. It all worked very well and Marren's cohorts were soon to apply their skills to the domestic stage with considerable success.[16]

But most Fine Gael faith rested in FitzGerald himself. He undertook a gruelling, three-week nationwide tour which consolidated his reputation with the party's rank-and-file and was on a par with his winter 1977/78 odyssey.

No doubt Fine Gael's fortunes had improved since the April poll, the main reason for this being mounting discontent with Fianna Fáil whose extravagant 1977 manifesto was falling apart. Public spending had grown enormously; the second oil crisis caused petrol shortages; although wage settlements were high, there was still industrial unrest, especially a postal strike dragging on since February, and a refuse-collection strike in Dublin continued during the actual polling. The government duly suffered in both the European and local elections, but Fine Gael did not benefit greatly and the results have been viewed as very disappointing for it and especially for FitzGerald and Prendergast[17] (not a view shared by the former Fine Gael leader in his autobiography).[18] Although the Fianna Fáil vote plummeted from 50.6% of June 1977 to 34.6%, Fine Gael's rose by only around 3%, and Labour was the real victor in the European contest. Fianna Fáil won five seats, Fine Gael and Labour four each, and two went to Independents. Labour's number of seats was a freak of the PR system, because it secured only 14.4% of the vote, as opposed to Fine Gael's 33%.

The two Fine Gael poll-toppers were Richie Ryan in Dublin (where Fennell did very well and lost only on the last count by a slender margin) and Mark Clinton in Leinster (where McDonald and Barnes polled badly). In Connacht-Ulster, Cooney and Staunton cancelled each other out, but McCartin was second in the first count. Munster was Fine Gael's best chance of a second seat, but T.J. Maher, former president of the Irish Farmers' Association, dashed expectations and ruined any chance Dukes had. Many local

Fine Gael officials campaigned for Maher, but at a meeting of the parliamentary party it was decided not to take disciplinary action in the matter. Tom O'Donnell won one of the Munster seats.

The local election performance provided some compensation for Fine Gael, however. It had done extremely well in 1974, winning 33.7% of the vote, and this was now raised to 35.2%. But the real significance of the result appeared only later in a collection of very capable new councillors who went on to become TDs in 1981-82. These were the younger generation FitzGerald and Prendergast had set out to win to Fine Gael's side; and among them were Gay Mitchell, Richard Bruton, Mary Flaherty, George Birmingham, Hugh Coveney, Bernard Allen, Madeleine Taylor, Ivan Yates, Brendan McGahon, Avril Doyle, Nora Owen and Alan Shatter.

The freedom and representation given to Young Fine Gael in FitzGerald's constitution were unique. It had two members on the national executive and a youth officer on each constituency executive. It achieved recognised status at the 1979 ard-fheis when Madeleine Taylor (daughter of Clare TD, Frank Taylor), the national executive delegate, was elected one of the two honorary secretaries of the organisation. Councillor Charlie Kelly, a Swinford solicitor, was elected non-parliamentary party vice-president. It was also at this ard-fheis that for the first time 12 members of the national executive, who could not be public representatives, were elected. In June 1979 Taylor and Mary Flaherty, another member of the executive of Young Fine Gael, were successful in the local elections.

The deaths of two Cork TDs (one Fianna Fáil, one Labour) in the summer of 1979 meant that there would be two by-elections after the Dáil resumption in October. Prendergast set about ensuring the best possible Fine Gael performance. Although the government was very unpopular, Fianna Fáil was expected to win the two easily, one of them being in Lynch's own Cork city constituency where in 1977 Fianna Fáil had nearly 59% of the vote (Fine Gael won 25% and Labour 10%). The other area, Cork North-East was a bit better for Fine Gael in 1977 (33% versus 48% for Fianna Fáil), but the party still had a major gap to bridge.

Prendergast commissioned extremely detailed opinion polls in September in each constituency. These revealed that a surprisingly large number of the electorate was undecided but otherwise they were not encouraging for Fine Gael, so the only hope was to work on the 'don't-knows', which would require policies with appeal and persuasive candidates. But Prendergast realised that the other information provided by the polls contained the means to success. There was discontent with the government over prices, taxation, unemployment, Northern Ireland, security, industrial unrest and insufficient pensions, in that order. There was also a perception that Fianna Fáil had too many seats and was too complacent, so the by-elections were seen as a chance to give a judgment on the government. The Cork city electorate regarded housing as a priority for a local TD, although not a government priority.

Fine Gael's new professional approach was underlined in the attention given to the choice of runners, its poll trying to measure not only its own candidates but Fianna Fáil's as well. Fine Gael had a choice of five candidates in Cork city: Blair, Lord Mayor Corr, and three aldermen, Allen, Coveney and Liam Burke. Burke pipped Blair in name identification in the poll and also topped the party list of who would best represent Cork. A Senator, he had been a TD from 1969 to 1977 and had outperformed Blair in the poll despite the latter just having had great publicity in the European campaign. Prendergast made sure that Burke was nominated at the selection convention.

In Cork North-East, those assessed were Councillor Michael Broderick and Tommy Sheahan, the former unsuccessful in the 1974 by-election, the latter a former Macra na Feirme president who was well-known to farmers. But Prendergast was interested in how Myra Barry, the 22-year-old daughter of local veteran TD, Dick, would do in the poll. She had been active in Young Fine Gael, was first chairperson of the Dublin Finglas constituency branch as a student teacher in St Patrick's College, Drumcondra, and was now teaching locally. She finished a close second to Broderick in the poll and

189

Prendergast thought that if she could do so well while not even being an aspiring candidate, she was the best bet. That Broderick had lost twice, in 1974 and 1977, also counted. Furthermore, Dick Barry had publicly stated that he would not run again.

So, Prendergast went to Cork to persuade her. Luckily, her parents were out when he arrived at her home. She was reluctant, believing that she had no chance of success, and Prendergast faced considerable scepticism among senior party figures. He based himself in Fermoy, in the heart of Cork North-East, aiming to prove to the organisation that one could achieve anything one set out to achieve. He also had to persuade the other Cork North-East TD, Paddy Hegarty, to support the campaign. At election time, relations between the Hegarty and Barry camps had always been tense, but with the father retiring at the next election and only one Barry to be faced then, Hegarty decided to cooperate.

Fine Gael used all its resources in the campaigns, FitzGerald playing a major role; he has been described as 'walking virtually every street and road of the two constituencies in the final three weeks'.[19] Despite government problems, Fianna Fáil was confident, but 'the politically impossible happened'.[20] Jack Lynch was humiliated and the considerable Fianna Fáil leads were wiped out. What was remarkable about the two results was how accurately the mid-September Fine Gael poll had measured the Fianna Fáil vote. The very skilful planning had reaped its reward. By carefully choosing the candidates and running a good campaign, Fine Gael had won over enough of the uncommitted and had significantly pushed up its 1977 vote. There was euphoria in the party and it was FitzGerald's greatest coup to date. Prendergast had proved to the organisation that the electorally impossible was feasible with proper planning. FitzGerald afterwards made it clear that he did not expect a general election for another two years, but that the party was on course, and only half the Cork swing, if repeated nationally, would make Fine Gael the largest party. There was much praise for the two directors of elections, Austin Deasy and Fergus O'Brien, but FitzGerald was the real hero.

The by-election results led to a move to unseat Jack Lynch

in Fianna Fáil which brought Charles Haughey to the top. The Dáil debate on his nomination on 11 December was expected to be a mere formality in view of the massive Fianna Fáil majority. But Garret FitzGerald had other ideas, because he deeply distrusted Haughey, believing him not fit to be Taoiseach. He also felt that some Fianna Fáil TDs had been intimidated into voting for him in his contest with George Colley. So, he stayed up until 5 am on the morning of the debate working on his speech.

FitzGerald delivered it in the Dáil some 12 hours later. He began by saying that he had known Haughey for 35 years and that relations between them had always been good, but that he had to set personal considerations aside in order to do what he saw as his duty. What he went on to say has been seen as significant for two reasons: (a) because it permanently embittered relations between the two men, and (b) because it harmed his own reputation as a politician who was 'uniquely' above the type of vulgar, personal abuse which is such a feature of Irish political life.[21]

FitzGerald referred to what he regarded as Haughey's 'flawed pedigree' in comparison to his six predecessors as Taoiseach, expressed his belief that Haughey wished to dominate rather than serve the state, that he did not have the authentic confidence of his own party (he called out the names of the 'genuine patriots' in Fianna Fáil: Colley, O'Malley, O'Donoghue, Wilson, Faulkner, Gallagher, Molloy and Woods), but was backed by 'the self-interested and the fatally misguided nationalists of his party'. The Fine Gael leader foresaw dangers to the state and predicted that the artificial majority put together to win Haughey the leadership would not long survive the pressures his 'flawed character' would put on it. He referred to Haughey's refusal to condemn the IRA in any way in the nine years since the Arms Trial, and avowed that he would be an obstacle to unity by consent, that his contraceptive legislation was blatantly hypocritical and that Fine Gael would benefit from his leadership because many Fianna Fáil voters would transfer their allegiance. Haughey listened to all this in silence, as did his family in the public gallery.

Much of what FitzGerald said proved prescient: Haughey

deeply and bitterly divided Fianna Fáil and was of electoral benefit to Fine Gael, but it has been asserted that FitzGerald had badly miscalculated by delivering his speech because, 'it was both unctuous and pompous, and it flung the most serious charges at Haughey in general terms without any specific proof or support adduced for them'.[22]   He afterwards explained that the phrase 'flawed character' referred to the Arms Trial and not to Haughey's private life and admitted that it had been careless of him to have used it. In his autobiography, FitzGerald acknowledged that the other phrase, 'flawed pedigree', which he described as 'an oratorical embellishment that must have owed something to the hour of the night at which I had drafted my remarks', was also inexcusably loose and open to easy distortion if taken out of the context in which it was used. He pointed out that other opposition speeches in the debate took a similar line to his own, Noel Browne being especially cutting, and concluded that:

> It will be for historians to judge whether placing my view bluntly on the record at that point was counterproductive or whether it may have contributed to my opponent's failure to secure an overall majority at any of the five subsequent general elections.[23]

Haughey seemed to steal Fine Gael's clothes by going on television on 9 January, 1980, to tell the people that Ireland had been living beyond its means, that government spending was too high and based on excessive borrowing, that industrial unrest would have to end and the country live within its means. Little wonder that Fine Gael notabilities were worried, as his message could woo their supporters more than his own. Their fear was that Haughey might decide to go to the country soon on a platform of fiscal rectitude, which was exactly the one on which Fine Gael intended to run, but they hoped not for another two years. Because Haughey was a different proposition from Lynch, it was decided to review the Fine Gael approach and another poll was commissioned, based on a countrywide sample. This showed a sudden surge in support for Fianna Fáil when contrasted with polls taken before the change in that party's leadership. It also revealed that Haughey was held in high esteem and that much was expected from him, even 45% of Fine Gael supporters displaying the belief that under him the government would do well. Fine Gael derived some encouragement from the high percentage holding Haughey's government responsible for the 1977 manifesto. The main issues needing government attention were seen as taxation, prices, housing, strikes, Northern Ireland, and the level of welfare benefits. The poll disclosed that Haughey rated well in comparison with FitzGerald and was seen by the electorate as being better equipped to handle the crucial economic issues with which it was so concerned, the belief being high that he would live up to 'his reputation as a financial wizard'.[24]

Haughey's policy on Northern Ireland was not an issue at this time and there was great worry within the Fine Gael leadership that he would seize the chance of a sudden election. So the front bench decided to take it easy on the government in case any excuse should be given for calling an election. Meanwhile, it intensified its own preparations for the contest which now seemed so imminent. The Fine Gael General Election Communications Committee was set up, for which Nealon assembled a group of experts to lay the formal groundwork. Marren, O'Herlihy, Heneghan, Jennings and Molloy, personal friends since the 1977 election, formed its core, and others were recruited from time to time to assist. They looked at all aspects of a campaign except party policy: posters (they studied samples from ten countries), advertising, propaganda, a leader's tour, special proposals for Dublin, how to equip and staff a press centre, music and how to appeal to youth. Subcommittees were appointed to take charge of each facet. Examining the idea of a countrywide tour, Seán Power, a Cork-based public relations man, thought a rail tour at the start of the campaign would be the best approach. He based it on the success of Harry S. Truman in the 1948 American presidential election and it had not been used since. It would enable Fine Gael to seize the initiative and was bound to get much media attention.

But Haughey sat tight. The February budget bore little relation to his January television address, yet Fine Gael was not reassured. Its uncertainty was reflected in the January issue of the *National Democrat* where FitzGerald urged preparedness for any occasion, but with a view to the long haul, and saw the main needs as perfecting the organisation, raising adequate funds and working out policies. Concerning the latter, Nealon in the party organ in February assured the faithful that preparations were well advanced in agriculture, health, education, social welfare, family and human rights. A major document on Dáil reform by John Bruton was approved by the party at the end of 1979.

But the main issue in Ireland in 1980 was reform of the income tax system. There had been huge anti-PAYE street demonstrations. FitzGerald was certain that a detailed tax reform programme, significantly reducing the amount the PAYE sector paid, would be sure to win an election. He turned to a past pupil of his from UCD, the economist Brendan Dowling, his economic adviser when he was Minister for Foreign Affairs and his and Peter Barry's informal adviser on economic issues since 1977. He was a tax expert, having recently written a report on the subject for the National Economic and Social Council. Dowling and the Fine Gael leader began examining tax reform in detail from early 1980.

FitzGerald was experiencing continued success in winning over the young and women's vote. Young Fine Gael held its second annual conference in January 1980 and he reiterated his commitment to allowing them complete freedom, despite fears that had been expressed that they could embarrass the national party. They thereupon decided to undertake a countrywide campaign to bring about the abolition of the status of illegitimacy.

A Fine Gael Women's Group was formally launched in February 1980. In the 1979 local elections, the number of women councillors in Fine Gael had increased by 17 to 52. This new group also doubled as the Women's Group of the European People's Party, Fine Gael's European allies. In his address to their first general meeting in May, FitzGerald urged them to stand for all decision-making positions in the party. Two of them had already been successful in the March ard-fheis that year: Madeleine Taylor held on to her honorary secretary position and Monica Barnes was elected one of the four vice-presidents, topping the poll in the process and beating a number of TDs.

Prendergast faced many problems in his internal restructuring, and TDs and their supporters were being often angered by his work with constituency organisations. This was made worse in 1980 by his urgent search for suitable candidates in case of a sudden general election. He later described his role in the difficult 1977-81 period as being 'to dig holes to bury certain people'. The COs were his vanguard, attending headquarters for regular meetings. Prendergast taught them how to do research and to canvass and how important it was to get transfers from people who supported other parties (he pointed out that only 16% of the TDs elected in 1977 won on the first count; the rest all depended on transfers). He faced a gruelling task, travelling all over the country, later remarking that 'he was closer to the COs than their own wives'.[25] Sometimes, he had to account for his actions to angry TDs at parliamentary party meetings.

By August 1980 Nealon and his group had worked out a detailed approach for an election campaign. Posters for the leader ('Garret for Taoiseach') and the constituencies ('Garret's Team') were ready. One-third of the FitzGerald posters would go up when the election was announced, a third would go with the candidate posters, and the balance would be held for his tour, polling day and special campaign occasions. FitzGerald's tour was believed to be vitally important; Nealon's group envisaged the election as a presidential- style contest between the two main leaders. Its advantages would be media publicity and a boost to the morale of the local organisations. Seán Power's suggestion of an initial train tour was accepted.

A Strategy Committee had also been established by FitzGerald to prepare for the election. He has written:

> My experience before becoming leader had convinced me that deputies trying to get themselves elected could not run a general election campaign effectively. What we needed were people from outside the party structure with a wide range of management and public relations skills who would

195

have learnt to work with the party leadership in the run-up to the election and who, given this experience, could then take on this task in conjunction with a small number of Senators and others with political experience, and with the professionals, Peter Prendergast and Ted Nealon.[26]

Its main purpose was to decide where outgoing TDs would stand because of the constituency revision carried out in April by the first ever Independent Commission. The main changes effected by this body were to increase the number of Dáil seats by 18, and the number of five-seaters from six to 15. The Strategy Committee was also responsible for finding other suitable candidates. As well as Nealon and Prendergast, FitzGerald himself, Senator James Dooge, the Mayo solicitor Charlie Kelly (who advised on the west), Seán O'Leary and Peter Barry were members.

Raising funds was another crucial aspect of the eventual campaign. In 1977, headquarters had spent £200,000, mainly on newspaper advertisements. Following FitzGerald's accession to the top, the problem of finance grew greatly, the new headquarters being costly with its much bigger organisation. FitzGerald was also paid a salary as a full-time leader, the same as that of a minister, as he himself had suggested. By 1978, headquarters was costing around £150,000 and two years later was seriously in debt. FitzGerald reorganised the long-established Capital Branch, the function of which was to underwrite deficits, by appointing Vincent Ferguson, a director of Fitzwilton, as chairman, and about a dozen other active members, most importantly the accountant Seán Murray. It functioned secretly, almost anonymously, with only the party trustees, nominated by FitzGerald, having the right to see its files (the trustees were Richie Ryan, Peter Barry and Sylvester Muldowney, a veteran member of the Branch).

In April 1980, Peter Barry set an aim of a half-a-million pound fund to fight an election. As well as the Capital Branch, the national executive and the parliamentary party agreed that they would levy the constituencies for £300,000 of that. Each Dáil seat was to raise £2,000 for headquarters. By the autumn the preparations for the general election were very advanced. Nealon's

196

group had a plan covering everything except the manifesto; the Capital Branch was writing to all sorts of businessmen seeking donations; Prendergast and the Strategy Committee were working away at the search for appropriate candidates.

Fine Gael faced a by-election in Donegal in early November in confident mood because of government disarray and the advanced state of its own general election preparations. Haughey had not lived up to his tough, decisive image with both unemployment and inflation rising rapidly since he had taken office. By November his government's budget deficit was nearly £200 million over the projected figure. He was fulfilling his promise of industrial peace by means of what have been termed 'extravagant settlements'[27] with every sectoral group. Agriculture was in the worst recession since World War II. It was no time for the government to fight an election, not even a by-election, but it had to because of the death of the Ceann Comhairle, Joe Brennan, during the summer.

Despite Fine Gael's optimism, based largely on its success in Cork of the year before, a September *Irish Times*/MRBI poll showed that, although support for the government was very low, neither Fine Gael nor Labour were benefitting, and there was a high percentage of undecided voters. A private opinion poll carried out by Fine Gael in Donegal brought more bad news: it was running third place (20%) to Independent Fianna Fáil (25%) and Fianna Fáil (45%). Prendergast also found that its candidate, Dinny McGinley, was not known in many parts of the county.

Fianna Fáil's campaign was thorough, the whole cabinet spending three weeks before the vote in Donegal, 'and vote-catching promises were flung about the county like snuff at a wake', it has been humorously remarked.[28] Its candidate, Clem Coughlan, was much better known than McGinley and while this alone (without cognisance of the opinion poll) should have caused a more cautious Fine Gael approach, FitzGerald confidently predicted victory on the eve of polling day. This despite Paddy Harte and Jim White, two Donegal TDs and FitzGerald's colleagues on the front bench, assuring him that Fine Gael would not win. While it was true that in 1977 the party had matched Fianna Fáil's share of the vote

(36%), Blaney's Independent Fianna Fáil had won 22% and his candidate was bound to transfer to Coughlan, so that the real Fianna Fáil vote was more than 50%. This was borne out in the by-election and Coughlan won on the third count. Prendergast later claimed that publicising McGinley as a winner had to be done to get him known and this may have been why the Fine Gael vote rose from the 20% in the October poll to 33% in the actual election, but both he and FitzGerald had miscalculated.

Following this setback, both men saw it as time for a major rethink, to find out what the electorate really wanted. To this end they decided, not on opinion polls, but on research into attitudes and predilections among the voters. 'A nationwide round of informal talk-ins with representative groups of people was planned for January 1981', it has been recorded.[29]

FitzGerald also decided to bring together into a single body the various committees preparing for the general election so that they could work on all aspects of strategy. He consulted his friend Derry Hussey, the former chairman of Dublin South-East constituency, and financial director of the Jones Group. He was not widely known in Fine Gael, although he had done a little work in the European campaign in 1979 in Dún Laoghaire. His wife, Gemma, had been an Independent Senator since 1977. FitzGerald wanted Hussey as head of the new 'Election Committee'; others on it were Murray, Nealon, Marren, Peter Sutherland, (a talented and energetic young barrister) Dooge and Prendergast. It first met at headquarters during Christmas week and spent two days analysing party faults and election needs. Eventually it came to be known as the Strategy Committee. About it, the observation has been made:

> This was the vehicle that would transform Fine Gael as a fighting force at election time, and play a pivotal role in the three general elections of 1981-82. As an electoral force the party was changing from well-intentioned amateurs to consummate professionals. A revolution was at hand.[30]

Garret FitzGerald has himself expressed the belief that 'this structure was one of the best organisational systems devised by a political party in independent Ireland'.[31]

198

A new move of FitzGerald's and Prendergast's was to ask Seán O'Leary to become national director of elections. This vital post had always been the preserve of a senior politician, but FitzGerald wanted it to be a full-time occupation. Like Prendergast and Nealon, O'Leary had failed to get elected, but on no fewer than four occasions, in his native Cork. He hardly seemed the ideal figure to undertake the direction of a successful national campaign, but FitzGerald thought that he was, and in his autobiography he has stated that O'Leary's 'qualities of warmth and vitality, political gut instinct, natural authority, toughness and joie de vivre, together with his excellent relationship with our national organiser, Peter Prendergast, equipped him ideally for this task'.[32]

Seán Murray, who had revamped the Capital Branch, was another central figure on the Strategy Committee because he was in charge of finance. Jim Dooge, a Fine Gael veteran and close adviser to Liam Cosgrave as well as to FitzGerald, was also on the Committee. A member of the Senate since 1961, and its Cathaoirleach (chairman) from 1973 to 1977, he was especially interested in Fianna Fáil's ability to run two able candidates along with outgoing TDs and to arrange the party vote geographically among them.

Prendergast was in charge of organisation, Marren was regional organiser for Dublin and Myles Staunton was the same for Connacht, Peter Kelleher for Munster and Peter Curran for Leinster. Nealon was responsible for publicity on the Committee, and two Dublin barristers, John McMenamin (speech-writing) and Peter Sutherland (co-ordination of policy statements with the front bench to be included in the manifesto), were also on it from the start. Vincent Ferguson was in charge of fund-raising. FitzGerald depended on Peter Barry to get parliamentary party approval for the new Committee, because deputies were bound to resent a group of non-elected people having so powerful a role. Barry was ideal for liaising with the elected TDs and Senators, because he was trusted by them, and together with Tom Fitzpatrick, he agreed to be on the new Committee. He has been seen as providing the vital link between the public representatives and the experts working behind the scenes.[33]

A reshuffle of the front bench was carried out in early 1981. In response to calls from within the party, those MEPs who were former ministers were invited to rejoin. Mark Clinton had decided to concentrate on Europe, while both Richie Ryan (Foreign Affairs) and Tom O'Donnell (Telecommunications and Broadcasting) were given their old portfolios. Peter Barry was transferred from Finance to become chairman of the Economic Group of Frontbenchers and General Election Coordinator; Paddy Harte moved from Security to Social Welfare, and John Bruton was given Finance. Following the rest of the reshuffle, the shadow cabinet looked like this: Jim Mitchell (Labour and the Public Service), Paddy O'Toole (Industry and Commerce), John Boland (Environment), Eddie Collins (Education), Dónal Creed (Defence), Austin Deasy (Transport), Michael Keating (Law Reform and Human Rights), Jim O'Keeffe (Security), Jim White (Fisheries), Tom Fitzpatrick (Health and Leader of the House). New junior frontbenchers were Myra Barry (Youth), John Donnellan (Public Works), Tom Enright (Consumer Affairs), Paddy Hegarty (Tourism), Enda Kenny (Western Development), Fergus O'Brien (Urban Affairs), Brendan Griffin (Arts and Culture) and Gemma Hussey (Women's Affairs). The latter was a surprise because she had been an ordinary member of Fine Gael since the early 1970s and was an Independent Senator for the National University of Ireland. Her appointment has been seen as FitzGerald's means of formally signalling his campaign to win women voters to Fine Gael.[34]

There was much speculation about an election from early 1981. From its annual capital public programme (12 January) and its budget (which was unrelated to the real condition of the public finances, and later in the year it would be seen how underprovided for many departments were), it was clear that Fianna Fáil was getting ready. A spring election seemed in the offing. An *Irish Times*/IMS poll of 24 January showed Fianna Fáil slightly ahead of Fine Gael and Labour combined, and Haughey's standing slightly up with FitzGerald's slightly down. Fine Gael now speeded up its readiness for the coming fray.

Selection conventions began in all constituencies on 11 January. The first candidates chosen in Kildare, where the absence of a sitting TD or Senator made the process easier, were Councillors Bernard Durkan and Patsy Lawlor. Alan Dukes became the third runner in this new five-seater. He had finished his time in Brussels with the ending of Richard Burke's commissionership at the end of 1980 and accepted FitzGerald's and Prendergast's persuasions to run in Kildare where his good reputation with the IFA helped him to get the third nomination. On 14 January, Nealon's Communications Committee produced a comprehensive, fully-costed (£380,000) campaign plan. The Stardust ballroom tragedy, occurring during and causing the postponement of the Fianna Fáil February ard-fheis, prevented that platform from being used as the unofficial launch of the general election campaign and gave Fine Gael more valuable time to carry on with its preparations.

The report of the marketing consultants, ICR Limited, on voters' attitudes and intentions, commissioned after the Donegal defeat, was presented to Prendergast later in February and has been described as 'a masterly insight into the mind of the electorate'.[35] It revealed a gloomy mood among the people: the recession was expected to get worse, with unemployment and inflation seeming set to rise; there was concern over government borrowing but, significantly, international factors were blamed rather than Fianna Fáil; greater national self-reliance was wanted (the fact that even farmers were buying vegetables in local shops was often cited); the main election issues were seen as inflation, employment and PAYE levels. Election manifestos were regarded with disbelief and Fianna Fáil's in 1977 was seen as a confidence trick (many referred to the return of car tax). Fianna Fáil was expected to win the next election because of its size. Fine Gael was not expected to become the biggest party; some saw it as possible for Fine Gael/Labour combined to win more seats than Fianna Fáil, but the ICR analysts saw no value in a pre-election agreement with Labour since it would lose Fine Gael support. Little difference was perceived between Fine Gael and Fianna Fáil; both were viewed as conservative, except on Northern Ireland, which was not considered to be an important election issue.

The attention was on personalities because of the absence of policy differentiation between the two main parties. FitzGerald was seen as dedicated, doing his best for the country, a believer in justice, but not as politically professional as Haughey. Apart from these general views, it was found that people knew very little about him. He was thought to be slightly to the left of his party's perceived right-wing position. Because of the widespread concern with the economy, ICR recommended presenting the prospect of an 'austere and idealistic' government, not unduly criticising Fianna Fáil but taking a positive approach, while slogans like 'The power is in your hands' and 'It's your country' were suggested as being most appealing, especially to the young.[36]

The Haughey government was now faring badly: economic problems were intensifying with an oil strike, a poor farm rescue EC package and a row over neutrality but, most ominously, a new hunger-strike in Northern Ireland from 1 March. Conversely, Fine Gael was making headway. A late March poll, commissioned by Prendergast, promised victory with Labour's help. So the party's ard-fheis, held shortly afterwards, tried to project 'a winning, professional image'.[37] John Kelly's barbed wit led the way in lampooning Fianna Fáil: Haughey was portrayed as an economic Mussolini who had been mercilessly exposed, Gene Fitzgerald at Finance was Rommel, 'the Desert Goat'. The high point for the huge 8,000 gathering was the leader's address. FitzGerald has been described as giving the faithful 'plenty of fighting, optimistic rhetoric' (the party was never stronger, more united or more determined and would lick Fianna Fáil whenever it had the guts to take them on; there would be radical tax reform; injustices and discrimination would be tackled), but he has been accused of being significantly lacking in policy detail.[38] Young Fine Gael and women made what has been termed 'spectacular progress'[39] at this ard-fheis. Madeleine Taylor from Clare and Nuala Murphy from East Cork were elected as the two honorary secretaries and Maria Stack, a 20-year-old medical student from Listowel, was chosen as one of the four vice-presidents.

It has been maintained that relations on the front bench were far from perfect at this time. The return of Ryan and O'Donnell was resented by some, this argument goes, while Ryan believed that FitzGerald cowed the entire shadow cabinet by his habit of interrupting - which Ryan would not stand for. Things have been seen as so bad that Senator Alexis Fitzgerald had to chair meetings; FitzGerald himself was considered to be a bad chairman, prone to dominate, often because he knew more about others' portfolios than they knew themselves, but this did not make for orderly gatherings. This supposed situation has been seen as having its amusing moments, however. An exasperated Michael Keating, unable to make himself heard, is reported to have shouted: 'This place is like the Muppet Show!', which provoked the puzzled response from FitzGerald: 'What's the Muppet Show?'[40]

Eighteen selection conventions had been completed by the end of March and a month later Prendergast planned to have settled another 12. Both he and FitzGerald were delighted with the emergence of new, younger candidates with no family history of public representation. As Prendergast saw it, 'members of the party now felt they belonged and had a real role', which strengthened their commitment.[41]

Fianna Fáil backbenchers, very perturbed that Fine Gael already had its campaign underway and most candidates selected, were pressing Haughey to call an election. The Northern hunger strike was disturbing the whole island and Bobby Sands, the republican prisoner and abstentionist Westminster MP, died on 5 May. The economy was worsening as Haughey spent huge sums to placate the electorate (the phasing out of food subsidies was reversed in April; incredibly, the building of Knock Airport was given the green light, despite the opposition of the experts in the relevant department). The time was up for the Fianna Fáil leader: the finance provided for the year would be nearly all spent by the end of the half-year (the exchequer returns would show this and a supplementary budget would be necessary), so he called the election for 11 June. Fine Gael faced a huge challenge (it was 38 seats behind Fianna Fáil) and its moment of truth had come. All would depend on the value of its election programme and the campaign mounted by the Strategy Committee and the revamped constituency organisations.

(iv) June 1981 general election

Only a few selection conventions were left; the organisation had been ready for weeks and was champing at the bit. It was to be the exact opposite of 1977; this time it was Fine Gael rather than Fianna Fáil that was better prepared and would seize the initiative. The first job FitzGerald faced was to get the go-ahead for his secret election manifesto, for which the parliamentary party was assembled. Its main plan was what has been described as 'a radical and imaginative tax reform package', which he and Dowling had worked out over the past year.[42] It had not been considered by the front bench, FitzGerald being almost obsessive about keeping it secret in case Fianna Fáil got wind of it.

He and Dowling did not discuss it on the phone, which was a sensible precaution resulting from a November 1980 incident when Prendergast accidentally picked up a conversation on his phone between two people who were clearly tapping into his line (he noted what they said, which included details of an earlier talk he had had with Bruton), and he concluded that both his home phone and those at headquarters were tapped. He and FitzGerald met the Gárda Commissioner, but were not assured that their phones were not tapped and this caused senior party members to be cautious with their phone conversations.

The election programme was readily accepted by the parliamentary party and was launched by FitzGerald the day after the Dáil was dissolved. It saw the economic crisis as the main issue. It proposed to phase out the budget deficit over four years and to bring down prices and costs by means of an 18-month anti-inflation programme. It was aimed to transform the investment situation via certain spending increases and tax cuts. It has been remarked that, 'Politically, Fine Gael hoped to tackle the problem without alienating the voters.'[43] So the standard rate of income tax was to be reduced from 35% to 25%, which would be paid for by a once-off increase in indirect taxation; grants were to be introduced for houses, energy and conservation; a £1,000 tax credit for people in rented dwellings and a low-cost mortgage scheme were also offered. Women working at home were to receive increased children's allowances; all welfare dependency allowances were to be paid to the dependent spouse, usually the mother, and half the married person's tax credit was to be paid directly to the spouse staying at home. The £101 million these proposals would cost was to be found by balancing extra revenue from five different sources. The cost of tax reform would be £263 million, taking into account increased health contribution charges (2.5% of all income) and a special 3.75% levy on all income over £8,500. 'The essence of the Fine Gael programme', it has been observed, 'was its tax reform package, designed in the words of a party advertisement "to give you more of your money to spend as you choose"'.[44]

It has been argued that the manifesto's 'novelty and attractiveness' put Fine Gael in front from the outset, as did its posters' campaign, initiated within hours of the election announcement and carried out with military precision, so that, 'people would have to revise their impression of Fine Gael as a sleepy, amateur party'. By the same score, Seán Power's 'rail safari' has been regarded as 'a truly brilliant publicity coup'.[45] Joe Jennings, CIE's press officer and a member of Nealon's Communications Committee, had provisionally booked a train months before in the name of an international company, not wanting Fianna Fáil sympathisers among his colleagues to know what was going on. On the first weekend of the campaign, FitzGerald did a two-day provincial tour on the 'Garret Express', accompanied by his wife, Joan, secretaries, a public relations team and news reporters. Nearly all the Dublin candidates were on the platform at Connolly Station to see him off. At each venue on the tour, the local faithful turned out. His press conferences on the train for the local media gave Fine Gael invaluable publicity in the provincial press.

The Strategy Committee was so well prepared that Ted Nealon had been able to drop out some months before to seek a nomination in Sligo-Leitrim. Liam Hourican, a former RTE reporter and press officer in Richard Burke's Brussels office, replaced him, and three public relations and advertising experts were added to the Committee: O'Herlihy, Heneghan and Molloy. It met every morning at eight o'clock in the Berkeley Court Hotel in Dublin where the director of elections, Seán O'Leary, was staying; the Committee analysed the morning papers and every aspect of the campaign and, after 26 May, when FitzGerald began a nationwide tour of the constituencies, it kept in touch with him and his tour managers and planned a schedule of speeches for all front-bench spokespersons.

The Capital Branch, especially Murray and Ferguson, were very busy, having some months before begun a quest for donations from business and the professions. Initially thousands were written to and gradually a list of 400 likely subscribers was built up, mainly over small business lunches attended by FitzGerald or other senior politicians. Once the campaign had started, these people were contacted. 'Absolute anonymity was assured, and the money flowed in', it has been maintained.[46] Average donations were less than £1,000, a few were around £5,000 and a small number were close to £10,000. There was no question of a quid pro quo being sought: Murray and FitzGerald decided to return a £10,000 donation because the company concerned was at the time seeking a government contract: 'It had not linked the issues but no chances were taken'. [47]

The remarkable figure of £500,000 was raised by the Capital Branch; a newspaper appeal raised a further £30,000 from the general public; the constituencies contributed about £100,000, so, instead of the projected £333,000 - later revised to £400,000 - headquarters was able to spend £600,000. The daily Strategy Committee meetings were chaired by Hussey and attended by Prendergast, O'Leary, Dooge, Hourican, Marren, O'Herlihy, Heneghan and Molloy. O'Leary knew the constituencies well and has been termed 'a brilliant strategist'.[48] Prendergast, through his COs and regional directors, knew intimately how the canvassing and vote spreading were going in each constituency. Marren was expert on the 11 Dublin constituencies. O'Herlihy, Heneghan and Molloy took care of the marketing and advertising.

All this expertise was needed because almost nobody understood the tax reform package. The meaning of tax credits, how they worked and who would get them, and the £9.60 per week for women at home, which was half the married person's tax credit, were real puzzles. Headquarters was bombarded with questions about them from party workers and the general public. O'Leary knew a little because he had been involved with FitzGerald and Dowling in some of the final policy meetings. The £9.60 idea quickly captured the public mind. Molloy, responsible for newspaper advertising, wanted simple ideas to be conveyed, but had to jettison many of his plans, and devote most of his efforts to explaining the tax proposals. O'Leary, too, had to prepare leaflets explaining the proposals to his Strategy colleagues and the office telephone staff.

FitzGerald faced the same task around the country. When his tour bus arrived at the edge of any town and the local candidates boarded, 'they dived on the leader like drowning men clinging to a raft', it has been humorously remarked.[49] While he wished to know how the campaign was going, all *they* wanted was to have the tax measures explained. He happily reached for pen and paper, totted and clarified, treating people on the streets 'to similar impromptu lessons'.[50] By the end of the first week, the problem lessened as all the activists had enough with which to get along.

In contrast to Haughey, FitzGerald was treated favourably by the press. An experienced RTE political correspondent described him as 'enormously appealing to the media - he's open and responsive, he knows the requirements in the press and because of his own background he knows people in the media on a personal basis'.[51] He was also more accessible than Haughey because he travelled on Fine Gael's press coach, whereas Haughey travelled around in helicopters or else by car ahead of the Fianna Fáil bus.

The two cut contrasting figures on tour. Haughey clearly enjoyed crowd contact and admitted that it was his favourite form of electioneering, while FitzGerald appeared less relaxed. It has been observed that he 'was an uneasy glad-handler, but he set to it with a grim fervour'.[52] Concerning the media cliché that he did not have the common touch, he himself has commented:

> In part this was a stereotyping exercise - woolly-headed academic versus practised professional - but there was an element of truth in it, for I have always been chary of all forms of populism and have perhaps been inordinately fastidious about the kind of artificial adulation of the leader that seems to be an inseparable element of party set-pieces, including party conferences and election meetings.[53]

Despite Haughey's acknowledged professionalism, FitzGerald's behaviour when meeting the public had its own special appeal. Mary Holland wrote of him that he:

> . . . treats everybody who questions him with infinite courtesy. He explains the details of the government's Youth Employment Agency to a nervous teenager, for example, as carefully as he might to a journalist on television. This takes time and it is doubtful whether most people, blinded by the television lights and buffeted by the crowd, can take in the fine print of what he is saying. It drives his aides, who are always wanting to push him on to the next stop, out of their minds.[54]

Holland also remarked on the curiosity that 'for a confirmed family man, he seems distinctly ill at ease holding a baby'.[55] A *Sunday Times* reporter perceived that while 'Haughey kisses babies and, even more enthusiastically, their mothers, FitzGerald shakes babies by the hand'.[56]

RTE programme-makers suggested a number of one-to-one debates between the rivals for the office of Taoiseach. Two radio programmes invited the two leaders to such a debate, but the most significant negotiations occurred in regard to a 'Today Tonight' television debate. The attempt had to be abandoned after two weeks of talks. Haughey held that the Labour leader, Frank Cluskey, had the right to take part in the debate. FitzGerald offered both a three-way and a two-way encounter, accused Haughey of being afraid, and remarked that RTE was not able to 'lasso him and drag him into the studio'.[57]

The eventual format, with each of the three leaders being

questioned separately by a team of journalists, was generally agreed to have been a failure, but it was also widely acknowledged that Haughey had done best. The four journalists who conducted the exercise were unimpressed by their interviews of the leaders. They found Haughey 'competent, cool, buoyant and excellently prepared'. Bruce Arnold, one of the four, thought FitzGerald's performance more honest than Haughey's; it 'led him into the much more real territory of argument and discussion, but made him, at the same time, more vulnerable'. Two of the other journalists on the team, Paul Tansey and Michael Mills, found Haughey used statistics selectively and found him impossible to interrupt. In Arnold's words, he 'defeated' them.[58] This suggests that he refused to enter into discussion with them, but browbeat them instead.

Although it ran a superb campaign, there was little chance of Fine Gael winning sufficient seats to form a government on its own, as FitzGerald knew, and the best that could be hoped for was 70 seats, which would have been a remarkable feat. The only way of keeping Fianna Fáil out was coalition. Both Fine Gael and Labour ran separate campaigns, but neither ruled out an alliance and each supported inter-party transfers. Policy differences were kept to a minimum. An *Irish Times*/MRBI poll published on 8 June showed a potential coalition 4% ahead of Fianna Fáil. FitzGerald's personal rating was 10% ahead of Haughey's and Fine Gael was doing well with the key electoral sectors: its leader was more popular with the young and the £9.60 idea had been well received in both rural and urban areas. There was so much gloomy economic data around during the campaign that FitzGerald, looking ahead to the huge and difficult problems awaiting the next government, joked, 'Whoever wins this election should have the first choice on going into opposition.'[59]

The face of the new Fine Gael party in the Dáil was bound to change because seven outgoing TDs were not seeking to return: Liam Cosgrave, Mark Clinton, Patrick Donegan, Richard Barry, John Mannion, Frank Taylor and Joan Burke. The early selection conventions meant that differences were healed by the time the campaign proper began, but it was not possible to keep the peace in some few constituencies. The final opinion poll in *The Irish Times* on 10 June found Fine Gael-Labour just 1% ahead of Fianna Fáil, with FitzGerald the same margin ahead of Haughey in popularity. The Fine Gael leader had much to be satisfied about at the end of the campaign, having masterminded the outmanoeuvring of the old enemy. He hoped for victory in the form of a coalition and had been careful over the three weeks to stress the common ground with Labour. But the real danger was a hung Dáil, with power in the hands of the Independents, the worst possible outcome for the country given the economic crisis. The opinion polls indicated such a possibility and so it was to prove.

The election result was inconclusive. Fianna Fáil won 45.3% of the vote and 78 seats, Fine Gael 36.5% and 65 seats, Labour 9.9% and 15 seats, the Workers' Party 1.7% and 1 seat, Independents 6.6% and 7 seats, including 2 H-Block hunger strikers (republican prisoners in Long Kesh in Northern Ireland). But despite this, it was a remarkable performance for the Fine Gael party. Not since 1927 had its Cumann na nGaedheal predecessor achieved a higher share of the vote; it had increased its Dáil representation by half, from 43 seats in 1977 to 65. There were 26 new TDs, many of them young and liberal, including six women deputies (as opposed to one in 1977), three of whom had risen to prominence via Young Fine Gael. Garret FitzGerald has described this phenomenon as 'an unprecedented influx of new blood into our political system'.[60]

The question now facing Fine Gael was whether to coalesce and seek to form a government, or to go into opposition. The Labour leader, Frank Cluskey, had lost his seat in the election, and Michael O'Leary was chosen to succeed him. He and FitzGerald discussed a coalition programme at the Dublin home of a mutual friend, Gay Hogan, and they were soon joined by their respective deputies, Peter Barry and James Tully. The agreement, which was reached after a week, included the full Fine Gael tax reform plan, food subsidies, a capital tax, a National Development Corporation and a Youth Employment Agency. FitzGerald also had talks with the Independent left-wing deputies, Jim Kemmy of Limerick and

Noel Browne of Dublin, about their possible support for his election as Taoiseach. As in 1973, Labour secured a greater share of ministries - four senior and three junior - than its proportion of Dáil seats would have given it. On 30 June, FitzGerald was proposed for Taoiseach by Oliver J. Flanagan and Ivan Yates, 'the father of the house and its youngest member',[61] and he was elected by 81 votes to 78, Jim Kemmy being his sole Independent supporter.

(v) Coalition, June 1981 - February 1982

One of the most surprising, and most commented-upon aspects of the Fine Gael members that Garret FitzGerald appointed to his cabinet, was the omission of former ministers Ryan, O'Donnell and Burke. The reason he himself put forward for his action was that he wanted his government 'to break new ground by bringing in fresh and younger faces rather than to be a virtual replica of the Cosgrave Government of the mid-1970s'.[62] Before offering his nominees their portfolios, he enquired of them if they were members of the Knights of Columbanus or any other secretive organisations and, if so, if they were willing to resign their membership. Why he did so, he has explained as follows:

> In our state, as distinct from the United Kingdom it was highly unlikely that Freemasonry played any role in politics; but there are comparable Roman Catholic organisations, membership of which is similarly not a matter of public knowledge, and I believed that ministers should not be members of any such organisation, because no one should ever feel they had reason to fear that their legitimate interests or common good might be adversely affected because any member of a government led by me owed private allegiance to such a body.[63]

The most remarkable appointment to office in the new cabinet was that of James Dooge to Foreign Affairs. Under the Irish Constitution, the head of government can choose two of his ministers from the Senate, but since the provision had been used only once before, most people were unaware of its existence. Dooge had decided not to seek re-election to the Senate in 1977, but

FitzGerald intended to choose him as one of his 11 nominees to that body, which would qualify him for his portfolio within two months, and in the meantime John Kelly would act as interim Foreign Minister. When Dooge's appointment was ratified by the Dáil in late October, Haughey attacked it as out-and-out croneyism; at least one commentator has observed that some disgruntled Fine Gael backbenchers felt likewise, but Dooge proved an outstanding Minister for Foreign Affairs, so that his leader's action was what has been described as 'triumphantly vindicated'.[64]

Deputy leader Peter Barry was invited to choose his post and opted for Environment. The 34-year-old John Bruton was made Minister for Finance. Despite his youth, he had been a junior minister in the Cosgrave government and since 1977 had been one of the party's most active and able front-bench members. The 36-year-old Alan Dukes, on his first day in the Dáil, was appointed Minister for Agriculture, his IFA and EC experience commending him highly in FitzGerald's eyes. John Kelly became Minister for Trade, Commerce and Tourism, having been shadow spokesman on Economic Planning. John Boland, also only 34, was the surprise choice for Education, as was Jim Mitchell, the same age, for Justice. Paddy O'Toole from Mayo was appointed Minister for the Gaeltacht and two veterans filled the remaining portfolios: Patrick Cooney became Minister for Transport, Posts and Telegraphs and Tom Fitzpatrick was given responsibility for Fisheries and Forestry. Another young man, only in his mid-thirties, Peter Sutherland, became Attorney General.

The Labour members of the coalition cabinet were Michael O'Leary (Tánaiste and Minister for Industry and Energy); Eileen Desmond (Health and Social Welfare); James Tully (Defence) and Liam Kavanagh (Labour and the Public Service).

Even before Garret FitzGerald presented his list of ministers to the Dáil for ratification, he had been made aware by a senior government official of the alarming state of the country's finances. So perturbed was he that he referred to it in the Dáil before presenting his cabinet:

Even in the brief time, I have learned something of the scale of the damage done. I have to say I am shocked to find the position is even worse than our most pessimistic predictions. I do not say that without careful consideration. It is not a propagandist remark; it is a factual remark. When the facts are disclosed, they will validate what I have to say. The scale of the mess is beyond anything that had to be faced previously.

Various departments had been totally under-provided for by the previous government and, although it was only the beginning of July, nine-tenths of the year's budget deficit had been spent. The new administration decided to act immediately and introduce a supplementary budget. A stringent commentator on Fine Gael in these years has remarked: 'It was a brave decision, not the kind of thing any government, especially a minority one, would willingly opt to do within a month of winning power.'[65]

John Bruton presented the 'mini' budget to a reconvened Dáil on 21 July. The details were astounding: the current budget deficit at the end of the half year was £457 million; if nothing was done, it would be £950 million or 9.5% of GNP by year's end (the highest it had been before this was 7.25% at the end of 1979). The newspapers described Bruton's measures to tackle the problem as 'savage' (excise duty on drink, tobacco and petrol was raised; the standard VAT rate went from 10% to 15%; CIE fares rose by 23%). While it has been conceded that these measures went some way towards 'checking the careering national finances', Bruton has been castigated for not dealing with what has been seen as the nub of the problem - public service pay, in turn due to the enormous expansion in that sector between 1977 and 1981, when 30,000 extra people were employed.[66] The government managed to get its budgetary provisions through the Dáil with the support of Independents Jim Kemmy and Seán Loftus, with the ill veteran Oliver J. Flanagan having to be brought from hospital to attend the vote. From then on, in relation to the economy, it was a matter of what has been described as 'desperate day-to-day crisis management'.[67]

If Gladstone's self-proclaimed political mission was to pacify Ireland, FitzGerald's was to end the agony in Northern Ireland.

When he came to power, the H-Block hunger strike was dragging on with all that it implied for the security of the island. He straightaway immersed himself in the problem. In his autobiography he deals in detail with his numerous contacts with the relatives of the hunger strikers and with the British. He is critical of both the way in which the IRA used the hapless families and of hamfisted British contacts with the IRA, and concludes:

> By early August I had in fact come under increasing pressure from a number of sources to wind down the confrontation with the British government. In the light of hindsight this note of caution had some justification. However, given the damage done by the continuation of the hunger-strike - and, I have to add, the human tragedy of these deaths, which I felt deeply despite my abhorrence of the violence these men had been involved in before being sent to jail - I was happier to have done too much rather than too little in attempting to bring it to an end, with whatever lack of success. Moreover, the scale of the efforts made on our side may in some degree have modified the potentially destabilising impact of this whole episode on domestic opinion, which would certainly have been aggravated had we shown a lack of compassion and concern.[68]

On 18 July, a march organised by the National H-Blocks Committee in Dublin degenerated into a riot, with over £1 million of damage being done to the neighbourhood of the British Embassy in Ballsbridge. Jim Mitchell, the Minister for Justice, dealt skilfully with what might have become a major security issue. It has been observed that he 'showed a striking sureness of touch in handling an ugly situation, defusing the threat with a nicely judged combination of fairness and restraint.'[69]

Once the true state of the public finances became known, Prendergast came increasingly to feel that another budget could not be got through the Dáil if it were to contain the kind of measures which the country needed. So he and FitzGerald began to consider the possibility of an early election to try to secure a clear majority.

A young TD from Dublin North-Central, George Birmingham, had urged his leader to seek such a mandate. Early October was considered a good time to go to the country, but when a commissioned opinion poll revealed that there was little chance of altering the Dáil arithmetic, it was decided to abandon the plan. At the end of October, Prendergast gave up his position as general secretary and became a special adviser to Bruton at the Department of Finance. He had achieved something of an organisational miracle in Fine Gael, but he declared that it would have been impossible without the commitment of FitzGerald and the dedication of the constituency organisers and public relations officers.[70]

As well as facing problems relating to the economy, security and Northern Ireland, this minority government also encountered trouble in the field of education. The decision to raise the primary school entry age to four-and-a-half proved controversial. John Boland, Minister for Education, had been a member of the Dublin Vocational Education Committee and he decided to go ahead with the measure because he believed that it had educational merit, but the Irish National Teachers' Organisation, worried about job losses, regarded it simply as a device to reduce public spending. Fianna Fáil tried to use the dispute to bring down the government and almost succeeded. Boland persisted with it but it created as many problems as it solved and it is difficult to disagree with the contention that it was an issue that should not have been taken up by a minority government and that it showed a lack of political experience.[71]

FitzGerald's famous declaration of his desire to lead a 'constitutional crusade' to eliminate sectarianism in the Republic's institutions and laws made during the course of a RTE radio interview on 27 September, has been described as 'an apparently unguarded response'.[72] It is claimed that he had not discussed it beforehand with cabinet colleagues,[73] but in his autobiography he explained that he had called together a conference on Northern Ireland on 24 and 25 August, attended by a number of ministers, at which the need for a general review of the Republic's Constitution was agreed. Shortly afterwards, in an interview he gave to *The Cork*

215

Examiner, he expressed the view that articles 2 and 3 were obstacles to better relations between the two parts of the island. He saw the radio interview as 'an opportunity to present the case for constitutional change directly to the people, in a far more effective way than would be possible through press reports of a Dáil debate or even in a necessarily static and formal ministerial broadcast'.[74]

In fact, he had long been a critic of the sectarian nature of the Irish Constitution, and his 1972 book, *Towards a New Ireland*, had argued for a pluralist state.

It has been asserted that this interview would have been extraordinarily outspoken and controversial from any Taoiseach, let alone the head of a minority government, and that it was as much a challenge to conservatives in his own party as to anyone else.[75] He has been warmly praised in the following terms: 'This was the radical FitzGerald, clearly willing to lead from the front, intent on breaking the conservative mould of Irish politics in dramatic fashion.'[76] FitzGerald himself regarded the rejection of his idea by Fianna Fáil, and the partitionist rhetoric in which it was expressed, as jettisoning once and for all 'the hackneyed argument' that there was no difference between Fine Gael and Fianna Fáil.[77]

Before examining the collapse of this short-lived and ill-fated government, mention should be made of some of its achievements, lest they be lost sight of in the shroud of crisis which seemed to envelope its activities. The Anglo-Irish summit in London on 6 November went a long way towards improving the relationship between the two governments (an inter-governmental council was set up) which had suffered from the way the previous meeting had been afterwards presented on the Irish side and from the tension generated by the hunger strike. A Youth Employment Agency had been quickly set up once the coalition came to power and its training programmes lessened the impact on the young of the harsh measures that had to be pursued in the attempt to solve some of the country's economic ills. A Housing Finance Agency was established to provide mortgages at fixed interest rates for people on lower incomes. Other innovations were the institution of a Combat Poverty Agency and a Curriculum and Examinations Board, and the system of higher education grants was reformed.

The preparations for the January 1982 budget caused government ministers much anxiety. The pledges to reduce public spending and reform the taxation system had enabled Fine Gael to get into office and these would have to figure in the budget now under construction. A week before it was due to be presented to the Dáil, O'Leary informed FitzGerald of Labour's outright opposition to cutting food subsidies, although this measure had earlier been agreed by the cabinet. A record 25% increase in social welfare payments was to compensate for the abolition of the subsidies. Footwear and clothing, heretofore exempt from VAT, were to have a rate of 10% imposed on them.

The coalition partners thereupon decided to work out a new series of budget proposals. It was decided to retain the subsidies on bread, flour and margarine, that on butter was to be reduced and the one on milk was to go. To finance the 25% social welfare increase, which was kept at that high level, the 15% VAT rate was to be increased to 18%. FitzGerald met Jim Kemmy and Noel Browne, both of whom declared that they would not support the abolition of food subsidies. He did not, because he could not, discuss the budgetary proposals with them. In a *Sunday Independent* interview a few days later, Kemmy made known his opposition to any major increases in VAT. FitzGerald felt that the two left-wing Independents would support the budget because food subsidies were merely being modified rather than abolished and because the huge social welfare increase would more than compensate for these changes and those in VAT rates for the poorer sections of society.

This budget, which levied an additional £330 million in taxes on the people, has been berated for taking the easier option of raising taxes rather than grasping the nettle of cutting public spending, but has been commended for at least seeking to return to 'the principles of good management in the state's finances, after the mad excesses of the Fianna Fáil years'. It has also been condemned as badly constructed and unduly negative, especially since it contained only a passing mention of the 25% hike in social welfare, the highest in the history of the state.[78]

When Bruton completed his presentation to the Dáil, Fergus O'Brien, the government Chief Whip, sought out the Independent deputies, Browne, Kemmy and Loftus and brought them individually to the Taoiseach's office. According to FitzGerald, Loftus said very little but did not convey the impression of strong displeasure with the budget. When he showed Browne and Kemmy that, overall, recipients of social welfare would benefit from the budget, Browne agreed to support the government, but Kemmy criticised its failure to increase capital tax and said that he was opposed to any lessening of the food subsidies. In FitzGerald's opinion, he refused to look at the budget as a whole, but concentrated on particular aspects of it. The Taoiseach consoled himself with the thought that, even if Kemmy voted against it, it would get through with the support of Browne and Loftus.

By the time of the first vote on the budget, FitzGerald was much less certain of Loftus's intentions, so that Kemmy's support became absolutely vital. He has recorded how on his way to the voting lobby, as he passed where Kemmy was sitting, he bent down to urge him to change his mind. Concerning this gesture, he has observed: 'This was perhaps an incautious action, which was inevitably observed and subsequently wildly commented upon.'[79] It certainly was! The following is an illustrative example:

> In the flurry and flux of so many people moving about and leaving their seats, nobody really noticed FitzGerald as he headed across to Kemmy in the no-man's-land between the government and opposition benches. Now he was actually kneeling on the bench in front of the Limerick man, talking earnestly and low to him. It was the posture of a supplicant. Suddenly the packed press gallery noticed it. Word was already out that Kemmy might not back the government. FitzGerald was pleading with him. He was shaking and distraught. Fianna Fáil deputies had also noticed the extraordinary scene. They began jeering and catcalling at FitzGerald. He drew up hurriedly from his kneeling posture, backing away, like a child caught with his hand in the cookie jar. It was an ignominious, embarrassing exposure of

the government's lack of political nous and professionalism.[80]

With both Kemmy and Loftus going into the 'no' lobby, the government lost the vote. It has often been asked if this narrow defeat (by the slenderest of possible margins) could have been avoided. It has been argued that government ministers believed that Kemmy would never vote to restore Haughey to office so that, to that extent, his support was presumed upon. Mary Flaherty had advised, at the first Fine Gael parliamentary party meeting in July 1981, that the Independents be informed about all potentially controversial issues to ensure that the government survived, a suggestion which should have been formalised.[81]

When FitzGerald reached Áras an Uachtaráin, President Hillery was not immediately available to accede to his request for a Dáil dissolution. While the Taoiseach waited, it seems that a number of Fianna Fáil frontbenchers had tried to make contact with the President by phone to urge him to refuse FitzGerald a dissolution and to call on Haughey to form an alternative government. This incident was to rebound on Brian Lenihan, the Fianna Fáil candidate in the 1990 presidential election. When FitzGerald returned to the Dáil, he announced that a general election would take place on 18 February.

There then followed a brief Fine Gael parliamentary party meeting at which FitzGerald and Bruton were given a standing ovation. Buoyed up by this reception, the leader was, in his own words, 'happy and exhilarated' at the subsequent press conference. In reply to a question as to why his government had not continued to exempt children's clothing and footwear from VAT, FitzGerald allowed his sense of humour to get the better of his judgment. He replied that that would enable women with small feet to buy children's shoes and thus evade the tax, while children with big feet would have to buy adults' shoes which carried the tax! Perhaps because of the late hour, the press failed to detect the whimsy in the reply and it was to be used relentlessly against him afterwards.[82]

(vi) General elections, February and November 1982

Fine Gael seemed to be facing an election in the worst of possible circumstances - defending a harsh budget which had brought about the collapse of the government. Although its new general secretary, Finbarr Fitzpatrick from Charleville, Co. Cork, had been appointed, he was not due to take up his duties for several weeks. Now he suddenly faced the onerous task of co-ordinating a general election campaign. The Strategy Committee rallied to the cause once again and the parliamentary party agreed to fight the contest on a vigorous defence of the defeated budget. Jim White of Donegal South-West decided to bow out of public life at this stage and Richie Ryan chose to devote all his time to his European seat.

The Strategy Committee's theme was that Ireland's financial survival was at stake and FitzGerald was to be presented as the leader who put country before party, power or office. This more or less gauged the mood of the electorate correctly, since it had now finally accepted that Ireland was facing a financial crisis.

All parties were equally unprepared for the February 1982 election, which has been seen as a contest 'with a one-dimensional aspect: more like a referendum on economic policy, with budgetary strategy as the specific issue'.[83] FitzGerald's instinctive reaction was to fight the election on an unchanged budget; Haughey accepted it as the main economic issue, but would not put forward a detailed alternative, while rejecting the coalition one out of hand, arguing that only a government in power could present a budget. But each party moved from its initial position. In order to secure a formal electoral alliance between Fine Gael and Labour, it was agreed that VAT on clothing and footwear would not apply to children under ten. This decision has been variously regarded as only 'one minor change'[84] or as marking 'a bodyblow to government credibility'.[85] The move in Fianna Fáil was much more profound: it was decided to accept the coalition budget's current deficit figure, and by agreeing to accept Department of Finance assistance, the party was committed to producing its own detailed alternative.

Fine Gael's selection conventions were quick and smooth

affairs and a team similar to the one in June 1981 was chosen. Constituencies in which there were problems were Louth, Sligo-Leitrim, Dublin South-West and, most of all, Kerry North, which had been the only one in the country not to return a Fine Gael TD in the June election. The Strategy Committee followed the same campaign pattern as in the previous contest; FitzGerald once again carried out a gruelling countrywide tour, and the Capital Branch came up with the necessary finance for a second time in eight months. An opinion poll published on 5 February was encouraging, with FitzGerald 20% ahead of Haughey as choice for Taoiseach and Fianna Fáil only 2% ahead of the coalition.

This poll showed that the electorate broadly accepted Fine Gael's contention that the country was in an economic crisis, so that Fianna Fáil was forced to fight the campaign on grounds of Fine Gael's choosing. When Fianna Fáil produced its own detailed alternative budget, the main feature of which was to bring forward the collection date of various corporate taxes (e.g., those on banks, insurance companies and so on), Bruton warned that it merely put off solving Ireland's economic problems for another year, and claimed that Fianna Fáil was again resorting to 'the use of funny money from the same accountancy stable as produced the 1981 budget'.

The current affairs magazine, *Magill*, published an article, based on a leaked Department of Finance document, which claimed to show that Fianna Fáil had seriously underestimated spending in its budget of January 1981, and which charged that it had deliberately falsified figures to justify a pre-election spending spree which caused a deep crisis in the country's finances. Bruton confirmed that the document was authentic, but was reluctant to charge Fianna Fáil with deliberately cooking the books, although he did say that the party was irresponsible in presenting such unrealistic estimates. Haughey responded by accusing the coalition of 'national sabotage' for allegedly leaking the document, and it has been asserted that Fine Gael did indeed pass it on to Vincent Browne, editor of *Magill*.[86]

It has been maintained that Labour was a liability to Fine

Gael in this election, and that party has been seen as running 'a kind of pantomime campaign', with Michael O'Leary's 'Oh yes, we are!' in coalition being contradicted by Michael D. Higgins's 'Oh no, we're not!'[87]

This time, unlike June 1981, there was a direct television debate between FitzGerald and Haughey, O'Leary accepting a separate interview. An *Irish Independent* journalist thought it was the Fine Gael leader's 'misfortune that his blinding command of statistics, and his incredible memory which enabled him to rattle off figures with impressive accuracy, are of little advantage on television'. Actually, research had shown that FitzGerald's 'wizardry with figures' in the June 1981 contest had been a marked disadvantage. It was generally agreed that Haughey's performance in the debate benefited him more, since his low standing in the polls meant that, in effect, he could move only upwards. Some journalists thought the debate a non-event.[88]

The outcome of the February 1982 election was another hung Dáil, but this time in Fianna Fáil's favour. Fine Gael's share of the vote had risen by almost 1%, but its number of seats declined from 65 to 63. There were three gains for the party to compensate for five losses: Maurice Manning in Dublin North-East, Gemma Hussey in Wicklow and Richard Bruton in Dublin North-Central. In fact, the performance of the Bruton brothers was remarkable. In Meath, John, despite being the architect of a harsh budget which resulted in the fall of the government, headed the poll with a quota and a half. Richard's achievement was even more astonishing in a constituency where Fine Gael, with only 32% of the vote, took two of the four seats, although Fianna Fáil had 51% of the vote. The credit was due to George Birmingham, who had first won a seat in Dublin North-Central only eight months previously. His daring and risky vote-splitting plan achieved its goal. It has been observed that Fine Gael's 'was a remarkable performance in the circumstances, given that the government had preached and even practised austerity during its seven months in office, and had fallen on the first budget in a decade that strove to face reality'.[89]

However, it has been argued that that achievement was

undone in an unseemly scramble for power, that there was little prospect of Fine Gael winning the support of all five socialist deputies (Jim Kemmy, Tony Gregory and three Workers' Party TDs), given the austere fiscal policies it was committed to, and that FitzGerald should not have tried. The Fine Gael leader has explained that a few days after the result, he attended and addressed as Taoiseach the annual conference dinner of the Confederation of Irish Industry. Although the majority of its members were traditional Fianna Fáil supporters, they told him of their unease concerning Haughey and were aghast at the prospect of a government led by Haughey being dependent on the support of the Workers' Party. They urged FitzGerald, in the economic and security interests of the state, to try to form a minority government. He was moved by this spontaneous and overwhelming vote of confidence, and against his better judgment, decided to compete for the marginal votes in the Dáil.[90]

Modifications were made to the budget to appease Labour's Administrative Council and to try to win the support of the socialist deputies. John Kelly wittily dubbed the courting of Tony Gregory by FitzGerald and Haughey as a case of 'a tail wagging two dogs'. The changes the coalition was prepared to implement in its budget made little impact on the Workers' Party or Gregory, and FitzGerald has observed:

> I soon regretted I had ever embarked on the course of seeking such unlikely support at the cost of modifying the budget proposals on which we had fought the election, although the actual performance of the Fianna Fáil government that now came to office proved even more alarming in some respects than anything I had foreseen when deciding to make the abortive effort to keep them out of office.[91]

Only 12 hours before the vote on the new Taoiseach, Labour's Administrative Council took the shock decision to pull out of coalition, although it agreed that FitzGerald's nomination should be supported. In the vote, the Workers' Party supported Haughey, as did Tony Gregory, who read into the Dáil record the remarkable deal he had agreed with Haughey as the price of his backing, a package which would cost the exchequer more than £100 million. Because of FitzGerald's own offer to the Dublin Central deputy, which was not even remotely akin to that of the Fianna Fáil leader, it has been maintained that 'Fine Gael TDs had little moral right to their shock/horror response or to their ridiculing of Haughey'.[92] A view worth recording is, the fact that the appalling problems of Gregory's constituency (poverty, neglect, unemployment, bad housing, a serious drugs problem) needed a deal like this to get any sort of attention was far more reprehensible than the more widespread criticism at the time that such an arrangement debased public life.[93]

Back in opposition, there were bitter recriminations within Labour concerning the absurd situation whereby its Administrative Council could dictate to its public representatives. It has been contended that some of the latter began to consider a more enduring arrangement with Fine Gael and that O'Leary and FitzGerald held talks later in the summer on the possibility of uniting Fine Gael and a number of Labour deputies to form a new social democratic party, but that they made little progress, FitzGerald never treating them too seriously.[94] Fitzgerald himself did not refer to such talks at all in his autobiography.

Shortly after his election as Taoiseach on 9 March, Haughey was toying with an audacious scheme to rid himself of his dependence on Gregory's support. Ireland's EC Commissionership was vacant because Michael O'Kennedy had returned to contest the February election. If a Fine Gael TD, from a constituency in which Fianna Fáil would be likely to win the subsequent by-election, could be persuaded to accept the appointment, this would secure the position of the new government. Ray MacSharry approached his fellow-Sligoman, Ted Nealon, but was flatly rejected. Albert Reynolds made a similar overture to Richard Burke, whom Haughey then met with a formal offer of the position. Burke accepted the job, but saw no reason to consult FitzGerald or the parliamentary party. FitzGerald, who learned of the move indirectly, was not hostile to Burke, but, according to one commentator, wanted his knowledge of the offer kept secret.[95] FitzGerald himself maintained that the request for secrecy came from Burke.[96]

The following day, at the parliamentary party meeting convened for that purpose, in a secret ballot on his leadership, only five members opposed FitzGerald's continuation in the position. The news concerning Burke, which had leaked out in a convoluted way, was brought up at the meeting and resulted in a bitter attack on him by his colleagues. So shaken was Burke by the onslaught that FitzGerald took him out to walk in the Dáil forecourt and tried to dissuade him from returning to Brussels. They returned to the meeting and Burke told his colleagues that he had changed his mind. He then notified Haughey. Fine Gael jubilantly believed that the Fianna Fáil leader's stroke had been stymied, but this was not to be the case. A few days later, on 30 March, Burke changed his mind again, accepted Haughey's offer and pre-empted his expulsion from the parliamentary party by resigning.

During the parliamentary party meeting at the end of March which analysed the election loss and the subsequent negotiations with the Independents, Austin Deasy revealed that he had been one of the five who had voted against retaining FitzGerald as leader. He had been a front-bench spokesperson from 1977 to 1981, but had not been given a ministry in the June coalition. He now gave vent to the anger and hurt he felt at that treatment, especially at not having been informed beforehand or been given any explanation. In fact, he repeated much of his criticism of his leader in a radio interview shortly afterwards, questioning his political judgment and criticising his government as being top-heavy with intellectuals and academics. However, he frankly admitted that FitzGerald was Fine Gael's greatest electoral asset.

When the new Fine Gael front bench was announced a few weeks later, Deasy was restored to it as spokesperson on Foreign Affairs. 'It was a testimony to the generous, open side of FitzGerald; he was no bearer of grudges', it has been remarked.[97] Promoted among others were Gemma Hussey, Paul Connaughton, George Birmingham, Michael Noonan and Nuala Fennell. There were no fewer than 24 on the new front bench, plus a further 18 shadow spokespersons, so that in all 42 out of the 63 TDs were involved.

Rather than dwelling on the somewhat inept loss of power, the party turned its attention to remedial action. George Birmingham, who had achieved the splendid two-seat coup in Dublin North-Central, criticised constituencies where seats were needlessly thrown away. Finbarr Fitzpatrick agreed and on his initiative a Constituency Review Committee was set up to analyse all problem and marginal constituencies. It consisted of Seán O'Leary, Enda Marren, Peter Kelleher and Frank Flannery, together with four TDs: George Birmingham, Michael Noonan, Paul Connaughton and Jim Mitchell. It targeted 20 constituencies and undertook a comprehensive five-month task to solve party shortcomings in them.

Meanwhile, and more immediately, the Dublin West by-election for Burke's vacant seat had to be fought. Fianna Fáil has been seen as having three advantages in this contest from the outset: all the cabinet would be involved in the campaign; it could ask for support to end the instability in the Dáil, and it had a well-known candidate in Eileen Lemass the wife of a former TD.[98] Jim Mitchell was the Fine Gael authority on this constituency. He carried out a poll to see the type of candidate the people wanted, and on the basis of its evidence suggested a long-time acquaintance of his own called Liam Skelly. The two had worked together in the last two elections and Skelly had been Burke's campaign manager in February. FitzGerald and Peter Barry attended the selection convention and Skelly was duly chosen.

John Boland was appointed director of elections and he threw himself enthusiastically into the task. Because of its importance, this contest became a mini-general election. The new tax year, which begins in early April, saw the harsh increases in PRSI (a feature of the coalition budget retained by Fianna Fáil) being implemented, which led in turn to a new trade union campaign for tax reform. The public purse strings were loosened in order to try to win Dublin West: there were some concessions on PRSI; children's allowance increases, due in July, were brought

226

forward to May; schools, sports centres, extra Gárdaí and employment were all promised to the constituency.

Fine Gael veterans like Peter Barry and Patrick Cooney, who had entered the Dáil with Burke in 1969 and felt that he had betrayed the party, led the way in campaigning in the by-election. Jim Mitchell, who had been generous to Burke in the past and felt especially let down by him, worked hardest of all. The strategy was to get Skelly identified with Mitchell so that his support would transfer to the new man. The PRSI protest proved a thorn in Haughey's side and Fine Gael played up his anti-British stance over the Falklands war and over Jim Prior's proposed new Assembly for Northern Ireland.

Haughey's 'stable government' tactic backfired because the people did not want to give him a clear mandate. Polling day was 25 May. After the first count Lemass had 39.7% of the vote, Skelly 39%. Workers' Party Tomás MacGiolla's vote transferred more than two to one to Skelly. It was an incredible result and has been dubbed 'Fine Gael's finest hour' because the party machine outmanoeuvred Fianna Fáil's, long regarded as unmatchable. It was the best possible response to the Burke debacle.[99]

In the Dáil, Fine Gael pursued a policy of pragmatic opposition to Fianna Fáil, although it may have agreed with the general thrust of its financial programme, on the grounds that Haughey was endangering the security of the state. From a very early stage, the party was aware of allegations of interference with the Gárdaí, of which the Minister for Justice, Seán Doherty, was accused. One member of the Fine Gael front bench, John Kelly, did not believe that his party and Fianna Fáil were mutually antagonistic. He was no longer happy with the idea of coalition with Labour and felt strongly that the issue of public sector pay had to be tackled. His party's support of the Labour demand for a National Development Corporation appalled him and in late April he resigned from the front bench, wishing to be free to speak his mind on issues as they arose. From the backbenches, he continued to urge a Fine Gael/Fianna Fáil alliance to deal with the national economic crisis.

The arrest in mid-August of a murder suspect in the apartment of the Attorney General caused Haughey to describe the event as 'grotesque, unprecedented, bizarre and unbelievable', from which Conor Cruise O'Brien coined the acronym GUBU to describe his government. The elements of GUBU have been discerned as follows: (a) in March the 'unnecessarily extravagant' Gregory deal; (b) in April, Haughey's election agent, Pat O'Connor, was charged with double-voting; (c) in May, the loss of Dublin West; (d) in June, allegations of telephone tapping, and (e) in August, the Attorney General, Patrick Connolly, was permitted to leave the country almost immediately after Malcolm MacArthur's arrest, then recalled and asked to resign. So, from September onwards, Fine Gael redoubled its efforts to drive the Haughey regime from office. By the end of that month the party was ready for a general election: the Strategy Committee had prepared a campaign plan, the funding was being collected and the Constituency Review Committee had reported.

In late October, two opinion polls published within a few days of each other showed Fine Gael and Fianna Fáil running neck and neck. Earlier that month, the Charles McCreevy motion of no confidence in Haughey revealed bitter internal divisions in that party. John Bruton had spent the summer working on policy and in mid-October the fruits of his labour were published in a document entitled *Jobs for the Eighties*. It has been described as 'a masterly analysis'[100] of the country's economic problems and contained a series of reforms for dealing with these. It formed the basis of the Fine Gael election manifesto and influenced greatly the programme of the second FitzGerald government.

The document forecast hard, deflationary times ahead. Public sector, civil service and Dáil reform were advocated; public sector pay would have to be controlled; its suggestions for privatisation could hardly have been very welcome to Labour. It has been adjudged 'a formidable, imaginative plan' but with two serious failings: it did not specify what exact facets of public spending and employment would be pruned and it failed to deal with tax reform and tax evasion.[101]

The so-called 'Dowra affair' at the end of September, involving Doherty's brother-in-law, contributed further to suspicions concerning the government. The death of a Fianna Fáil TD and the serious illness of another had left the government in a very vulnerable position. There were further rumours of political interference with the Gárdaí, and FitzGerald and Mitchell were in receipt of more definite information that journalists' telephones were being tapped. At the end of October, Michael O'Leary resigned as Labour leader and left the party, joining Fine Gael five days later. Labour's negative and indecisive stance on coalition was his main reason for his action. The Workers' Party saw this as a chance to exploit Labour confusion, and Tony Gregory felt he could take advantage of O'Leary's move in Dublin Central. The parliamentary party decided that the time was ripe for a no confidence motion in the government. The calculation was correct, because the Workers' Party supported it and the country faced its third general election inside of 18 months.

The Fine Gael election machine was ready for its best campaign ever. There was no disagreement among the contenders on the central issue. Fianna Fáil's *The Way Forward* adopted as its programme for this election, borrowed a favourite slogan of Fine Gael from the February election campaign, and the economic plan it contained adopted that which the coalition had pursued since June 1981. Although this ensured that the economy would not be a major issue between Fianna Fáil and Fine Gael, it rearoused doubts about Fianna Fáil's credibility on economic issues. In what has been termed this 'latest in a series of policy somersaults',[102] Haughey was returning to the austere course he had advocated in January 1980, but which he had failed to pursue.

Fine Gael's programme was based on a summary of its *Jobs for the Eighties*, published in October, which saw unemployment as the main problem. It reiterated its commitment to phasing out the current budget deficit in four years and to continuing the constitutional review initiated as part of FitzGerald's 'constitutional crusade'.

Because of the broad agreement on it, for the first time in

229

the three elections of 1981/82 the economy was not the chief campaign issue and focus for debate. The belief seemed to be more or less shared by all parties that what happened at constituency rather than national level would decide this election. The quality of candidates, their strategic placement in the constituencies, the skilful use of vote management based on organisational ability - these would be the decisive factors. Fine Gael's Constituency Review Committee's directives were followed carefully and selection conventions went smoothly, apart from a few difficulties in Dublin South-West, Roscommon and Cork North-Central.

Nationally, it was an election where themes (credibility, trust, stability) seemed to count for more than issues because of the congruence between the parties. The abortion question, the first to be raised in the campaign, shows this. Fianna Fáil tried to use it to undermine Fine Gael's claim to being the party of credibility. Three days before the election was announced, Fianna Fáil produced its formula for the proposed amendment to the Constitution to protect the life of the unborn foetus, and FitzGerald quickly welcomed the move. Haughey maintained that Fine Gael could not be trusted to go ahead with such a measure because Labour had made it a precondition of coalition that the amendment be dropped. Dick Spring, the new leader of the Labour party, denied this and the Pro-Life Amendment Campaign's (PLAC) acceptance of FitzGerald's assurance that there would be no delay meant that it did not become an issue.

The uneven nature of the first half of the campaign resulted from Fine Gael's tactical decision not to seize the initiative. Its strategy was two-pronged: initially it emphasised how much inter-party agreement there was on the main issues, while for the second part of the campaign it directed its attention to differences in policy approaches. It feared peaking too soon because polls both before and in the middle of the contest showed Fine Gael-Labour well ahead of Fianna Fáil.

Fianna Fáil tried to switch attention onto the issue of Northern Ireland and to attack FitzGerald's credibility, his strongest point. Gerry Collins, the Minister for Foreign Affairs, accused the

Fine Gael leader of permitting himself to be used by the British for their policy purposes in Ireland. Using a London *Times* article of 9 November, he asserted that James Prior, the Northern Ireland Secretary, had used FitzGerald to get the Duke of Norfolk's support for his devolution proposals. FitzGerald replied that the allegation was false and that he had spoken informally with Norfolk to try to get the legislation under which the Northern Ireland Assembly was established amended since it proposed to exclude the SDLP's Seamus Mallon because he was a member of the Irish Senate.

During the second part of the campaign, most of all Fianna Fáil's efforts went into attacking FitzGerald's role in Anglo-Irish relations, alleging that he was allowing the British to use him and was colluding with them, and that both the government and the media in Britain were interfering in the election to ensure Haughey's defeat. 'It was something of a political conspiracy theory, rationalised out of circumstantial rather than factual evidence and relying on minor political figures like the Duke of Norfolk', it has been observed.[103]

Fianna Fáil based its accusations of collusion on remarks Prior was supposed to have made in the United States, to the effect that FitzGerald would soon propose an all-Ireland court and police force. Prior denied making such remarks (which would have implied that he knew beforehand of FitzGerald's intentions), but said that he had referred to newspaper reports which suggested that such proposals would be made by the Fine Gael leader. It had been a precedent of the three elections for the party leaders to deliver only one major speech on Northern Ireland and when FitzGerald made his on 18 November he fulfilled the earlier newspaper speculations. The effect has been perceived as follows: 'In doing so, despite major misgivings inside his own party, he made Fine Gael's security proposals a central campaign issue and one that gave new impetus to a flagging controversy conducted in a histrionic manner by the Fianna Fáil leader.'[104]

There was nothing new about these proposals. They were first raised with the British government during the June 1981-January 1982 coalition, and in his Dimbleby lecture on the BBC on

20 May 1982, FitzGerald publicly advocated them. Indeed, Fianna Fáil had been in favour of an all-Ireland court since the mid-1970s, and only months before the Minister for Agriculture, Brian Lenihan, had supported the principle in the Senate. Now, Haughey abruptly dismissed the idea as no longer Fianna Fáil policy. The Fine Gael proposals for cross-border security included an all-Ireland security council, court and prison system and a new police force separate from both the Gárda Síochána and Royal Ulster Constabulary. Haughey claimed to be terrified by such proposals and in the last days of the campaign an embittered tone entered the contest with relations deteriorating between himself and FitzGerald.

In a final cynical twist to the plot linking FitzGerald and Duke of Norfolk, Haughey insisted that by meeting him, FitzGerald had lunched with 'a trained British spy'; in evidence, Norfolk's career was presented, he having been head of intelligence in the British Ministry of Defence until 1967. The purpose of playing the green card was to raise the morale of traditional Fianna Fáil supporters and its full effect could be seen in the last weekend of the campaign with the distribution of leaflets in some constituencies which asked, 'Do you want the RUC policing our streets?'

There was again a lot of disagreement about a television confrontation, Fine Gael being this time more wary, unlike June 1981 when FitzGerald had issued the challenge. Fianna Fáil's enthusiasm for it on this occasion (the challenger is usually the keenest for such a showdown) was not only a measure of its satisfaction with how Haughey had performed in February, but also a reflection of its lack of confidence about winning the election. *The Irish Independent* thought FitzGerald 'right to be cautious about such a programme because, with all his experience, he is still a hesitant debater on the box, too careful about getting his statistics right to have time for the cut and thrust of instant controversy. Mr Haughey shows more zest for such things'. *The Irish Press* believed that Fine Gael was fighting shy of the debate and that, although FitzGerald had little to gain from facing his rival on television, he would lose a lot of respect if he refused. This time it was generally accepted that FitzGerald emerged victorious, and it has been observed that 'Haughey's failure to repeat some of the accusations against FitzGerald that had marked his recent press conferences aroused much comment'.[105]

The reason for FitzGerald's success was a new willingness on his part to accept the advice of his party strategists to stay away from statistics and accept the limited nature of a television debate of this kind. He was well rehearsed, anticipated many of Haughey's points and was a more effective performer.

Fine Gael employed vote management extensively in this election, including 'Good Morning' leaflet drops in many constituencies seeking support for particular candidates in particular areas. When the ballot boxes were opened on 25 November, the initial tallies seemed to indicate that Fine Gael would draw level with Fianna Fáil. But this extraordinary prospect was not to be realised. However, the result revealed a further outstanding breakthrough for the party. For the third time in 18 months its vote had increased again, to a record 39.22%, higher even than that of Cumann na nGaedheal in 1923 as it embarked on the historic task of establishing the country's first independent government. The number of seats was up by seven on February, from 63 to 70, only five short of Fianna Fáil's total. It has been contended that:

> The key to the party's success was Garret FitzGerald, who in five years had transformed the party at every level, taking it close to becoming the largest single party and to a position where it could challenge Fianna Fáil's monopoly role as the natural party of government.[106]

New Fine Gael TDs after the November 1982 contest were Michael O'Leary, Monica Barnes, Fintan Coogan, Avril Doyle (a member of a family long associated with the party, the Beltons of Dublin), Dick Dowling, Joe Doyle and Brendan McGahon. One outgoing seat, Dublin West, was lost, while eight new ones were gained: Clare, Dún Laoghaire, Dublin Central, Dublin South-Central, Galway West, Kildare, Sligo-Leitrim and Wexford.

(vii) 1982-87 Coalition: (a) preliminaries and beginnings

There is no disputing the point that by agreeing to enter a

coalition, Fine Gael was committed to compromising on its policies.[107] By their very nature, coalitions could not function, or indeed be formed, without this degree of compromise. The location where the Fine Gael and Labour leaders held their discussions, the Good Shepherd Convent on Eglinton Road in Donnybrook, Dublin, was an unusual one, but it was a tranquil setting and, more importantly, it remained unknown to the media. The two leaders did not know each other well; there was a big age gap between them (FitzGerald was 56 and Spring just 32), and on some issues their respective parties had totally opposing policies. Although Fine Gael had won more than four times the number of seats Labour had in the election, the party could not form a government on its own. The only feasible alternative was a coalition with Labour, because no one in the two larger parties apart from John Kelly believed in a grand alliance between them.

The two principals negotiated alone, consulting advisers and other members of their parties, but not involving them directly in the talks. Capital tax, a National Development Corporation (NDC), the budget deficit, and referendums on abortion and divorce were the sticking points. It has been maintained that FitzGerald was personally well disposed to many of Labour's demands but would not have been able to get his party to accept them.[108]

Labour wanted the NDC to have a working capital of £500 million. The accommodation reached on this issue was that £200 million equity capital, to be used over a period of years, would be provided for it. Fine Gael wished to eliminate the budget deficit over four years; Labour was worried about the impact on public services of the withdrawal of so much funding. The compromise was five years. Half the Labour request on capital taxation was conceded. A Dáil and Seanad committee on marriage breakdown was agreed, rather than a referendum on divorce, which Labour wanted, but Fine Gael's determination to honour its commitment regarding an anti-abortion amendment was carried. Competitiveness as the key to job creation by means of increased productivity and incomes restraint was pure Fine Gael dogma, as were Dáil and public service reform and the creation of the post of Ombudsman.

234

After nearly two weeks of intensive discussion, the programme was agreed. It was accepted by a special delegate conference of the Labour Party in Limerick on 12 December, and by the Fine Gael parliamentary party in Dublin on the same day. John Kelly, who was opposed to the principle of coalition with Labour, voted against it, being especially unhappy with the residential property tax, and he made his position public.

Once again Labour had four ministries: Spring, Tánaiste and Environment; Barry Desmond, Health and Social Welfare; Liam Kavanagh, Labour; Frank Cluskey, Trade, Commerce and Tourism. Peter Barry and James Dooge advised FitzGerald about his appointment of Fine Gael ministers. Because EC and Northern Irish affairs were so vital, he wanted someone on whom he could rely totally and chose Peter Barry, who fulfilled the duties of Foreign Affairs splendidly.

He decided not to return John Bruton to the Department of Finance for a number of reasons. Because so many harsh measures would have to be adopted, which inevitably would cause friction with Labour, he felt that Bruton's pugnacious temperament would not be the best for the job. It has been contended that FitzGerald took this decision in Bruton's own interest, because he saw him as a future leadership challenger, but that Bruton took some persuading that this was the case and not that it was a retrospective judgment on the January 1982 budget.[109] Instead Alan Dukes was appointed to Finance, FitzGerald believing that his equanimity and imperturbable manner would cause less problems with Labour. Bruton became Minister for Industry and Energy.

Giving Gemma Hussey Education and Michael Noonan Justice engendered some surprise, because both were relative newcomers to the Dáil. But making Austin Deasy Minister for Agriculture was the biggest surprise of all. This former teacher knew almost nothing about his brief, but FitzGerald chose him because he knew he would prove a resolute and persistent negotiator in EC agricultural forums. Deasy was to have a turbulent interaction with the IFA and proved to be a relentless critic of that organisation's inconsistencies.

Former ministers Patrick Cooney and Paddy O'Toole were reappointed, Cooney to Defence and O'Toole to the Gaeltacht, acquiring Fisheries and Forestry in addition. Jim Mitchell, who had been Minister for Justice in the June 1981 to January 1982 coalition, was now given Communications. John Boland was also switched, from Education to the Public Service. This appointment has been seen as showing FitzGerald's commitment to reform in the bureaucracy.[110]

Tom Fitzpatrick became the new Ceann Comhairle; Seán Barrett the government Chief Whip (he was also Minister for State at the Department of the Taoiseach), and Peter Sutherland Attorney General. Peter Prendergast was appointed government Press Secretary and Joe Jennings head of the Government Information Service.

As an immediate cost-cutting exercise, the government decided to end the practice of providing state cars for its junior members, at a saving to the exchequer of around £2.5 million per year. The next such measure announced - introducing a charge for the school transport scheme - produced a furious response. In vain did Gemma Hussey protest that she was merely introducing a scheme agreed and planned by the previous government, and she was attacked from all sides. It was decided to exclude the children of people who received social welfare from the charge. Fiscal rectitude was to prove unpalatable medicine for most of the general public.

There was no disguising the huge task the new government faced. The official figures published at the beginning of 1983 revealed that the deficit figure targeted by Fianna Fáil for the previous year was underestimated by an incredible almost 50%! Differences within the coalition on how to deal with the problem very quickly became apparent, with Fine Gael's priority of cutting public spending not being shared by Labour. It has been lamented that 'the easier option of increasing taxation, rather than cutting spending, was adopted.'[111] On 7 January, large increases in the excise duties on alcohol, tobacco and petrol amounted to a mini-budget in themselves.

Although it appeared that the budget deficit for the year would be more than £900 million, in a radio interview, Alan Dukes intimated his intention to reduce it to £750 million and the following day Jim Mitchell, at Communications, declared that CIE workers possibly would face a wage cut of 10% that year. From his hospital bed, Dick Spring of Labour disclaimed such aspirations, arguing that no consensus had been reached in government on such matters. A formal government statement shortly afterwards upheld Spring's position, expressed concern about over-deflating the economy and was something of a public admonishment of Dukes. It has been maintained that many Fine Gael backbenchers would have been nearer to the Tánaiste than to the Minister for Finance on this issue.[112] It was a dilemma that was to plague the coalition again and again during its tenure of office.

In contrast to his colleagues, Hussey and Dukes, Michael Noonan had the most auspicious of all possible starts to his ministerial career. On 20 January he made the dramatic announcement that the Haughey administration had unwarrantedly tapped the telephones of journalists Geraldine Kennedy and Bruce Arnold, and that Ray MacSharry had secretly recorded a conversation he had had with a party colleague, Dr Martin O'Donoghue. He also made known that the Gárda Commissioner and Deputy Commissioner would be retiring on 1 February. These startling disclosures were the fruits of a comprehensive, month-long enquiry carried out by Noonan's officials at the Department of Justice. His calm and measured media performance won him widespread plaudits.

(vii) 1982-87 Coalition: (b) tackling the financial mess

A stern critic of the second FitzGerald government's fiscal performance has argued that because of the chaos in Fianna Fáil and the high standing of the coalition following the telephone tapping revelations, the opportunity existed in the February 1983 budget for really significant cuts in public expenditure. Ministers were later to look back with regret, this argument goes, that instead of taking this approach, there were large tax increases, VAT rates were raised substantially and a residential property tax was introduced.[113] Although this latter imposition has generally been regarded as Labour-inspired, FitzGerald has explained that the initiative was his, on the grounds that it seemed ridiculous to him that since 1977 wealthy people in big houses made no payment for local services.[114]

His response to the charge of too little, or virtually no action, outlined above, was the following:

> As a government new to office we had an evident temptation to take the toughest possible budgetary action at the outset, blaming it (with good reason in this instance!) on our predecessors. But in the light of the deeply depressing Department of Finance projections for an undeflated economy, such a course of action carried the risk of precipitating a collapse of economic activity. Might it not be wiser economically, whatever about the politics, to act with more restraint?[115]

The new Taoiseach emulated his predecessor's action of early January 1980 by addressing the country on television on 18 March 1983, on the serious economic crisis it faced, but he has been accused of failing to confront realities in that speech, and the reason he did not do so, it has been maintained, was because there was a fundamental dichotomy in the coalition over the central issue: Fine Gael stood for cutting public spending, Labour for high public expenditure; Labour wanted more capital taxation, Fine Gael, recalling the electoral harm the wealth tax had done to its candidates in 1977, definitely did not. In the disagreement between the two, it was the smaller party which called the shots. So, while Dukes and Mitchell did their best, and there were 'piddling' savings here and there, the big nettle of public service pay was not grasped. Eventually it dawned on Labour that no capital tax was Fine Gael's bottom line, but if it forbade spending cuts and Fine Gael gainsaid tax hikes, 'the result was utter stagnation and inertia'.[116] This is the case for the prosecution, as it were.

The case for the defence was best presented by Garret FitzGerald himself. He acknowledged that there were indeed differences between the parties, which were greatly exacerbated by the financial crisis with which the government was trying to cope. FitzGerald felt that the informal government conferences in the relaxed atmosphere of Barrettstown Castle, Co. Kildare, greatly helped to defuse tension. He expressed resentment at leaks to the press from Labour ministers' aides, which he felt had the purpose of keeping the anti-coalition element in that party happy, and which invariably conveyed the impression that the credit for saving the country from much harsher measures was due to Spring and his party colleagues in government. FitzGerald affirmed that this was

> particularly galling for Fine Gael ministers, whose concern for the preservation of these services and for minimising the impact of spending cuts and tax increases on the less well-off was in fact just as great as that of their Labour Party colleagues.[117]

He referred to his Carlow speech in September 1983 when, with the following year's budget in mind, he expressed the desire for a further narrowing of the budget deficit by means of spending cuts rather than increases in tax, and urged the high-spending semi-state bodies to shape up to the tough economic circumstances in which the country found itself. Spring's public response was that this did not rule out searching for means other than cuts and that the five-year commitment to phasing out the current budget deficit was conditional on protecting and creating employment. 'His point was valid, but it did not help that he felt it necessary to make it in this way at this time' was FitzGerald's rueful comment.[118]

So, while there is no dispute about inter-party tensions in this government, were they so severe as to prevent any sort of constructive action in the economic sphere? Was a really serious start to tackling the budget deficit postponed for another year and the 1984 budget merely a 'neutral' one which was mainly concerned to prevent discord between the coalition partners?[119] A more detached and authoritative contention is that the FitzGerald government did indeed make some headway, as the following statistics show: the consumer price index, which increased by one-fifth in 1981, rose by only one-twentieth in 1985; the balance of payments deficit decreased from a stunning 14.7% of GNP in 1981 to 3.6% in 1985; although the total public foreign debt maintained its quick increase, the rate of the rise in foreign borrowing was brought down in 1984 and 1985. The conclusion was that 'these were not insignificant achievements', but they were negative in that they were simply beginning to compensate for previous inexcusable performances.[120]

The clash between John Bruton and Frank Cluskey over Dublin Gas epitomised, it has been argued, the differing Fine Gael and Labour approaches.[121] This privately owned company had a reputation for inefficiency and poor management. The natural gas from the newly developed Kinsale gas field was the responsibility of An Bord Gáis, a state enterprise, but Dublin Gas was bound to play a crucial role in its distribution in the capital. Cluskey wanted Dublin Gas to be nationalised; Bruton and some of his cabinet colleagues were opposed to such a move on the grounds of the amount of public money that would be involved. His view prevailed and Cluskey resigned from the government. 'I regretted losing a colleague whose courage, social commitment and political skill I had come to appreciate over the years and whom I regarded with affection - tinged at times with frustration at his occasional stubbornness!', FitzGerald has remarked.[122] Ironically, because of persistent management problems at Dublin Gas, the company was taken over by An Bord Gáis some two-and-a-half years later.

FitzGerald has recorded that his administration wished to confine public service pay to a 1% increase in 1985 but that, faced with the danger of a widespread strike, it eventually agreed to a 4.5% arrangement. The 1984 budget had reduced the number of income tax bands from six to five and this rationalisation was continued in 1985 with a further reduction from five to three; the number of VAT bands was also brought down from six to two, the top rate was cut from 35% to 23% and VAT on newspapers from 23% to 10%. The Social Employment Scheme, introduced in late 1984, which provided a year's work for the long-term unemployed, was an immediate success, and has since continued to be so.

Because of various factors, a tough budget was required in 1986 to bring the government's spending back into line with its intended targets. Sizable expenditure cuts were made; taxes were raised again, but on the financial institutions; a deposit interest retention tax was introduced as also was a new tax on life assurance companies. This budget actually afforded £120 million worth of tax relief to PAYE workers and has been described as Dukes's 'most creative' effort yet.[123]

Because of the lack of any economic growth, and the decline in sterling and the US dollar, it was decided to devalue the Irish pound within the European Monetary System (EMS). It was a brave if risky decision. However, the combination of the quick devaluation and the pay restraint of 1987/88 led to a stability which caused a major influx of funds. This, in turn, brought interest rates down and kept them low in the late 1980s and early 1990s.

However, the unexpected and steep downturn in the Irish economy which occurred in 1986 meant that more harsh measures would have to be undertaken in the election year budget of 1987 if the current deficit was to continue to be cut. It was inter-party disagreement over these that caused the collapse of the government.

(vii) 1982-87 Coalition: (c) social issues

In the early 1980s a number of anti-abortion groups came together to form the Pro-Life Amendment Campaign (PLAC) with the aim of having incorporated into the Irish Constitution a provision that would prevent abortion being legalised in Ireland. In late April 1981 FitzGerald promised a delegation from this organisation that Fine Gael in government would hold a referendum to have an amendment to this effect inserted into the Constitution. He did so because of his personal abhorrence of abortion and because he believed that the people of the whole island were deeply opposed to it. But he has recently remarked, with the benefit of hindsight:

> What I failed to appreciate at that time was the extraordinary difficulty of drafting a constitutional amendment that would have the desired effect, given, first, that any such amendment must constitutionally be interpreted by the Supreme Court and, second, the need to make continued provision for the termination of pregnancies in cases where

the life of a mother was at risk.[124]

When he next met PLAC representatives in December 1981, he informed them that the amendment they sought would be incorporated into the general review of the Constitution which he had announced in his radio interview of late September, a move they had little enthusiasm for because they wished their request to be treated separately and speedily. During the February 1982 general election campaign, FitzGerald was again pressed by the PLAC and gave an assurance that during the life of the next Dáil he would do what was necessary to extend constitutional protection to the unborn child. But Fianna Fáil formed the next government and the matter rested until, just two days before it fell from power in early November, it produced its proposed formula for the amendment required by the PLAC. It read: 'The State acknowledges the right to life of the unborn and, with due regard to the equal right to life of the mother, guarantees in its laws to respect and, as far as practicable, by its laws to defend and vindicate that right.'

Fine Gael welcomed this wording without reservation and it has been maintained that political opportunism inspired this decision on its part because, being certain that a general election was imminent, it did not want to risk being accused of being 'soft on abortion' and thereby losing votes.[125] But FitzGerald has argued that he accepted it because, on the face of it, it did not appear sectarian (press reports had referred to consultations with the Protestant Churches in October) and it was positive in nature.[126] He regarded its being produced at that particular time as an election ploy and his decision did at least have the merit of preventing abortion becoming an issue in the November 1982 campaign. During that contest he committed Fine Gael, if it was returned to power, to bringing the amendment before the country by 31 March 1983 and it was duly incorporated into his coalition's 'Programme for Government'.

In January 1983, Peter Sutherland, the Attorney General, presented FitzGerald with his formal legal view that the Fianna Fáil formula was much too ambiguous. FitzGerald was guided by him.

The Labour members of cabinet had already made it clear that they would not support the Fianna Fáil wording and FitzGerald, before presenting Sutherland's reservations to the ministry as a whole, met his Fine Gael cabinet colleagues to discuss their dilemma. They knew that they would be accused by Fianna Fáil of breaking solemn election commitments, of wavering in their anti-abortion attitude, and they were not at all certain of getting an alternative wording through the Dáil. However, they all quickly agreed to accept Sutherland's decision. FitzGerald's retrospective gratitude for their solidarity was clear when he affirmed: 'The fact that, faced with a clear moral issue of this kind, none of my colleagues hesitated about taking a decision bound to arouse deep - and dangerous - controversy was, and remains today, for me a source of great pride.'[127]

Michael Noonan and Sutherland worked hard to find an alternative draft, which Noonan then put to the various churches, the Catholic Church alone rejecting any changes in the Fianna Fáil formula. On 9 February, Noonan introduced the second stage of the Amendment Bill in the Dáil, where he made it known that the government had an open mind on its wording.

Following a Fine Gael parliamentary party meeting of 15 February, at which Sutherland presented his objections to the Fianna Fáil formula, it was officially announced that the government was seeking an alternative wording. The reaction from the pro-amendment side was predictably hostile and a debate which had displayed little enough tolerance and reason up to that point deteriorated significantly. Fine Gael backbenchers were submitted to a stream of letters and personal representations and the more conservative deputies were becoming distinctly uneasy. Often they were accused of being less than wholehearted in their opposition to abortion. Not surprisingly, they became impatient for the government to produce its alternative wording. More and more, Catholic priests were preaching against any change in the original formula. The draft which was presented to the parliamentary party in late March ('Nothing in this Constitution shall be invoked to invalidate any provision of a law on the grounds that it prohibits

243

abortion') proved unacceptable to some members, most notably Oliver J. Flanagan, Alice Glenn, Tom O'Donnell, Liam T. Cosgrave and Michael Joe Cosgrave. The PLAC also rejected it, as did the Catholic Church, but all the other churches endorsed it.

The bitter and divisive debate now intensified and the parliamentary party itself fell victim to the general malaise. Rural deputies were subject to constant and extraordinary pressure from members of the PLAC, especially those who belonged to the Society for the Protection of the Unborn Child (SPUC). At a meeting of the parliamentary party in late April on the day before the final, decisive vote in the Dáil, eight members declared they would not accept the government's draft. (These were Flanagan, O'Donnell, the two Cosgraves, Glenn, Joe Doyle, Godfrey Timmins and Michael Begley.) They agreed to abstain in the vote on the government's wording - which was defeated - and they supported the original Fianna Fáil formula, while the rest of the Fine Gael TDs, except for Barnes and Shatter, who opposed, abstained in that vote. Four Labour deputies also supported the Fianna Fáil draft, which was carried.

The referendum was to be held on 7 September. The summer campaign, in which Fine Gael officially did not take part, was a sorry affair, carried on far more on emotional rather than rational lines. Few would dispute FitzGerald's own opinion that no one came well out of the whole business: the Catholic bishops seemed to bow to a minority, right-wing element of their own flock; Fianna Fáil exploited the occasion to make political capital at the expense of the government and ignored any moral dimension; Labour, too, was deeply divided, despite the sagacity of its leadership's position from the beginning. FitzGerald himself deeply regretted accepting the original referendum proposal, although he felt that nothing he could have done would have changed the minds of a significant minority in both government parties.[128] It has to be conceded that his own reputation was damaged and the prospects for his 'Constitutional Crusade' dented by this unfortunate experience.

It has been contended that of the 36 Fine Gael TDs elected

since June 1981, only a small number could be described as possessing a radical outlook. Belonging to this group were Barnes, Richard Bruton, Coveney, Flaherty, Manning, Owen and Shatter, and at the meeting in Malahide in July 1984, which was held to analyse the direction of the party following the elections to the European Parliament, these deputies urged wide-ranging reforms on such matters as child care, contraception, the court system, illegitimacy, marriage breakdown and joint property rights. But the party has been diagnosed as suffering from schizophrenia as regards social reform, the ailment being particularly evident in February 1985 in relation to the Family Planning Amendment Bill, the purpose of which was to change the existing law, which confined the use of contraceptives to married couples, to make them available to everyone over the age of 18. It has been asserted that ministers Barry and Cooney were apprehensive about the measure and that many in Fine Gael, with the bruising experience of the abortion amendment still fresh in their minds, were anxious for no further confrontations with the Catholic Church.[129] However, the Bill was navigated safely through the Dáil, despite the fact that the three Fine Gael TDs - Flanagan, Glenn and O'Donnell - did vote against it.

The removal of the constitutional ban on divorce had been Fine Gael policy since 1978. During its brief period in office in 1981/82, FitzGerald's attempt to establish an all-party committee on the question came to nothing because of Fianna Fáil opposition. But in July 1983 a Joint Committee on Marital Breakdown did come into existence. It took two years to report, and the fruit of its labours was a majority recommendation in favour of the ending of the constitutional ban and the introduction of some measure of divorce in certain circumstances.

Clearly there were divisions within Fine Gael on this issue. John Kelly contended that a referendum on divorce would be defeated because of the opposition of the Catholic Church, Fianna Fáil and some in Fine Gael. In November 1985, on a RTE current affairs programme, FitzGerald declared himself in favour of holding such a referendum. In early December, Cooney stated in the Dáil that he and a majority of the Fine Gael TDs were opposed to divorce. Almost immediately, his leader repudiated such a view.

Following consultations with the various churches in February, March and April 1986, the government published its proposals: remove the constitutional prohibition; permit the courts to grant divorce; allow remarriage where it could be shown that a previous union had failed for at least five years, where there was little likelihood of a reconciliation, and where provision had been made for the dependent spouse and children. The Bill was designed, in FitzGerald's own words, 'to meet a genuine and widely held concern that in introducing a restricted form of divorce we might be starting on a slippery slope towards "easy divorce"'.[130]

Both Fine Gael and Labour were committed to campaigning to have the referendum carried, although individual members were allowed not to participate on grounds of conscience. The Catholic Church was opposed, while Fianna Fáil initially declared itself to be neutral. Successive opinion polls had shown a majority of the people in favour of divorce, the timing seemed right and the proposal appeared certain to be carried.

But on 12 May at a private Fine Gael meeting in Longford, Cooney, now Minister for Education, firmly condemned the referendum, despite an agreement reached in the parliamentary party that the amendment would not be opposed. It has been maintained that Cooney's stance made it difficult for his fellow Fine Gael TDs, especially in rural areas, to openly support their government's proposal.[131] In the debate on the amendment in the Dáil, Fianna Fáil members rendered ridiculous the supposedly neutral stance of their party, with Dr Michael Woods likening divorce to a Frankenstein stalking the land. In late May, Cooney again proclaimed his opposition at an anti-divorce meeting in Longford and shortly afterwards his party colleagues Paul Connaughton and Patrick Hegarty announced that they would be voting against the proposed amendment. In fact, the majority of Fine Gael TDs did not take part in the campaign.

Two factors have been seen as turning public opinion around in the weeks before the referendum. One was the great pressure both the Catholic hierarchy and priests put on their followers to reject the amendment. The second was the very effective strategy of the anti-divorce lobby in causing deep unease among the public concerning the possible effects of divorce on property rights and social welfare entitlements. On polling day, Fine Gael advertisements appeared in the newspapers consisting of a picture of FitzGerald and a caption urging support for the amendment, but it was all to no avail. The proposal was rejected by a vote of 63.5% to 36.5%.

The outcome has been seen as a catastrophic defeat for the government, but most of all for FitzGerald himself.[132] He has been criticised for rushing the issue and for not putting in place beforehand such pro-marriage and pro-family items as family courts, conciliation services and an older marriage age, which would have deprived anti-amendment campaigners of much of their ammunition. He himself has argued that he wished the 1987 general election to be fought on the fiscal issue only and that he did not want the divorce question acting as a distraction from the crucial need to continue to try to rehabilitate the Irish economy.[133]

There were bitter conservative-liberal clashes at the parliamentary party postmortem, but Peter Barry took the sensible attitude that a political party had to change with the times if it were to survive. Adopting a fighting stance, FitzGerald committed the party to pursuing the course of social reform as long as he was its leader.

(vii) 1982-87 Coalition: (d) Northern Ireland

The security dimension of the Northern Irish situation was a drain on public resources during the term of this administration, as of its predecessors. In December 1983, Don Tidey, the chief executive of the Quinnsworth supermarket group, was kidnapped by the IRA with a view to extorting a large ransom for his release. The attempt was foiled and, after an intensive three-week operation, Tidey was found and released, but at the tragic cost of the lives of a Gárda officer and a soldier. In March 1984, Dominic McGlinchey, leader of a breakaway faction from the IRA, called the Irish National

Liberation Army (INLA), was recaptured by the Gárdaí, having absconded some months before while on bail pending a Supreme Court hearing. He was extradited immediately to Northern Ireland.

However, it will not be for this aspect of its Northern Irish policy that the second FitzGerald government will be remembered, but for the remarkable new ground it broke in Anglo-Irish relations. When it took office, those relations were at one of their lowest ebbs ever, as a result of the Haughey government's reaction to the Falklands conflict. In Northern Ireland itself, since the H-Blocks crisis, Sinn Féin had been making rapid electoral progress at the expense of the SDLP.

FitzGerald saw a new Anglo-Irish arrangement as a means of counteracting this growth in support for the IRA and envisaged, as a preliminary to this, consultations between all the constitutional nationalist and, ideally, Unionist parties on the island. John Hume, leader of the SDLP, informed him that he was going to propose to his forthcoming party conference a coming together of the constitutional nationalist parties in Ireland to work out the nationalist proposals which would be put to Northern Unionists with a view to finding a political solution to the Northern impasse. But FitzGerald wished for a wider framework to such a forum. He wanted it to be open to direct Unionist participation or at least receptive to having the Unionist case presented to it.

Expecting that Haughey at the Fianna Fáil ard-fheis at the end of February 1983 would endorse the narrower SDLP proposal, FitzGerald presented his own broader suggestion to his cabinet on 22 February. He was surprised by the largely negative reaction of his colleagues, with only Barry and Noonan supporting him. The other ministers feared that the Taoiseach's obsession with Northern Ireland might distract him from what they regarded as the extremely urgent domestic situation. Immediately, the persistent FitzGerald, with the help of Chief Whip Seán Barrett, set about persuading his colleagues individually. He stressed that if they did not act quickly on his proposal, Haughey would pre-empt them by publicly accepting Hume's idea. Succeeding in his persuasion, he announced his initiative on 24 February and wrote to the leaders of the other parties to invite their participation. Out of the consultations between the party leaders which followed was born the New Ireland Forum, which held its first meeting in Dublin Castle on 30 May 1983.

The Fine Gael delegation to the Forum consisted of eight members. Along with FitzGerald himself were Peter Barry, Paddy Harte, John Kelly, Enda Kenny, Ivan Yates, David Molony and Maurice Manning.

Their initial addresses to the new body showed the differing emphases of FitzGerald and Haughey. The Fine Gael leader referred to the necessity to examine any structure which would guarantee and give expression to the two identities in Ireland, while Haughey saw the purpose of the Forum as working out the basic nationalist position which would then be presented to an all-party conference established by the Irish and British governments; this would act as a prelude to British disengagement from Ireland.

While the Forum's deliberations continued, an Anglo-Irish summit was held at Chequers in early November 1983. FitzGerald had met Thatcher in the margins of a number of European Council meetings before this and the main drift of Irish policy had been to try to interest her in the possibility of a major initiative in relation to Northern Ireland during her second term of office. During the November meeting, FitzGerald argued the need for such an initiative to deal with the alienation of the nationalist minority in Northern Ireland by presenting them with an alternative focus of loyalty within that statelet. He himself felt after this encounter that he had achieved his main purpose of ensuring that the North would be one of Mrs Thatcher's priorities during her second period in power.[134]

Relations between the Fine Gael and Fianna Fáil leaders during the Forum were good, in contrast to their many bitter clashes since 1979. An occurrence from just before Christmas 1983 illustrates this improved personal relationship. There had been a leak to one of the newspapers and, at a Forum meeting, Spring fiercely attacked Haughey as the source. The Fianna Fáil leader became very upset at this accusation and had to be helped from the room in an emotional state. He afterwards explained that the controversial book *The Boss*, which had just been published, had caused him and his family deep distress. That afternoon, both FitzGerald and Spring realised that they had told the *Sunday Tribune* newspaper that the book would be part of their Christmas reading. FitzGerald thereupon telephoned the editor of the *Sunday Tribune*, Vincent Browne, and asked him not to include *The Boss* in either his or Spring's Christmas reading list.

It was almost a full year before the report of the New Ireland Forum was launched. During that time it received a wide range of submissions. Garret FitzGerald's comment on its historic nature is worth giving in full:

> It had been an unprecedented episode in Irish political history. In the course of 11 months the three main political parties in the Irish state, together with the constitutional nationalist party of Northern Ireland, had met on almost a hundred occasions, including over fifty leaders' meetings, to establish a considerable measure of common ground on the most divisive national issue.[135]

The report offered three possible options: unity, a federal/confederal arrangement or joint authority but, significantly, also declared nationalist Ireland's willingness to discuss other alternatives. Fianna Fáil had wished the unitary state model to be presented as the only way forward and, in his press conference following the report's publication, Haughey announced that 'the only solution is as stated in the report: a unitary state with a new constitution'.

Despite the differing party emphases in the Forum report, it acted as what has been described as 'a major catalyst to the Anglo-Irish process', leading to the Chequers summit of 19 November 1984.[136] The alacrity with which the government took up the report's suggestions with the British, and the complex negotiations which followed have been covered in extensive detail in FitzGerald's autobiography.[137]

It was not what took place at the 19 November Chequers summit itself but what occurred at the press conferences afterwards that attracted most attention and notoriety. The communiqué agreed at the meeting described the exchanges on Northern Ireland as 'extensive and constructive', but the negative nature of much of the discussion convinced the Irish delegation that any agreement the British were likely to reach would be very limited in scope. It was agreed that Thatcher would give a press conference at five o'clock and that FitzGerald would follow with one at the Irish Embassy at six.

FitzGerald was briefed about the Thatcher press conference by an Irish diplomat who had had to leave the British press conference before it ended in order to be in time to speak with FitzGerald before he began his. What the diplomat had to say about Thatcher's remarks was by and large positive and encouraging. But when the Taoiseach began his own session with the press, it very quickly became apparent that Thatcher's constructive attitude for most of her press conference had been rendered irrelevant by the manner in which she had dismissed the three Forum options. He was in an obvious dilemma, not having heard her actual remarks, could not understand why the three models should suddenly have reappeared in controversial circumstances because they had already been formally rejected by the British in July, and he was especially anxious to limit any further possible damage.

The reaction in Ireland to Thatcher's haughty and FitzGerald's apparently incompetent press conference performances was one of outrage. The significant new development pointed to by the communiqué, whereby stress was laid on the need to recognise and respect the nationalist minority's identity and reflect it in the institutions of Northern Ireland, was lost in the furore. In the Dáil debate which followed, a jubilant Fianna Fáil launched scathing attacks on FitzGerald, but he had decided to endure such short-term humiliation in the interests of the more constructive longer-term action of getting the Anglo-Irish negotiations back on the rails.

On 21 November, in his opening address to the Fine Gael parliamentary party, FitzGerald was at pains to stress the real progress that had been made at the Chequers summit. However, he was subjected to widespread criticism for his press conference performance. In response, he acknowledged that Thatcher's remarks had been regarded as 'gratuitously offensive', a phrase that was unfortunately leaked to the press with the impression that this was what he actually thought of Thatcher's comments.

It has been observed that the Irish response of 'outraged indignation' to Thatcher's curt 'out, out, out' dismissal of the three proposed alternatives of the New Ireland Forum was 'natural if immature', but that, fortunately, FitzGerald,

> despite the devastating humiliation, refused to indulge in the vindictive diatribe designed to appeal to the more primitive instincts of the indigenes. His dignity in duress rightly earned him immense credit. His reward would come just over a year later when, after patient and tenacious diplomacy, FitzGerald had the satisfaction of signing with Mrs Thatcher the Hillsborough Agreement of 15 November 1985.[138]

It was certainly to FitzGerald's immense credit that he did not give in to domestic pressure at the time, but that he instead doggedly pursued the Anglo-Irish process to a triumphant conclusion. The steps on the long and tortuous road to Hillsborough are explained best by FitzGerald himself.[139] The Anglo-Irish Agreement, signed there on 15 November 1985, which for the first time gave the Dublin government a say in the internal affairs of Northern Ireland, has been justly described as 'an incredible breakthrough'.[140] It was widely welcomed in Britain and Ireland and Fianna Fáil's abrupt rejection of it revealed that party to be out of touch with Irish public opinion. Fine Gael, it now seemed, was 'the republican party'.

The Agreement offered the hope of the beginnings of a solution, if not a complete answer in itself, and the prospect that an end to the Northern tragedy might at last be coming into sight. If any settlement is ever to be reached, it has to be something along the lines sketched by the Hillsborough Accord. From an Irish point of view, what must ultimately be achieved is agreement between Belfast and Dublin, but consensus between London and Dublin was a necessary forerunner to that because Belfast refused to talk to Dublin as long as it felt it was fully protected by London. It has been remarked that Hillsborough 'could come to be regarded as having launched a historic process of genuine conciliation between Britain and Ireland.'[141] It may well be Garret FitzGerald's greatest contribution to Irish political life and must give him immense satisfaction since it was achieved on a question that was one of his basic reasons for being in politics.

(vii)   1982-87 Coalition: (e) public relations and electoral fortunes

The *Irish Times* political columnist, John Healy, labelled the background strategists and advisers to the FitzGerald government the 'national handlers' at a very early stage in the life of the new administration. It was extraordinary how widely used the term came to be and how it came to signify powerful operators dictating to a bumbling Taoiseach. It was an image that could not have been further from the truth.

The widespread reorganisation which had taken place in Fine Gael after 1977, and the remarkable electoral surges of the party, particularly after 1979, had received extensive media attention. Peter Prendergast was an object of much scrutiny, and the development which occurred was correctly attributed to him and to the team of public relations and media experts assembled by Ted Nealon. Following the general election success of November 1982, the focus was on the members of the Strategy Committee: Flannery, Heneghan, Hussey, Marren, Molloy, Murray, O'Herlihy, O'Leary and Prendergast. It began with a cover story in the current affairs magazine *Magill* in December 1982 entitled 'How the Fine Gael whizz-kids sold us a Taoiseach'.

Bill O'Herlihy and Pat Heneghan had a public relations business, Enda Marren a legal practice, and Frank Flannery was chief executive of the Rehabilitation Institute. These four socialised in a pub off Lower Mount Street in Dublin and have been dubbed the 'Scruffy Murphy set'.[142] From the time that the coalition took office, Fianna Fáil members regularly complained in the Dáil about the sway which advisers and 'faceless men' held behind the scenes. There were accusations of political patronage when any of the former Fine Gael strategists received public appointments and contracts. There were a small number of such made and granted, but the idea of Fianna Fáil making accusations about political favouritism was a sick joke. To take just one example: when Haughey became Taoiseach, there was a staff of 76 in his department which, in less than a year, had swollen to 174. Haughey and Fianna Fáil were obsessed with Prendergast in particular. They rightly identified the enormous contribution of the Strategy Committee to Fine Gael's success and believed that if they could drive a wedge between it and the government, their path back to power would be greatly facilitated.

In December 1982, the government appointed a Communications Strategy Committee, the purpose of which was to advise on how government decisions should be presented and published. John Boland was the chairman, Ruairi Quinn, Minister for Labour, was also a member, as were the Fine Gael and Labour general secretaries. The rest of this body comprised Prendergast, the Government Press Secretary, and his assistant, Labour's Fergus Finlay, Joe Jennings, head of Government Information Services, and Flannery, Molloy and O'Herlihy. It can be seen that where the Committee's advice was sought and followed, the government experienced a public relations triumph, while where it was not, the opposite was the case.

One notorious example was the 19% pay increase to be awarded to TDs, ministers and judges in November 1983. The Committee counselled against paying such a large amount at once, but the government chose to disregard its advice. The result was what has been justifiably called 'one of the coalition's major public relations gaffes'.[143] The public, not surprisingly, did not think very highly of a government preaching pay moderation awarding itself so much, and it look a long time to live down the bad publicity.

Worse still was how the cabinet presented its decision, taken in early August 1984, to reduce the subsidies on butter, milk and bread by half. The money such a cut would realise was needed to service American dollar loans because of the increasing strength of that currency. The Committee was not even referred to; it was left up to civil servants to explain the measure; everyone else had gone on holiday. There were personal extenuating circumstances in FitzGerald's case: his wife Joan was very ill at the time and they were going to France next day for a much-needed holiday. An exhausted cabinet, weary from devising cost-cutting measures and working out a national plan, simply had not anticipated the storm that would break. There was no minister available to the media to explain or defend the decision and Fianna Fáil made hay. Boland and Spring waged a belated media campaign, but the damage had been done.

By contrast, the presentation of the three-year national plan in October 1984 was an outstanding public relations success, thanks to the Communications Strategy Committee. It was responsible for the sober but optimistic title, *Building on Reality*, and for the stylish launch in the ornate ballroom of Iveagh House, Dublin, by FitzGerald and Spring, before an invited audience of all the sectoral interests, and with television cameras present.

Another impressive coup for the Committee was the manner in which the 1985 budget was presented. In contrast to the traditional formula, the Committee decided that the good news should be given first: concessions in income tax, improvements in PAYE and VAT bands, and a 6.5% social welfare increase. The panel of experts assembled by RTE reacted with surprise and approval and the public, too, was convinced, at least for some months!

A new RTE authority and director general were due for appointment in March/April 1985. The leading contenders for the position were Muiris MacConghail, Vincent Finn and John Sorohan. The first-named was clear favourite and was expected to be approved by the Minister for Communications, Jim Mitchell. Frank Flannery, already a member of the authority, was expected to be appointed its new chairman. It was the role of the outgoing authority, appointed by Fianna Fáil in 1980 and of a pronounced pro-Haughey hue, to choose the new director general. Haughey canvassed it for support for Sorohan, determined to frustrate the coalition's MacConghail-Flannery plan. When it appeared that Sorohan would be the authority's choice, Mitchell intervened to postpone the appointment of a new director general until a review of RTE had been carried out. Fianna Fáil accused him of politicising the station and the authority and, while there was real merit in his move, its timing was purely political. The row which ensued saw FitzGerald giving guarantees of no political interference in RTE. It meant neither MacConghail nor Flannery could now be appointed.

Heartened by this success, Fianna Fáil intensified its attack on whom it perceived as the background strategists. Fine Gael backbenchers were angry at all the attention they were getting and their own inability to win FitzGerald's ear. The hostility towards the background team was quite unjustified because their main role had been completed with the November 1982 election success, and it was very unpleasant personally for the men concerned. Then a *Magill* article by Olivia O'Leary in May 1985 presented FitzGerald as the puppet of the 'national handlers'. In some ways the latter now became the architects of their own downfall because in this article they claimed all the credit for the 1982 success. In the words of Enda Marren: 'We brought a no-win, no-hope party to power'. The article provoked a furious reaction within the Fine Gael parliamentary party and organisation and dominated discussion at the ard-fheis which took place in Cork shortly afterwards.

At a parliamentary party meeting in Dublin soon after this, the role of the advisers was attacked by a number of TDs, although FitzGerald accurately defined their function as purely helping with presentation and with no input whatsoever into policy. As a result of the anger expressed, the committees were set aside. FitzGerald realised how the pit had been prepared and how they had tumbled into it. He described the Fianna Fáil concentration on the advisers as one of its cleverest achievements and has been reported as saying, 'They have kept it up since we came into government, and now they have half our own party believing it too'.[144]

The disappearance of the advisers was a deep and soon-felt

loss. The opinion polls had Fianna Fáil way ahead. The government was being assailed from all sides and was roundly trounced in the June local elections. The Communications Strategy Committee was reassembled and advised that FitzGerald open the new Dáil session with a wide-ranging serious of proposals. The greatest hit among these was a house improvement grants scheme. The proposals were well received by the media and meant that the government seized the initiative at the beginning of the new Dáil term.

When the advisers were not involved, the results were plain to see. An example was the special Leinster/Dublin Fine Gael organisation conference held in Kill, Co. Kildare on 7-8 December. It was a flop, being poorly presented and sparsely attended. Not everyone in the parliamentary party welcomed the advisers' demise. Peter Barry regarded them as professional experts who had given unselfishly of their time to help Fine Gael and he felt that they had been very badly treated. He persuaded them to return, but FitzGerald warned them about the media.

Fine Gael had a dismal record in the by-elections during this period. In Donegal South-West in May 1983 its vote declined by 8%, while Fianna Fáil's climbed to 56%, despite the division within the party caused by the tapping and bugging scandals. In November of that year Fianna Fáil easily won the by-election in Dublin Central caused by the death of George Colley, although the constituency organisation was deeply divided between anti- and pro-Hagheyites. The new £50 water charges which had been introduced into Dublin hardly helped Fine Gael's cause. Fianna Fáil also comfortably won the Laois-Offaly by-election in June 1984, with the Fine Gael vote dropping by almost 8% again.

However, its performance in the mid-1984 European elections provided some consolation for the party. In January 1984, four Constituency Review Committees were set up by FitzGerald, based on the European electoral divisions. In Munster, where Fine Gael had run four candidates in the 1979 contest, it was now decided to have only two, one based in Limerick and the other in Cork. The outgoing MEP, Tom O'Donnell, was the automatic choice for Limerick, and the other candidate chosen was Tom Raftery, Professor of Agriculture in University College, Cork. It proved a wise strategy and both men were elected.

In Dublin, Mary Banotti was selected as a candidate because her northside base would balance Richie Ryan's on the southside of the city, and she would also have an appeal for women and young voters. Again, this approach proved successful and both candidates were returned. The party could not improve on its single-seat position in both Connacht-Ulster and Leinster, but its increase from four to six European seats represented a 50% improvement, although its share of the vote declined by 1%. While Fine Gael could be happy with its Euro-elections performance, the detailed constituency review yielded evidence of a decline in the west of the country (perhaps not surprising in view of the party's more liberal direction under FitzGerald) and, more alarmingly, in Dublin, especially in working-class areas.

The local government elections, held in June 1985, were little short of a disaster for Fine Gael. The party won only 30% of the vote, in contrast to Fianna Fáil's 46% and, for the first time in many years, lost its superior position in Dublin to its arch-rival. If such a result were to be repeated in a general election, Fine Gael stood to lose as many as 40 seats, worse even than its performance in 1977.

The opening months of 1986 proved an unrelieved disaster for Fine Gael. A new political party, the Progressive Democrats (PD), was born on 21 December 1985. Although largely ex-Fianna Fáil in personnel, its chairman was Michael McDowell, former chairman of FitzGerald's own Dublin South-East constituency executive. But the policy espoused was pure Fine Gael: public spending cuts, reducing the current budget deficit, tax reform, backing private enterprise, and separating church and state. The new party had an immediate appeal for disenchanted followers of FitzGerald's party. An *Irish Independent* poll of 17 January 1986 showed Fine Gael back at its core 29% support of 1977. The PD already had 19% backing, acquired more or less evenly from the two major parties.

A Fine Gael transfer switch to the PD would be disastrous for Labour and this poll revealed that, while 24% of Fine Gael voters said they would give their second preferences to Labour, 22% promised theirs to the PD. With more Fianna Fáil TDs joining the new party, the possible disintegration of its major rival must have cheered Fine Gael. It has been asserted that many in Fine Gael privately welcomed the emergence of a potentially more compatible coalition partner, and a *Magill* survey of 38 of the party's backbenchers in February showed that a majority of them preferred coalescing with the PD rather than with Labour. This survey also revealed significant Fine Gael backbench discontent with Labour's performance in government.

But an *Irish Times* opinion poll on 10 February contained alarming overtones for Fine Gael. While its own support was as low as 23%, the new, barely two-month-old O'Malley party was at 25%. Fine Gael chairman, Kieran Crotty, acknowledged that every one of the party's seats was now at risk. Even more shocking was the fact, revealed by the poll, that 47% of PD support had been formerly Fine Gael, while only 31% had been formerly Fianna Fáil. The electoral prospects looked bleak for FitzGerald.

(vii) 1982-87 Coalition: (f) last lap and assessment

The final stage of this government was to be a traumatic time for Education Minister Gemma Hussey. Because of the difficulty of keeping down the level of the budget deficit and government borrowing, in the face of a recommended very large increase in teachers' pay, the administration pleaded inability to pay. In the course of a radio interview, Hussey questioned the morality of pressing so substantial a pay claim at a time when the whole community was being forced to cut back. She was fiercely assailed by teachers' representatives for this remark. As well as this, the government had decided, in view of the marked decline in the number of primary-school pupils, to close one of the teacher training colleges, Carysfort in Dublin. Before Hussey had informed the head of Carysfort of this decision, news of it leaked out and she confirmed it when questioned in the Dáil. Another storm broke around her. Barry Desmond, at Health and Social Welfare, had a similar experience when his announcement of a number of hospital closures, provoked an uproar in the Dáil. Both he and Hussey were condemned for failing to consult beforehand with the interests concerned.

When the Fine Gael parliamentary party next met, the cabinet came under fire for blundering on the two most crucial electoral questions - education and health. Those members in whose constituencies the closures were to be made were particularly vociferous. Liam Skelly attacked Gemma Hussey on RTE radio that evening and Maurice Manning caught the mood of TDs well when he referred to the ghost of Ernest Blythe still haunting the party.

It had always been FitzGerald's intention to undertake a cabinet reshuffle in the lifetime of his government because he wished to give leading members of his party the widest possible experience in office and young backbenchers the opportunity to serve for a time before the next election. The reshuffle was later than intended because of the delay in concluding the Anglo-Irish Agreement and he did not turn his mind to it until early 1986. He was also especially anxious that the re-election prospects of some members of his government would not be damaged by their being associated in the public mind with cutbacks which were necessitated by the extremely grave economic situation.

An obvious candidate for transfer was Alan Dukes who, as Minister for Finance, was the most associated in the eyes of the public with the tough budgets that had had to be implemented from 1983 onwards. The measures he introduced in January 1986 have been described as his 'most creative' because of the tax relief offered to PAYE workers for the first time.[145] FitzGerald decided to return John Bruton to Finance, knowing how disappointed he was not to receive that appointment in 1982. The Taoiseach felt that John Boland and Michael Noonan had done excellent jobs in their respective ministries and deserved experience in other major posts. Since Gemma Hussey was under pressure because of the Carysfort and teachers' pay imbroglios, and because her seat was a marginal one, it was FitzGerald's intention to transfer her from Education to a new Department of European Affairs, believing that Peter Barry would have more than enough to occupy him with Northern Ireland and the other duties of Foreign Affairs. He also felt that Barry Desmond, who had undertaken the many unpopular cuts in Health, needed to be moved for his own sake.

FitzGerald's intention to transfer Desmond to Justice, Noonan to Industry and Commerce, Dukes to Education and Boland to Health and Social Welfare has been seen as 'an imaginative redeployment'.[146] Spring agreed with him as to the advisability of moving Desmond, but the latter refused the suggestion outright. Another obstacle was that Dermot Nally, Secretary to the Government, informed FitzGerald that if he was to appoint a Minister for European Affairs, Foreign Affairs would have to be divided in two and a separate Secretary appointed to the new Department. The Desmond crisis was soon leaked to the media, Spring informed the Taoiseach that he had no alternative but to back his deputy leader, and the government appeared in danger of collapsing.

A compromise emerged whereby Desmond was willing to give up the Social Welfare half of his portfolio, having concentrated mainly on Health anyway during his tenure of office. Boland was given Environment, Dukes Justice, Patrick Cooney Education, and Paddy O'Toole Defence, while retaining the Gaeltacht. FitzGerald offered Social Welfare to Hussey, which deeply disappointed her, because she regarded her transfer from Education as a demotion. She had become the victim of Desmond's obduracy. There was dismay among Fine Gael backbenchers when the new team was belatedly announced to the Dáil amid much Fianna Fáil barracking. FitzGerald himself has admitted that this botched reshuffle was damaging to him personally and to his administration.[147]

Worse was to follow. Two Fine Gael junior ministers, Dónal Creed and Michael D'Arcy, were dropped and replaced by Avril Doyle and Enda Kenny. FitzGerald informed the Dáil that he had 'accepted the resignations' of the two demotees mentioned, but on the following Sunday on RTE radio both denied having given him their resignations. FitzGerald has since explained that when he informed them of their demotions, one accepted without complaint, while the other protested and, not wishing to make matters worse for them, he did not specifically ask them to submit their resignations in writing, assuming that they would do so automatically. Since they did not do so and repudiated his Dáil statement, he was forced to dismiss them and had afterwards to apologise to the House for misleading it.

The autumn 1986 Dáil session was a torrid one for the coalition. The exchequer returns published at the end of September showed the likelihood of a significant overrun in borrowing for the year. Interest rates rose and there was much unease in the markets. In order to restore confidence in the government's determination to continue to control the deficit and reduce borrowing, FitzGerald proposed to the cabinet that it should announce that the deficit for 1987 would be held at the level budgeted for in 1986 (7.4% of GNP), that borrowing for 1987 would be less than the 11.8% budgeted for in 1986, and that there would be no increase in the tax burden. This would clearly imply significant spending cuts, at which the Labour ministers demurred, but so serious did FitzGerald consider the situation that he pressed for a majority decision, something he had never previously done, despite the clear party division on the question. This did not augur well for an agreement on the estimates for the 1987 budget.

Both parties' backbenchers began to exert increasing pressure on their respective ministers. Liam Skelly was pressing for government support for the development of a bus station, shopping centre and underground railway complex in the middle of Dublin. Alice Glenn, who failed to secure reselection at the constituency convention in Dublin Central, resigned the party whip. Oliver J. Flanagan, who everyone knew had not long to live, attended the Dáil to vote on the Extradition Bill and his appearance provoked a spontaneous round of applause. He had been in the Dáil for no fewer than 43 years by that stage. The survival of the government depended on the casting vote of the Ceann Comhairle on a number of occasions during the final months of 1986 because its small majority had evaporated due to defections from both the partners.

No agreement could be reached within the cabinet over the estimates for the 1987 budget. The Fine Gael ministers believed that the deficit and borrowing had to be reduced by more than 1% of GNP in order to preserve confidence and they were not prepared to see any further increases in the taxation burden. Their Labour colleagues were not willing to concede the spending cuts that would be required to achieve such a target. An amicable parting of the ways was agreed upon for 20 January 1987.

Despite the enormous obstacles that it faced, the government's achievements were considerable. It had come close to reducing by half the level of borrowing/GNP ratio that Fianna Fáil had bequeathed to it, and it had brought down the ruinously high inflation rate that it had inherited, to less than 5% and falling. It had also managed to more than halve the rate at which public service pay increases had been running in 1982. The arrangement signed at Hillsborough has been described, without exaggeration, as 'probably the most significant achievement in Anglo-Irish relations since 1922'.[148]

The Minister for Communications, Jim Mitchell, went a long way towards dealing with waste and inefficiency in the public transport facilities of CIE, Irish Shipping and B&I. John Boland's achievements in public service reform deserve a special mention. Because of the growing discontent with the performance of the public service, FitzGerald gave him that portfolio in December 1982, the first time the Department had had its own separate minister.

Boland faced a formidable task and needed to be determined and astute to overcome or bypass the opposition he would encounter. He had to move cautiously through the minefield of bureaucratic resistance and operate with stealth in hostile territory. His creation of the Top Level Appointment Committee (TLAC) in January 1984 instituted what has been termed 'a major change in appointment procedures'[149] and succeeded in implementing a recommendation, which the Devlin Report thought could be done immediately, 15 years after it had been proposed! The TLAC aimed to see that promotions were based on merit. Boland was likely to meet such entrenched resistance that he had to resort to the device of getting cabinet acceptance without circulating proposals to the other departments, as was the normal procedure which, it has been maintained, 'would have guaranteed another 15 years delay!'[150] Boland's work has been seen as a brave and potentially revolutionary endeavour to solve the problems that frequently resulted from the appointments of unsuitable people to the top posts because of limited competition. It was also an attempt to deal in advance with the difficulties that inevitably would occur when the many talented young people recruited in the 1970s would find themselves frustrated in their promotion prospects if the latter depended on seniority, as hitherto had been the case.[151]

Even an unrelenting exposer of any Fine Gael shortcomings in the 1977-87 period, paid it this warm tribute:

> In the long term, however, FitzGerald and his party may be remembered for something else, something that a country ought to be able to take for granted but which Ireland seemed in danger of losing in the early eighties. He provided honest government. There were no scandals, no outrageous cases of nepotism or patronage. The administration of justice and the Gárdaí were above reproach. Of course, this is a negative achievement - the prevention or avoidance of abuses - but after the debilitating scandals and sinister machinations of the GUBU days, FitzGerald's government was like a breath of fresh air.[152]

Conclusion

(i) Image: from conservative to liberal/progressive?

Although during the mid-1920s Cumann na nGaedheal enjoyed a strong position in Irish politics, with most of the electorate supporting the Treaty, it did not become the country's leading party. Failure in this regard suggests that mistakes must have been made which militated against a growth in popularity.

It hoped to appeal initially to a broad spectrum of public opinion, but was discernibly a conservative party by the end of its tenure of office. The reduction in the old age pension in 1924 by Ernest Blythe, government non-interference in the economy, and limited action on protective tariffs, all seemed to connote a right-wing party. Examination of Cumann na nGaedheal's electoral support shows that it became closely identified with the better-off sections from the end of the 1920s, and this has led to the view that its reaction to the economic recession in the late 1920s and early 30s was as much responsible for its core support as was its stance on the Treaty.[1]

The party attempted to build up a countrywide organisation by circularising businessmen and requesting them to form local branches, which was all very well while Cumann na nGaedheal was in power, but by the middle of the 1940s it evoked little response. In 1946, a Fine Gael journal maintained that the party advocated chiefly thrift in social welfare expenditure, no state interference and the promotion of private enterprise. During the 1948 general election campaign, John A. Costello declared that Fine Gael 'stood for the ordinary decent people and in particular for the middle class'. The fact that its ard-fheis was held in the middle of the week until 1969 suggests the presumption that not many of the delegates would be from the working class. For these reasons it seems that there was some basis for the impression that Fine Gael appeared to be a conservative party.

But the party never openly proclaimed itself conservative and preferred to be perceived as classless and national, without an ideology. This was how W.T. Cosgrave presented it at the first Cumann na nGaedheal convention. In the late 1940s, Richard Mulcahy defined Fine Gael as 'national party', unlike Clann na Talmhan and Labour which were 'sectional parties'. In 1964, Gerard Sweetman denied that it was either right - or left - wing but a centrist party, and John A. Costello objected in the same year to Fianna Fáil categorising it as a conservative party.

Sometimes, members asserted that Fine Gael was a party of the left. In March 1963, Anthony Barry TD described it as 'slightly left of centre' and a year later James Dillon claimed that he was 'a radical of the centre', adding that they were all socialists at heart but not intellectually, because they knew that socialism did not work. In May 1964, Liam Cosgrave stated that it was well-known that for a party to secure and maintain support, it had to be slightly to the left, adding that this did not mean any doctrinaire socialist adherence. 'Such attempts to claim the mantle of a party of the left must, of course, be seen in the context of an essentially populist political culture which frowns upon the expression of ideological conflict', it has been observed.[2]

However, during the 1960s more sustainable views were put forward for Fine Gael being a party of the left in a more conventional sense. Declan Costello and Garret FitzGerald were prominent figures in this move. In the early 1950s, Costello had called for government intervention in the running of the economy and at the end of the decade he urged the party to move 'openly and firmly to the left', by advocating such policies as economic planning by the state and greater taxation and social welfare payments. Costello was the prime mover behind the *Just Society* proposals of the 1960s.

FitzGerald inherited his mantle, arguing in 1968 that Fine Gael and Labour were left-wing parties and that the future would be theirs. He saw his party as differing from Fianna Fáil because it sought genuine economic planning and systematic public sector activity. Fine Gael was also unlike Labour because of its national rather than sectional nature and because it was free from the reactionary influence of the trade unions, in FitzGerald's eyes.

When FitzGerald became leader, he tried to put his ideas into practice. In July 1983, he described Fine Gael as liberal and progressive and built on a conservative base, but there can be little doubt that during the years of his leadership, the perception of conservatism was greatly diluted.

(ii) Nationalist?

Those who supported the Treaty were accused of betraying the nation during the Dáil debates on that agreement. The charge was repeated with renewed vigour by their opponents when Cumann na nGaedheal accepted the outcome of the Boundary Commission in 1925 and the financial settlement of the following year with Britain. During their final years in office, members of the party determinedly defended Ireland's membership of the Commonwealth and resolutely opposed Fianna Fáil's dismantling of the Treaty in the 1930s. This led to their being depicted as 'West British'.

In October 1932, Seán MacEntee spoke of W.T. Cosgrave as being at one with the well-known traitors of Irish history and announced that, Fianna Fáil would have his name spat upon. The IRA justified its disruption of Cumann na nGaedheal meetings by declaring that there would be no free speech for what it termed 'traitors'. While Cumann na nGaedheal benefited the political system by integrating ex-Unionists into the new state, it possibly damaged its own standing by so doing.

In fact, although Fine Gael resorted to less aggressive rhetoric than Fianna Fáil, its attitude to Irish independence was effectively the same. The second point of its founding manifesto of September 1933 declared that Fine Gael 'maintains the fundamental right of the Irish people to decide for themselves at all times their own constitutional status'. However, its first point stated that it stood for voluntary unification as the most important issue in Irish politics, a tone quite distinct from that used by Fianna Fáil.

During its Blueshirt phase, some elements in Fine Gael were stridently nationalistic, General O'Duffy being most bellicose on the topic. In 1922, he had declared that if Unionists opposed Sinn Féin's plans, they would have to be given the lead, by which he presumably meant that force would be used against them. In August 1934, he saw Britain as strengthening its position in Northern Ireland and proclaimed that if this led to war, he would be involved with the vast majority of the Blueshirts.

Differences between Fine Gael and Fianna Fáil attitudes to the national question became harder to distinguish as time went on. Fine Gael's commitment to Commonwealth membership did much to mark it out from other parties, but then it seemed to play the lead in the withdrawal from that connection. It was as enthusiastic as any of the participants in the Mansion House Committee opposed to partition at the end of the 1940s. Costello proposed a motion in Dáil Éireann in 1948, which was seconded by de Valera and passed unanimously, urging the British to evacuate Northern Ireland and allow unity to come about. This motion further pledged the determination of the Irish people to continue the struggle against 'the unjust and unnatural' division of their country until it was successful.

When British troops were deployed in Northern Ireland in 1969, it was the leader of Fine Gael who stated the deepest reservations. At the May 1971 ard-fheis, it was decided to use 'the Six Counties' rather than Northern Ireland in all motions where the name was used, the former appellation traditionally signifying that one rejected the right of the Northern Irish state to exist. A 1978 survey showed little divergence in attitude among supporters of the three main parties, although it did reveal slightly less sympathy among Fine Gael followers for the IRA and slightly less antagonism among them to partition.

Indications occurred that the bipartisan approach on Northern Ireland had ended after 1977 when Garret FitzGerald became leader of Fine Gael and Charles Haughey of Fianna Fáil. Indeed, even during the years of the shared approach, it was found from interviews with senior politicians in the late 1960s and mid-70s that there were basic differences between Fine Gael/Labour on the one hand and Fianna Fáil on the other. In the 1980s, Fianna Fáil went back to the notion of British withdrawal, while Fine Gael, though by no means exonerating the British, tended to emphasise conciliation between the two traditions on the island as a prelude to any sort of political union.

This caused a renewal of Fianna Fáil's attempts to depict Fine Gael as British puppets (especially in the November 1982 general election), but such an approach paid less political dividends in more recent times. 'While there are still undoubtedly many electors who have inherited a traditional aversion to Fine Gael, dating originally from the early years of the state and based upon its perceived softness on "the national question", Fine Gael seems to have overcome its image as a party of suspect Irishness as far as most voters are concerned', it has been well concluded.[3]

(iii) Clericalism?

For much of its existence Fine Gael has had the reputation of being Ireland's political party most influenced by the clergy. Like most facets of its image, this aspect too can be traced from the 1922-32 period. In 1922, however, those in favour of the Treaty prepared a secular pluralist constitution for the new state and opposed any efforts to give it a more Catholic tone. A certain amount of ex-Unionist support was won by Cumann na nGaedheal, but the party was extremely respectful of the hierarchy. Education was given into Church control and legislation on divorce and censorship was closely in line with Roman Catholic teaching.

Backers of the Treaty in general had been supported by the Church in the 1922-3 period and Cumann na nGaedheal's constituency organisations saw many priests involved. In the 1932 general election the party emphasised its adherence to the Catholic Church and questioned Fianna Fáil's.

Fine Gael followed the hierarchy's stance on the Spanish Civil War, while Fianna Fáil took a neutral stand. Members made no objections to the Catholic tone of de Valera's 1937 Constitution, although this was so different from the 1922 document, which they had consistently and stubbornly defended. In fact, at times they criticised the 1937 Constitution for not being Catholic enough. For example, referring to the private property provision, Patrick McGilligan expressed Fine Gael's desire to have the hierarchy involved in its interpretation.

In 1949, John A. Costello referred to Ireland as 'one of the oldest and most Catholic nations in the world', and two years later, Dr T.F. O'Higgins, defending the government's attitude in the Mother and Child controversy, stated that because the bishops had informed the cabinet that the scheme was contrary to Catholic teaching, 'the government, a Catholic government of a Catholic country, harkened to the hierarchy'.

Seán MacEoin, at the 1955 Fine Gael ard-fheis, got a motion in favour of legalising Sunday opening of public houses withdrawn on the basis that the bishops had opposed it and that finished the matter. 'I, for one, am not prepared to get a stroke of a crozier for any publican', was how he rather picturesquely put it. It has been maintained that from the 1930s to the 1970s it is unlikely that Fine Gael had much attraction for Protestants and liberals.[4]

But changes occurred in this as in other features of the party's appearance in the 1970s and again Garret FitzGerald was to the forefront. When in May 1971 Fianna Fáil, after consulting with the Catholic but not the other Christian authorities, proposed establishing community schools, which would have led to Catholic control over the previously non-denominational vocational schools, FitzGerald opposed the move. 'We are not prepared to see the schools we established handed over to the ecclesiastical authorities of one church', he told *The Irish Times* in May 1971. In 1972, his *Towards a New Ireland* argued that a major barrier to Irish unity was the not unreasonable Protestant fear, given the record of the Republic, that public law would be used to enforce private morality in a united Ireland.

Following his elevation to the leadership, and especially after the 1981 general election had returned a more youthful parliamentary party more in tune with his views, he returned to this question. His 'constitutional crusade' of the autumn of 1981 aimed to achieve a basic reassessment of church-state relations in Ireland. In the Dáil, the following year, he asserted that this was what now marked a major difference between Fianna Fáil and Fine Gael:

Fianna Fáil has been visibly untouched by liberalising forces

270

in Irish society, because its members find no inspiration, as I have done, in social democracy and because the great majority of them find little attraction in pluralism but adhere to the old vision of a single-ethos society. So long as they remain an unreconstructed party in these matters, not open as Fine Gael has been to a new vision of our society, there will remain a fundamental political division between our parties.

Fine Gael certainly shows a more open approach than Fianna Fáil to issues such as divorce (a referendum on the constitutional ban was called for at its 1983 ard-fheis and held three years later), contraception (first discussed at a Fine Gael ard-fheis in 1971) and other such questions. It managed to attract to its ranks women active in the feminist movement in the early 1970s, and the growth in its support in Dublin in the early 1980s seemed to have come from the liberal middle class.

It tends to have more liberal supporters than Fianna Fáil. A MRBI survey in January 1984 found concerning divorce being permitted in certain circumstances, 67% support among Fine Gael followers as opposed to 57% among Fianna Fáil, and on the question of contraceptives being available to all, there was a 36% Fine Gael support and 29% Fianna Fáil.

What occurred in relation to the anti-abortion amendment of September 1983 reflected the position of the two major parties. The form of wording which Fianna Fáil devised and supported was backed by the Catholic bishops and the various pressure groups seeking the amendment, but rejected by all the non-Roman Catholic religious groups. At first Fine Gael accepted the Fianna Fáil formula but then produced a version more acceptable to the Protestant and Jewish faiths. However, in the Dáil vote in April 1983, eight Fine Gael TDs opposed their own party's wording.

The episode showed Fine Gael to be now less prone to clericalism than Fianna Fáil, but also revealed that the party was divided over whether the state's laws should reflect a Roman Catholic ethos, and FitzGerald suffered, because he was the first to promise the Pro-life Amendment Campaign, in April 1981, to hold a referendum on whether a constitutional ban on legalising abortion should be imposed. Although no longer markedly influenced by clergy, Fine Gael is by no means an anti-clerical party.

(iv) 'The party that was always right'!

'Fine Gael is a party which has always preferred to be right than to be popular', it has been asserted.[5] This seems to have been the case in the Cumann na nGaedheal era with the government often bringing in harsh measures just before elections, appearing to see itself as the strict doctor obliged by circumstances to administer unpalatable medicine to an unwilling patient, and the more the latter protested, the more correct the diagnosis proved!

The former Unionist, Bryan Cooper, who supported Cumann na nGaedheal in the Dáil in the 1920s, remarked at one time that Kevin O'Higgins would feel obliged to examine his conscience if he ever became popular. That also seems to have been the mood following the 1977 defeat when Fine Gael appeared to laud itself on having told the truth to the people about the economic conditions and lost rather than have competed with Fianna Fáil in lavish offers to the electorate.

It is a way of thinking which has been well analysed as follows:

> At its best, this can be seen as a noble determination to put the national interest first no matter what the consequences for the party. At its worst, it is inclined to come across as an arrogant belief that Fine Gael knows better than the Irish people what is good for them, so that if the people keep preferring Fianna Fáil, that is a reflection on the poor judgement of the electorate rather than a reason for Fine Gael to change in any way.[6]

The party has had adherents who prefer upright opposition to compromising government. T.F.O'Higgins affirmed in 1944: 'We belong to an organisation with a magnificent record; our future can be moulded on our past. We have a clearcut view and have the confidence born from having been consistently right'. Along with this has gone a tendency to look down on Fianna Fáil's efforts to court popular support and a belief that that party's only motivation is the desire for power which it satisfies by appealing to the people's greed.

So Fine Gael perceives itself as patriotic and selfless and Fianna Fáil as dishonest, patronage-mongers and exploiters of the people's materialistic instincts. If that is the way to win a majority, Fine Gael would prefer to be without it. On the other hand, there are sometimes indications of a reluctant admiration for Fianna Fáil's skill in taking the pulse of the people in contrast to Fine Gael's lack of it. General Richard Mulcahy, in March 1946, distinguished between his party's 'inability to be politically-minded' and Fianna Fáil's 'knack of doing the popular thing, or doing the unpopular thing in the popular way'.

Since 1977, vigorous efforts have been made to alter this attitude. Fine Gael's vote has increased in working-class areas of Dublin with the advent of younger TDs willing to involve themselves fully in community and constituency work. However, the view of the party as socially superior still clings to it and analyses of supporters' backgrounds confirm this.

It has been maintained that Fine Gael ard-fheiseanna sometimes give the impression of a party desirous of doing some good for the disadvantaged rather than a party with roots in that stratum of society.[7] This has sometimes provided a target for critics such as John Healy who commented that the decision to charge for school transport in 1983 was due to the feeling that all the nonsense about educating the masses endangered the chances of the 'best people' getting their offspring into university. While there is little doubt that such suggestions are groundless, Fine Gael has never quite managed to free itself from such a line of attack. The party's attempt to portray itself as classless and all-embracing has been made more difficult as a result.

(v) Resilient

In the August 1923 general election, Cumann na nGaedheal secured just over 39% of the vote. It was a performance that was not to be equalled until almost 60 years later. Electorally, Cumann na nGaedheal never again reached that high-point, and indeed the ten years of its existence witnessed a steady decline at the polls, with the exception of the second general election in 1927. Fine Gael's electoral graph for its first 15 years was consistently downwards, so that the whole period from 1923 to 1948 could be seen as one of persistent decline.

After World War II, Seán Lemass uttered the taunt: 'Fine Gael is finished, why do they not just lie down and die?' But, in fact, Fine Gael proved to be the party that would not lie down and die and this resilience has proven to be one of its most abiding characteristics.

Participation in government from 1948 to 1951 led to a spectacular recovery in Fine Gael's electoral fortunes. By 1954 its vote had increased by a huge 60% on its 1948 performance and, while it declined fairly sharply in 1957, between then and 1973 it rose steadily, so that in the latter year Fine Gael's vote was no less than 75% higher than what it had been in 1948.

That the party survived two extremely long 16-year periods in the opposition wilderness is eloquent testimony to its resilience. Other parties which seemed to promise so much at their inception, such as Clann na Poblachta and Clann na Talmhan, came and went, but Fine Gael endured.

The last two decades have been the most successful in the party's history and it seems to have undergone and absorbed change much more so than its major rival, which perhaps equips it better to face the future.

BIOGRAPHICAL SKETCHES

(a) W.T. Cosgrave

William T. Cosgrave was born in Dublin in 1880, the son of Thomas Cosgrave, TC, PLG, of 174, James's Street, Dublin. To date, four generations of the Cosgrave family have been represented in Irish public life. W.T., together with his brother Philip and his uncle P.J. Cosgrave, attended the first convention of Sinn Féin which was held at the Rotunda, Dublin in 1905. Arthur Griffith, founder of the organisation, was his revered mentor, exemplar and abiding influence. W.T. formed a Sinn Féin branch in Dublin's Usher's Quay ward, and he was elected to the Corporation as a Sinn Féin councillor in 1909. He became Chairman of the Corporation's Finance Committee in 1916, while he continued to be an energetic worker on behalf of Griffith's organisation.

His proposal to Dublin Corporation in July 1911 that the eminent Celtic scholar, Kuno Meyer, be made a freeman of the city was unanimously carried. When, as a result of the anti-German hysteria engendered by the First World War, a motion to expunge the name Meyer from the list of honorary burgesses was passed at a Corporation meeting in March 1915, W.T. Cosgrave protested vehemently. In the course of a long and eloquent letter, he declared that:

> In a country rent almost in twain by different schools of politics, and distracted by sectarian prejudice, the associations which have undertaken the preservation of the native language have attracted all that is best of every shade of political and sectarian thought.[1]

Cosgrave joined the Volunteers on their formation in 1913, and was a lieutenant with 'B' Company, 4th Battalion, which under Vice-Commandant Cathal Brugha undertook to establish a stronghold within the scattered complex of the South Dublin Union on Easter Monday 1916. Brugha had curiously chosen to occupy a timber-built structure, which W.T. persuaded him to abandon in favour of a less assailable, substantial stone-walled building, the Nurses' Home, and which was in a tactically more advantageous position. Cosgrave assisted in giving first-aid treatment to Brugha, who was seriously wounded when the retaliatory offensive took place. W.T. and his brother Philip, who fought with the Marrowbone Lane garrison, were court-martialled on 5 and 6 May respectively and sentenced to death, both sentences later being commuted.

In 1917, after the general release of internees, Sir Philip Vane, who was in charge of the counter-attack on the Union during Easter week, informed W.T. of his having reported that the position held by the 'rebels' in the Nurses' Home was 'impregnable'.

Released in June 1917, he was elected an abstentionist Sinn Féin MP for Kilkenny in a by-election in August 1917. He was arrested and imprisoned again in May 1918 under the so-called 'German Plot' allegations. In the general election of December 1918, he was elected for North Kilkenny. Like the rest of the Sinn Féin members who were released by April 1919, he attended the second session of the first Dáil and was made Minister for Local Government in the new Sinn Féin administration, a post in which his many years experience as a councillor and alderman were to be of great benefit.

His Ministry was one of the most successful of the first Dáil. As a result of the January and June local elections of 1920, Sinn Féin controlled 28 of the 33 county councils and 72 of the 127 town and city corporations. These bodies transferred their allegiance from the British Local Government Board to Cosgrave's Department of Local Government. The success he achieved from 1919 to 1921 was quite astounding given that he and his staff were 'on the run' for most of that period. His able Assistant-Minister, Kevin O'Higgins, was to remain a close ally from this time until his murder in 1927 at the age of 35.

Despite the success of his Department, Cosgrave was under no illusions as to where real power still lay in Ireland and he was realist enough to know that independence would have to be negotiated and compromises would have to be made. He wanted the strongest possible Dáil delegation to go to London and was astounded when de Valera announced to his cabinet colleagues that he would be remaining in Dublin. W.T. Cosgrave was unique in that he made his opposition to de Valera's decision known in the Dáil when, on 14 September 1921, he introduced a motion proposing that de Valera should lead the delegation. Declaring that they were sending a team to London, in a memorable and oft-quoted phrase, he said that he could not see the sense in keeping their ablest player in reserve.[2]

In the immediate aftermath of the signing of the Articles of Agreement in London, he played a crucial role. When de Valera told the members of the cabinet who were not part of the London delegation that the Ministers who had signed the Articles would have to resign, Cosgrave urged that they should at least be given the chance to defend themselves first. His subsequent support for the Articles in the cabinet - he was the only non-signatory in the government to vote for them - meant that acceptance in cabinet was by the narrowest of margins, four votes to three. His speeches during the protracted Dáil debates on the Treaty - incisive, practical, reasonable and, at times, humorous - were among the finest in favour of the settlement.

Indeed, a strong sense of humour was one of the hallmarks of this quiet man. A life-long friend was the gifted and witty, Dublin-born, Dr Oliver St John Gogarty. W.T. had earned a reputation for devoutness, and the impious Gogarty liked to tilt at this aspect of his character during afternoon visits which he and Michael Collins paid to Cosgrave's home, 'Beechpark', Templeogue, near the Dublin foothills. 'I often thought that that pair of rascals took more delight in shocking me than in talking serious business when they came out to tea', Cosgrave told one of Gogarty's biographers.[3]

Cosgrave was a member of both Griffith's Dáil Government and Collins's Provisional Government from January 1922 onwards. After the outbreak of the Civil War, when Collins became Commander-in-Chief of the army in July, Cosgrave took over as Chairman of the Provisional Government, and when Griffith died suddenly in August, he was also installed as Acting-President of the Dáil. During the Civil War he held a number of key ministries as

Richard Mulcahy, the Minister for Defence, and O'Higgins, the Assistant Adjutant-General, were concerned with the successful prosecution of the military campaign. His uncle, P. J. Cosgrave, was murdered during that bitter conflict.

William Cosgrave was a TD for Carlow-Kilkenny from June 1922 until September 1927, when he was also elected for Cork City. He then resigned from his former constituency and represented Cork City until his retirement from politics in 1944.

When the Civil War ended in May 1923, to Cosgrave fell the onerous task of initiating the recovery from six years of ruinous warfare and setting the nascent state on its feet. His place in history ultimately depends on his performance as a state-builder. The Civil War left a legacy of simmering violence which was never far below the surface and all of his decisions were taken in that strained atmosphere. He had to cope with the inevitable, deflating experience which the reality of independence brings, when it is appreciated how complex the social, economic and political problems, once thought to be simply because of foreign rule, actually are. Cosgrave experienced much tougher conditions than any other leader in independent Ireland. Many of his measures were institutional and therefore unexciting, but none the less crucial and have remained ever since as cornerstones in the structure of the state.

He was a most modest and deliberately self-effacing leader. When, in his capacity as head of the Irish government, he first met James Craig, Prime Minister of Northern Ireland, he is reputed to have said: 'I've been pushed into this. I'm not a leader of men'. Dónal O'Sullivan, clerk and historian of the Free State Senate, remarked of Cosgrave that in the midst of colleagues such as O'Higgins, Mulcahy, Hogan and McGilligan, all highly educated men of strong personalities, he was never more than primus inter pares. Subsequent views have tended to be along similar lines, but more recently it has been argued that this image was misleading and needed modification.

It is certainly true that he never aspired to be a charismatic leader. He always stressed that he was the captain of a team and emphasised his consultation with ministers before taking decisions. He perceived his role as that of a chairman. One of his criticisms of de Valera's 1937 Constitution was that it robbed ministers of their independence. Nevertheless, he displayed vigorous leadership actions at times. He inherited his first cabinet when he assumed control in September 1922, but when he formed his Executive Council after the August 1923 election, he demoted Eamon Duggan, a Treaty signatory and Minister for Home Affairs under Griffith, to the rank of Parliamentary Secretary. Likewise, in 1927, James A. Burke, who had been Minister for Local Government and Public Health since 1923, was demoted to Parliamentary Secretary in the Department of Finance.

Of his performance in the 1920s, it has been acutely observed that 'Cosgrave's capacity to survive as leader during this troubled decade is itself a measure of his political acumen and strength within his cabinet'.[4] His leadership survived such crises as the 'army mutiny' and the Boundary Commission disillusion, the resignations of three ministers and no fewer than 11 elected members of his own party. Kevin O 'Higgins has often been seen as the 'strong man' of the first Cumann na nGaedheal government, but this view fails to explain how Cosgrave survived in power despite his second-in-command's death. His achievements on the domestic front from 1923 to 1932 have been well summarised as follows: he selected the first generation of post-independence civil servants, oversaw the establishment of the formal institutions of the state, including a police force which remained unarmed during and after a Civil War, carried through Griffith's policy of reconciling the Southern Unionists, deliberately choosing a chairman style of leadership, but the fact remains that he survived more, and more serious cabinet crises than any of his successors, holding together a group with a great diversity of views in the process.[5]

The cabinet files for his period as Irish leader reveal what has been well described as his 'patient, positive and intransigent commitment to the furtherance of Irish independence'.[6] The Free State's joining the League of Nations, the posting of ambassadors to various countries, the work of the Irish delegations at the

279

different Imperial Conferences, the elimination of the right to appeal to the Privy Council and the securing of the right to use a native Irish seal on official documents are the well-known achievements in this area. But there were other lesser-known but none the less significant developments, such as the Compensation Commission, the ending of the British tradition of appointing judges to honorary positions, the diminution in the role of the Governor-General and indeed the discontinuance of many of the forms of the old elitism (the so-called 'flight from the top hat', which putatively has been a feature of the arrival of Fianna Fáil in office, was in reality occurring in the Cosgrave era).

The first leader of independent Ireland showed himself capable of remarkable magnanimity. A government document from near the end of the Civil War reveals his concern for de Valera's personal safety:

> I do think I must again mark my apprehension as to Mr de Valera's safety. I have no hesitation in pledging my word and that of the government and Oireachtas that every precaution and safeguard in our power will be taken to secure his life and that of his followers, but it must be quite understood that they have stirred up a storm it is not easy to quell. While, therefore, I deem it my duty to refer to this matter, which I mention not as a threat or even as a reason for coming to terms or any other reason whatever, I am prepared to and will do my duty to him and to all his associates.

Possibly during the conduct of the world's countless civil wars had there ever been a comparable expression of concern of one leader for the safety of the other. Indeed, no history of the period should omit mention of this extraordinary and little known act of humanity by W.T.

Before the February 1932 general election the ever-realistic and patriotic Cosgrave, expecting defeat, made representations to the British on behalf of a prospective Fianna Fáil government through the Irish High Commissioner in London. He advised the British against an aggressive or unduly tough policy towards such an administration in Ireland. For a parallel to this exceptionally high-minded gesture there is only Arthur Griffith's surrender in October 1917 of the presidency of the organisation, which he founded and valiantly sustained for 12 years, to Eamon de Valera.

W.T. Cosgrave led Fine Gael in opposition from 1935 until his retirement in 1944. He was not as successful in this role as he had been in government. In his defence it must be pointed out that he took the leadership at a time when the party was divided and weakened by the Blueshirt experience and when World War II broke out, domestic political controversy was perforce dampened. As he extended so much cooperation in the cause of national defence and survival, it was extremely difficult for him to mount an effective opposition to the party in power.

On retirement from public life he was enabled to give an extended expression to his innate love for horses, and being so deeply ingrained with a sense of duty, he consented to giving service, which was long and valuable, as Chairman of the Racing Board.

He died on 16 November 1965. Not for him a plot among illustrious souls of the nation in Glasnevin, since self-effacement had prescribed the unpretentious Goldenbridge Cemetery in Inchicore, Dublin.

The author of a thesis, 'William T. Cosgrave and the Foundation of the Irish Free State 1922-23', Brian A. Reynolds of Illinois State University, has reported on an interview given him on 16 July 1971 by Fianna Fáil's one-time General Secretary, Senator Thomas Mullins. The Senator, who had been an Irregular in 1922, and who had a sentence of death on him commuted by the end of the Civil War is quoted as having said:

> Cosgrave was a tower of strength; if it were not for him the Irish Free State would have cracked under the loss of Griffith and Collins. He was a law and order man who held the State together. Once he firmly believed he was right, during the Civil War, he refused to compromise the integrity of the State. He beat us in the Civil War and brought us to our knees.

281

From an erstwhile enemy, this was a singularly honourable acknowledgement of and testimony to the courage and determination of the country's leader who had declared that 'the rule of democracy' should be maintained no matter what the cost.

W.T. Cosgrave is in many ways Ireland's forgotten prime minister, an intensely private man and an elusive figure. Opinions on him vary from his being a first among equals to his having been a firm leader who knew his own mind. He certainly deserves recognition as the founder of the modern Irish state. A recent appraisal of him argued that he had leadership thrust upon him in dreadful circumstances, which reinforced his natural caution; that he was fundamentally a conservative, and that he had a basic decency, a sense of the duties of one who serves on behalf of the public and a steady judgement in governmental matters. He was most of all a moderate who had to, and reluctantly did accept the fact that for civilised public life to survive, moderates must be prepared to resort to extreme means.[7] It was mainly thanks to William T. Cosgrave that utter anarchy was not loosed upon the Ireland of his time.

(b) Kevin O'Higgins

Kevin O'Higgins was born in Stradbally, Co. Laois, in 1892, and he attended four schools before entering St Patrick's College, Maynooth. On deciding that the priesthood was not his métier, he set about acquiring arts and law degrees. While still a student in University College, Dublin, he joined the Irish Volunteers and was imprisoned in 1918 on grounds of complicity in the 'German Plot'. He was elected MP for his native county in the general election, held at the end of that year, and when the first Dáil cabinet was formed in April 1919, he became Assistant to the Minister for Local Government, William T. Cosgrave. Notwithstanding the awesome constraints militating against it, the clandestine skeleton Department courageously operated by these two men was conspicuously successful. Thus began a close working relationship that was to endure through eight turbulent and eventful years for Ireland.

O'Higgins possessed a streak of political realism similar to that of his senior colleague. He acknowledged that by agreeing to negotiate with the British, Sinn Féin had compromised on its unequivocal demand for a republic. His speech in support of the Treaty, which reflected intense powers of concentration, and a capacity for logic remarkable in a man not yet 30 years of age, was one of the most thorough and lucid treatments of the case for the agreement. His expressed belief that the evolution of the British Commonwealth 'must be towards a condition not merely of individual freedom but also of equality of status' was to prove most prophetic. It has rightly been remarked that he, most of all, played a leading part 'in transforming his instinctive feeling about the Commonwealth into accomplished fact' in the decade after the Treaty.[8] His plea that the lives of people should not be sacrificed to the dictates of doctrine displayed the deep-seated pragmatism of the man: 'The welfare and happiness of the men and women and the little children of this nation must, after all, take precedence of political creeds and theories'.

In Collins's Provisional Government, which was charged with the task of taking over the running of Irish affairs from the Dublin Castle authorities, O'Higgins was appointed Minister for Economic Affairs. At the end of 1922, he captured the precarious nature of the existence of the cabinet of which he was a member in a memorable declaration:

> The Provisional Government was simply eight young men in the City Hall standing amidst the ruins of one administration, with the foundations of another not yet laid, and with wild men screaming through the keyhole.

During the Civil War he accepted his full share of the responsibility for the extremely harsh measures to which the government had to resort, even when these involved the execution by way of reprisal of Rory O'Connor, who, a year before, had been groomsman at his wedding. His own father, a dispensary doctor, while at home with his wife and two daughters, was murdered by a party of Irregulars on Sunday 11 February, 1923, simply because he procreated '... a son who did what he believed to be his duty'.[9]

In the first Cosgrave government he was appointed Vice-President of the Executive Council and Minister for Home Affairs (later Justice). Because the restoration of law and order was of such primary importance, it was understandable that O'Higgins appeared to dominate the political scene. A remarkable man of extraordinary calibre, he has been regarded as 'an unflinching political realist'.[10] He was endowed with great courage, intelligence and self-control, and his work-rate astonished his contemporaries. So great was the impression that he made on people, that he was soon being referred to as 'the Irish Mussolini'. Such an appellation was most misleading because, although he could be authoritarian at times with his colleagues and with the Dáil, he was an unqualified believer in the democratic process.

Violence and lawlessness of kinds continued to be widespread in Ireland after the Civil War. O'Higgins sought and secured far-reaching powers (including the reintroduction of flogging) to counteract this malignancy, and so effective was he that by the end of 1924, return to normality was considered sufficient to permit the freeing of the Civil War internees. His handling of the army crisis in 1924 was incisive, consistent and impartial. In this he succeeded in establishing civilian control of the state's military forces, a principle he eloquently summarised himself when he told the Dáil: 'Those who take the pay and wear the uniform of the state, be they soldiers or police, must be non-political servants of the state'.

It is said that O'Higgins fainted when he learned that the Boundary Commission would not bring an end to the partition of his country. Believing that the price of Irish unity meant recognising the devotion of Unionists to the British Crown, he resurrected Arthur Griffith's idea of a dual monarchy between the two islands. In London in November 1926 as leader of the Irish delegation to the Imperial Conference, he paid an extempore visit to Edward Carson, who suggested he should take up the idea with the Prime Minister of Northern Ireland. O'Higgins then approached Leo Amery, Secretary of State for the Dominions. Having cleared the proposal with his cabinet colleagues in Dublin, O'Higgins again met Amery in early December, and the Dominion Secretary then proceeded to outline proposals to his own cabinet in Westminster.

The British were distinctly unenthusiastic about the idea and Sir James Craig expressed his outright opposition to it. O'Higgins's untimely death in July 1927 meant that nothing more came of his initiative.[11] In the light of more than 20 years instability and the deaths of almost 3,000 people since 1969, it must be strongly regretted that not more attention was paid by the British at the time to one of the most constructive attempts to solve the Irish question for once and for all.

John A. Costello, who attended the 1926 Imperial Conference as part of the Irish team, later declared that O'Higgins was the dominant figure there and that indeed he was outstanding among world statesmen at the various conferences, greatly impressing the British, Canadians and others present.[12]

The 1926 Conference, presided over by the elderly Lord Balfour with, in O'Higgins's words, 'a smile like moonlight on a gravestone', was significant for its declaration that the members of the Commonwealth were free and coequal partners. This was incorporated into law in the 1931 Statute of Westminster, a development to which O'Higgins contributed so much but which he did not live to see.

The extensive abuse of alcohol was a problem in Irish social life, with which O'Higgins was much concerned. Following the recommendations of an impartial commission of inquiry, appointed by him, he promoted the Intoxicating Liquor Act undaunted by strong opposition, especially from the licensed vintners, just before the 1927 election.

On Sunday morning, 10 July 1927, before he left his home in Cross Avenue, Booterstown, Co. Dublin, to walk unaccompanied to nearby Booterstown Avenue Church for 12 o'clock Mass, he kissed his wife, his two little girls and some dolls good-bye. Within minutes of his departure he was intercepted by three gunmen intent on assassination. He had tried to run for cover but six bullets lodged in his body and one in his head, ensured that he was doomed. The first person to find the stricken blood-soaked victim, still conscious, as he lay on the roadside was an old comrade, Eoin MacNeill. After five hours of horrible pain, stoically borne, and during which he repeatedly forgave his murderers, Kevin O'Higgins died in his home, at the early age of 35. Although a book published in the mid-1980s revealed the names of the three killers, his daughter, Mrs Una O'Higgins-O'Malley stated that his family never wanted to know their identities or have them punished.[13]

He has been described as the finest speaker in the Dáil of his time and the few quotations from him, which this brief sketch contains, may help to bear this out. He has also been seen as sharing Collins's physical and moral courage. His view of human nature, especially in its Irish embodiment has been diagnosed as deeply pessimistic:

> Able, energetic, fearless, stern, dedicated to his concept of the common good, he refused to be cowed, even by the murder of his father, from his duty to inculcate a sense of responsibility into the reluctant natives. Few men in Irish public life have cherished so exalted a sense of the mission of the statesman to reform public morality and improve the quality of the civic culture.[14]

According to J.J. Walsh, one of his government colleagues, he 'won much respect, much hatred and little popularity' and, indeed, another of his political contemporaries has asserted that if ever he found himself popular he would examine his conscience! Again, it has been concluded that 'he sought to cram the task of a century or more, forging a national character cleansed from the mark of the serf, into a few years', for which 'he naturally roused fierce resentment among the intended beneficiaries'.[15]

His policy of replacing the armed Royal Irish Constabulary with the unarmed Gárda Síochána was part of his determination to eradicate militarism and to impose a civilian stamp on Irish culture. His bravery seemed boundless and he turned down General Eoin O'Duffy's demands to arm the Gárdaí when two members of the force were murdered, only months before he himself became a victim. He refused to carry arms himself for his own protection or to have armed guards.

What might have been his role, had he lived, is as difficult to assess as it is for Collins. One eminent historian who has described him as the most brilliant and fearless of the politicians who had come to power since the Civil War, had no doubt that the pattern of Irish politics would have been very different had Kevin O'Higgins not been cut off in his prime.[16]

(c) Other Cumann na nGaedheal Ministers

(i) Eoin MacNeill

Eoin MacNeill was born in Glenarm, Co. Antrim, in 1867. He received his schooling at St Malachy's College, Belfast, and afterwards studied at both the Royal University of Ireland and University College, Dublin. He was the inspiration behind and a founder member and first secretary of the Gaelic League, which was set up in 1893. His work on its behalf took him all over the country and he was the editor of its first newspaper, *An Claidheamh Soluis*, until 1903, when he was succeeded in that position by Patrick Pearse. He was appointed Professor of Early and Medieval Irish History at UCD in 1908.

His article in *An Claidheamh Soluis*, entitled 'The North Began,' on 1 November 1913, which commented on the example that the Ulster Volunteer Force set for nationalist Ireland, led to the founding of the Irish Volunteers, with MacNeill himself as the organisation's first president. He was friendly with Sir Roger Casement, who was also brought up in Co. Antrim, and The O'Rahilly, who was treasurer of the Volunteers. Although a supporter of the Home Rule party, MacNeill opposed Redmond's call, in September 1914, for the Volunteers to join the British army.

He was against the idea of using the Volunteers to stage a rising against the British during the First World War. The two circumstances in which he would agree to military action were if the authorities attempted to suppress the organisation or if conscription were to be imposed on Ireland. For this reason the IRB kept its plans for a rising and its intention of using the Volunteers for that purpose secret from him. He tried to call off the Rising at the last moment. His countermanding order in the *Sunday Independent* on Easter Sunday, 1916, was a devastating blow to the plans of Pearse, MacDermott and MacDonagh, but all of them, in the final hours of their lives, took pains to exonerate him from any of the consequences of his action. Similarly, during his own court-martial and always afterwards until his own death, MacNeill upheld the honour and good faith of his former comrades.

He was sentenced to life imprisonment after the Rising but was released in 1917 and was elected to the executive committee of the reorganised Sinn Féin. He was returned for both Derry City and the National University of Ireland (NUI) in the December 1918 general election. He was re-elected for the NUI in the May 1921, June 1922 and August 1923 elections. In the first Dáil government he was appointed Minister for Finance, and then Minister for Industries. He was imprisoned in Mountjoy, along with Arthur Griffith, after 'Bloody Sunday', 21st November 1920.

He supported the Treaty and occupied the unenviable position of Speaker in the Dáil during the bitter debates about that agreement, as a result of which he suffered from insomnia. He became Minister without Portfolio and then Minister for Education in the Provisional Government, occupying that position in the Executive Council as well until 1925. He was also first President of Cumann na nGaedheal.

MacNeill was appointed Free State representative to the Boundary Commission in 1925. Like Griffith and Collins and the other signatories of the Treaty and indeed like all of nationalist Ireland, he expected that there would be large transfers of territory to the 26 counties, but the other two members of the Commission decided on only slight border adjustment. Because, like the other commissioners, he had signed a pledge of confidentiality, MacNeill did not feel at liberty to inform his government of this. His honourable stance was not shared by his Unionist counterpart and when, as a result of a leak, the ultra-Conservative and Unionist newspaper, the *Morning Post*, reported that there would be little change effected by the Boundary Commission, the storm that ensued in Ireland caused MacNeill to resign, not only from the Commission, but from his Ministry as well.

He was defeated in the first 1927 election and retired from

politics. The following year he became the first president of the Irish Manuscripts Commission and was president of the Royal Irish Academy from 1940 until 1943. He died in 1945.

His brother, James, was Free State High Commissioner in London from 1922 until 1928 and was then appointed Governor-General of the Free State until his resignation in 1932. One of Eoin MacNeill's sons, Brian, took the anti-Treaty side in the Civil War and was killed in the fighting in Sligo in 1922. Another son, Hugo, fought on the pro-Treaty side and went on to become a lieutenant-general in the Irish army. Professor Michael Tierney, Professor of Greek at UCD, a Cumann na nGaedheal TD and Senator, and later President of UCD, was Eoin MacNeill's son-in-law.

Eoin MacNeill was a man who possessed a broad range of abilities and accomplishments. His early love of Irish history and literature was to remain a life-long passion with him and he became an eminent scholar in the area of early and medieval Irish history. But he was also a man of action and was deeply involved in the Gaelic League, the Irish Volunteers, the first Dáil and the first independent Irish government. His multifaceted talents have been well explored and revealed by Professors F.X. Martin and F.J. Byrne in their edition of a collection of essays on MacNeill called *The Scholar Revolutionary* (1973), and by Professor Michael Tierney's biography, *Eoin MacNeill: Scholar and Man of Action* (1980).

(ii) Earnán de Blaghd (Ernest Blythe)

Earnán de Blaghd was born in Lisburn, Co. Antrim, in 1889. He came from a Protestant and staunchly Orange background and was a most unlikely convert to Irish nationalism. His nationalism belonged to the broad Sinn Féin tradition as moulded by Arthur Griffith in the early 20th century. He believed absolutely in the need to restore the Irish language to general and widespread use if independence were to have any real meaning. He has left three volumes of autobiography, all in Irish: *Trasna na Bóinne* (1957), *Slán le hUltaibh* (1970) and *Gaeil Á Múscailt* (1973).

Instead of entering the British civil service, he took a job in the Department of Agriculture and Technical Instruction in Dublin in 1905. He became very friendly with Seán O'Casey, under whose influence he became a member of the IRB, and he also joined the Gaelic League. He contributed to W.P. Ryan's newspaper, *The Peasant*, a widely-read supporter of the Irish-Ireland movement. De Blaghd's main interest, career-wise, was journalism and in 1909 he got a job with the *North Down Herald*, a Unionist weekly published in Bangor. He became an organiser for the IRB in Ulster.

As Unionist resistance to the 1912 Home Rule Bill hardened in that province, de Blaghd kept his conversion to the cause of Irish independence secret from his own people. He went to live in Corca Dhuibhne, the west-Kerry Gaeltacht, to acquire fluency in Irish in 1913. He made a living by working as a farmhand for the family of Thomas Ashe. Among those with whom he became friendly in west Kerry were Desmond FitzGerald and The O'Rahilly. He became an organiser for the Irish Volunteers and was ordered to leave the country by government edict in July 1915. Arrested a month before the Rising for not complying, he was imprisoned in Brixton, where one of his fellow-inmates was Sir Roger Casement.

After 1916 he continued to organise the Volunteers and was arrested and confined in Cork and then in Belfast. He was elected to the Sinn Féin executive in 1918 and to the Dáil, the same year, for North Monaghan, which he continued to represent until 1933. He was appointed Director of Trade and Industry in the first Dáil in April 1919, supported the Treaty and became Minister for Local Government 1922-23, Minister for Finance 1923-32, Minister for Posts and Telegraphs 1927-32, and Vice-President of the Executive Council 1927-32, following the murder of Kevin O'Higgins.

A conservative in economic matters, he is still remembered in Irish political folklore for reducing the old-age pension in his 1924 budget. His work for the Irish language, as Minister for Finance from 1923 until 1932 has been seen as his 'greatest single monument'.[17] He did not agree that the state's revival effort should have no element of compulsion - he insisted that strong state support was crucial for its success, and he was to remain blunt and uncompromising in this attitude. When his old friends in Fine Gael openly ended their support for compulsory Irish in 1966, he dissociated himself from the move in articles in the *Irish Independent* newspaper.

His achievements in the cause of the Irish language were many: he made possible Galway's Irish-language theatre, Taibhdhearc; he initiated An Gúm, the Irish language publishing company; he gave special assistance to all-Irish schools; he established state-aided Gaeltacht courses, and introduced housing grants and other measures to benefit the Gaeltacht. Whatever modest success there has been in language revival in this country is owed to him.

He spent from 1934 to 1936 in the Senate and then retired completely from politics. He was Director of the Abbey Theatre from 1941 until the 1970s. Although there has been some controversy about his performance in this role, he guided the Abbey through the difficult years after the disastrous fire of 1951, and was concerned with developing a bilingual acting tradition in the process.

De Valera appointed him president of Comhdháil Náisúnta na Gaeilge in 1943. In this position, he undertook a scheme to get state support for Irish language magazines and newspapers. Comhdháil produced a blueprint for a Gaeltacht Development Board in 1952, leading eventually to Roinn na Gaeltachta in 1956 and Gaeltarra Éireann in 1957. De Blaghd edited the *Leader* and wrote for *Inniu* (founded in 1943) and for the *Sunday Independent* (in Irish).

His Ulster Protestant background gave him a unique insight into the whole problem of partition. In 1955 he published *Briseadh na Teorann* (*The Smashing of the Border*). He accepted that partition was there at the wishes of Northern Protestants and not at the behest of the British government. He argued that the only way to end it was to persuade a few hundred thousand Protestants to vote for its abolition and he urged friendship and contacts with Unionism. He linked the failure of the majority tradition to assimilate the Ulster planter tradition, as it had assimilated other foreign traditions, to the decline in Irish culture and language and

291

especially to the failure of 19th-century nationalist leaders to appreciate its importance. His views on partition proved unpopular at the time he expressed them but have since become commonplace in Irish nationalist attitudes, especially since the late 1960s.[18]

Earnán de Blaghd was never afraid of courting unpopularity. His decision to go against his ethnic progenitors is perhaps the most conclusive evidence of this facet of his character, but instances can be found throughout his entire life. As early as 1922 he was advocating a policy of consistent conciliation with Ulster Unionists, something that was not seriously considered by nationalist Ireland until almost 50 years later and which even today does not find widespread acceptance among Irish nationalists. His austere financial policies in the 1920s won him little popularity with the Irish people in general but he remained an unwavering disciple of public fiscal rectitude. He was almost unique in his party for his opposition to the Irish PR electoral system, believing that it militated against the formation of stable governments. Many of his decisions as manager of the Abbey Theatre were strongly criticised by the literary establishment of his time. When Fine Gael changed its attitude towards compulsory Irish, de Blaghd did not hesitate to express openly his disagreement with his old colleagues. Although one may disagree with many of his views, one cannot but admire the tenacity with which he defended and expressed them.

There was a granite quality in the man which may be seen from the following anecdote. On a visit to Northern Ireland, he commended the government there for its control of the B-Specials, saying that otherwise they would wreak havoc in nationalist areas. Returning to Dublin, he emerged from the railway station to be greeted with the abusive epithets 'Presbyterian bastard!' from a non-admirer. 'Wrong on both counts!' was de Blaghd's imperturbable reply!

(iii) Desmond FitzGerald

Desmond FitzGerald was born in London in 1888 to parents who had emigrated from Cork and Kerry. A lover and writer of poetry, he joined the Imagist group of poets in London, which

292

included Ezra Pound, who became a life-long friend. He enrolled in the Gaelic League in London where he met his future wife, Mabel McConnell, who came from a Belfast Unionist family. Her father, John McConnell, was managing director of Dunville Distilleries, which also included among its directors James Craig, father of the future prime minister of Northern Ireland. She worked at one time as secretary to George Bernard Shaw with whom she afterwards maintained a regular correspondence. Desmond and Mabel married in 1911 and went to live in Brittany in France.

They returned to Kerry in 1913 where they met The O'Rahilly and Earnán de Blaghd, who introduced FitzGerald to the Volunteers and the IRB. On a visit to Belfast in 1913, he met James Connolly and Sir Roger Casement. He was expelled from Kerry in 1915 and went to live in Bray, Co. Wicklow. The reason for his expulsion seems to have been related to his wife's decision to keep hens in order to meet the shortages caused by the First World War. She read in a Department of Agriculture leaflet that egg production would improve if the hens were fed late at night, and her wavering lantern, seen by the RIC barracks across the bay, convinced the police that FitzGerald was making contact with German U-boats.[19]

He was imprisoned for six months in 1915-16 for anti-recruitment activities but was set free in time for the Easter Rising. He joined in the attempt to have it called off but then took his place in the General Post Office garrison, as adjutant to The O'Rahilly, who also disapproved of the insurrection and was to perish during it. FitzGerald managed to evade arrest at the GPO, but he was arrested a few days later and sentenced to life imprisonment in Dartmoor. From there he was transported to Maidstone by train, chained to de Valera. He was released in mid-1917 but was again jailed in Gloucester in 1918 under the 'German Plot' allegations.

He was elected for the traditionally Unionist constituency of Pembroke in Dublin in 1918. In June 1919 he was appointed Dáil Director of Publicity and was responsible for the publication of the *Irish Bulletin*, an underground daily newspaper established to combat British propaganda and to state the Irish case to the world.

He insisted that everything it contained be factual and verifiable and before long journalists found it to be so reliable that they were making use of its material throughout the world. It was an extraordinary achievement that it was compiled and published in such difficult circumstances as the British authorities, realising the amount of damage it was causing them, sought relentlessly to suppress it. It had a major influence in attracting international support for Irish independence, a factor which greatly contributed to the eventual British agreement to a truce and negotiations.

FitzGerald was arrested and imprisoned again in 1921. He went to London as part of the Treaty delegation from October to December of that year and took the pro-Treaty side in the split that followed. He became ex-cabinet Minister for Publicity in January 1922 and Minister for External Affairs in August 1922, retaining that portfolio in the Executive Council from 1923 to 1927.

He oversaw Ireland's joining the League of Nations from April to September 1923, attended the Imperial Conference in October of that year, registered the Treaty as an international agreement at the League of Nations in 1924, and established an Irish legation in Washington also in that year, the first diplomatic mission abroad to be established by a Commonwealth member. He was part of the Irish team led by Kevin O'Higgins at the 1926 Imperial Conference, which fought successfully for the principle of equality of status among the dominions.

FitzGerald was switched to Defence following the June 1927 election, where he remained until 1932. Patrick McGilligan became Minister for External Affairs in succession to the murdered Kevin O'Higgins, and at the Imperial Conference in 1930, he was well assisted by the experienced Desmond FitzGerald, who by that time was a veteran of the 1923 and 1926 dominion gatherings. The Irish and Canadian campaign to have the sovereign independence of the Commonwealth countries formally recognised was brought to a successful conclusion at this conference and led to the Statute of Westminster the following year.

Desmond FitzGerald represented Dublin County from 1923 to 1932; he was elected for Carlow-Kilkenny in the 1932 and 1933 elections, but was defeated in 1937. He contested Dublin County again in 1944 but was unsuccessful, Liam Cosgrave being elected there for the first time that year. He was a member of the Senate from 1937 to 1943. He died in April 1947. His son, Garret, who was later to lead Fine Gael, has written about his father:

> All of us had loved, admired and respected our father, and had found enormous stimulation in his company - drawing in different degrees according to our individual interests on his literary, philosophical and political talents, but all enjoying equally his company, his irrepressible sense of humour and his extraordinary fund of anecdotes. To live up to his standards of integrity, emulate fully his patriotism and sense of public service, or replicate the combination of physical and moral courage for which he was so highly regarded by many of his contemporaries, would be impossible; but at least these qualities gave us something to which to aspire.[20]

(iv) Patrick Hogan

Patrick Hogan was born in June 1891 at Kilbrickle, Loughrea, Co. Galway. He received his schooling at St Joseph's College, Ballinasloe, and afterwards attended University College, Dublin. He qualified as a solicitor in 1915. He became a member of the Irish Volunteers and was interned in Ballykinlar during the Anglo-Irish war. He was returned to the Dáil, unopposed, for Galway in the May 1921 general election, along with Padraig Ó Máille, George Nicholls, Liam Mellows, Dr Brian Cusack and Professor J. Whelehan.

He took the pro-Treaty side and his contributions during the Dáil debates on the agreement were among the most cogent. He expressed his complete faith in the arguments and abilities of Griffith and Collins, its two chief negotiators and signatories, contended that it was the best deal that could have been reached in the circumstances, that it secured the substance of freedom and that forms of government did not matter, and that the oath it contained was unobjectionable, because the allegiance was to the Constitution of the Irish Free State.

On 4 and 5 January 1922 he took part in an informal meeting of a group of TDs from both sides which attempted to reach a compromise agreement on the Treaty before the Dáil vote on it took place. A consensus was achieved and put to the leaders of each side but came to nothing when turned down by de Valera and could not avert the fatal divide which was to follow. Hogan was appointed to both Griffith's Dáil Cabinet and Collins's Provisional Government in January 1922, his innate talents finding both an early recognition and outlet.

He became Cumann na nGaedheal Minister for Agriculture in 1923 and occupied that position until the party lost office in 1932. He has been described as 'an outstanding Minister for Agriculture' and 'a man of exceptional drive and ability'.[21] He himself defined what he was doing, with characteristic outspokenness, as 'helping the farmer who helped himself and letting the rest go to the devil'.

There is no doubt that his attitude greatly influenced the government's general economic policy in the 1920s, as it depended greatly on agriculture as the means to economic growth. Hogan himself expressed the belief in early 1924 that 'national development in Ireland for our generation at least, is practically synonymous with agricultural development.' He was influenced by George O'Brien, the gifted young Professor of Economics at University College, Dublin, who wrote a magnificent obituary of Hogan when he was tragically killed in a car crash in 1936.[22]

In many ways, Hogan was the unqualified success of the Cumann na nGaedheal period in government. He was not wedded to any one particular political or economic dogma. His 1923 Land Act provided for the completion of land purchase. Determined to improve breeding and marketing standards in Irish agriculture, he passed a series of Dairy and Livestock Breeding Acts which met with far from widespread popularity. Of these it has recently been written that:

> The reputation of Irish agricultural produce had suffered in
> the First World War, when farmers took advantage of the

boom conditions on the British market to deluge consumers with substandard produce. Hogan's insistence on improved standards of cleanliness, packaging, marking and honest description of the quality of produce caused culture shock to many farmers weaned on more relaxed ethical standards.[23]

He was probably the best platform speaker of his party and was also a noted wit. When a heckler at a public meeting which he was addressing shouted at him 'How many toes has a pig?', his lively reply was, 'Take off your shoes and count!' On another occasion, when he was speaking in public in favour of wheat-growing, a heckler shouted : 'What about hay?' 'I'm talking about human food now. I'll come to your variety later', was Hogan's rejoinder.

Patrick Hogan took part, along with W.T. Cosgrave, in the first meeting with the leaders of the Centre Party, James Dillon and Frank MacDermot, in June 1933, with a view to uniting Cumann na nGaedheal and their party. He had little confidence in Eoin O'Duffy's leadership of Fine Gael and chose to retire to the backbenches in September 1933. From then until his untimely death in 1936, he became increasingly detached from public affairs and concentrated on building up his solicitor's practice in Co. Galway.

In November 1934, he attacked O'Duffy for his views on Northern Ireland and for having praised Hitler in a recent speech. He expressed disgust at O'Duffy's having described Hitler as the greatest man Germany ever had. 'Hitler stood for the crude militaristic dictatorship of Germany and O'Duffy stood for the same thing according to that statement', he said.[24]

Patrick Hogan's tragically premature death in 1936 was an incalculable loss to Fine Gael. Indeed it was the pro-Treaty party's great misfortune to have lost so many of its most talented members in the 1920s and 1930s. Patrick Hogan was arguably Ireland's most successful Minister for Agriculture, and James Dillon, who occupied that portfolio in the two inter-party governments in the 1940s and 1950s, consciously modelled himself on his Cumann na nGaedheal predecessor and frequently quoted many of his precepts. His daughter, Brigid Hogan-O'Higgins, who was married to Michael

O'Higgins, brother of Tom and son of Dr T. F., was a TD for East Galway from 1957 to 1969 and for Clare-Galway from 1969 to 1977.

(v) Fionán Lynch

Fionán Lynch was born in Cahirciveen, Co. Kerry, in 1889. He attended both Rockwell College and Blackrock College before becoming a student in University College, Dublin. He was a teacher for a while and later became a barrister.

Lynch participated in the 1916 Rising, fighting with the Dublin Brigade of the Irish Volunteers, and was afterwards imprisoned. He went on hunger-strike twice in 1917, in May and November, following which he was released. He was in jail again in 1918-19 under the 'German Plot' allegations.

He was elected a Sinn Féin TD for Co. Kerry in December 1918 and again in May 1921. He represented Kerry as a Cumann na nGaedheal and then a Fine Gael TD from 1922 to 1937 and sat for Kerry South from 1938 to 1944. He resigned from political life in October 1944.

Lynch served as Assistant-Secretary to the Treaty delegation in London from October to December 1921, and on taking the pro-Treaty side, became Minister for Education in the Provisional Government in 1922. A brigadier in the Free State army during the Civil War, he commanded a unit of the Dublin Guards in Co. Kerry. His appointment as Minister for Fisheries in the first Cosgrave government in September 1923 lasted until 1927 and he was Minister for Lands and Fisheries until March 1932.

During the Blueshirt era, Lynch spoke at public meetings with General O'Duffy and they were attacked by a crowd in Tralee in October 1933. He was elected Leas Ceann Comhairle of the Dáil in 1938. Fionán Lynch became a judge of the High Court following his retirement from active politics in 1944.

(vi) John Marcus O'Sullivan

John Marcus O'Sullivan, a native of Killarney, Co. Kerry, was born in 1881. Following schooling at St Brendan's College,

Killarney, and Clongowes Wood College, he entered University College, Dublin, and he did post-graduate courses in the universities of Bonn and Heidelberg. The latter institution awarded him the degree of D.Phil in 1906. He was appointed to the chair of Modern History (that is British and European history) in University College, Dublin.

John Marcus O'Sullivan was a Cumann na nGaedheal and then Fine Gael TD for Co. Kerry from 1923 to 1937, and sat in the Dáil for Kerry North from 1937 until 1943. He lost his seat in the 1943 general election, and his constituency, North Kerry, was to be a Fine Gael black spot for many years to come.

He was Parliamentary Secretary to the Minister for Finance 1924-25, and succeeded Eoin MacNeill as Minister for Education in November 1925 when MacNeill resigned from the cabinet as a result of his involvement in the Boundary Commission. O'Sullivan retained that portfolio until Cumann na nGaedheal fell from power in 1932. He introduced the Vocational Education Act in 1930, which established a general network of vocational schools around the country and gave poorer children an opportunity to acquire a secondary education. He was the Irish delegate to the League of Nations in 1924 and from 1928 to 1930.

O'Sullivan continued to be Fine Gael shadow spokesman on Education until he left politics. Although he had responsibility for the government attempt to revive the Irish language through the primary schools in the 1920s and although he supported the element of compulsion, he sympathised with the Irish National Teachers' Organisation's criticism of the policy in the late 1930s and early 1940s. He was one of the most trenchant Dáil critics of the approach of the Fianna Fáil Minister for Education, Tomás Derrig, to the use of compulsion in the language revival effort.

John Marcus O'Sullivan wrote a number of books and articles in German. He died in 1948.

(vii) James Fitzgerald-Kenny

James Fitzgerald-Kenny, who came from Co. Mayo, was born in 1877. He went to Downside Public School in England and became a student at University College, Dublin. He was called to the Bar in 1899, an advancement which led to his becoming a King's Council. He was also a landowner.

Fitzgerald-Kenny was a keen advocate of the revival of the Irish language and an active member of the Gaelic League. He was elected as a Cumann na nGaedheal TD for South Mayo in June 1927 and at every subsequent election until 1944, when he lost his seat. He was Parliamentary Secretary to the Minister for Justice from August to October 1927 and succeeded the murdered Kevin O'Higgins as Minister for Justice, retaining that position until Cumann na nGaedheal's defeat in the 1932 general election.

He was nominated to the national executive of the newly-formed Fine Gael party by W.T. Cosgrave in September 1933. In December of that year, and because General O'Duffy was absent, he was the main speaker at the inaugural public meeting of the League of Youth at Westport, Co. Mayo. He was described by Conor Maguire, Attorney-General to the second Fianna Fáil government, as 'the gloomy Dean of the Dáil'.

James Fitzgerald-Kenny served as Senior Counsel on the Western Circuit, where he was the revered mentor of Patrick Lindsay, who was also a Fine Gael TD for Mayo. Fitzgerald-Kenny lived at Clogher House, Claremorris, Co. Mayo.

(viii) Michael Hayes (Micheál Ó hAodha)

Michael Hayes was born in Dublin in 1889. He was a pupil of the Christian Brothers' School, Synge Street, Dublin, and subsequently studied at University College, Dublin. He was appointed Assistant-Professor of French in UCD in 1912, lectured there in modern Irish from 1933 to 1951 and was Professor of Modern Irish at the University from 1951 until 1960.

He joined the Irish Volunteers when they were formed in 1913, and for his part in the 1916 Rising suffered imprisonment. To him went the role of Sinn Féin Director of Elections for the National University of Ireland constituency in 1918. He was interned in Ballykinlar during the Anglo-Irish war in 1920-21. Hayes was a TD for the National University of Ireland from 1921 until 1933. He was pro-Treaty Minister for Education and briefly for Foreign Affairs in the Provisional Government in 1922, and the position of Ceann Comhairle was occupied by him from 1923 to 1932.

As Speaker of the Dáil, Michael Hayes was Chairman of the Civil Service Commission which did the new state great service by instituting high ethical standards for recruitment to the civil service. Some of his appointees progressed to distinguished civil service careers.

His casting vote as Ceann Comhairle saved the Cumann na nGaedheal government from defeat in August 1927, when Fianna Fáil entered the Dáil for the first time, and the opposition combined to vote against the Cosgrave government.

He lost his National University of Ireland seat in 1933 but was elected to the Senate, remaining a member of that chamber until 1965. He was Leader of the Senate from 1948 to 1951 and again from 1954 to 1957. He was for many years chairman of the standing committee of Fine Gael.

Professor Michael Hayes died in 1976.

(d) Richard Mulcahy

Richard Mulcahy was born in Waterford in 1886. He received his schooling at Mount Sion Christian Brothers' School, Waterford, and at the Christian Brothers' School, Thurles. Although his formal education ended in 1902, when he embarked upon a career in the Post Office, he continued to study and was eventually to earn promotion to the engineering division of the same official body. Moving to Dublin in 1908, he tutored himself for matriculation and then enrolled in Kevin Street and later Bolton Street technical schools.

Mulcahy read Arthur Griffith's *United Irishman* avidly and it shaped his philosophy. He regarded Griffith as his ideological mentor, like many of his generation:

> It was Griffith who most fully painted in his weekly writings for us the traditions and resources of Ireland, portrayed its mission, and gave us for practical purposes our dream, our

sense of work and opened for us work's widespreading scope.[25]

Shortly after arriving in Dublin he joined the Irish Republican Brotherhood (IRB) and when the Irish Volunteer organisation was formed in November 1913, he was among the 3,000 who enlisted at the first mass meeting in the Rotunda Rink in Dublin. A member of the Gaelic League since his Thurles days, he joined the Keating Branch in Dublin, where he met such future comrades-in-arms as Cathal Brugha, Thomas Ashe and Michael Collins.

He was a member of C Company of the Dublin Brigade of the Volunteers and he worked his way up through the ranks, becoming first lieutenant on the eve of the 1916 Rising. During Easter week, he was second-in-command to Thomas Ashe, commandant of the Fingal Volunteers, Fifth Battalion, Dublin Brigade. Their attack on the RIC barracks at Ashbourne, Co. Meath, was one of the few successful military actions of the Rising. Denis McCullough later remarked that Mulcahy was the only one to come out of 1916 with a military reputation. Certainly the Ashbourne action was the prototype for the guerilla campaign fought by the Volunteers from 1919 to 1921.

After the Rising, he was interned in Frongoch in Wales, from where he was released in December, 1916. He then enrolled as a medical student in University College, Dublin, and survived on a student's allowance from the Prisoners' Dependants' Fund. He rapidly became captain of C Company and then O/C of the Second Battalion of the Volunteers. Following the funeral of Thomas Ashe, at the end of September 1917, in which Mulcahy played a leading organisational part, the Dublin battalions were reorganised into the Dublin Brigade and he was appointed O/C. The next month he became Director of Training of the Volunteers. When in March 1918, a General Headquarters Staff was set up to oversee all aspects of Volunteer activity, Mulcahy was the choice for the position of chief-of-staff.

Nominated for the Clontarf constituency for the general election of December 1918, he began to fill a more active role in

302

Sinn Féin. Returned as one of the 73 successful Sinn Féin candidates in that election, it was he who introduced the 'Democratic Programme' at the meeting of the first Dáil on 21 January 1919. During the course of his speech he said:

A nation cannot be fully free in which even a small section of its people have not freedom. A nation cannot be said fully to live in spirit, or materially, while there is denied to any section of its people a share of the wealth and the riches that God bestowed around them to make them living and to sustain life in them.

This speech has been seen as containing 'the core of Mulcahy's political philosophy' and as representing 'the guiding principles which would inform his political career'.[26]

Appointed Minister for Defence in the Dáil cabinet from January to April, he was assistant Minister for Defence to Cathal Brugha from April 1919 onwards. As Brugha chose to continue his own business and to grant his salary to Mulcahy, the latter was thus able to become a full-time chief-of-staff. In this capacity he was largely responsible, along with Collins, for directing the revolutionary struggle over the next two years. He spent most of that time 'on the run', with more than 20 offices and hiding-places in and around Dublin. Often he barely escaped arrest, fleeing through windows or gardens, and on at least one occasion, by nonchalantly walking through a Black-and-Tan cordon. That he and Collins avoided capture was vital for the morale of the IRA, as the Volunteers came to be called.

It has recently been written of him:

Mulcahy's concern for his officers and his men was readily apparent in his communications with them. His caution frustrated some; his insistence on procedure annoyed others. But he patiently reiterated the reasons for his actions, and even those who disagreed, had to admit that he wanted to understand their point of view, their concerns, their problems.[27]

Tom Barry, in his *Guerilla Days in Ireland*, described him as a calm, unhurried, meticulous man who was always courteous and friendly, regardless of the pressure he was under, and Seán Ó Muirthuile referred to his tireless devotion to his task and his fairness to all.

Mulcahy's position on the Treaty was that it contained the means to achieve full independence gradually and peacefully. But he desperately wanted to maintain a united national front and worked unceasingly to try to bring this about. He, who was in a better position than anyone else, except Collins, to assess the military campaign waged by the Volunteers, remarked during the debates on the Treaty in the Dáil: 'We have not been able to drive the enemy from anything but from a fairly good-sized police barracks', thus showing how realistic he was about the possibility of a complete military victory over the British.

During the six months between the Dáil ratification of the Treaty and the outbreak of the Civil War, Mulcahy tried frantically to find a compromise that would maintain Volunteer unity. 'His patient and methodical personality would serve him well in this quest', his biographer has observed.[28] However, it proved to be a hopeless pursuit.

When the fighting broke out, Mulcahy became chief-of-staff of the National Army, while remaining as Minister for Defence. He and Collins resumed their old partnership, Collins being general commander-in-chief. They were responsible for raising, equipping and training a force to win the conflict and for deciding on the strategy to be pursued. When Collins was killed on 22 August, 1922, Mulcahy succeeded as military chief. He was not daunted by such callous scribbling on walls as 'Move over, Mick, make room for Dick', but stuck doggedly to his task.

In the August 1923 general election, standing in the Dublin City North, constituency, he received an outstanding 22,205 first preference votes, which represented 40% of the valid poll. It is a record that has not been equalled since. Mulcahy was successful in all subsequent elections until 1937, when he lost his seat, but was elected to the Senate in the same year. Re-elected to the Dáil for Dublin North-East in 1938, he was again unsuccessful in 1943. Elected for Tipperary the following year, he was a TD for that constituency until 1961, when he retired from public life, to which he had devoted 43 years.

The attempt to professionalise and demobilise the army, after the Civil War, led to the so-called 'army mutiny' in 1924. (For details of the crisis in the army see Chapter 1 of this book.) As Minister for Defence, Mulcahy became the principal target for the enmity engendered by the dissatisfaction on all sides and he was the primary victim of the crisis. Against his better judgement, he was persuaded to or pressurised into meeting the dissident officers, whom he cautioned about using the army for political purposes. As before in 1922, he desperately wished to prevent a split and to be able to hold the army together. A request from the dissident group (known as the 'old IRA') in October 1923 that Mulcahy preclude the demobilisation of certain officers, was regarded by him as being highly improper and irregular.

Following incidents in November, when between 60 and 70 officers at the Curragh were arrested, tried and removed from the camp as a result of their refusing to accept demobilisation papers, the cabinet set up a demobilisation committee consisting of MacNeill, Blythe and Joseph McGrath. The committee upheld Mulcahy's decisions but, as he regarded it as encouraging the dissidents, relations between him and his cabinet colleagues were strained.

The crisis reached a climax in early March 1924, when the dissident officers issued an ultimatum to the government demanding, among other things, the suspension of demobilisation and the reorganisation of the army. The cabinet's response was to arrest the two signatories of the ultimatum. During the Dáil debate which followed, McGrath, who was Minister for Industry and Commerce, rejected the government's policy, blamed Mulcahy's department for the crisis, and resigned from the government. He afterwards defended the dissident officers at Cumann na nGaedheal party meetings, asserting that what had occurred was not a mutiny but a dispute between two rival secret organisations, the IRB and the old IRA.

The possible influence of the IRB in the army especially

worried O'Higgins and Hogan. The cabinet, fearing the army command was tainted by this association, appointed Eoin O'Duffy, the Gárda Commissioner, overall commander of the Free State defence forces. This decision upset Mulcahy, but he held his counsel, refraining also from defending himself against McGrath's charges at Cumann na nGaedheal meetings, as he considered this course would prove the least harmful to the government. However, his silence enabled McGrath to persuade both party and government that his interpretation was correct and he was delegated to work out a compromise with the dissidents. When the cabinet agreed to establish a committee of enquiry to investigate McGrath's charges against the Department of Defence, the dissidents repented for and withdrew their ultimatum, asserting that their intention had been to expose 'a serious menace to the proper administration of the army' and declaring their allegiance to the state.[29]

The government accepted this interpretation and Mulcahy called in vain for much harsher treatment for the dissidents. The evidence shows that their intentions were far from being as innocuous as their ultimatum-withdrawal statement avowed. Intelligence reports warned Mulcahy of the gravity of the situation and the army arrested 11 dissident officers in a Dublin public house on his orders, neither O'Duffy nor the rest of the cabinet having been consulted. When the cabinet immediately demanded the resignations of the heads of the army, Mulcahy resigned in protest.

Both he and the dismissed generals accepted the government's decision and called on the officer corps to give absolute obedience to the civilian authorities. The following observations ring true:

> By acknowledging the right of the cabinet to dismiss the generals, the army showed that it had progressed from a politicised volunteer force to a professional, disciplined military body. Ironically, this evolution was primarily the work of the army council and the Minister for Defence, those very men who were now being dismissed because of the alleged undisciplined, political spirit which the cabinet believed animated the military.[30]

Mulcahy himself regarded the 1924 army crisis as disastrous in that it reduced the prestige of the government and left the 'directing force, in the parliamentary party and in the government, completely denuded of those people and names who stood for the Griffith approach and policy, in relation to industrial development'. The incident has been seen as a personal catastrophe for Mulcahy because, although he would again serve in government and eventually lead Fine Gael, he would never again enjoy the prestige and power that he had in 1924.[31]

He had dedicated himself to the creation of an army, which would give unquestioning loyalty to any democratically elected Irish government and would not interfere in politics. His resignation and those of his generals, when the government demanded it, clearly displayed the extent of his success. It has been well remarked that:

> Mulcahy fought the Civil War to uphold the principle of majority rule and affirm the right of the people to choose a government that would carry out their will. He would not, two years later, repudiate those principles for personal ambition or power.[32]

He made no attempt to split Cumann na nGaedheal in 1924 and set himself up as a rival to Cosgrave, but remained steadfastly loyal to government and party. On the contrary, he played an important role as mediator, defusing hostility within the party and bringing about a compromise. It is no surprise that W.T. Cosgrave later praised him for his 'great qualities or restraint and self-sacrifice'.

He remained active in Cumann na nGaedheal and chaired the Commission of Enquiry into the Gaeltachtaí. The members of Cumann na nGaedheal elected him to the executive committee of the party in 1926, and the following year he was returned to the cabinet as Minister for Local Government and Public Health.

When de Valera (whom he always blamed for causing the Civil War) came to power in 1932, Mulcahy, like many of his colleagues, felt that basic rights were under threat. Disrupted public election meetings and attempts to wreck his platform strengthened this fear. He became a member of the national executive of the

Blueshirts, not because of any enthusiasm for fascism, but because he feared a replay of the Civil War. As well as safeguarding the rights to free speech and free assembly, the Army Comrades Association wished to foster Irish culture and 'patriotic idealism by honouring the memory of all the heroic dead who worked and suffered for Ireland and especially of Griffith, Collins and O'Higgins'. These aspirations were dear to Mulcahy as well.

During World War II, he endorsed his party's support for neutrality and believed a national government was called for to deal with the crisis. He was one of the Fine Gael participants in the defence conferences, de Valera's sop to the opposition. He found these frustrating and meaningless and indeed advised his party to discontinue its involvement in them until de Valera's attitude changed.

He succeeded W.T. Cosgrave as leader of Fine Gael in 1944. Once again his commitment, dedication and hard work were in evidence and he inspired by example. The party's fortunes were at a low ebb when he took over, and he toiled unceasingly to arrest and reverse the decline. He travelled all over the country organising, speaking at meetings and giving encouragement. When he became leader, he told his TDs he was willing to go to any part of the country and he spent years travelling Ireland on behalf of the party.

He urged Fine Gael TDs to concentrate on being conspicuous in order to increase impact on their constituencies. He exhorted them to ask more questions in the Dáil, to become more involved in community issues and to get more publicity in the local press. All his hard work bore fruit in that Fine Gael's number of seats increased from 30 to 50 over a ten-year period.

The first inter-party government was his brainchild and its formation again afforded evidence of his lack of self-aggrandisement. He brought the parties together, and, although as leader of the largest he could have rightfully claimed the position of Taoiseach, he selflessly stood aside and persuaded John A. Costello to fill the post. As Minister for Education he spoke only on that brief and did his utmost to ensure the success of this first inter-party arrangement.

The Irish language and Irish culture formed an integral part of Mulcahy's national vision. One of his first actions as Minister for Education was to double the grant to the Irish Folklore Commission. He believed it the duty of society to provide for the cultural and spiritual, as well as the material well-being of the nation. He always thought in terms of the common good. So as leader of Fine Gael he would not oppose for the sake of opposition or criticise for personal or party advancement. The nation was of paramount importance to him, and not the party or individuals. In this he was typical of the leaders of the Gaelic League and early Sinn Féin.

He also occupied the position of Minister for Education in the second inter-party government. He retired from politics in 1961, having served Ireland for nearly half a century, and he died in 1971. John A. Costello paid him the following, fitting tribute:

> In any situation where there appeared to be conflict between his personal and his public interests, he unhesitatingly left aside all his own interest. He was a man of idealistic principle. He served his country well, but was not appreciated. I personally have never come across any man who was so selfless in public or national affairs.[33]

(e) John A. Costello

John A. Costello was born in Dublin in June 1891 into a middle-class family which was pro-Parnell. He attended O'Connell Schools, North Richmond Street, Dublin, studied history, languages and literature in University College, Dublin and later law at King's Inns. The 1913 lock-out in Dublin directed his attention to social ills. He graduated in 1914 and practised law, often defending nationalist prisoners. He decided to enter politics in 1921, having been involved in the activities of the republican courts since 1919.

Of an extremely pragmatic outlook, he regarded the Treaty as mainly a means to political and social development. He was appointed assistant to the Law Officer of Collins's Provisional Government in 1922. He believed the June 1922 election was overwhelmingly for the Treaty in that the people ignored the Collins-de Valera pact in order to give a clear verdict on the agreement with Britain. He acted as assistant to the Attorney General, Hugh Kennedy, from 1923 to 1926.

Costello was a firm believer in the evolutionary potential of the Treaty and the new government immediately turned its mind to that, despite pressing social and economic domestic problems and the Civil War. He acted as a legal constitutional adviser to the government in its efforts to establish legations in Washington, the Vatican, Berlin and Paris, and in its striving to join the League of Nations and to become a member of the Council of the League. He was Attorney General from 1926 to 1932.

He was present at the 1926 and 1929-30 Imperial Conferences. At the 1926 gathering he tried to convince General Hertzog of South Africa that demanding the right for the dominions to secede from the Commonwealth would be an inadvisable course to pursue. He was sure that the British would not go that far, but that they would concede a certain amount, including the co-equality of the dominions. He found the Canadians to be particularly good friends of Ireland and was especially impressed by MacKenzie King.

John A. Costello was first elected to the Dáil in 1933 for Dublin County and for the Dublin Townships constituency from 1937 to 1943. He was defeated in the 1943 general election, but was re-elected the following year and was successful again in 1948 when he contested Dublin South-East. He continued to represent that constituency until 1969 when Garret FitzGerald took over from him. During Fine Gael's long sojourn in opposition between 1932 and 1948, he built up a reputation as an outstanding Senior Counsel.

Costello emerged as a compromise choice for Taoiseach in the inter-party government which was formed after the 1948 general election. He was acceptable to the Labour party (it was William Norton who suggested him for the post) because of the liberal social views he had displayed while on the boards of a number of hospitals, and Clann na Poblachta welcomed him because of the great respect his fellow barrister, Seán MacBride, had for him.

Costello himself has explained that Richard Mulcahy, who was Fine Gael's leader at the time, was the prime mover behind the inter-party arrangement. He has also averred that a number of Labour TDs would have been happy for Mulcahy to have led the government. He has remarked that Mulcahy's service to his country has not been appreciated and that he never met so selfless a public man.[34]

On the day the results of the 1948 election were declared, Mulcahy consulted Daniel Morrissey about the idea of forming an inter-party alternative government to Fianna Fáil and Morrissey advised him to get in touch with the other party leaders, which he did the following day. They were enthusiastic about the suggestion, and when William Norton suggested Costello for Taoiseach, Mulcahy got in contact with him. At first Costello was appalled by the notion, but pressure was brought to bear on him. He and Mulcahy met with Patrick McGilligan and Dr T.F. O'Higgins and then all the parties' representatives requested him to lead the government.

It was mainly the appeals made by O'Higgins at Mulcahy's house which made up Costello's mind. He has reflected that 'Mulcahy, as usual, put public before his own interests'. He sought counsel from his own friend, Arthur Cox, who advised him to go ahead. He had to make a big financial sacrifice to become Taoiseach and he was worried about the impact upon his family, but he decided to agree to accept the nomination. He has described his selection by the Dáil to become the leader of the government as his 'proudest moment'.[35]

He was also very proud of the economic achievements of the 1948 to 1951 administration. It introduced a capital budget separately from the current budget, thus recognising in Ireland for the first time that the budget was an important part of economic policy as well as having the purpose of balancing the country's finances. The economic philosophy of J.M. Keynes was introduced into Ireland in this way. The Irish Export Board was also set up during this government's tenure because, in Costello's own words, exports were seen as 'the basis of a growing upward swing in the rate of production and a higher standard of life leading to social progress for all'.[36] The establishment of the Industrial Development Authority was regarded by him as one of the most important contributions of all of the 1948-51 period. The first inter-party government instituted the practice of attracting foreign capital to Ireland, a policy opposed by Fianna Fáil at the time although this, like many other of that administration's measures, was adopted by de Valera's party when it returned to power.

The declaration of the Republic, in which he himself played such a key role, was probably Costello's first government's most memorable achievement, and he regarded it as its most significant. He saw it as ending the confusing constitutional position between Ireland and Britain or, as he more colourfully put it: 'The pirouetting on the point of a pin was over'.[37] Sadly, his hope that it would take the gun out of Irish politics was not to be realised. From the outset, he viewed the Treaty as containing the means to full independence and the 1948 declaration was a pinnacle in that agreement's potential.

Although his initial premiership was to end in controversy, it has been observed that 'even those who differed most sharply from him admitted his skill and patience as a chairman who could, most of the time, bring order and reasonable harmony into the proceedings of his variegated and highly temperamental team.'[38] Indeed, the government of which he was leader was an extraordinarily disparate grouping. An early advocate of a coalition arrangement, he had little chance of being more than chairman in the 1948-51 period. Agreements had been made between the parties before he took office and he had to abide by these. The allocation of ministries had been decided by the parties before he agreed to become Taoiseach and the parties continued to treat portfolios as at their own disposal. To try to resolve some of the differences that arose in cabinet and perhaps also to shorten the length of, and avoid possible bitterness in ministry meetings, he tried to use the cabinet committee system which had worked so well in Britain. That concerned with economic planning was particularly successful.

John A. Costello was very conservative in religious matters

and deferred completely to the Catholic hierarchy on the 'Mother and Child' controversy in 1951. In fact, it has been asserted that he was 'more aggressive in his deference to his church authorities than any of his predecessors.'[39] He was afterwards to state to the Dáil:

> I am an Irishman second; I am a Catholic first. If the hierarchy gives me any direction with regard to Catholic social teaching or Catholic moral teaching, I accept without qualification in all respects the teaching of the hierarchy and the church to which I belong.

He was shocked when Dr Noel Browne, Minister for Health, made the disagreement public. 'The public never ought to have become aware of the matter', he told the Dáil.

When the second inter-party government was formed in 1954, Costello again became Taoiseach. This was a much less diverse arrangement from the point of view of the number of parties involved and, with his own political prestige enhanced, he was in a stronger position than he had been during Ireland's first experiment with a coalition administration. He would have preferred Patrick McGilligan to have again taken responsibility for Finance, but, for health reasons, McGilligan chose to become Attorney General. Conscious that some ministers were not as resourceful as they had been during their first period in office (ministers and departmental officials knew each other by now and did not spark off each other as much as before to stimulate policy initiatives), Costello tried to urge on particular incumbents and to promote certain schemes of his own. This led to Gerard Sweetman, Minister for Finance, complaining of undue interference by the Taoiseach.[40] Indeed it has been contended that Costello was in 'spirited disagreement' with Sweetman's policies.[41]

He was a vigorous supporter of his son, Declan, probably the most articulate exponent of Fine Gael's *Just Society* policy in 1964. The *Irish Times* journalist who interviewed him in 1967 saw John A. Costello as most of all humane and with a genuine concern for social progress. At that time he declared that if he were Taoiseach again he would devote himself to the formulation and implementation of a coherent social programme, mobilizing all the

313

country's human and material resources to create the maximum national wealth so that all would be enabled to live full lives. He believed that the *Just Society* enshrined such an approach and that all parties would be forced to adopt that programme as future elections would turn on social questions.[42]

He did not contest the 1969 general election. An energetic backbencher for the ten years before his retirement from active politics, he has been described as speaking on the 1968 referendum issue 'with undiminished vigour'.[43] He is a unique phenomenon in Irish political life, a man who was twice Taoiseach while never having been leader of his party.

(f) Patrick McGilligan

Patrick McGilligan came from a political background as his father was an anti-Parnellite MP for South Fermanagh from 1892 to 1895. He was born in Coleraine, Co. Derry, in April 1889. He attended a local primary school and then St Columb's Derry, and Clongowes in Co. Kildare. He went to University College, Dublin, where he studied classics. He contracted TB and spent a year in an English sanatorium while still a student. His subsequent spare frame gave an impression of frailty to which the extraordinary energy and creativity he displayed throughout his multifaceted career gave the lie.

He had an outstanding academic career at UCD, going on to do the Master of Arts Degree and Higher Diploma in Education. Contemporaries at UCD, and afterwards to become well-known in various areas of Irish public life were John A. Costello, Patrick Hogan, Conor Maguire, George O'Brien, Arthur Cox, Frank Cruise O'Brien, Joseph Brennan, Thomas Bodkin and J.J. ('Ginger') O'Connell, who became his brother-in-law. McGilligan was a secondary teacher for a short time in Cork and afterwards in St Patrick's Academy in Armagh.

He joined Sinn Féin in 1917 and was particularly influenced by Arthur Griffith's message of non-violent nationalism. He became an assistant in classics in UCD in October 1918 and began to study law. He was also asked to contest the strongly-Unionist

314

constituency of North Derry in the 1918 general election. Following the death of his father in 1917, he had moved his mother and the rest of his family to Dublin, and their house was frequently raided by the Black-and-Tans during the Anglo-Irish war. His admiration for Griffith's policies and his commitment to peaceful political means meant no direct involvement for him in the military campaign between 1919 and 1921, and also guaranteed his support for the Treaty.

He acted as a barrister and press censor for Collins's Provisional Government in 1922. Becoming especially friendly with Kevin O'Higgins, he was made his private secretary when O'Higgins became Minister for Home Affairs in the Cosgrave government from September 1922. Six months later he was appointed secretary to the new Irish High Commissioner in London, James MacNeill. He participated in the 1923 Imperial Conference in London, standing in for Eoin MacNeill who, although a delegate, seldom attended the meetings because of the demands of his Education ministry. He was elected to the Dáil for the first time in late 1923 in a by-election for the National University of Ireland constituency. He served for this constituency until it was abolished by de Valera's 1937 Constitution. When Joseph McGrath resigned over the army crisis in 1924, McGilligan succeeded him as Minister for Industry and Commerce, testimony to the remarkable reputation he had built up though still short of 35 and so few years in public life.

His greatest and most memorable achievement in this portfolio was the Shannon Scheme. He always insisted that the credit should go to T. J. McLaughlin, the engineer involved, rather than to himself, but it is highly unlikely that the project would have had state support without his backing and the skilful way he manoeuvred it through the Department of Finance. Initially, he raised it in cabinet when Ernest Blythe, the Minister for Finance, was absent, so that that Department's officials were unaware how far advanced it was at cabinet level, and then he persuaded Blythe to champion the scheme. The Shannon enterprise set a precedent which was to be followed repeatedly in the years to come.

Patrick McGilligan favoured industrial protection, in which Griffith had so strongly believed, but he made little progress in this area, largely because of the opposition from Department of Finance officials. Dr Garret FitzGerald believes that had McGilligan succeeded in this endeavour, not only would industrialisation have been advanced by almost a decade, but the subsequent electoral imbalance between Fine Gael and Fianna Fáil might have been reversed - or at least avoided - because the protection it introduced from 1932 onwards won for Fianna Fáil the support of the new industrialists and industrial workers.

After the September 1927 general election, McGilligan became Minister for External Affairs, as well as retaining Industry and Commerce. He expanded his new Department, opening legations at the Vatican, in Paris and Berlin, and consulates in New York and Boston. His experience of the 1923 and 1926 Imperial Conferences stood him well in the preparations for that of 1930, at which the Irish delegation took the lead. Journalists at the time and historians since have paid tribute to McGilligan's crucial role in having the sovereign independence of the dominions enshrined in the Statute of Westminster. Garret FitzGerald has applauded the confidence, constitutional knowledge and intellectual dominance, which the team McGilligan led, displayed at the 1929-30 meetings.

The long experience of Dáil opposition from 1932 to 1948 was a frustrating one for Patrick McGilligan. He also had to build up his career at the Bar to support a growing family. He was probably not an intuitive politician and has been described as being hopeless at constituency work and as having no interest in party organisation. He was a most trenchant - some would think corrosive - critic of Fianna Fáil in the Dáil and never had personal relationships with any of it members. He was a very popular lecturer in UCD, where he became Professor of International and Constitutional Law. Both as a lecturer and practitioner, he was a vigorous defender of the rights of the individual.

Although it was suggested before the formation of the 1948 inter-party government that he become Attorney General, Labour, in particular, was anxious to see him being made Minister for

Finance. By an irony of history, he found himself in charge of the officials who had frustrated so many of his endeavours in the 1920s. Without his influence and cooperation, many of the activities and achievements of Seán MacBride at External Affairs and James Dillon at Agriculture would not have been possible. However, he opposed MacBride in 1949 over the issue of breaking the link with sterling. The achievement of which he was proudest was the introduction of the first capital budget in 1950. By now he was a convinced Keynesian and this separate capital budget has been described by Garret FitzGerald as 'one of the most striking innovations introduced by the first coalition government.' Although he was most reluctant to accept conventional Finance thinking, his officials regarded him as the most intelligent Minister under whom they had served up to that time.

He returned to the Bar in 1951. For health reasons he turned down the onerous Finance portfolio in 1954 and was content to become Attorney General, but when he learned that Gerard Sweetman was Costello's choice for Finance, he privately regretted not taking the job and was critical of Sweetman's deflationary policies.

He supported the *Just Society* policy, the leading proponent of which in the 1960s was Declan Costello. He was defeated in the 1965 general election, at the age of 76, losing his Dublin North-Central seat (which he had held since the abolition of the NUI constituency in 1937) to Luke Belton. He died in 1979.[44]

Patrick McGilligan's public life spanned six decades of the history of the independent Irish state to which he contributed so much, initially by extracting the maximum amount of freedom contained in the Treaty (John A. Costello described his work at the 1929-30 Imperial Conference as 'truly colossal' and declared that, 'nobody worked harder or thought harder than Paddy McGilligan'), and then shifting Irish economic horizons by his familiarity with Keynes and his advocacy of the adoption in Ireland of planning based on the doctrines of this economist. A TD from 1923 to 1965, he was one of the longest-serving public representatives ever in his country's history.

(g) Other Inter-Party Government Ministers

(i) Dr T.F. O'Higgins

Thomas F. O'Higgins was a brother of Kevin O'Higgins and two of his sons, Tom and Michael, were Fine Gael TDs for many years. He was born in Stradbally, Co. Laois, in 1890. He attended Clongowes Wood College and afterwards University College, Dublin, where he studied medicine. His first medical practice was in Portlaoise and he became an organiser for Sinn Féin and the Volunteers in South Kildare from 1917 onwards. He was imprisoned twice, in Mountjoy and Ballykinlar, during the Anglo-Irish war.

He joined the Free State army in May 1922 and became Director of Medical Services in 1924. He resigned his commission in February 1929 and was elected to the Dáil for North Dublin the following month. He represented Laois-Offaly from 1932 to 1948. In the latter year he was elected for Cork City for the first time, while his son, Tom, was elected for Laois-Offaly the same year. Dr T.F. was re-elected for Cork City in 1951.

He was a founder-member of the Army Comrades' Association in February 1932 and was elected its president in August of that year. He saw it as the primary purpose of the organisation to defend the right of free speech. He resigned the leadership in July 1933 because of the many pressing demands on his time and was succeeded by General Eoin O'Duffy. He was involved in the series of meetings during the summer of 1933 which led to the formation of Fine Gael, was a member of the party's first national executive and of its front bench in the Dáil.

As a gesture of defiance, he and Desmond FitzGerald, among other Fine Gael TDs, wore their blue shirts in the Dáil in September 1933. In February 1934, he threatened to break up de Valera's meetings if Blueshirt meetings were disrupted. He declared:

> They would see that every man could express his opinion in public without fear. They did not want any blackguardism, but if there was, and if the other side broke gobs, they

would also break gobs. They had the material and they would use it.[45]

He was elected vice-president of Fine Gael at the March 1935 ard-fheis. After the outcome of the 1948 general election became known, he played a crucial role in persuading John A. Costello to lead the inter-party government. In that government he was Minister for Defence until early March 1951 and then Minister for Industry and Commerce until the government's collapse. Although his own personal preference would probably have been for Irish membership of the North Atlantic Treaty Organisation in 1949, the continued existence of partition prevented his advocating it.

Dr T. F. O'Higgins retired from active politics in 1954 on grounds of health, but his son, Tom, served in the second inter-party government.

(ii) Seán MacEoin

Seán MacEoin was born in Bunlahy, Co. Longford, in 1894 and was a blacksmith by trade. He joined the Irish Volunteers in 1914, was Commandant of the First Battalion, Longford Brigade in 1919 (later promoted to Vice-Commandant Longford Brigade IRA), leader of a flying column in 1920-21 and was one of the heroes of the War of Independence. He led an ambush on Black and Tans and Auxiliaries at Ballinalee in November 1920 in which 20 of them were killed.

He foiled an attempt to capture him in January 1921 and led an ambush at Clonfin the following month in which a British army officer and two Auxiliaries were killed and 17 Auxiliaries surrendered. Because of his chivalrous treatment of prisoners, he acquired the nickname of 'the gentle Blacksmith of Ballinalee'. He was wounded and captured at Mullingar in March 1921 and was condemned to death. In the May 1921 election, he was returned to the Dáil unopposed. The British were most reluctant to release him under the terms of the truce negotiated in July 1921, but the Irish were adamant that there would be no cease-fire unless he was set free.

MacEoin was then appointed O/C of the First Midland

Division of the IRA. Part of his area included South Fermanagh and in February 1922 he oversaw raids into Northern Ireland in which 40 Special Constables and Fermanagh Unionists were taken and held as hostages for the release of a number of Monaghan IRA men who had been captured in the North. Both groups were set free.

Seán MacEoin seconded the motion, proposed by Arthur Griffith, approving the Treaty in the Dáil on 19 December 1921. When the commander of the Irregulars in Sligo 'proclaimed' a public meeting which was to be addressed in the town by Griffith on 16 April 1922, MacEoin conspicuously led an armed escort which resolutely ensured that the President was enabled to speak without molestation. Griffith and Collins were among the guests at his marriage in June 1922 to Alice Cooney, aunt of former Minister for Justice, Paddy Cooney.

He was appointed GOC of the Western Command of the Free State forces during the Civil War and Chief of Staff in 1923. He was re-elected to the Dáil in June 1922, but did not take part in the August 1923 contest, devoting himself instead to his army career. He left the army in 1929 and was elected for Cumann na nGaedheal for Sligo-Leitrim in a by-election the same year. He won a seat in Longford-Westmeath in 1932 and was re-elected in all subsequent elections until his retirement from public life.

He was one of the founders of the National Defence Association in 1929 and was assiduous in ensuring the welfare of ex-army men. He was involved in the Blueshirts in the 1930s. He twice contested presidential elections unsuccessfully for Fine Gael - against Seán T. O'Kelly in 1945 and de Valera in 1959 - but polled well on each occasion.

MacEoin was Minister for Justice from 1948 to 1951, Minister for Defence in 1951 and held the same portfolio in the 1954-57 inter-party government. He has been described as having the old-fashioned, pious Catholic attitude to such issues as the legalising of adoption and Sunday opening of public houses, which arose during his tenure of office. He did not want to involve the Church in any sort of public dispute. He also opposed the introduction of the shortened birth certificate on the grounds that it would encourage promiscuity. His was an uncomplicated attitude to political matters: if the hierarchy had pronounced on a question, they should be obeyed and that was the end of the matter.[46]

General Seán MacEoin, hero of the Anglo-Irish war and Fine Gael veteran, retired from politics in 1959. He died in 1973.

(iii) Daniel Morrissey

Daniel Morrissey was born in Nenagh, Co. Tipperary, and he attended the town's Christian Brothers' School. He worked as a labourer on the Great Southern Railway and afterwards as an insurance agent. A trade-union official from 1916 onwards, he organised the Irish Transport and General Workers' Union in his native county and became a member of its executive.

Morrissey was elected as a Labour TD in June 1922 for Tipperary and was re-elected in all subsequent elections until his retirement from public life in 1957. He served for the Tipperary North constituency from 1948 to 1957. He was Labour Chief Whip in the Dáil between 1923 and 1928, and Leas Ceann Chomhairle from 1928 until 1932.

He grew gradually closer to Cumann na nGaedheal and in 1931, he and another Labour deputy, Richard Anthony, defied the Labour Whip and voted for the Cosgrave government's establishment of a military tribunal to deal with the increasing lawlessness in the country. The two men were expelled from Labour for this action, but Morrissey was re-elected in the 1932 election as an Independent Labour candidate.

He joined Cumann na nGaedheal in 1933 and was re-elected for that party in the general election of that year. When the Fine Gael party was formed, he was nominated onto its national executive by W. T. Cosgrave.

Morrissey became partner in an auctioneering firm in Nenagh and later set up his own auctioneering company in Dublin, retaining business connections in the trade unions. His was a significant role in the preliminaries which led to the first inter-party government. It was he whom Richard Mulcahy first canvassed about the possibility of forming such a government. Advising Mulcahy to go ahead, Morrissey's former Labour and trade-union associations did much to smooth the course of the subsequent talks.

He was Minister for Industry and Commerce from 1948 to 1951 and Minister for Justice for three months in 1951. During his term of office such significant advances took place as the establishment of the Industrial Development Authority and Córas Tráchtála and the nationalisation of Córas Iompair Éireann. He also took part in the negotiation of the Anglo-Irish Trade Agreement in 1948 and in discussions with the government of Northern Ireland concerning the Great Northern Railway.

Because of ill health, he did not take a ministry in the 1954-57 inter-party government and he retired from politics in 1957. Daniel Morrissey died in 1981.

(iv) Tom O'Higgins

Tom O'Higgins was born in 1916, that momentous year in Irish history. A son of Dr T.F., nephew of Kevin, and, also, a descendant of T.D. Sullivan of the Irish Parliamentary Party, who wrote such patriotic ballads as 'God Save Ireland' and 'Deep in Canadian Woods', it was hardly surprising that he should have entered politics. Perhaps what was surprising was that he did not enter active politics until the age of 32, choosing instead to concentrate on his legal career, having been called to the Bar in 1938.

He was first elected to the Dáil for Laois-Offaly in 1948, his brother Michael also making his Dáil debut for Dublin South-West on the same occasion, while their father, who had moved from Laois-Offaly, was returned for Cork City. Although only six years in the Dáil, Tom O'Higgins was appointed Minister for Health in the second inter-party government in 1954.

It was a sensitive portfolio, given the controversy in which the precedent administration had become embroiled as a result of the Mother and Child scheme. O'Higgins's fellow-barrister, John A. Costello, told him that his job was to 'take health out of politics'. Securing the passage of the amended Mother and Child scheme through the Dáil provided O'Higgins with great satisfaction. He was also responsible for the establishment of the very successful Voluntary Health Insurance scheme or VHI.

However, the exercise of office by the government of which he was a member was by no means an easy one in the middle of possibly the most depressed decade, economically, of the independent Irish state, and he remembers Costello looking wearily around the cabinet table and asking: 'What's the bad news today?'[47]

In 1957, O'Higgins was so perturbed by the dreadful economic slump that he wrote a memorandum urging the government to declare a new policy for development and to call on all parties supporting it to express their loyalty to the administration. Sent to ask Seán MacBride to propose a motion of confidence, he found him most amenable, yet some weeks later MacBride put down a no-confidence motion which caused the fall of the second inter-party government. Why MacBride acted in the way he did has since remained a mystery to O'Higgins.

Nevertheless, he wished to propose MacBride as a united opposition candidate to contest the 1966 presidential election against de Valera, but Liam Cosgrave thought little of the suggestion. O'Higgins then proposed John A. Costello but it was put to him that it would be bad politics to attempt promoting a man who was old enough to have participated in the 1916 Rising, but did not, against its senior surviving commandant. Then Pat Lindsay suggested that O'Higgins himself should be the Fine Gael candidate, and other front bench members backed this proposal strongly, and O'Higgins reluctantly agreed to run.

Despite this initial disinclination, he has stated that he enjoyed the campaign, especially the 'huge friendly crowds'. His adviser and speech-writer, Michael Sweetman, presented O'Higgins, only slightly more than half de Valera's age, as a man for the new generation and the new Ireland then developing. To general amazement, O'Higgins came within one half of one per cent of defeating de Valera.

His remarkable performance greatly enhanced his standing in Fine Gael and many in the party may well have looked to him as an alternative leader, but he has rejected suggestions of tensions between Liam Cosgrave and himself and declared that relations between them were always cordial.[48] He has remarked, however, that divisions within Fine Gael over the amendment to the Offences Against the State Act left the party deeply traumatised.

As a presidential election was due in 1973, he thought that proposing Liam Cosgrave as Fine Gael's candidate might be a way of healing the internal rifts. But when he approached Cosgrave, he was firmly rejected and, instead, he again reluctantly agreed to allow his name to go forward. Shortly afterwards a general election was called and, as he had made known that he would contest the presidency, he felt obliged to announce that he would not be seeking to get elected to the Dáil. He regretted that circumstances conspired against him in such a way but it was some consolation to him that the pre-electoral arrangement with Labour, for which he had worked so hard, came to fruition. In fact, it was he who chaired the long Fine Gael-Labour meeting which produced the agreed programme which removed Fianna Fáil from power after 16 years.

Tom O'Higgins has expressed the view that the Fine Gael-Labour coalition victory damaged his own presidential campaign, because at public meetings he discovered that he was being blamed for the increases in taxation in the government's first budget. He also felt that the publication of an opinion poll showing him an easy victor over Erskine Childers harmed him and he has admitted that he and his strategists underestimated the effectiveness of Childers's campaign. Following the loss of his second election for president, Tom O'Higgins retired from active politics.

Following six months practice at the Bar, he was appointed to the Bench and, a year later, to the highest legal office in the land, Chief Justice. After ten years in that position, he became the Irish Judge in the Court of Justice of the European Communities, from which he retired at the end of September 1992.

(v) Gerard Sweetman

Gerard Sweetman was from an Anglo-Irish background and

was born in Dublin in 1908. He attended Downside College in England before entering Trinity College, Dublin. He qualified as a solicitor and joined the firm of George Fottrell and Sons, 30, Lower Baggot Street, Dublin, becoming a senior partner in the practice.

He contested the 1932 general election for Cumann na nGaedheal in Carlow-Kildare but was unsuccessful. He was prevented by poor health from contesting another election until 1943, when he again failed to make it to the Dáil, but he was elected to the Senate in the same year. He was returned to the Dáil for the Kildare constituency in 1948 and he acted as Fine Gael Chief Whip during the first inter-party government.

In this capacity he took on a key organisational function within Fine Gael and he was to continue to act in this capacity until his tragically premature death in 1970. It was a position 'for which his forceful personality well fitted him', according to Garret FitzGerald, who has described him as 'a man of exceptional energy'.[49]

Sweetman was appointed Minister for Finance in the second inter-party government, when Patrick McGilligan declined the post, because of failing health. He could do little about the evil of increasing inflation apart from the time-honoured response of cutting government expenditure and increasing taxation. However, he achieved some success in closing Ireland's trade gap in that he reduced the balance of payments deficit from £35 million in 1955 to £14 million in 1956. But he had to resort to extreme measures, including tough import levies, to do so.

He has been seen as over-reacting to the crisis and his two deflationary budgets have been regarded as sending the Irish economy deeper into recession.[50] It should be remembered that the second inter-party government bequeathed to Fianna Fáil the man most capable of preparing a programme for economic development. T.K. Whitaker had been selected at the young age of 40, by Gerard Sweetman, to fill the cardinal post of Secretary of the Department of Finance.

It has been contended that Sweetman played the key role in the election of James Dillon as leader of Fine Gael in 1959 when

General Richard Mulcahy retired. He did not wish John A. Costello to get the position, it has been argued, because Costello had made it known that he would fulfil the role in a part-time capacity only, as he wished to continue his legal practice. There was ill-feeling between Liam Cosgrave, the other contender for the leadership, and Sweetman, so this argument goes, because as Minister for Finance, Sweetman had imposed betting taxes which were deeply opposed by W.T. Cosgrave, who resigned his position on the Racing Board in protest.[51]

Sweetman has been described as 'a vigorous conservative' and 'a pragmatically conservative businessman'.[52] He had little sympathy for the *Just Society* policy of the mid-1960s and the increasing liberal element within the party. It has been maintained that he was prepared to swallow whatever differences he had with Liam Cosgrave and to back him in his bid for the leadership in 1965, in order to keep Declan Costello out. He grew closer to Cosgrave after he became leader and it has been asserted that his was the dominant influence on Cosgrave from 1966 to 1970.[53] Of this period Garret FitzGerald has written concerning Sweetman:

> He was not an ideological right-winger but rather a politician with a business orientation and a practical interest in winning power for his party. He was tough and had little instinctive sympathy with the younger generation, least of all with the liberal youth of the 1960s. He had no malice in him and did not bear grudges, but in what he conceived to be the interests of the party he could be quite ruthless. My relationship with him was combative but not unfriendly. When from time to time we were in agreement on an issue he would tell the rest of the front bench good-humouredly that when we two agreed, no further argument was necessary.[54]

Gerard Sweetman was tragically killed in a car accident in Co. Kildare in February 1970.

(vi) Patrick Lindsay

Patrick Lindsay was born in Dublin on 18 January 1914. He

326

was reared in the townland of Doolough, Co. Mayo, on a small farm. In his recently published memoirs, he told of an incident that occurred in his home when he was five. There was a discussion going on about the maiden name of the wife of the local landlord. The young Lindsay was hungry and somewhat impatient as the talking continued, and when somebody suggested that the lady's name was Miss Eager, he interjected: 'Whatever her maiden name is, I'm very eager for my supper'! From this his father could see his son's interest in language and the youngster was soon provided with stimulating reading material such as Lord Macauley's essays, the novels of Charles Dickens, Charles Kickham and so on.[55]

He attended the primary school in the local village of Geesala, on the shore of Blacksod Bay, and afterwards Doolough National School. At the age of 13, he won a scholarship to St Mureadach's secondary boarding-school in Ballina, Co. Mayo. On his first visit to Ballina, he attended, with his father, an election rally at which W.T. Cosgrave was the main speaker. 'Somehow or other I felt, while listening to this frail little man with a quiff in his hair, speaking of affairs of the country which I, of course, did not understand, that there was a sadness, a sad prophetic tone in his voice as to what might ultimately happen in this country', he has written.[56]

Lindsay had a successful sojourn in St Mureadach's, from which he won a scholarship to University College, Galway. He was actually expelled from his secondary school for offences he did not commit (as he claimed himself!), but was allowed back because he threatened to 'take the soup'![57]

He studied Classics in University College Galway. While there, he became active in the Blueshirt movement and has described himself as 'an unrepentant Blueshirt'.[58] It was only the intervention of his Professor of Classics, Fr Tom Fahy, which prevented him from going to Spain with Eoin O'Duffy's Irish Brigade to fight on the side of Franco.

When he graduated from UCG, he taught for two years at the Royal School, Cavan. He then moved to Dublin where he did part-time teaching and where he was befriended and helped by

Michael Tierney, Professor of Greek at University College, Dublin, a former Cumann na nGaedheal TD for North Mayo. He began to study Law at UCD in 1943, where one of his professors was Patrick McGilligan, and he then spent two years in the King's Inns, being called to the Bar in 1946. In the Law Library, he found John A. Costello particularly helpful.

Patrick Lindsay practised as a barrister on the Western Circuit and among those who impressed him, and whom he has always regarded as one of his mentors, was the former Cumann nGaedheal Minister for Justice, James Fitzgerald-Kenny, who was a Senior Counsel on that Circuit. Lindsay himself took silk in 1954. He was appointed Master of the High Court in 1975 and retained that position until 1984. In this capacity, he saw his role as 'the protector of the lawful rights of the small man or woman against the banks, the insurance companies and, worst of all at times, the Revenue', to use his own words.[59]

He first contested a Dáil seat for the constituency of North Mayo in the 1937 general election, but was unsuccessful. He was to meet a similar fate in the 1938, 1943 and 1948 general elections. He has recorded one abiding memory from the aftermath of the 1948 campaign. The formation of an inter-party government was an uncertainty right up to the last minute. Lindsay was on circuit in Galway on the day the Dáil met and has recounted the following:

> I drove into Tuam and I saw there the large physique of a man, a civic guard, who was standing on the footpath. I pulled in *diagonally* and lowered my window.
>
> 'Guard, is there any news from Dublin?' 'At ten-past-five this afternoon, Mr John Aloysius Costello was elected Taoiseach of this country'.
>
> I knew by the way that he said it, that this really meant something to him and I said: 'Guard, would you like a drink?'
>
> 'We'll have two'.
>
> 'Will you wait a minute, until I park this car?'
>
> 'Leave it where it is. We have freedom for the first time in sixteen years'.

We had more than one drink that day.[60]

Unlucky again in a by-election in 1952, he was returned to the Dáil for North Mayo in the 1954 general election. John A. Costello's second government created a Department of the Gaeltacht and in June 1956, Lindsay was appointed Parliamentary Secretary to the Departments of the Gaeltacht and Education. In October, when the new Roinn na Gaeltachta came into existence, he was made the state's first Aire na Gaeltachta.

His tenure of office was short and the resources at his disposal were meagre. He regarded his two main achievements as extending grant-aid to areas bordering on the Gaeltachtaí which suffered similar social problems, and appointing Seán Glynn as Assistant-Secretary to his Department, seeing him as understanding the Gaeltacht's problems well and as attempting to solve them.[61]

Despite Fine Gael losing ten seats in the 1957 general election, Lindsay held his comfortably. He travelled the country with Seán MacEoin in the 1959 presidential campaign and he had a very high regard for this old Fine Gael veteran. He lost his seat in the 1961 general election but was successful in the Senate election which followed and he became Leas-Cathaoirleach of that body. 1965 was the last general election in the old North Mayo constituency in its then form, and Lindsay and Tommy O'Hara achieved the outstanding result of taking two seats for Fine Gael. He was returned to the front bench as spokesman on Education and Transport and Power.

In this capacity, he opposed the closure of the small one- and two- teacher schools and in the course of a lyrical speech in the Dáil on the opportunities children walking to school had of observing the onset of spring, he mentioned that they could see the frogs jumping on the road after heavy rain. In his own words: 'Fianna Fáil, never ones to look a gift-frog in the mouth, seized on the speech and used it afterwards to jeer me'.[62]

Pat Lindsay did not contest the 1969 general election in North Mayo, because the redrawn boundaries had carved up his traditional areas of support. Instead, he stood in Dublin North-Central, where he polled strikingly well and was only narrowly defeated. He remained active in Fine Gael, but his contesting North-Central in 1973 was once more unavailing. Appointed Master of the High Court in 1975, he retired from that position in 1984.

Pat Lindsay's wife, Moya Brady from Cavan town, whom he married in 1952, died in 1977. Their three children are Alison, John and Erris. If any public figure deserved the familiar epithet, 'a great character', Pat Lindsay did. His powerful physique (John Healy used to refer to him as 'the Great Congest'), but more so his great warmth, energy, wit and joie de vivre left a lasting impression on all who met him. His gifts as a raconteur were unsurpassed and oft-times he was 'wont to set the table on a roar' in many an establishment. He died in July 1993.

(h) James Dillon

James M. Dillon was one of the outstanding political figures of modern Ireland. He was born in Dublin in 1902 into a family which had been prominent in Irish politics for most of the 19th century. His grandfather, John Blake Dillon, was a leading member of Young Ireland, a friend of Thomas Davis, and was involved in the Rising of 1848. Later he was exiled to the US before returning and becoming an MP for Tipperary. Unfortunately he died of cholera before he could make any real impact in the House of Commons. James Dillon's father, John Dillon, was a leading member of the Irish Party at Westminster. One of the great figures of the House of Commons he was jailed on a number of occasions for his part in the Land War. He played a part in most of the major reforms which benefited Ireland in the late 19th and early 20th centuries and it was he who led the Irish Party after the death of Redmond. It was his tragedy to see his life's work swept away in the election victory of Sinn Féin in 1918.

Coming from this tradition, James Dillon vowed never to be part of either of the Sinn Féin parties and entered the Dáil as an Independent TD for Donegal in 1932. Within a year his opposition to the policies of de Valera and Fianna Fáil led him to become Deputy Leader of the new National Centre Party which won ten seats in the 1933 election. In September of 1933, just over a year in politics, he became a Vice-President of Fine Gael on the foundation of the party. Later, as recounted in the text, he was to resign on the issue of neutrality in 1942 and was to serve twice as Minister for Agriculture from 1948 to 1951 and 1951 to 1954 and then in 1959 became Leader of Fine Gael, a position he held until 1965. He retired from politics in 1969 after 37 unbroken years in Dail Éireann, all but five of those years as a TD for Monaghan.

James Dillon is often and rightly referred to as the greatest orator of 20th century Irish politics. He was one of the few politicians who drew large crowds, either as a platform speaker or in Dáil Éireann. But there was much more to James Dillon than his masterful oratory. He had a superb grasp of a wide range of issues and a view of life based on deeply rooted and fervently held convictions. These convictions included a passionate attachment to civil and individual liberty, to the supremacy of parliament, a respect for tradition and settled values combined with a radical approach on many economic and social questions. Most of all was his fearless independence of mind, this last trait in particular he showed to the full when alone he defied all parties and public opinion to oppose Ireland's neutrality in World War II. He did this because he believed that the Second World War represented a battle for the survival of democracy and parliamentary values against the barbarism of Nazism. It was a display of moral courage never equalled in Irish politics.

(i) Liam Cosgrave

Liam Cosgrave, son of W.T., who was President of the Executive Council from 1923 to 1932 and leader of Fine Gael from 1935 to 1944, was born in Dublin in April 1920. He went to the Christian Brothers' School, Synge Street, Dublin and to Castleknock College and afterwards studied at the King's Inns. He was called to the Bar in 1943 and to the Inner Bar in 1958. He served in the Irish army from 1940 to 1943, firstly with the rank of private and then as a commissioned officer.

He was returned to the Dáil for Dublin County in 1944 at

the youthful age of 23 and served for that constituency until 1948. He represented Dún Laoghaire-Rathdown from 1948 until his retirement in 1981. 'Unlike some of his colleagues, he was a full-time and very dedicated politician', it has been remarked,[63] and it is universally accepted that he was an outstanding constituency representative throughout his entire public career.

When the country's first inter-party government was formed in 1948, Cosgrave was appointed Parliamentary Secretary to the Taoiseach and to the Minister for Industry and Commerce. Because of Seán MacBride's distrust of the Secretary to the Government, this official did not attend cabinet meetings and to Cosgrave fell the responsible and sensitive task of recording these conferences, in his capacity as Government Chief Whip.

A *Leader* profile in February 1954 described him as a man of independent disposition who was never afraid to speak his mind, although he never publicly disagreed with his cabinet or party colleagues. Elevated to ministerial status at the early age of 28 after only five years in the Dáil, he must have made a strong impression because in the second inter-party government he was given the portfolio of External Affairs. He was only 34.

In this capacity, he oversaw Ireland's formal admission to the United Nations Organisation in 1955 and guided his delegation through the stormy session of 1956 when the Suez and Hungarian crises threatened world peace. That first Irish delegation to the United Nations was a capable and versatile one. It was led by the experienced and knowledgeable diplomat, Frederick H. Boland and one of its permanent officials was the gifted Dr Conor Cruise O'Brien.

When Richard Mulcahy retired as leader of Fine Gael in 1959, Cosgrave took part in the contest to succeed him against James Dillon. Although the voting figures for leadership contests in Fine Gael are never made public, it is believed that the number of votes each candidate received was very close, with Dillon emerging victorious.

Cosgrave was chairman of his party's policy committee which in 1964 produced the *Just Society* paper. His intervention on behalf of the proposals it contained, at the 1964 ard-fheis, is regarded as having been crucial in getting them accepted by the party as a whole. He afterwards said that he regarded the *Just Society* document as a radical change from anything that had been put forward before. He also saw it as unusual for an opposition party to produce such a detailed policy as it lacked the skilled, technical advice available to a government from its civil servants.[64]

When James Dillon resigned the leadership of Fine Gael following the 1965 general election defeat, Liam Cosgrave was unanimously chosen to succeed him. He became the leader of the party in which his father had been such a key figure in the year of his father's death. At 45, he was the youngest to become leader until Alan Dukes was elected to that position in 1987.

In an interview, given in 1966, he declared his open-mindedness on the question of coalition, considering that its having given Labour experience for the first time of responsibility in government to be one of the very important results of the first inter-party arrangement.[65]

In fact, it has been argued that a factor of major influence on him was that he spent most of his political life in opposition. 'Especially galling for him were the long years after 1957, when it looked as if the failure of the opposition to form a common front would leave Fianna Fáil in power forever'. This feeling was further seen as especially strong in a man with his fundamental suspicion of and aversion to what he saw Fianna Fáil as standing for.[66]

The remarkable success of Tom O'Higgins's presidential campaign in 1966 received a significant input from Cosgrave and must have been a substantial boost for Fine Gael's new leader. However, the result of the 1969 general election must have been a deep disappointment to him because, although his party gained three seats, Fianna Fáil was returned with an overall majority.

It is generally believed that he was close to Garret FitzGerald and the liberal wing of the party in the early years of his leadership (during his first ard-fheis speech as leader he described himself as 'slightly left of centre'), so much so that the *Irish Times* journalist, John Healy, coined the term 'FitzCosgrave' to convey the

333

closeness of the cooperation between the two. However, so this argument goes, following the 1969 defeat he moved closer to Gerard Sweetman and the conservative wing, fearing a threat to his leadership from his erstwhile allies.[67]

It is debatable whether much importance should be attached to this question of which influence guided Liam Cosgrave. As seen from the 1954 *Leader* profile already referred to, he had early gained the reputation of being very much of independent mind. It has been asserted that only he in Fine Gael wanted to support the referendum in 1968 by which Fianna Fáil attempted to change the Irish electoral system.[68] But his statements in the Dáil at the time certainly contradict this assertion.

He played a significant role in the 1970 arms crisis, when he went in early May to the Taoiseach at the time, Jack Lynch, and informed him that he had received information which implicated ministers in illegal arms dealing. He received widespread praise for approaching Lynch privately and there seems to be no doubt that Lynch was forced to act by Cosgrave's threat to make public his information.

The Fianna Fáil government's Offences Against the State (Amendment) Bill of 1972 caused deep divisions within Fine Gael and appears to have provoked something of a crisis for Liam Cosgrave's leadership. He was sympathetic with the general thrust of giving the Gárdaí greater powers. It has been contended that the primary influence on him was his father and his father's values and that this explains his almost obsessive preoccupation with law and order and what he regarded as the state's chief institutions - especially the army, the courts and the police.[69]

Because his attitude to this piece of legislation differed from that of most of his front bench and party, he was in danger of being replaced as leader, it has been asserted.[70] However, the recollections of some of the Fine Gael shadow cabinet at the time are not in agreement on the point. Garret FitzGerald has indeed maintained that Cosgrave was virtually isolated in his support for the government measure, but Tom O'Higgins has recalled that he himself, his brother, Michael, and FitzGerald supported Cosgrave, while Patrick Cooney, Richard Burke and Richie Ryan opposed him. Nevertheless, he acknowledged that supporters of the Bill were in a minority.[71] Cosgrave's own clear recollection is that only Patrick Donegan and Richard Burke backed his stance.

Whatever the attitude to Cosgrave's leadership, the moment was never forced to its crisis because the Dublin explosions on 1 December 1972, which killed two people and left over 80 injured, rallied the party behind its leader and, following a RTE interview, he emerged with his position strengthened. In a little over three months later he was head of the government.

He has been seen as filling a constructive role in negotiating the coalition agreement with Labour before the February 1973 general election. Opinions on his performance as Taoiseach vary. One view is that he saw himself as chairman of the cabinet rather than as its chief and that he let ministers get on with their responsibilities and that he did not interfere with them.[72] Another is that he was an effective and firm leader of his government but that even his Labour Ministers saw him as fair.[73] Like his father, his leadership and style were no doubt quiet, low-key but none the less able for that.

It has been observed that, like his father, he had 'a passion for law-and-order, and a desire for well-regulated economic prosperity, an unobtrusive toughness in government, and a deep distrust for republicanism, radicalism and Britain'.[74] The inclusion of Britain in his list of distrusts must be questioned, because he played a very prominent part in the Sunningdale Conference in 1973, which paved the way for the power-sharing executive in Northern Ireland which lasted from January to May 1974.

The period during which he presided over the government was one of considerable unrest and uncertainty caused mainly by the twin calamities of the Northern troubles and the quadrupling of oil prices. 'His courage under fire stood the country in good stead', it has been remarked,[75] and he has been credited with displaying 'endless patience in difficulty'.[76]

Cosgrave's premiership was not without its share of controversy. His approach to social issues was basically conservative and this explains 'his opposition to any change in the contraception laws (even when this meant voting against his own government without telling them in advance) and his support for the conservative educational policies of his Education Minister, Richard Burke'.[77] His handling of the President Ó Dálaigh resignation has also been criticised as has his speech at the May 1977 Fine Gael ard-fheis where he referred to 'blow-ins' and attacked those whom he saw as undermining the forces of law and order.

However, it is probably the case that he presided over the most harmonious coalition government ever in the history of the state. His reputation as a Taoiseach will probably improve in retrospect, it has been argued, in that he was decisive, had a clear, uncomplicated view of the direction of his administration, had an immediate rapport with at least a section of the voters and was in quiet control of his cabinet. These qualities, it is further contended, have appeared relatively rarely since he left office.[78]

Following the failure of the coalition to secure re-election in 1977, Liam Cosgrave resigned as leader of Fine Gael. He retired from the Dáil in 1981, having spent nearly 40 years and virtually all his adult life in active politics. He was succeeded as one of the Fine Gael TDs for Dún Laoghaire by his son Liam T. Cosgrave, who represents the fourth generation of Cosgraves to have served in Irish public life.

(j) Other Coalition Government Ministers 1973-77:

(i) Richie Ryan

Richie Ryan was born in Dublin, in November 1929. He received his schooling at the Christian Brothers' School, Synge Street, Dublin. Afterwards he attended University College, Dublin and the Incorporated Law Society and qualified as a solicitor. He was a member of Dublin Corporation from 1960 to 1973.

Richie Ryan first reached the Dáil by winning a by-election in 1959. He came from a background that was strongly Fianna Fáil, and often remarked that while many were in Fine Gael because of their antecedents, he was there because of personal conviction. He was returned at every general election since 1961 until he became elected a Member of the European Parliament (MEP) when he decided that his career lay in that sphere.

It has been maintained that he was a formative supporter of the *Just Society* programme in 1964 but that shortly afterwards he became estranged from the liberal wing of Fine Gael.[79] His rise in the party ranks was rapid and he was appointed a member of the front bench in 1966. At first he was shadow Minister for Health and Social Welfare and then for Foreign Affairs.

After the 1969 general election he remarked that 'the Irish people have disgraced themselves again by their crass inability and cowardly unwillingness to use the ballot box to get rid of a government which most of them detested'.[80]

It came as a surprise to him, but was probably a measure of the confidence Liam Cosgrave reposed in him, that he was appointed Minister for Finance in 1973. It has been remarked that in his new ministerial role his natural reforming instincts came to the fore.[81] He made a courageous attempt to impose some taxation on wealth and on farmers and he it was who piloted the capital taxation measures through the cabinet. For this legislation he was to be reviled in some quarters as 'Red Richie'.

But he faced difficulties no other Irish Minister for Finance before him had to confront, because of the massive leap in world oil prices from the end of 1973. He bore the brunt of the challenge which this development presented. His strong social conscience convinced him that the poorer sections of society had to be protected from the worst effects of the recession and this explains the large increase in government social welfare expenditure during his term of office.

He argued that the increase in Ireland's foreign debt was justified in order to prevent the economy sinking further into recession. It was firmly believed at the time, and not just in Ireland, that the slump was a temporary phenomenon and that governments could spend their way out of it. By 1976, Ryan announced that Irish foreign borrowing had reached its limit and he succeeded in reducing slightly government expenditure as a proportion of GNP and in bringing down foreign borrowing significantly between 1976 and 1977. For his brave attempts to wrestle with the country's daunting economic problems he was dubbed 'Richie Ruin'. It seemed that no matter what he did he could not win. In view of the amount of public spending that occurred after he left office, his performance from 1973 to 1977 may be seen in retrospect as positively ascetic.

Bad luck appears to have dogged Ryan's political career. His ministerial spell coincided with the disastrous oil crisis; he was asked by Liam Cosgrave to be Fine Gael's director of elections for the catastrophic 1977 campaign, for the result of which he had to carry much of the blame, and he was out of the country on official business when Cosgrave announced his resignation as leader of Fine Gael, so that the other aspirants to the top position in Fine Gael had a head-start on him. Had circumstances been otherwise, there is no doubt that he would have been in a much stronger position to challenge for the leadership.

He was re-appointed to his old front bench position of Foreign Affairs by Garret FitzGerald in the autumn of 1977. He was elected to the European Parliament in June 1979, heading the poll in the Dublin City constituency, a strikingly impressive performance given the odium that was heaped on him while he was in office. He was removed from the front bench by FitzGerald following his becoming a MEP, but was restored to his old shadow portfolio in January 1981 following Fine Gael's failure to win the by-election in Donegal two months before. It must have been a surprise and disappointment to him that he was not appointed to the Fine Gael - Labour coalition government that was formed in July 1981. Richie Ryan chose not to contest the February 1982 general election but to concentrate instead on the European Parliament. He was again successful in the 1984 Euro-elections and was appointed to the European Court of Auditors in 1986, for a seven-year period of responsibility.

(ii) Patrick Cooney

Patrick Cooney was born in Dublin, in March 1931, but he

has spent much of his life in Athlone, Co. Westmeath. He attended Castleknock College, University College, Dublin and he studied law at the Incorporated Law Society of Ireland in Blackhall Place, Dublin. A member of the Fine Gael Youth Group in the 1960s, he was an enthusiastic supporter of the *Just Society* proponents within the party. He contested unsuccessfully the three general elections held in the 1960s and was elected to Westmeath County Council in 1967.

Successful in a by-election to the Dáil in 1970, he was appointed to the Fine Gael front bench after only two years in the House as spokesman on Justice. He was a trenchant opponent of the Offences Against the State (Amendment) Bill in 1972, asking how the Minister for Justice could 'come into this Parliament and ask it to support a Bill the like of which can only be found on the statute books of South Africa'.

When the Fine Gael-Labour coalition won a majority in the 1973 general election, Cooney was appointed Minister for Justice, on only his third year in the Dáil. He enacted some legislation which was very beneficial to the community in general. His 1974 Adoption Act repealed the section of the 1952 Act which prevented a couple in a mixed marriage adopting, or orphans of such a marriage being adopted. When the Supreme Court ruled that the 1935 Control of the Importation, Sale and Manufacture of Contraceptives Act was unconstitutional, Cooney's attempt to amend the Act was defeated in the Dáil in July 1974.

But most of his period in office was taken up by the subversive threat which he unflinchingly confronted, despite threats of assassination. He gave the police force wider powers of arrest and detention and increased the penalty for membership of illegal organisations. There were many allegations of Gárda brutality and Cooney has been accused of increasing the possibility of such occurring by extending the maximum period of detention without trial from two to seven days.[82] A recent historian has remarked that neither he, nor his leader, showed much concern about the charges of Gárda misbehaviour, and has further observed that: 'However exaggerated, cynical or opportunistic many of these allegations

339

were, some incidents left a nasty taste in the public mouth'.[83]

He was a shock loser in the 1977 general election and was only a few hundred votes behind Gerry L'Estrange for the final seat. He was probably the victim of the generous campaign he ran in the election in an effort to ensure two Fine Gael seats.

Cooney was the Leader of Fine Gael in the Senate from 1977 to 1981. Returned to the Dáil in the June 1981 election, he was appointed Minister for Transport and Communications in the coalition government formed afterwards. He had little chance to make his mark in his new Department, as the coalition lost power after only six months in office. However, when Fine Gael and Labour again formed a government after the November 1982 general election, he became Minister for Defence. In the cabinet reshuffle of early 1986, he was transferred to Education.

As Minister for Defence he introduced the Courts-martial Appeal Bill which set up an appeal system from courts-martial. He also defended the Irish army's taking part in the British Legion's Remembrance Day ceremonies. In October 1983 he authorised the army's participation for the first time in Poppy Day ceremonies in St Patrick's Cathedral, Dublin. He defended his action as follows: 'But we must remember that the point of the ceremony is to commemorate Irishmen who died in the cause of peace. Thousands did so in the First World War to safeguard small nations and in the Second in the fight against fascism'.[84]

Cooney was against the removal of the constitutional ban on divorce and publicly clashed with his leader, Garret FitzGerald, on more than one occasion over the issue. Although the official government position on the June 1986 divorce referendum was neutral, individual Fine Gael TDs were permitted to express their opposition in a personal capacity only but not as members of the party. First at a private party meeting in Longford and then twice at public meetings, Cooney made it very clear that he was against the change being proposed by the referendum.

He was unsuccessful when contesting the European election for Connaught-Ulster in 1979, but was returned as a Member of the European Parliament for the Leinster constituency in 1989. Since

340

that time he has chosen to concentrate on European rather than on domestic politics.

(iii) Mark Clinton

Mark Clinton was born in Kells, Co. Meath in February 1915. He attended the Christian Brothers' School, Kells; Warrenstown Agricultural College and University College, Dublin, where he took Diplomas in Social Science and Agricultural Science. He was estate manager, Peamount Hospital, Newcastle, Co. Dublin before entering the Dáil.

Mark Clinton served on a large number of public bodies during his career. He was a member of Dublin County Council from 1955 to 1973, vice-chairman of that body 1956/57 and 1967/68, and chairman 1957/59 and 1968/69. A member of Dublin County Committee of Agriculture also from 1955 to 1973, he was its vice-chairman 1962/63 and 1964/65, and chairman 1965-68. Also on Dublin Vocational Education Committee from 1955 to 1973, he acted as its chairman from 1970 to 1973. Clinton was also a member of the Dublin Health Authority from 1960 to 1971, and of the Eastern Health Board between 1971 and 1973 (chairman, 1972-73).

He was first elected to the Dáil in 1961 and represented Dublin County from 1961 to 1969, and Dublin County North from 1969 to 1981. He was Fine Gael opposition front-bench spokesman on Local Government, Agriculture and Defence. When the coalition government was formed in 1973, Mark Clinton was appointed Minister for Agriculture by Liam Cosgrave.

He proved to be a most impressive and successful Minister for Agriculture. His Department had acquired a vital importance with Ireland's recent membership of the EEC. Agriculture ministers from the various member states met regularly to discuss the Common Agricultural Policy (CAP) which decided the prices farmers received for their produce. Each fought for the best possible deal for his own country and Mark Clinton was a tough and determined negotiator on behalf of Irish farming interests. Under him Irish agriculture achieved levels of prosperity that were never before thought possible.

When Garret FitzGerald became leader of Fine Gael in 1977, he wished to have Clinton as his deputy leader, but the latter declined the invitation.

He was elected a MEP in the 1979 Euro-elections for the Leinster constituency. He did not seek re-election to the Dáil at the 1981 general election, deciding to concentrate instead on the European parliament. He was again successful in the 1984 Euro-elections for Leinster.

Mark Clinton retired as a MEP in 1989. A quiet, dignified, reserved man, he at all times displayed unfailing courtesy in public life.

(iv) Peter Barry

Peter Barry was born in August 1928 in Cork into the famous tea-importing and wholesaling family of that city. He attended the Model School, Cork and the Christian Brothers' College, Cork.

His father, Anthony Barry, was a Fine Gael TD for Cork City from 1954 to 1957 and 1961 to 1965, and was Lord Mayor of Cork for 1961-62. Peter was elected to Cork Corporation in 1967 and was Lord Mayor of his native city in 1970-71.

Peter Barry was first elected to Dáil Éireann in 1969 and has been successful in all general elections since then. He acted as front bench spokesman on Labour from 1970 to 1973 and became Minister for Transport and Power in the government formed in 1973. In this capacity he had the agreeable duty of presiding over the bringing ashore of oil and gas from the Bantry Bay field in his native heath. He was appointed Minister for Education at the beginning of December 1976 when Richard Burke was nominated to the EEC Commission.

He considered contesting the Fine Gael leadership on Liam Cosgrave's retirement in 1977, but withdrew when it became clear to him that Garret FitzGerald had a majority. He proposed FitzGerald for the leadership at the parliamentary party meeting at which he was unanimously elected Cosgrave's successor. He then became deputy leader of the party and was appointed spokesman on Economic Affairs and the Public Service. In January 1981, he was made General Election Co-ordinator, which meant that he was given responsibility for the organisation as it prepared for the electoral contest of that year. Barry provided a vital link, along with Tom Fitzpatrick, between FitzGerald's new party administrators and the parliamentary party. He was popular with the TDs and Senators, who liked and trusted him.

He took part in the negotiations which preceded the formation of FitzGerald's first coalition and was consulted by him on possible membership of that government. It has been contended that FitzGerald offered him the Finance portfolio in July 1981, but that he turned it down at least partly because he was aware that his leader preferred John Bruton for Finance.[85] He occupied the position of Minister for the Environment in the 1981-82 administration.

With Jack Lynch's retirement from politics in 1981, Peter Barry became the dominant political figure in the Cork area. He also participated in the talks which led to FitzGerald's second government, again advised his leader on his cabinet and was appointed Minister for Foreign Affairs, a position for which, it has been remarked, he proved an inspired choice.[86]

The following laudatory comment was made of him in 1983:
Although a man of personal financial substance, having taken over a lucrative family business with a long history, he shows surprisingly liberal instincts and steers clear of the tight professional/religious coteries to which such merchant princes are often drawn.[87]

There has certainly never been anything retrogressive about him. 'Any political party must change with the times, or else it dies', he has been cited as declaring at the parliamentary party meeting in the aftermath of the defeat of the divorce referendum in 1986.[88]

As Minister for Foreign Affairs, he supported the idea of the New Ireland Forum from its inception and was one of the eight Fine Gael delegates to the Forum. He also played a crucial role in the extremely complex process which led to the signing of the historic Anglo-Irish Agreement at Hillsborough in November 1985.

Peter Barry contested unsuccessfully the election to choose Garret FitzGerald's successor in 1987, from which Alan Dukes emerged victorious.

(v) Richard Burke

Richard Burke was born in March 1932, in Brooklyn, New York. He attended the Christian Brothers' School, Thurles, Co. Tipperary and afterwards studied at University College, Dublin, and the King's Inns, Dublin, qualifying as a barrister.

His first venture into politics was as a member of the Christian Democratic Party founded by Seán Loftus in the early 1960s. He joined Fine Gael in the mid-sixties and was elected to Dublin County Council in 1967. He was elected to Dáil Éireann in 1969 and was appointed to the front bench straightaway by Liam Cosgrave. He was Fine Gael Chief Whip for three years and then spokesman on Posts and Telegraphs.

For part of his career he was a secondary teacher and when the coalition government was formed in 1973, Burke was made Minister for Education. He promised many educational reforms and was very popular with the media, because he was articulate and immensely able intellectually. However, owing to the economic crisis, the finance was not available for many of his proposed reforms and he clashed with the teachers' unions.

He was an extremely conservative Minister for Education, resisting the development of non-denominational schools, which were sought by parents in two areas of Dublin, and defending the denominational basis of Irish schooling. He also joined with his leader in voting against his own government's 1974 Contraceptive Bill.

He let it be known at an early stage that he wished to be his government's nominee to the EEC Commission. He was strongly opposed for this position by Labour's Justin Keating, who was Minister for Industry and Commerce and who had Garret FitzGerald's backing. However, with Liam Cosgrave's support,

Burke won the nomination and took up his new post in January 1977.

At the new Commission, he was given responsibility for taxation, transport, consumer affairs and relations between the Commission and the European Parliament. He promoted some reforms, especially in the area of transport, but it has been contended that he was only a minor figure in the Commission and that he did not succeed in making any real impact.[89]

When he completed his four-year term as European Commissioner, he went to Harvard University in the United States in January 1981 to take up a fellowship in international affairs. In March, Garret FitzGerald invited him to return to domestic politics, which he did in mid-April, becoming an adviser to the front bench on European affairs.

An attempt was made to find a niche for him in the Dublin North-East constituency but this was successfully resisted by the sitting TD for that area, Michael-Joe Cosgrave. He was then accommodated in Dublin West, mainly thanks to the efforts of Jim Mitchell. However, Brian Fleming, another Fine Gael candidate in that constituency, did his utmost to prevent Burke being nominated for Dublin West. As things turned out, Fleming need not have worried. It was a remarkable achievement for Burke and a great tribute to the constituency workers in Dublin West, that he took a third seat for Fine Gael in this five-seater in the June 1981 general election.

In the coalition government that was afterwards formed, Burke expected to be given the Foreign Affairs portfolio. On the morning of the day that FitzGerald was to announce his new cabinet, in a radio interview on RTE, Burke made it clear that he expected the appointment. After all, he had been invited to return from the United States to rejoin the front bench, although he was not a member of the Dáil. It must have been a deep disappointment to him that he was offered nothing.

He began to practise at the Bar as a junior counsel and was appointed a director of a number of public companies. In the February 1982 general election, he repeated his creditable feat in

Dublin West of the previous June. The Fianna Fáil government under Charles Haughey which was formed after that election was dependent for its survival on the support of the Independent TD, Tony Gregory. Haughey decided to offer Burke the position of Irish EEC Commissioner, hoping to win the subsequent by-election in Dublin West. The offer was made in March and Burke accepted, resigning from Fine Gael in the process.

(vi) Patrick S. Donegan

Patrick Donegan was born in Monasterboice, Co. Louth in October 1923. He received his schooling at the Christian Brothers' School, Drogheda, Co. Louth, and Saint Vincent's College, Castleknock, Co. Dublin. His occupations have been a company director, a miller, a farmer and a publican.

He was an alderman on Drogheda Borough Council from 1956 to 1973; a member of Louth County Council from 1955 to 1973, and its chairman from 1967 to 1973; a member of Louth County Committee of Agriculture from 1956 to 1973, of Drogheda Harbour Board 1956-58, and of the North-Eastern Health Board 1971-73. Patrick Donegan was also a member of the Federated Union of Employers, of the Irish Grain and Agricultural Merchants' Association and of the Joint Labour Committee Provender Milling Industry for many years.

He was first elected to the Dáil for Louth in the 1954 general election. He lost his seat in 1957 but was successful in the Senate election of that year on the Agricultural Panel. Returned to the Dáil again for Louth in 1961, he represented that constituency until his retirement from active politics 20 years later.

Donegan was Fine Gael front-bench spokesman on Agriculture from 1961 to 1966 and on Industry and Commerce from 1966 to 1973. Throughout the Offences Against the State Amendment Bill crisis in Fine Gael in 1972, he firmly supported his leader's stance. During the Cosgrave government, Donegan was Minister for Defence until December 1976; Minister for Lands from then until February 1977, and Minister for Fisheries from February to July 1977.

346

As Minister for Defence he was deeply involved in the struggle against subversion and armed aggression of those years and the high-point of his ministerial career was the capture of the arms ship, the 'Claudia'. The low point was his description of President Ó Dálaigh as a 'thundering disgrace' in a speech at an army barracks in the autumn of 1976, after which he offered to resign. It was an unfortunate blot on an otherwise long, distinguished and unblemished public career.

Patrick S. Donegan retired from active politics in 1981, the same year as Liam Cosgrave, his former leader to whom he had been so close and loyal for so much of his political career.

(vii) Tom Fitzpatrick

Tom Fitzpatrick was born in February 1918, at Scotshouse, Clones, Co. Monaghan. He received his schooling at St MacCartan's College, Monaghan, and afterwards studied at University College, Dublin, and the Incorporated Law Society, Blackhall Place, Dublin.

He was a member of Cavan Urban District Council, to which he was first elected in 1950, and of Cavan Vocational Education Committee. A member of the Senate from 1961 to 1965, he was first elected to the Dáil in the latter year and was returned at each election between then and his retirement from active politics in 1987.

Fitzpatrick was quickly appointed to the Fine Gael front bench, on which he served until 1973. He was made Minister for Lands in the Cosgrave coalition and occupied that ministry until the cabinet reshuffle of 1 December 1976, when he was transferred to Transport and Power.

Because he had been a senior member of the party since the mid-sixties, he was regarded as a potential leader by many who thought that there would have to be a compromise choice between the Cosgrave and FitzGerald sides of Fine Gael. But at 60, Fitzpatrick considered himself to be too old for the position and withdrew his name from the contest to succeed Liam Cosgrave.

In fact, he was one of Garret FitzGerald's closest advisers

in the 1977-81 period. His new leader appointed him to the various committees that he formed during those years and depended on his persuasive influence and manner to get many of his organisational innovations accepted. He was front bench spokesman on the Environment from the autumn of 1977 until January 1981, when he took over Health and was also made shadow-Leader of the House.

He would almost certainly have been Ceann Comhairle had not the first FitzGerald coalition's position in the 22nd Dáil been so tenuous. Instead, he served as Minister for Fisheries and Forestry from July 1981 until February 1982. He was Ceann Comhairle during the second FitzGerald government from December 1982 until February 1987.

Tom Fitzpatrick held a number of key positions in the Fine Gael organisation, including those of national organiser, chairman of the national executive and vice-president. As such, he was an enormously influential figure. As a very skilful broker and mediator, he smoothed over divisions and disagreements within the party and often played a crucial role in bridging the gap between liberals and conservatives from the 1960s until the 1980s.

(viii) Tom O'Donnell

Tom O'Donnell's uncle, Richard O'Connell, was a Commandant of the Mid-Limerick flying column of the IRA during the Anglo-Irish War 1919-21, and was subsequently a Cumann na nGaedheal TD for Limerick from 1924 until 1932.

Tom was born in Limerick in August 1926. He attended the Christian Brothers' School, Charleville, Co. Cork, Crescent College, Limerick, St. Patrick's College, Thurles, Co. Tipperary, and University College, Dublin.

He was a teacher for a period in a number of secondary schools in Dublin. He worked with Canon Hayes on the national executive of Muintir na Tíre and he edited the organisation's journal, *Landmark*, for three years.

O'Donnell was first elected to the Dáil in the 1961 general election, winning the seat formerly occupied by John Carew. He was a supporter of the *Just Society* development in the party in

1964. He was appointed to the Fine Gael front bench in 1969 and was given responsibility for Transport and Power.

When the party secured office along with Labour after the 1973 general election, Tom O'Donnell became Aire na Gaeltachta, or Minister for the Gaeltacht. He could boast of many significant achievements during his term of office and he emerged from his ministerial experience with much distinction. His warm and genial personality made a deep and lasting impression on the public.

In October 1977, he was appointed to the front bench as spokesman on Transport and Communications, his old brief. He was Fine Gael's only successful candidate in the Munster constituency in the June 1979 elections to the European Parliament. He was afterwards relieved of his front bench responsibilities by Garret FitzGerald but these were restored to him in January 1981.

He must have been disappointed not to have been given a ministry in the July 1981 coalition government as he had topped the poll in Limerick East and had helped bring in Michael Noonan, the first time ever that there were two Fine Gael TDs in that constituency. His organisation in East Limerick was deeply critical of what it saw as this failure on FitzGerald's part and the *Limerick Echo* banner headline read *Shame on you, Garret*. It has been argued that O'Donnell had traditionally been on the right wing of Fine Gael more because of a sense of alienation from the liberal Dublin set than because of ideological conviction.[90]

However, this assertion seems difficult to sustain in view of his consistently conservative position on the various social issues that arose during the period of the 1982-87 government, and it is likely that his age and personal outlook, which was probably shared by the majority of those who voted for him, were more relevant factors.

He clashed with the party leadership over the anti-abortion amendment in 1983. He voted for the Fianna Fáil wording and abstained in the vote on the Fine Gael formula. His sister, Bernadette Bonnar, was one of the leading organisers of the Pro-Life Amendment Campaign. He also cast his vote against his party's Family Planning Bill in 1985 and divorce referendum Bill the following year.

He was a member of the Committee on Secondary Legislation of the European Community. He did not contest the 1987 general election, concentrating instead on his career in the European Parliament, to which he was again returned in the 1984 Euro-elections in the Munster constituency. He retired from active politics in 1989.

(ix) Oliver J. Flanagan

Oliver J. Flanagan was born in Mountmellick, Co. Laois, in May 1920 and he attended the National School in that town. He was elected to Laois County Council in 1942 and was a member of that body until his retirement from active politics. He was also a member of the Midland Health Board and of Laois Vocational Education Committee. He was one of the longest serving TDs ever, having been elected to the Dáil for the first time in 1943 and having retained his seat thereafter until his retirement in 1987.

He was originally elected as a Monetary Reform candidate, and then as an Independent, joining Fine Gael in 1950. In the second inter-party government, which held power between 1954 and 1957, he was appointed Parliamentary Secretary to the Minister for Agriculture and Fisheries, James Dillon, for whom Flanagan had an enduring admiration.

He was front bench spokesman on Lands from 1958 until 1969. During the Cosgrave coalition, he became Parliamentary Secretary to the Minister for Local Government in 1975, and in December 1976, he was appointed Minister for Defence when Patrick Donegan was transferred to the Department of Lands. He was not reappointed to the Fine Gael front bench when Garret FitzGerald became leader in 1977. Although he proposed FitzGerald for Taoiseach on 30 June, 1981, it has been argued that he represented a very different tradition within the party from that for which FitzGerald stood.[91]

Flanagan was a member of the Knights of Columbanus and always championed the position of the Roman Catholic Church on issues as they arose in Irish public life. In this he probably differed little from most of his fellow-TDs for perhaps three decades or more of his public life. He voted against his own government's Contraceptive Bill in 1974 as did a number of other Fine Gael deputies in the Dáil. He was conferred with the Knighthood of St Gregory the Great by Pope John Paul 1 on 21 September 1978.

In the vote on the anti-abortion measure in the Dáil in 1983, he supported the Fianna Fáil wording. When Garret FitzGerald said that that formula could endanger the lives of Irish women, Flanagan accused him on radio of trying to terrorise the mothers of Ireland. Along with Alice Glenn and Tom O'Donnell, he also voted against his government's 1985 Family Planning Amendment Bill.

His health had not been good during his last Dáil term and his long public career came to an end in 1987. His vote was always huge in his Laois-Offaly constituency until 1977 and he consistently topped the poll there. There is little doubt that the view that his reputation as a constituency worker was unrivalled, still holds good.[92]

Oliver J. Flanagan was one of the most colourful figures on the Irish political stage. There was a streak of the actor in him and his turn of phrase frequently entertained Dáil and public alike. His tongue-in-cheek remark on a 'Late Late Show' that there was no sex in Ireland before television is by now legendary and belongs to a different, almost forgotten era. Irish political life is somewhat poorer for his passing.

(k) Garret FitzGerald

Garret FitzGerald's father was Desmond FitzGerald, who was Cumann na nGaedheal Minister for External Affairs from 1923 to 1927 and Minister for Defence from 1927 until 1932. His mother, Mabel McConnell, came from a staunchly Unionist Belfast family, but was converted to Irish nationalism mainly through the Gaelic League. Both his parents were members of the GPO garrison during the 1916 Rising and also took part in the subsequent independence struggle. They differed strongly over the Anglo-Irish Treaty, and during the Civil War which followed, his mother chose to give up her active political role.

351

Garret was the youngest of four sons and was born in Dublin, in February 1926. He went to the Jesuits' Belvedere College, Dublin, and afterwards attended University College, Dublin, where he obtained a degree in French and History. He was then employed by Aer Lingus, firstly as an administrative assistant and subsequently as research and analysis officer.

In 1950, he was made directly responsible for economic planning in the national airline. This was a new area for him, but he went on to study economics at postgraduate level in UCD and before long he had a broad knowledge of how the Irish economy functioned.

In the early 1950s he entered the field of journalism, having to write under a pseudonym because he was still a semi-state company employee. It has been observed that the quality of Irish journalism improved in many ways during the 1960s but that FitzGerald, 'at first virtually single-handed, was already pioneering in the 1950s as *analyst* of the *Irish Times*, a new level of sophistication in public economic comment'.[93] From 1959 to 1973, he wrote weekly for the *Irish Times* and became the country's leading commentator on the economy. Following the publication of his autobiography in 1991, he has resumed this journalistic role and writes a feature each Saturday for his old newspaper, with a roving brief to write on whatever topic he wishes.

Taking up the offer of a fellowship from Trinity College, Dublin, in 1958, he resigned from Aer Lingus. Three years later he set up his own economic consultancy practice which he merged shortly afterwards with the Economist Intelligence Unit, and he was managing director of this until 1972. He also widened his journalistic horizons, becoming the Irish correspondent of the *Financial Times* and then of the *Economist*. He also became a lecturer in economics in UCD.

He was invited to join Fine Gael in 1964 by Declan Costello, who was working on the ideas which were soon to become known as the *Just Society* programme. There was nothing at all unusual about FitzGerald joining Fine Gael. After all, his father had been a TD for the party until 1943. What was surprising was that he was almost 40 before he involved himself in active politics.

In his autobiography he tells how, when he was 22, he and his wife, Joan, canvassed in the 1948 general election for the Fine Gael candidate, John A. Costello, in what is now the Dublin South-East constituency. They assured the middle-class residents in Waterloo Road that Fine Gael supported Ireland's remaining in the British Commonwealth. When Costello, as Taoiseach, took Ireland out of the Commonwealth and declared a republic, FitzGerald was disillusioned and decided to drop out of politics until the 1960s. The inter-party government's opting not to join NATO and the anti-partition campaign it engaged in in tandem with Fianna Fáil, further disenchanted him.[94]

It has been remarked that Irish Catholic attitudes to social issues changed in the 1960s and that very clear evidence of this was the rejection by Catholics at that time of what other Catholics had done in Ireland in the 1940s and 1950s In an article in the Jesuit periodical *Studies* in 1965, FitzGerald argued that in some ways Catholic thinking in Ireland had been a long way behind Catholic thought in other countries. He believed this was particularly the case in relation to social welfare, and he expressed the view that in the 1930s and 1940s the Catholic Church in Ireland had gone astray in its thinking on such issues.

Around the same time, Declan Costello, in a lecture to the Dublin Institute of Catholic Sociology, maintained that Irish social conditions at the time showed that the influence of the Church on government thinking had been to prevent ameliorative action being taken and that Catholic social principles could be unjustly used to uphold the existing unfair situation. He observed that attempts at social reform had been attacked on Catholic grounds, as had the reformer, while the conditions he tried to improve were accepted without criticism. [95] It is little wonder that two such like-minded men should have been drawn together and that FitzGerald should have joined with Costello in trying to persuade Fine Gael to accept their ideas.

He was invited to stand as a Fine Gael candidate in Dublin South-East in the 1965 general election, but turned down the offer mainly because Joan, his wife, did not wish him to enter active politics.

That election was the first to receive extensive television coverage and RTE employed FitzGerald to analyze the results as they came in. How he discharged this task has been described as follows:

> One member, in particular, of the panel of experts had displayed indefatigable energy with an almost unbroken ten-hour performance. It stood him in good stead when he launched his own political career in the Senate election a few weeks later. In a cloud of statistics and high-velocity opinions, Garret FitzGerald had arrived in the political arena.[96]

Following his election to the Senate, Liam Cosgrave appointed FitzGerald to the Fine Gael front bench of that House and he participated in full party front bench meetings. He worked closely with his new leader and played an active role in Tom O'Higgins's 1966 presidential campaign.

However, for reasons which are still not clear, relations between Cosgrave and FitzGerald cooled thereafter. FitzGerald himself suggested two possible causes. One was the growing influence of the conservatively-minded Gerard Sweetman on the Fine Gael leader. Another was that in 1967, Brendan Halligan of Labour informed FitzGerald of his party's renewed interest in coalition with Fine Gael, but intimated that Labour would not serve under Cosgrave as Taoiseach, a fact which FitzGerald felt in duty bound to communicate to his leader.[97]

He stood for the Dáil in the Dublin South-East constituency at the 1969 general election and topped the poll. Appointed shadow spokesman on Education, he frequently spoke in the Dáil on numerous other issues as well, so much so that an *Irish Times* cartoon of the time showed a Fine Gael front bench consisting of 21 Garret FitzGeralds! In 1971, he was moved to the shadow Finance portfolio.

FitzGerald's contributions during the arms crisis debates in the Dáil in 1970 received widespread attention and he played a major role on the Committee on Public Accounts which tried to investigate how £100,000, voted by the Dáil in 1970 for the relief of distress in Northern Ireland, had been spent.

The tension between the liberal-social democratic and the conservative wings of Fine Gael came to a head in 1972. FitzGerald saw himself as one of the targets of Liam Cosgrave's 'mongrel foxes' speech at the party's ard-fheis in May of that year. He records that he considered leaving the platform but decided against it.[98] The debate within the party on its response to the Offences Against the State (Amendment) Bill, where Cosgrave was reluctant to follow his colleagues' line on voting against it, led to FitzGerald afterwards accusing him of 'having neither led, nor been led' on the Bill.[99] However, he subsequently accepted that his leader's position on this particular piece of legislation had been the right one to have adopted.[100]

As shadow Finance spokesman, FitzGerald's success over George Colley in a television debate during the early 1973 general election campaign was perceived as significantly affecting the overall result of the contest. When Fine Gael and Labour afterwards formed a government, FitzGerald was appointed Minister for Foreign Affairs.

The importance of that Department greatly increased with EEC membership. The new Minister had soon acquired an outstanding reputation. His impact on European Foreign Ministers and officials was astounding and was due mainly to his ability, idealism, hard work, and the ease with which he could speak French. The manner in which he presided over the EEC Council of Ministers meeting in Dublin in 1975 enhanced his country's reputation. It was to his advantage that Ireland's early experience of the EEC was mainly good.

Because of his maternal background, Garret FitzGerald always felt close ties with Northern Ireland, visiting his cousins in that part of the island throughout his life. When he entered the political arena, he established informal links with both nationalist and Unionist politicians there. In his book, *Towards a New Ireland*, which was published in 1972, he contended that if Unionists were ever to be persuaded into a united Ireland, a determined effort would have to be made to change the predominant ethos in the southern Catholic state.

When he became Foreign Minister 'contacts with political leaders of both communities in the North were developed in a structured way', as he himself expressed it.[101] His central involvement in both the pre-Sunningdale and actual Sunningdale discussions is recorded at length in his autobiography as is the depressing sequence of events which led to the collapse of that hopeful initiative.[102] He had no doubt about where the fault lay: 'The failure of the British government to give adequate support to the Executive that it had caused to be established by a democratic process, and its incapacity to maintain essential services, led to a complete collapse of self-confidence amongst the pro-Assembly Unionists'.[103]

In his first speech to the Dáil as Fine Gael leader, he summarised his feelings about the 1973-77 period in relation to Northern Ireland thus: 'My greatest pride is a remark by a Northern politician that our government had won more respect from both sections in the North than any previous government had won from either'.

When Liam Cosgrave resigned after the June 1977 defeat, Garret FitzGerald was unopposed for the leadership of his party. No previous Fine Gael leader had served so short a Dáil apprenticeship before being elevated to the primary position.

FitzGerald appointed Peter Prendergast, a marketing executive, to reorganise and promote the party. This turned Fine Gael into a professional political structure which, already by 1981, had an organisation to match that of Fianna Fáil. This was a notable achievement in that FitzGerald had been elected leader as a man of ideas and not as one noted for his organisational skills.

It has been maintained that his comments during the Dáil debate on the nomination of Charles Haughey as Taoiseach, in December 1979, have been the cause of grave personal embarrassment to FitzGerald since then.[104] However, his own observation on the matter in his recently-published autobiography would seem to contradict this view: 'It will be for historians to judge whether placing my view bluntly on the record at that point was counterproductive or whether it may have been contributed to my opponent's failure to secure an overall majority at any of the five subsequent general election'.[105]

The improvement in party organisation and FitzGerald's personal appeal, as well as disillusionment with Fianna Fáil, explain Fine Gael's impressive showing in the June 1981 general election. In his published memoirs, he paid this tribute to the party's rank-and-file and to the ordinary people of Ireland:

> I was very often deeply moved by the enthusiasm of so many of our party workers engaged in the patriotic work of electioneering and in other less dramatic tasks to be performed between elections; their efforts, and, of course, those of activists of other parties, which ensure the alternation of governments so vital to the preservation of democracy from corruption and the abuse of power, deserve far more recognition than they ever received from the general public. And I could not fail to be heartened by the warmth of so many ordinary Irish people, uninvolved in politics, who frequently feel moved to express their appreciation of those who take part in the democratic process. Without the reward of such enthusiasm and such sporadic public gratitude the political process would often seem thankless.[106]

His handling of the appointment of his first government has been criticised as insensitive and inept because he did not allow himself sufficient time to consult with his colleagues.[107] But he himself has insisted he saw each of his ministerial nominees individually (rather than collectively, as Liam Cosgrave had done) in order to have a private word with each one.[108] It has to be admitted that his manner of appointing his junior team was less than felicitous.

He faced the twin problems which had plagued this country for the previous decade, those of the economy and Northern Ireland, firmly. His RTE radio interview of 27 September 1981 generated

357

a major debate and was remarkable for being the first time in the history of the Irish state that a Taoiseach had declared that there were sectarian aspects to our society and had pledged himself to getting rid of these.

It has to be conceded that there was a certain amount of political inexpertness in his handling of the January 1982 budget, which led to the fall of his first, short-lived administration. Despite this, he led another skilful, energetic and gruelling election campaign (his second in only a little over eight months), and the result was quite extraordinary for Fine Gael given the austerity it had been preaching and practising in office, and the fact that it had fallen on its tough budget.

FitzGerald has since expressed regret that he became involved in the horse-trading that followed the February 1982 election in the effort of forming a government. But the bizarre series of crises through which the brief Haughey government staggered, the damage which was done, during it, to Anglo-Irish relations and indeed to the idea of political credibility in this state must, in retrospect, restore to Garret FitzGerald whatever standing he may have felt he had lost.

The November 1982 general election was the third in less than 18 months and FitzGerald's most successful. Much of the credit for winning for Fine Gael 39.2% of the vote cast and bringing the party within striking distance of Fianna Fáil for the first time in half a century must go to him personally.

His second administration experienced its crests and troughs. Deeply disappointing for him were the so-called 'pro-life' amendment to the Constitution in 1983 and the failure of the divorce referendum in 1986, both of which severely damaged his self-proclaimed 'constitutional crusade'. Constant wrestling with the almost intractable problem of the public finances must have taken a heavy toll on him. His cabinet reshuffle of early 1986, also, turned out to be something of a vexation.

But if there were disappointments, they were more than compensated for by accomplishments. The alarming slide in the public finances was halted and turned around and Fianna Fáil was converted to financial orthodoxy to such an extent that Fine Gael in opposition after 1987 was able to support that party's fiscal policy in government.

Because his mother was from a northern Presbyterian-Unionist background, and his father had southern Catholic nationalist antecedents, FitzGerald was possessed of a deep-seated desire to see the two peoples on the island of Ireland reconciled. A colleague of his in the Cosgrave coalition, Justin Keating, had shown no interest at all in the Sunningdale process, because he was convinced it was premature. Of FitzGerald he has written: 'Garret was full of optimism, and consequently of hurt when it failed. But he was right in his optimism, because a decade later things had moved and the Anglo-Irish Agreement was the great triumph of his lifetime'.[109]

FitzGerald was primarily responsible for moving the things to which Keating referred. He patiently and painstakingly laid the foundations in that minefield of a terrain which is Anglo-Irish relations. He convened the New Ireland Forum, but while he negotiated with the other nationalist parties, he was preparing the way for the eventual talks with the British. He displayed extraordinary persistence and dedication in his relations with the latter, most notably after Mrs Thatcher's 'out, out, out' dismissal of the three main Forum options.

His own personal preference was for the joint-authority model but, in the end, he had to settle for less than that. However, that is not to detract from the historic nature of his achievement - a real say for the first time for the Republic in what happens in the North, i.e., in a part of the United Kingdom. The Anglo-Irish Agreement was his crowning glory and is likely to remain his political monument.

Garret FitzGerald is a deeply religious man. He has been described as 'a devout and thoughtful Catholic on the liberal wing of the Church' and as 'a phenomenon not uncommon on the continent, but hitherto rare in Ireland - the Catholic intellectual, who has thought deeply about issues connected with his faith and has come up with solutions that might not coincide with those current among the hierarchy.'[110]

He would probably admit himself that he talks too fast and his students in UCD must have had a feverish time at his lectures! He has been regarded as being too optimistic but that characteristic is not necessarily a drawback in either public or private life. Finally, he is probably also a bit self-absorbed and does not always notice those around him and that could have caused misunderstandings, and even offence, among some of his colleagues.

(l) Other Ministers in the FitzGerald Governments

(i) John Kelly

John Kelly was born in Dublin in 1931. He received his schooling from the Benedictines of Glenstal Abbey, Co. Limerick, and afterwards attended University College, Dublin, Germany's Heidelberg University, Oxford University and the King's Inns, Dublin.

He had an outstanding academic career in the area of law. Among his publications were *Princeps Iudex* (Weimar, 1957), *Fundamental Rights in the Irish Law and Constitution* (Oxford, 1976), and *Studies in the Civil Judicature of the Roman Republic* (Oxford, 1976). He inaugurated a new series of the legal periodical, *The Irish Jurist*, of which he was editor from 1966 to 1972.

John Kelly was Professor of Roman Law and Jurisprudence at UCD before his appointment as a minister and was perhaps the most distinguished lecturer in recent memory at the University. His lectures on what might be regarded as the somewhat dry subject of Roman Law attracted students from other faculties besides his own.

His first entry into politics was as a Fine Gael candidate for the Dublin South-Central constituency in the 1969 general election. He failed to get elected on that occasion but was successful in the election to the Senate shortly afterwards.

He was returned to the Dáil in the 1973 general election. In the coalition government, he was appointed Parliamentary Secretary to the Taoiseach. He also served as Parliamentary Secretary to the

Minister for Defence from 1973 to 1975 and to the Minister for Foreign Affairs from 1975 to 1977. He was Attorney General for a few months in 1977, following Declan Costello's appointment to the High Court.

Shadow spokesman on Industry and Commerce from 1977 to 1981, he was made Minister for Trade and Tourism in the first FitzGerald government. (At Labour's request, the old Department of Industry and Commerce was divided up, something about which Kelly was unhappy.) He also acted as Minister for Foreign Affairs for James Dooge until the latter's appointment to that portfolio could be ratified by the Dáil in October 1981.

John Kelly resigned from the Fine Gael front bench in April 1982, because of his opposition to any further coalition with Labour. He felt that the nature of the Labour party had changed greatly since the years of the Cosgrave coalition and had taken a distinct lurch to the left. From the back benches he argued repeatedly for a reconciliation between Fine Gael and Fianna Fáil, 'Siamese twins', as he regarded them.

He was a member of the Fine Gael delegation to the New Ireland Forum in 1984, having been very involved in policy formation in relation to Northern Ireland for many years. He decided to retire from active politics in 1987 and his tragically premature death occurred in 1991, at the young age of 59.

In terms of his political philosophy, John Kelly has been seen as an old-fashioned devotee of self-help and of small business enterprise.[111] He was indeed wont to call for a renewal of the principles of Arthur Griffith in Fine Gael.

He was the wittiest and most brilliant performer the Dáil has seen for decades. Even political opponents crowded into the Dáil chamber to hear him speak, although they knew they themselves were as like as not to be the butts of his brilliant barbs.

At the March 1981 ard-fheis he ridiculed Charles Haughey as 'an economic Mussolini' who had been remorselessly exposed, and derided Gene FitzGerald as 'Rommel, the Desert Goat'. His description of Brian Lenihan as 'the Bismarck of the lobster pots' has passed into the political folklore of the country.

But his oratorical powers were not used simply to laugh to scorn. He was always ready to acknowledge and praise the good work of the opposition. He has been described as 'one who never accepted anything unquestioningly,' as having been 'for years a glittering star in the political firmament', and as possessing a voice that was always 'clear, courteous, rational and humane'.[112] His death has been a tremendous loss to Irish public life.

(ii) James Dooge

James Dooge was born in Birkenhead, Cheshire, in July 1922. He went to the Christian Brothers' School, Dún Laoghaire, Co. Dublin and afterwards attended University College, Dublin, Iowa University (USA), the Agricultural University of Wageningen in Holland and the University of Lund, Sweden.

He was an assistant engineer on the main river improvement schemes with the Office of Public Works from 1943 to 1946 and a design engineer with the Electricity Supply Board from 1946 until 1958. He was Professor of Civil Engineering at University College, Cork, between 1958 and 1970 and held the corresponding position at UCD from 1970 until his appointment as Foreign Minister was formally approved by the Dáil in October 1981. Professor Dooge is a hydrologist of worldwide repute and a member of numerous academic and international organisations, such as the Royal Irish Academy, the International Council of Scientific Unions and the Institution of Engineers of Ireland.

James Dooge was elected to Dublin County Council in 1948 and was its chairman in 1950-51 and 1953-54. He became a Senator in 1961 and was to remain a member of the Senate until 1977. He was Leas-Cathaoirleach of that chamber from 1965 to 1973 and Cathaoirleach from 1973 to 1977.

It was in the Senate that he first worked with Garret FitzGerald, the two becoming close friends, and to whom he was an adviser from 1965 onwards. They were both members of the coalition election committee formed to organise the Fine Gael-Labour endeavour to retain power after the 1977 general election. When FitzGerald became leader of Fine Gael, Dooge was his confidant and foremost counsel on policy. He was a member of the Strategy Committee which orchestrated the three successful general election campaigns for Fine Gael in 1981-82 and he took a direct part in the negotiations on the coalition agreement with Labour in 1981.

His nomination as Minister for Foreign Affairs caused a major surprise in the Dáil when FitzGerald announced his new cabinet on 30 June 1981. However, during his brief tenure of that portfolio, James Dooge acquired an outstanding reputation. His enormous intellectual ability, calm judgement, and the fact that he did not have a political career of his own to pursue have been seen as contributing to this achievement.[113] It is to be regretted that he had so short a time to exercise his abundant talent.

He again advised FitzGerald during the negotiations with Labour in late November - early December 1982. His leader wished him to return to Foreign Affairs in this second coalition, but Dooge declined for health reasons. He was appointed chairman of the Committee on Institutional Affairs of the European Community in July 1984 and again discharged his duties with distinction.

(iii) Alan Dukes

Alan Dukes was born in Dublin in April 1945. He attended Coláiste Mhuire, Parnell Square, Dublin, and later studied at University College, Dublin. He had a spectacular academic career at UCD, where one of his lecturers in Economics was Dr Garret FitzGerald.

He was the chief economist of the National Farmers' Association (now the Irish Farmers' Association) from 1967 to 1972. As such he was deeply involved in the debate which preceded the referendum on EEC membership in May 1972. The following January he was appointed to take charge of the Brussels office of the IFA, representing that organisation in its dealings with the EEC Commission. In January 1977, he joined the team of Richard Burke, who had been appointed Ireland's EEC Commissioner. His time in Brussels provided him with an almost unique understanding of the workings of the Common Agriculture

Policy (CAP), on which he is an accepted authority.

Garret FitzGerald persuaded his former student to contest the June 1979 elections to the European Parliament for Fine Gael in the Munster constituency. In his first ever electoral contest, he secured 21,510 votes and was not eliminated until the eighth count, when there was only a difference of 8,000 between the number of votes cast for him and those for Fianna Fáil's Noel Davern, who was ultimately elected.

In March 1981, he resigned his position on the EEC Commission staff, and he was invited by the Kildare constituency executive to go forward in the impending general election. In the June 1981 contest he was elected on the last count without reaching the quota.

He was appointed Minister for Agriculture on his first day in the Dáil. The only other politicians before him to have had the honour of being made full ministers on their Dáil debuts were Dr Noel Browne of Clann na Poblachta, and Dr Martin O'Donoghue and Kevin Boland of Fianna Fáil.

In the February 1982 general election, Alan Dukes became the first ever Fine Gael candidate to exceed the quota in the Kildare constituency. He was front bench spokesman on Agriculture between March and December 1982. Garret FitzGerald consulted him during his negotiations with Dick Spring before the formation of the December 1982 coalition.

In that government he was allocated the primary Finance portfolio by his leader, and faced the unenviable and Herculean task of putting the public finances in order. There was a very early clash between Dukes and the Labour leader over this issue. Department of Finance officials urged on him the necessity of reducing the current budget deficit with the greatest haste and by the maximum possible amount. Dick Spring took public issue with the figure Dukes mentioned and early disagreement between Fine Gael and Labour thus became manifest.

Garret FitzGerald has since recorded that he felt the Finance officials were overstating the case and that he was able to secure independent international verification that this was so.[114] He, his

Minister for Finance, and the Labour leader were able to arrive at a compromise figure, but the incident illustrates the deep division that existed between the coalition partners on how soon and by how much to curb public spending. It was a discord which was to recur frequently over the next four years, making Dukes's already onerous assignment doubly so, and which finally led to the collapse of the government.

Alan Dukes campaigned actively against the so-called 'pro-life' constitutional amendment in 1983. Three years later, as Minister for Justice, he was responsible, along with FitzGerald and Spring, for bringing forward the proposals for a referendum on an amendment to the Constitution to remove the ban on divorce. In the campaign which followed, he worked energetically to try to ensure that the government proposal would be carried.

When Garret FitzGerald came to plan his cabinet reshuffle in early 1986, one of his chief concerns was to ensure that ministers' future political prospects would not be damaged by being identified in the public mind with the financial cuts which were necessitated by the country's grave economic situation. Dukes, who in FitzGerald's own words, 'had the most unpopular job of all in Finance', was naturally a prime candidate for movement and he was allocated the Justice portfolio.[115]

From the three-cornered competition to succeed Garret FitzGerald as leader of Fine Gael in March 1987, Alan Dukes emerged victorious. His had been a meteoric political career: elected to the Dáil on his first attempt; a minister on his first day in the House; Minister for Finance after scarcely 18 months a TD; leader of Fine Gael after a Dáil apprenticeship of less than six years; the party's youngest ever leader.

Alan Dukes's intellectual brilliance is widely recognised. On television he appears a reserved and distant man and this has caused him to be labelled a 'bureaucrat' and even a 'technocrat' but all who meet him attest to the warmth and geniality of his personality.

(iv) John Bruton

John Bruton was born in May 1947, in Dublin. He attended the Jesuit Clongowes Wood College, Co. Kildare, and subsequently studied Economics at University College, Dublin, where one of his lecturers was Dr Garret FitzGerald. He also studied at King's Inns, Blackhall Place, Dublin.

He was secretary of the Fine Gael youth group in the middle of the 1960s and was prominent in the 'Young Tiger' section of the party at that time. He was elected to the Dáil for the Meath constituency in 1969, at the young age of 22, not having gone through the usual local authority apprenticeship beforehand. Three years later he became front bench spokesperson on Agriculture.

In 1973, he was appointed Parliamentary Secretary to the Minister for Education, in which capacity he served until 1977. He was also Parliamentary Secretary to the Minister for Industry and Commerce from 1975 to 1977. Following Fine Gael's return to opposition in 1977, Bruton assumed his previous responsibility as shadow spokesperson on Agriculture.

He then dedicated a lot of his time and considerable energies to a wide-ranging and innovative policy statement on reform of the Dáil and Seanad, particularly stressing the need for the Dáil to have very much greater control over public expenditure. This desire to make the state's parliamentary institutions more effective and accountable has remained an abiding passion with him.

In January 1981, he was appointed Fine Gael's spokesperson on Finance, a position which gave his manifest talents and abilities much greater scope. It has been maintained that, in this post, he soon became the high priest of financial rectitude.[116] His contribution in the Dáil on the January 1981 budget made a strong impression on media and public alike.

During the general election campaign in June of that year, he was very much to the fore in drafting his party's economic and taxation policies. He especially emphasised the necessity of getting the public finances into shape. His mastery of the economic issues and the direct manner in which he faced difficult questions on them throughout the entire campaign were most impressive.

When Garret FitzGerald came to select his cabinet members, Peter Barry was the first to be offered the Finance portfolio, but he opted instead for Environment. It has been remarked that 'Bruton virtually chose himself for Finance, given that he had been one of the most active and able frontbenchers in the previous Dáil.'[117] His leader has since observed that although he was young for the job by any standards, he was 'a very serious and principled politician as well as being imaginative and innovative, and also both generous and strong-willed'.[118] No Irish Minister for Finance has ever been appointed at such an early age as John Bruton.

It was an extraordinary achievement and no doubt a great honour for one so young, but it was a poisoned chalice that was being proffered to his lips. On his first day in office the following dreadful scenario was unfolded for him at an emergency meeting with the Secretary of the Department of Finance: 90% of the year's budget deficit already spent, although only little over half the year had passed; a number of government Departments grossly underprovided for in the year's estimates; key government services in danger of running out of money within a short time; some semi-state bodies, having been allowed to run at a loss, needing substantial injections of capital. The country faced a major economic crisis.

Immediate action was needed, and within two days Bruton was circularising government colleagues on the need for an emergency meeting to curtail excess spending and to consider other financial measures. On 21 July, he presented a supplementary budget to a reconvened Dáil, the main purpose of which he saw as ensuring that Ireland remained an independent economy. What this emergency packet achieved marked, in Garret FitzGerald's words, 'a good start to the process of bringing our finances under control'.[119]

Although having the onerous responsibility for Finance, John Bruton also managed to instigate some of the key reforms in parliamentary procedure, which he had outlined when in opposition.

His January 1982 budget statement was broadcast live by RTE for the first time ever, but it contained few tidings of joy. One of its provisions, that extending the new 18% VAT rate to all footwear and clothing, which had previously been zero-rated, was to prove unacceptable to some of the Independent deputies whose votes against the budget brought the government down. However, it has been rightly remarked that Bruton had succeeded 'in reintroducing the principles of good management into the state's finances, after the mad excesses of the Fianna Fáil years'.[120]

Although campaigning on something of a draconian budget, Fine Gael performed remarkably well in the general election which followed. The unparalleled government collapse, the fact that it had been prepared to introduce such harsh budgetary measures and was sticking by them, shocked the people into realising the extent of the financial crisis the country faced. In personal terms, the February 1982 general election was a triumph for Bruton, in that he topped the poll in his Meath constituency with a quota and a half.

Back in opposition, he once again shadowed on Finance. The Fine Gael policy document, *Jobs for the Eighties*, which was published in the run-up to the party's October 1982 ard-fheis, was mainly his work and has been described as 'a masterly analysis of the problems facing the economy' and as proposing a large range of reforms.[121] It formed the basis for the party's election manifesto in November 1982 and for many of the subsequent coalition government's policies.

Briefly stated, it revealed the sorry state of the public finances, the alarming inflation and unemployment levels, and the enormous national debt. It advocated strict control of current and capital spending and an economic and social plan for a number of years ahead. Specific budgets for semi-state companies were proposed. The need for cost-competitiveness to attract foreign industry was stressed, and tax and social insurance reductions for the lower paid to encourage people to work were urged. Major reform of the public sector, radical proposals for employee shareholding in industries, a National Development Corporation, support for agriculture and work schemes for the young unemployed were all further parts of this redoubtable and imaginative plan.

When Garret FitzGerald came to form his second

government in December 1982, he decided not to reappoint Bruton to Finance. Knowing that tough budgetary decisions lay ahead, FitzGerald felt that Bruton's somewhat pugnacious temperament might not be the best for ensuring smooth relations with Labour. The Fine Gael leader was also of the opinion that if Bruton were to be associated for another four to five years with harsh fiscal policies, his political prospects could be severely blighted. For FitzGerald had no doubt that he was a potential future leader of the party.

But in his Industry and Energy portfolio, Bruton was faced with many tough decisions during the lifetime of this the third coalition in which he served. The question of whether to nationalise the almost bankrupt Dublin Gas Company has been seen as essentially 'a clash of two men who epitomised the different approaches of Fine Gael and Labour', Bruton and Frank Cluskey.[122] But this is to ignore the fact that most of the cabinet, including some of Cluskey's Labour colleagues, favoured retaining Dublin Gas in the private sector.

John Bruton also had chief responsibility for dealing with the collapse of Irish Shipping and the Insurance Corporation of Ireland. As has already been mentioned, parliamentary reform was one of his chief interests and he introduced the debate on this issue in January 1984, which eventualised in the establishment of a whole series of new joint Dáil and Seanad committees to discuss specific policy areas in detail. He was also strongly in favour of broadcasting Dáil proceedings.

In the cabinet reshuffle of January 1986, Bruton was returned to the Department of Finance. Later he campaigned vigorously in the divorce referendum. In August 1986, he and FitzGerald took the controversial decision to devalue the Irish pound within the European Monetary System, the eventual result of which was a major influx of funds which helped to bring Irish interest rates down.

When Garret FitzGerald resigned as leader of Fine Gael in 1987, John Bruton took part in the contest to succeed him together with Peter Barry and Alan Dukes, the last mentioned emerging successful. In 1990, Bruton replaced Alan Dukes as Fine Gael leader.

(v) Gemma Hussey

Gemma Hussey was born Gemma Moran in November 1938, in Dublin. She attended Loreto Convent, Bray, Co. Wicklow and Mount Anville, Dublin, before entering University College, Dublin.

She was first elected to the Senate as an Independent candidate on the National University of Ireland panel in 1977. Although less closely involved in the women's movement than her colleague, Nuala Fennell, she made several attempts as a Senator to have new legislation on rape introduced.

Notwithstanding her membership of Fine Gael and married to Derry Hussey, one of the devotees who helped reshape the party after 1977, she remained an Independent in the Senate until 1980. She was appointed to the Fine Gael front bench as spokesperson on Women's Affairs in January 1981 by Garret FitzGerald, albeit not yet a member of the Lower House. She was Leader of the Senate during the July 1981 to February 1982 government.

Gemma Hussey was first elected to the Dáil in the February 1982 general election for the Wicklow constituency. While she was a member of the Board of the Abbey Theatre, she was a coauthor of a report on women in broadcasting, and she was Fine Gael front bench spokesperson on the Arts, Culture and Broadcasting from June to November, 1982. She took the initiative in opposing the government's decision to close Ardmore Studios in Bray. She also suggested that ministerial Mercedes be replaced by more modest cars as a cost-saving measure.

From the time of her entry into the Dáil, she gave much evidence of her ability to handle the complications of the House's procedure and the intricacies of a wide range of subjects. She was given responsibility for the Department of Education in December 1982, even though she was less than a year in the Dáil. According to Garret FitzGerald, she was astonished to be offered this portfolio, but he had no doubt that 'she would tackle it with vigour and imagination, initiating reforms that were long overdue'.[123]

370

But, unfortunately, because of the shocking state of the public finances, too much of Gemma Hussey's time and energy had to be devoted to finding ways of reducing the Education budget. Within a few weeks of taking office, she had the unenviable task of introducing charges for the school transport system. Because it affected every village and townland in the country, this particular issue was considered to be akin to political suicide and the new Minister found herself assailed from all sides. It was a veritable baptism of fire for her, but she persevered with her scheme, although the government decided to exclude the children of social welfare recipients from the new charges.

In 1983, she campaigned actively against the so-called 'pro-life' amendment to the Constitution.

Between 1980 and 1986, years of economic crisis in this country, enrolments in third-level educational institutions increased by a staggering 40%. In large measure, this was facilitated by Gemma Hussey's securing increased government provision for higher education in 1984. She justified it, in times of severe cutbacks in public spending, on demographic grounds, by pointing to the need to cater for the rapidly expanding number of young people in the educational system. It was a farsighted approach. In 1984, also, as a result of her negotiating the allocation of resources from the European Community Social Fund, annual grants of £300 were provided for around one-third of school-leavers, who undertook employment-preparation courses.

In late 1985, the government was faced with a large increase in teachers' pay and pleaded inability to meet this demand. Hussey, whose proposed educational reforms were often stymied because of lack of finance, questioned on the radio the morality of so substantial a pay claim at a time of national stringency when the community as a whole was having to suffer severe restraints. The response from the teachers' unions was one of almost hysterical indignation. This dispute remained unsettled by the time she was moved from the Education ministry, but she was to become embroiled in another in early 1986.

Because the number of primary-school pupils was due to

decline significantly, the government decided to close one of the primary teachers' training colleges, Carysfort, in Dublin. Somehow, this information leaked out before relevant authorities were informed and all sorts of charges were hurled at the Minister for Education. As a result of this unfortunate experience, because the teachers' dispute was still raging and because she occupied a marginal seat, FitzGerald decided to move her in his cabinet reshuffle of early 1986.

His intention was to create a special Department of European Affairs for her. Although reluctant to leave Education, she was certainly attracted to her proposed new post. But two problems arose which prevented FitzGerald's plan for her coming to pass. One was Barry Desmond's adamant refusal to be moved from Health. The other was that Dermot Nally, Secretary to the government, informed the Taoiseach that his proposal for Hussey would necessitate dividing the Department of Foreign Affairs in two and the creation of a separate secretariat for the new European Affairs Department.

The result was that Gemma Hussey became Minister for Social Welfare, which she regarded as demotion from Education, and in which she would have little time to distinguish herself before the next general election. She had been the victim of a cabinet reconstitution that went wrong. Late in 1986, she played a very active role in the divorce referendum in an attempt to ensure that the measure would be carried.

From 1987 to 1989 she was front bench spokesperson on Education. Following defeat in the 1989 general election, she retired from politics.

(vi) Austin Deasy

Austin Deasy was born in Dungarvan, Co. Waterford, in August 1936. He was a pupil in the Christian Brothers' School, Dungarvan, before taking up studies in University College, Cork. He worked for some years as a secondary school teacher.

He was elected to Waterford County Council and Dungarvan Urban District Council in 1967. Unsuccessful in his attempts to be elected to the Dáil in the 1969 and 1973 general elections, he also failed to win a Senate seat in 1973, but was, that year, nominated a member of the Upper House by Liam Cosgrave.

Deasy was returned to the Dáil in the 1977 general election and on his debut was elevated to the front bench as spokesman on Fisheries, a duty which he performed until January 1981, when he was given responsibility for shadowing on Transport. He was a very active front-bencher and made a strong impression in the Dáil, so that it was generally expected that he would be made a minister in the July 1981 coalition government. To his deep disappointment, he was not.

At the end of March 1982, during the parliamentary party postmortem on the general election defeat of the previous month, Austin Deasy made no secret of his displeasure with his leader, with the political insouciance which had caused the party to lose power and with how he felt he himself had been treated in July 1981. Declaring that he had been one of the five TDs who had voted against Garret FitzGerald in the poll on the leadership the previous week, he conveyed that his exclusion from the government in July 1981, hurt him less than not having been informed beforehand of the decision. Despite this attack on FitzGerald, he was chosen as spokesman on Foreign Affairs in the new front bench of June 1982, and once again he made impressive use of his brief.

An extremely hard-working, professional politician, Deasy maintained his position at the top of the Dáil poll in Waterford over the three general elections in 1981-2 and this in a constituency which witnessed several changes in personnel and party balance. To his own personal, and, indeed, probably public astonishment, he was made Minister for Agriculture in December 1982.

Garret FitzGerald has given a number of reasons why he selected Deasy for this particular role. One was that he felt his independence of mind and sense of 'grass roots' feeling would be valuable assets to the cabinet. Another was that, although Deasy had no special knowledge of the Agriculture area, FitzGerald felt that because of the pressure on the Common Agriculture Policy, 'what we needed in this Department in the period immediately ahead was a tough negotiator', and he believed that Deasy had 'the requisite qualifications'.[124]

Because of the importance of the dairy sector to Irish agriculture and to the economy as a whole, much of Deasy's, and, indeed, of FitzGerald's attention in 1983-4 was taken up with the threat of a severe cutback in the EC milk superlevy. FitzGerald has recorded how he and Deasy, whom he described as one 'who never wanted to flinch from a fight', ran a high-profile campaign to secure exemption, or at least special treatment for Ireland within the proposed milk quota and superlevy regime. Concerning the outcome of their labours, the *Irish Times* remarked that it was difficult to see how Ireland could have done better.[125]

Deasy has been seen as having a tempestuous relationship with the Irish Farmers' Association, and as being 'a fearless critic' of that organisation's inconsistencies.[126] When FitzGerald came to reorganise his cabinet at the beginning of 1986, he decided to retain Austin Deasy at Agriculture because 'he had won the respect of the farming community without bending to their often excessive demands'.[127]

(vii) Michael Noonan

Michael Noonan was born in Foynes, Co. Limerick, in May 1943. He attended Glin Secondary School, Co. Limerick, before his admission to St Patrick's Teacher Training College, Drumcondra, Dublin, in which he qualified as a primary-school teacher.

A member of Limerick County Council since 1974, he was first elected to the Dáil in the June 1981 general election. He soon established himself as a TD with a distinctive contribution to make. He spoke on a varied range of subjects, and it was clear that he was heading for rapid promotion. In June 1982, he was advanced to the front bench as spokesman on Education by Garret FitzGerald, who had noted his debating skills from the back benches during the first, short-lived coalition with Labour.

Michael Noonan's vote rose steadily over the three general elections in 1981-2. He was a surprise choice as Minister for Justice in December 1982, because he had been in the Dáil for only

18 months by that time and he had not been a junior minister in the first FitzGerald government.

Concerning his assignment to Justice, FitzGerald has remarked: 'I judged that he had the combination of qualities needed to tackle sensitively and successfully the subversion of our security system for party purposes. . .and to restore the independence of the Gárda Síochána by securing the force against the kind of political interference that had become a source of public concern during the previous nine months'.[128]

The investigation Noonan carried out into illegal telephone tapping in December 1982 and January 1983 led to the resignations of the Gárda Commissioner and Deputy-Commissioner. He made a very good impression during the public revelations of this scandal, handling them in an able, coherent and detached manner. His ministerial career had a most auspicious inception.

In the autumn of 1983, he introduced a new Criminal Justice Bill to attempt to cope with the massive growth in non-political crime over the preceding 30 years. One aspect of the measure which was subjected to lively debate was that which proposed to give to the Gárdaí the power to detain suspects for up to 12 hours. A number of Fine Gael back-benchers approached the Bill from a civil liberties point of view and during the many months of Dáil discussion on the matter, Noonan had to do battle with critics ranged behind rather than in front of him and in general dealing with their arguments in a good-humoured, genial manner.

Perhaps his most difficult task while in control of Justice was handling the anti-abortion amendment to the Constitution. He managed to extricate the government from the Fianna Fáil wording and to put forward an alternative formula which he regrettably failed to get the Dáil to accept.

An enthusiastic supporter of the New Ireland Forum from the initiation of that concept, he also participated in the negotiations which led to the historic Anglo-Irish Agreement in 1985. He was sent by FitzGerald to the United States to publicise the accord there, doing so with considerable skill and great success.

When the Taoiseach came to consider reshuffling his cabinet

at the beginning of 1986, he felt that Noonan had done an excellent job as Minister for Justice and was entitled to be given experience in some other major position. Accordingly, he appointed him to Industry and Commerce for the last year of the government's tenure of office.

Michael Noonan has become a very popular figure with the media. He is very eloquent, with an original turn of phrase, and a penchant for colourful and humorous imagery.

(viii) Jim Mitchell

Jim Mitchell was born in October 1946, in Dublin. He received his schooling at St James's Christian Brothers' School, James's Street, Dublin, and the Vocational School, Inchicore, Dublin, and subsequently he studied at Rathmines College of Commerce and Trinity College, Dublin.

He joined Fine Gael in 1967 and was the party's candidate in the Dublin South-West by-election in 1970 at which he failed to get elected. Over a long period he gave encouragement to Declan Costello to re-enter the Dáil and in 1973 invited him into his own Dublin South-West constituency to contest the general election of that year. As it turned out, it was at the expense of his own candidature, because Costello took the one seat won by Fine Gael. Mitchell was to display the same amazing generosity nearly ten years later, when he invited Richard Burke to return to the Dáil via his own Dublin West constituency.

Jim Mitchell was elected to Dublin Corporation in 1974 and has been a member of that body ever since. When he became Lord Mayor of Dublin in 1976 he was, at the age of 29, the youngest ever holder of the office. He was once again the Fine Gael candidate in the Dublin South West by election in 1976, and again failed to be elected, but he was returned to the Dáil for the new constituency of Dublin-Ballyfermot in the general election of the following year.

He was directly promoted to his party's front bench as spokesman on Labour. In January 1981, he was given responsibility for the Public Service as well. His installation as Minister for

Justice in June 1981 came as a surprise, because he had never handled that brief in opposition. He was only 34. Garret FitzGerald has recorded: 'I believed he would be sound on security and liberal on law reform. What I did not allow for was his unbounded enthusiasm, which prompted him to arrive in our bedroom at all hours of the night to brief me on urgent security matters. But, Joan and I soon became accustomed to these incursions'.[129]

His reaction to the protest march by supporters of the H-Block hunger strikers to the British Embassy in Dublin in mid-July 1981, in which much damage was done to neighbouring property, won him widespread acclaim. It has been noted that he 'showed a striking sureness of touch in handling an ugly situation, diffusing the threat with a nicely judged combination of firmness and restraint'.[130]

Jim Mitchell had joined the Guinness computer staff in the early 1970s and his skill in this area came into good use for the first FitzGerald government on at least one occasion. This was when the intention to tax short-term social welfare benefits was being frustrated by officials in the Department of Social Welfare, and one of their arguments being that their computers were not compatible with those in the Department of Finance. Mitchell's expertise as a computer analyst was called upon and he, after a long, late-night wrangle, succeeded in persuading the relevant official of the technical possibility of the proposal.

In March 1982, Richard Burke accepted Charles Haughey's offer of a second term as Ireland's EEC Commissioner. Following this news being made public, Garret FitzGerald has written concerning the subsequent parliamentary party meeting: 'Jim Mitchell, who with his usual generosity had accepted Dick Burke as a fellow-candidate in Dublin West in the recent election and had worked extraordinarily hard to get him elected as a third Fine Gael TD in a five-seat constituency, was predictably furious at Dick's acceptance of the nomination'.[131]

For the by-election which followed Burke's departure, to Mitchell was entrusted the task of finding a candidate who would retain the seat for Fine Gael. He met the requirement in the person of Liam Skelly who, like Mitchell himself, was born and lived in the constituency and whose background was remarkably similar to Mitchell's own.

In December 1982, FitzGerald appointed Mitchell to the Department of Communications because it was responsible for a large number of state enterprises and because Mitchell's 'dynamism and determination would, I believed - correctly, as it turned out - make a major impact on many of these loss-making bodies'.[132] Mitchell showed how seriously he took his assignment when, early in 1983, he warned that CIE workers might have to take a 10% wage cut that year.

At the end of June 1983, he told CIE that no overrun on its £86 million grant for the year would be permitted and he instructed the board of the company to reduce spending by 12% over the subsequent five years. He displayed his determination to do his share in eliminating the budget deficit by putting an end to inefficiency and waste in the publicly owned transport facilities.

The appointment of the RTE Authority in 1985, for which he had chief responsibility, showed his own, his leader's and, indeed, the whole cabinet's desire to ensure that boards of state bodies would be strong and politically independent.

Jim Mitchell was not moved from Communications in the cabinet restructuring of early 1986, because FitzGerald felt that he was doing an exceptionally good job there, and should be left to complete the task he was undertaking of reforming the former loss-making enterprises under his control, and, also, because he already had the experience of a period in the Department of Justice behind him.

(ix) John Boland

John Boland was born in Skerries, Co. Dublin, in November 1944. He attended the Christian Brothers' School, Synge Street, Dublin, following which he studied at University College, Dublin. While at UCD he was editor of the magazine *Awake* and was closely identified with Gerry Collins, and his student political organisation known as 'the machine', but he himself was not involved in any party political organisations at the time.

When he graduated from UCD, he became a sales representative for Pan Books. He was elected to Dublin County Council in 1967, at the young age of 23, and unsuccessfully contested the 1969 general election in the old North Dublin constituency. He was, however, elected to the Senate in 1969. He was chairman of Dublin County Council in 1971-2, 1976-7 and 1979-80. John Boland has the distinction of being the youngest ever chairman of Dublin County Council and the youngest elected Senator.

Again unsuccessful in the North County Dublin constituency in the 1973 general election, he succeeded in getting himself re-elected to the Senate in that year. However, four years later he was returned to the Dáil for the first time. Garret FitzGerald has recorded how, when he was canvassing support in the leadership contest of 1977, his telephone call to Boland sticks in his mind particularly, because the latter interrogated him for almost half an hour on his intentions as leader. This meticulousness on Boland's part impressed him so that he resolved to find a place for him on his front bench if he were chosen as leader.[133] So, in the autumn of 1977, John Boland became spokesman on Health and Social Welfare.

He was very successful in this role and gave his opposite number, Charles Haughey, a difficult time, especially on the Family Planning Bill in 1979. His front bench responsibility was changed to Environment in January 1981, a brief in which he again performed well, especially in the debate on the Stardust tragedy.

His appointment as Minister for Education in July 1981 caused some surprise. He had no familiarity with the conduct of this office and it was thought that his somewhat caustic style would not be connotative of the diplomacy which the post was considered to demand. But his 'political intuition and ability to see around corners' outweighed in FitzGerald's view such possible minuses as his relative youth (he was only 34), his lack of experience in the area and his putatively pugnacious manner.[134]

The first issue he took up in his new role was the proverbial hot potato in political terms. The idea of raising the primary-school entry age to four-and-a-half had been around for some time and Boland, as a former member of Dublin County Vocational Education Committee, had no doubt about the educational merit of the proposal. In fact, correspondence reaching his Department suggested that a majority of the general public agreed with him, but when he proceeded to implement the measure for the following autumn, the full wrath of the Irish National Teachers' Organisation was unleashed upon him. Dismissing the education merit argument, the INTO countered that it was merely a crude, cost-cutting measure which would mean job losses, and a bitter debate ensued, the government eventually having its way in a tense Dáil division in early November.

FitzGerald selected him as director of elections for the crucial Dublin West by-election of late May 1982. For nearly two months he devoted his extraordinary energy to orchestrating a memorable campaign which achieved a victory for Fine Gael, something considered virtually impossible at the outset.

In December 1982, John Boland became Minister for the Public Service. FitzGerald felt that reform in this area was long overdue and had been neglected because the Department of the Public Service had been combined with the Department of Finance under a single minister. So he decided to make it a separate domain with its own political head and he concluded that Boland had the requisite qualifications to carry out the necessary reforms: 'I knew that he would not allow himself to be bullied, or cajoled by the civil service into backing off from what needed to be done'.[135]

He faced a formidable task. 'A gritty performer with a dash of the street fighter in his make up'[136] he needed to be determined and astute to overcome, or circumvent all the opposition he would encounter. He had to move with extreme care through the minefield of bureaucratic resistance and operate with stealth in hostile territory.

His creation of the Top Level Appointment Committee (TLAC) in January 1984 instituted what has been described as 'a major change in appointment procedures' and succeeded in implementing a recommendation which the Devlin Report thought could be done 'at once' 15 years after it had been proposed![137] The TLAC aimed to see that promotions were based on merit. Also, secretaries of departments were now not to serve for more than seven years and not beyond the age of 60. These changes have been seen as going to the very heart of civil service culture. In order to avoid the entrenched resistance that he was sure to have met, Boland had to resort to the device of getting cabinet acceptance without circulating his proposals to other departments, as was the normal procedure and which, it has been well remarked, 'would have guaranteed another 15 years delay!'.[138]

Boland's was a brave and potentially revolutionary endeavour to solve the problem that frequently resulted from the placing of unsuitable people in the top positions because of limited competition. It was also an attempt to deal in advance with the difficulties that would inevitably occur when the many talented young people recruited during the 1970s would find themselves frustrated in their promotion prospects if the latter depended on seniority, as was hitherto the case:

> How to mobilise this massive reservoir of talent, how to harness its potential idealism, how to prevent it from vegetating, how to save it from the corrosive cynicism induced by the techniques perfected by the forces of resistance, presented a major managerial problem, of the utmost significance for the national interest. Boland's initiatives counted as a major innovation, and not only in civil service terms.[139]

Achieving change in any Irish institution is a notoriously difficult undertaking, and it has been observed that one 'can only marvel at the tenacity and idealism of those who sustained the Sisyphean struggle against the forces of resistance and inertia.'[140] The best measure of the hugeness of the task that Boland undertook was the fact that no less a politician than Seán Lemass 'half conceded defeat in his effort to improve matters. . .That Boland got the idea "off the ground" where Lemass failed must count as a notable achievement'.[141]

When rearranging his cabinet in early 1986, FitzGerald decided that Boland deserved an opportunity to exercise his talents in another major department 'where his toughness and drive might achieve worthwhile results in the year ahead'.[142] Accordingly, he gave him responsibility for the Department of the Environment.

John Boland was Fine Gael spokesman on the Environment from 1987 to 1989 and lost his seat in the 1989 general election.

(x) Paddy O'Toole

Paddy O'Toole was born in January 1938, in Doolough, Co. Mayo. He attended Doolough National School, Coláiste Einde, Galway, St. Patrick's Teacher Training College, Drumcondra, Dublin, and University College, Galway.

He worked for some time as a primary-school teacher and was encouraged to become involved in politics by Pat Lindsay, former Mayo TD and Master of the High Court, and one of the most stimulating ever figures in Fine Gael. He was first elected to Mayo County Council in 1974 and became a member of Ballina Urban District Council the same year.

He had been an unsuccessful candidate in the 1973 general election, but was successful in the Senate election of that year. O'Toole was elected to the Dáil in 1977 and was delegated to serve as Fine Gael spokesman on Consumer Affairs in October that year. In January 1981, he was given responsibility for Industry and Commerce and joined his party's front bench. When the coalition government was formed in July 1981, O'Toole, whom FitzGerald has described as 'a gentle westerner and Irish-speaker', was appointed Minister for the Gaeltacht. When FitzGerald came to form his second government in December 1982, he felt that O'Toole's command of Irish justified his retaining the Gaeltacht assignment, but he also allocated additional responsibility to him for Forestry and Fisheries.[143]

In the cabinet reshuffle which occurred in January 1986, Paddy O'Toole was made Minister for Defence, but was also left in charge of Gaeltacht affairs.

NOTES

Chapter I: Cumann na nGaedheal 1923 - 32

1. J.J. Lee, *Ireland 1912-1985: Politics and Society* (Cambridge University Press, 1989), p. 107.
2. *ibid.*, p.162.
3. Warner Moss, *Political Parties in the Irish Free State* (Harvard, 1933), pp. 133,135.
4. Ronan Fanning, *Independent Ireland* (Dublin, 1983), p. 109.
5. F.S.L. Lyons, *Ireland since the Famine* (London, 1973), p. 481.
6. Lee, *op. cit.*, p. 129.
7. M.G. Valiulis, *Almost a Rebellion: the Irish Army Mutiny of 1924* (Cork, 1985).
8. Oliver MacDonagh, *Ireland: the Union and its Aftermath* (London, 1977), p. 107.
9. R.K. Carty, *Party and Parish Pump: Electoral Politics in Ireland* (Ontario, 1981), p. 98.
10. Lee, *op. cit.*, p. 119.
11. Michael Gallagher, *Political Parties in the Republic of Ireland* (Dublin, 1985), pp. 44,67.
12. James Meenan, 'From free trade to self sufficiency', in Francis MacManus (ed.), *The Years of the Great Test 1926-39* (Cork, 1967), p. 70.
13. *ibid.*, pp. 69-72.
14. *ibid.*, pp. 72-3, 75, 78-9.
15. Lee, *op. cit.*, pp. 117-20.
16. *ibid.*, pp. 110,124-7.
17. Ronan Fanning, *The Irish Department of Finance* (Dublin, 1978), pp. 105-110.
18. Terence Brown, *Ireland: a Social and Cultural History* (London, 1985), p. 15.
19. Lyons, *op. cit.*, p. 496.
20. *ibid.*, pp. 609-10.
21. MacDonagh, *op. cit.*, pp. 125-7.
22. Francis MacManus, 'The literature of the period', in MacManus (ed.), *op. cit.*, p. 116.
23. Basil Chubb, *The Government and Politics of Ireland* (London, 1970), pp. 256-7.
24. MacDonagh, *op. cit.*, pp. 128-31; 136-7.
25. Oliver MacDonagh, *States of Mind* (London, 1983), pp. 117-19.
26. Brown, *op. cit.*, pp. 49-50.
27. *ibid.*, p. 52.
28. *ibid.*, p. 53.

29. S. Ó Catháin, 'Education in the new Ireland', in MacManus (ed.), *Great Test.*

30. Brown, *Social and Cultural*, pp. 68-9.

31. J.H. Whyte, *Church and State in Modern Ireland 1923-79* (Dublin, 1980), pp. 38-9, 41.

32. Brown, *op. cit.*, pp. 69, 75-7.

33. Lyons, *Famine*, p. 447.

34. *ibid.*, p. 510.

35. MacDonagh, *Union*, p. 114.
    Lee, *Irl. 1912-85*, p. 156.

36. Lee, *op. cit.*, p. 156.

37. *ibid.*, p. 171.

38. Carty, *Party and Parish Pump*, p. 89.

39. Cornelius O'Leary, *Irish Elections 1918 - 1977: Parties, Voters and Proportional Representation* (Dublin, 1979), p. 25.

40. Carty, *op. cit.*, p. 106.

41. Maurice Manning, *Irish Political Parties: an Introduction*(Dublin, 1972), pp. 18-19.

42. Michael Gallagher, *Electoral Support for Irish Political Parties* (London, 1976), pp. 9-10, 30, 32-3.

43. K.B. Nowlan, 'President Cosgrave's last administration', in MacManus (ed.), *op.cit.*, pp. 17-18.

44. Lyons, *op cit.*, p. 479.

45. Lee, *op. cit.*, pp. 173-4.

46. Carty, *op. cit.*, pp. 151-2.

Chapter 2: Fine Gael and the Blueshirts 1932 - 37.

1. J.A. Murphy, *Ireland in the 20th Century* (Dublin, 1975), p. 75.

2. Gallagher, *Political Parties*, p. 45.

3. Maurice Manning, *The Blueshirts* (Dublin, 1970).

4. Gallagher, *Political Parties*, pp. 102-5.

5. Manning, *Blueshirts*, pp. 69, 74-5.

6. Gallagher, *Political Parties*, p. 46.

7. Manning, *Blueshirts*, pp. 99-100.

8. Dónal O'Sullivan, *The Irish Free State and its Senate* (London, 1940), pp. 296, 330-31, 334, 336-8, 340-42, 418-27.

9. Manning, *Blueshirts*, chs. VI, VII and VIII *passim*.

10. *ibid.*, p. 147.

11. *ibid.*, p. 160.

12. *ibid.*, p. 162.

13. *ibid.*, p. 182.

14. *ibid.*, p. 187.

15. *ibid.*, pp. 191-6.

16. Manning, *Blueshirts*, p. 229.
17. *ibid.*, p. 230.
18. *ibid.*, p. 231.
19. David Thornley,'The Blueshirts', in MacManus (ed.), *Great Test,* p. 51.
20. Lyons, *Famine,* p. 528.
21. MacDonagh, *Union*., pp. 110-11, 113.
22. Gallagher, *Political Parties*, p. 62.
23. *ibid.*
24. Manning, *Parties*, p. 21.

Chapter 3: A Period of Prolonged Decline: 1937 - 48.

1. Manning, *Parties*, p. 21.
2. Fanning, *Independent Ireland*, p. 163.
3. Lee, *Irl 1912 - 85*, p. 271.
4. *ibid.*, pp. 209-10.
5. *ibid.*, pp. 214-15; Murphy, *Ireland*, p. 110.
6. K.B. Nowlan, 'On the eve of the war', in K.B. Nowlan and T.D. Williams (eds.), *Ireland in the War Years and After, 1939 - 51* (Dublin, 1969), p. 4.
7. *ibid.*, p. 7.
8. *ibid.*, p. 8.
9. T.D. Williams, 'Ireland and the war', in Nowlan and Williams (eds.), *op. cit.*, p. 15.
10. G.A. Hayes-McCoy, 'Irish defence policy, 1938 - 51', in Nowlan and Williams (eds.), *op. cit.,* pp. 41, 43, 44, 49.
11. J.A. Murphy, 'The Irish party system 1938 - 51', in Nowlan and Williams (eds.), *op. cit.*, p. 153.
12. Lee, *op. cit.*, p. 237.
13. Murphy, *'Irish party system'*, pp. 148, 151-2.
14. Lee, *op. cit.*, p. 241.
15. Murphy, *'Irish party system'*, p. 153.
16. Lee, *op. cit.*, p. 241.
17. Gallagher, *op. cit.*, p. 47.
18. Chubb, *Government and Politics*, pp. 81-2.
19. Gallagher, *Electoral Support*, p. 34.
20. *ibid.*, p. 35.
21. Murphy, *'Irish party system'*, pp. 152-3.
22. J.A. Murphy, 'Put them out! Parties and elections, 1948 - 69', in J.J. Lee (ed.), *Ireland 1945 - 70* (Dublin, 1979), p. 3.

Chapter 4: Two Periods in Government: 1948 - 57.

1. Lee, *op. cit.*, p. 299.
2. *ibid.*
3. Fanning, *op. cit.,* p. 166.
4. *ibid.*, p. 167.

5. Lyons, *Famine*, p. 563.
6. Fanning, *Independent Ireland*, p. 173.
7. Lyons, *op. cit.*, p. 567.
8. Fanning, *op. cit.*, p. 175.
9. Murphy, *Ireland*, p. 128.
10. *ibid.*, p. 129.
11. Fanning, *op. cit.*, p. 176.
12. Gallagher, *Political Parties*, p. 49.
13. Patrick Lynch, 'The Irish economy in the post-war era', in Nowlan and Williams (eds.), *Irl. in War Years*, p. 187.
14. Fanning, *Finance*, p. 406.
15. Fanning, *Independent Ireland*, p. 170.
16. Fanning, *Finance*, pp. 436, 439.
17. *ibid.*, p. 457.
18. *ibid.*, p. 458.
19. *ibid.*, p. 460.
20. *ibid.*, pp. 448, 455-6.
21. Lynch, *'Irish economy in post-war era'*, in Nowlan and Williams (eds.), *op. cit.*, p. 198.
22. Lee, *Irl. 1912 - 85*, p. 303.
23. MacDonagh, *States*, pp. 122-4.
24. Dónal McCartney, 'Education and language, 1938-51', in Nowlan and Williams (eds.), *op. cit.*, pp. 85-6, 92.
25. Whyte, *Church and State*, pp. 135, 141, 153.
26. *ibid.*, p. 207.
27. *ibid.*, pp. 199, 201, 205-10.
28. Fanning, *Independent Ireland*, pp. 182-3.
29. Whyte, *op. cit.*, pp. 217-20, 223-6, 228-9.
30. *ibid.*, p. 232.
31. *ibid.*, p. 235.
32. *ibid.*, p. 237.
33. Gallagher, *op. cit.*, p. 49.
34. Lee, *op. cit.*, p. 319.
35. *ibid.*, p. 322.
36. Murphy *'Irish party system'*, in Nowlan and Williams (eds.), *op. cit.*, p. 162.
37. Lyons, *op. cit.*, p. 580.
38. *ibid.*
39. Fanning, *Finance*, p. 504.
40. *ibid.*
41. Murphy, *Ireland*, p. 142.
42. Fanning, *Finance*, p. 511.
43. Murphy, *Ireland,* p. 137.

44. Gallagher, *Political Parties*, p. 50.
45. Lee, *Irl. 1912-85*, p. 327.
46. *ibid.*, pp. 327-8.
47. K.T. Hoppen, *Ireland since 1800: Conflict and Conformity* (London, 1989), p. 180.
48. Manning, *Parties*, p. 25.

Chapter 5: Prolonged Opposition Once More: 1957 - 73.

1. Gallagher, *op. cit.*, p. 50.
2. *ibid.*
3. O'Leary, *Elections*, pp. 25-6.
4. *ibid.*, p. 30.
5. *ibid.*, p. 31.
6. *ibid.*, p. 48.
7. *ibid.*, pp. 48-9.
8. Lee, *op. cit.*, p. 330.
9. O'Leary, *op. cit.*, p. 53.
10. *ibid.*, p.54.
11. Fergal Tobin, *The Best of Decades: Ireland in the 1960s* (Dublin, 1984), p. 49.
12. *ibid.*
13. O'Leary, *op. cit.*, p. 62.
14. Tobin, *op. cit.*, p. 51.
15. *ibid.*, p. 46.
16. *ibid.*
17. Fanning, *Independent Ireland*, p. 204.
18. Tobin, *op. cit.*, p. 46.
19. *ibid.*, p. 47.
20. *ibid.*, pp 47-8.
21. Peter Mair, *The Changing Irish Party System: Organisation, Ideology and Electoral Competition* (London, 1987), pp. 184-6.
22. *ibid.*, p. 205.
23. Manning, *op. cit.*, p. 29; Gallagher, *op. cit.*, p. 51; Fanning, *op. cit.*, p. 198, mistakenly included Liam Cosgrave among Costello's opponents.
24. Tobin, *op. cit.*, pp. 134-5.
25. *ibid.*, p. 136.
26. *ibid.*, p. 135.
27. Gallagher, *op. cit.*, p. 52.
28. Tobin, *op. cit.*, p. 136.
29. *ibid.*, p. 142.
30. *ibid.*
31. Garret FitzGerald, *All in a Life: an Autobiography* (Dublin, 1991), pp. 75-6.
32. Tobin, *op. cit.*, p. 142.

33. Tobin, *Decades,* p. 142.
34. *ibid.*, p. 143.
35. *ibid.*, p. 152.
36. *ibid.*, p. 154.
37. *ibid.*, p. 186.
38. *ibid.*
39. O'Leary, *Elections*, pp. 66-8; 69.
40. *ibid.* p. 70.
41. *ibid.*, p. 71.
42. Tobin, *op. cit.*, p. 216.
43. O'Leary, *op. cit.*, p. 72.
44. Tobin, *op. cit.*, p. 215.
45. *ibid.*
46. O'Leary, *op. cit.*, p. 73.
47. Gallagher, *Political Parties*, p. 52.
48. O'Leary, *op. cit.*, p. 73.
49. Gallagher, *op. cit.*, p. 52.
50. FitzGerald, *Life*, pp. 105-6.
51. Gallagher, *op. cit.*, pp. 52-3.
52. Patrick Lindsay, *Memories* (Dublin, 1992), pp. 198-9.
53. FitzGerald, *op. cit.*, pp. 106-9.
54. Chubb, *Government and Politics*, p. 82.
55. O'Leary, *op. cit.*, pp. 77-8.
56. Brian Harvey, *Cosgrave's Coalition* (London, 1977), p. 11.
57. O'Leary, *op. cit.*, p. 78.
58. *ibid.*, p. 80.
59. Gallagher, *Electoral Support*, p. 38.
60. *ibid.*, p. 39.
61. *ibid.*, p. 66.
62. Mair, *Changing Party System*, p. 211.
63. *ibid.*, p. 121.
64. *ibid.*
65. *ibid.*, p. 122.
66. *ibid.*
67. *ibid.*
68. *ibid.*, pp. 123-4.

Chapter 6: Coalition Government 1973 - 77

1. Lee, *Irl 1912-85*, p. 469.
2. Stephen O'Byrnes, *Hiding behind a Face: Fine Gael under FitzGerald* (Dublin, 1986), p. 12; Harvey, *op. cit.*, p. 29.
3. Lee, *op cit.,* pp.475-6.
4. FitzGerald, *op. cit.*, pp.293-4.

5.   O'Byrnes, *Face,* p. 10.
6.   Harvey, *Coalition,* p. 30.
7.   *ibid.,* p. 32.
8.   *ibid.,* p. 33.
9.   *ibid.,* p.33-4.
10. *ibid.,* p. 34.
11. *ibid.,* p. 42.
12. *ibid.,* p. 61.
13. *ibid.,* p. 130.
14. *ibid.*
15. *Irish Times,* 7 October 1991.
16. Harvey, *op. cit.,* pp. 130-31.
17. *Irish Times,* 7 October 1991.
18. Lee, *Irl. 1912-85,* p. 481.
19. O'Leary, *Elections,* p. 84.
20. Harvey, *op. cit.,* p. 75.
21. O'Leary, *op. cit.,* p. 81.
22. *ibid.,* pp. 81-2.
23. Harvey, *op. cit.,* p. 86.
24. *ibid.,* pp. 157-8.
25. Whyte, *Church and State,* p. 414.
26. Gallagher, *Political Parties,* p. 53.
27. Harvey, *op. cit.,* p. 137.
28. Gallagher, *op. cit.,* pp. 53-4.
29. Whyte, *op. cit.,* p. 394.
30. Lee, *op. cit.,* p. 476.
31. Harvey, *op. cit.,* p. 115.
32. *ibid.,* pp. 116,118.
33. *ibid.,* pp. 93-7.
34. *ibid.,* pp. 98-9.
35. *ibid.,* p. 100.
36. *ibid.,* p. 101.
37. *ibid.,* p. 102.
38. *ibid.,* p. 106.
39. O'Leary, *op. cit.,* p. 83.
40. Lee, *op. cit.,* pp. 482-3.
41. O'Leary, *op. cit.,* p. 86.
42. O'Byrnes, *op. cit.,* p. 2.
43. Brian Farrell and Maurice Manning, 'The election', in Howard Penniman
     (ed.), *Ireland at the Polls: the Dáil Elections of 1977* (Washington, 1978),
     p. 133.
44. *ibid.,* pp. 133-4.

45. Maurice Manning, 'The political parties', in Penniman (ed.), *Irl. at the Polls 1977,* pp. 90-91.
46. O'Byrnes, *Face,* p. 4.
47. Farrell and Manning, 'The election', in Penniman (ed.), *op. cit.,* p. 138.
48. *ibid.,* p. 144.
49. *ibid.,* p. 150.
50. *ibid.,* pp. 150-51.
51. O'Leary, *Elections,* p. 110.
52. Manning, *op. cit.,* p. 87.
53. *ibid.,* p. 88.
54. *ibid.,* p. 89.
55. Harvey, *Coalition,* p. 64-5.

Chapter 7: The FitzGerald Years: 1977 - 87

1. FitzGerald, *Life,* p. 322.
2. O'Byrnes, *op. cit.,* p. 7.
3. FitzGerald, *op. cit.,* p. 322.
4. O'Byrnes, *op. cit.,* p. 9.
5. *ibid.,* p. 10.
6. *ibid.,* pp. 13-14.
7. FitzGerald, *op. cit.,* pp. 13-14.
8. O'Byrnes, *op. cit.,* p. 14.
9. *ibid.,* p. 16.
10. *ibid.*
11. FitzGerald, *op. cit.,* p. 19.
12. O'Byrnes, *op. cit.,* p. 19.
13. *ibid.,* p. 21.
14. *ibid.,* p. 22.
15. *ibid.*
16. *ibid.,* pp. 34-5.
17. *ibid.,* p. 36.
18. FitzGerald, *op. cit.,* pp. 337-8.
19. O'Byrnes, *op. cit.,* p. 42.
20. *ibid.*
21. *ibid.,* pp. 45-6.
22. *ibid.,* p. 47.
23. FitzGerald, *op. cit.,* pp. 339-41.
24. O'Byrnes, *op. cit.,* pp. 48-9.
25. *ibid.,* pp. 54-5.
26. FitzGerald, *op. cit.,* p. 355.
27. O'Byrnes, *op. cit.,* p. 59.
28. *ibid.,* p. 61.
29. *ibid.,* p. 64.

30. O'Byrnes, *Face,* p. 65.
31. FitzGerald, *Life,* p. 355.
32. *ibid.*
33. O'Byrnes, *op. cit.,* pp.65-6.
34. *ibid.,* p. 69.
35. *ibid.,* p. 72.
36. *ibid.,* p. 73.
37. *ibid.,* p. 74.
38. *ibid.,* p. 75.
39. *ibid.,* p. 76.
40. *ibid.,* p. 77.
41. *ibid.,* p. 78.
42. *ibid.,* p. 83.
43. Joseph O'Malley, 'Campaigns, manifestos and party finances', in Brian Farrell and Howard Penniman (eds.), *Ireland at the Polls 1981, 1982 and 1987: A Study of Four General Elections* (Washington D.C., 1987), p. 36.
44. *ibid.*
45. O'Byrnes, *op. cit.,* p. 86.
46. *ibid.,* pp. 88-9.
47. *ibid.,* p. 89.
48. *ibid.*
49. *ibid.,* p. 90.
50. *ibid.,* p. 91.
51. John Bowman, 'Media coverage of the Irish general elections of 1981 - 82', in Farrell and Penniman (eds.), *op. cit.,* p. 172.
52. O'Byrnes, *op. cit.,* p. 91.
53. FitzGerald, *op. cit.,* p. 357.
54. Bowman, *op. cit.,* pp. 172-3.
55. *ibid.,* p. 173.
56. *ibid.*
57. *ibid.,* p. 178.
58. *ibid.,* p. 179.
59. O'Malley, *op. cit.,* p. 40.
60. FitzGerald, *op. cit.,* p. 359.
61. O'Byrnes, *op. cit.,* p. 102.
62. Fitzgerald, *op. cit.,* p. 364
63. *ibid.,* p. 361.
64. O'Byrnes, *op. cit.,* p. 119.
65. *ibid.,* p. 114.
66. *ibid.,* pp. 115-16.
67. *ibid.,* p. 117.
68. FitzGerald, *op. cit,* pp. 367-75.

69. Lee, *Irl. 1912-85,* p. 507.
70. O'Byrnes, *Face,* pp. 119-20.
71. *ibid.,* p. 122.
72. Brian Farrell, 'The context of three elections', in Farrell and Penniman (eds.), *Ireland at the Polls 1981, 1982 and 1987,* p. 12.
73. O'Byrnes, *op. cit.,* p. 123.
74. FitzGerald, *Life,* pp. 375-8.
75. Farrell, *op. cit.,* p. 12.
76. O'Byrnes, *op. cit.,* p. 124.
77. FitzGerald, *op. cit.,* p. 378.
78. O'Byrnes, *op. cit.,* pp. 127-30.
79. FitzGerald, *op. cit.,* pp. 396-7.
80. O'Byrnes, *op. cit.,* pp. 131-2.
81. *ibid.,* p. 133.
82. FitzGerald, *op. cit.,* pp. 397-8.
83. O'Malley, 'Campaigns', in Farrell and Penniman (eds.), *op. cit.,* p. 41.
84. *ibid.,* p. 42.
85. O'Byrnes, *op. cit.,* p. 139.
86. *ibid.,* p. 145.
87. *ibid.,* p. 146.
88. Bowman, 'Media coverage of 1981-2 general elections' in Farrell and Penniman (eds.), *op cit.,* p. 183.
89. Lee, *op. cit.,* p. 508.
90. FitzGerald, *op. cit.,* p. 402.
91. *ibid.,* pp. 403-4.
92. O'Byrnes, *op. cit.,* p. 157.
93. Lee, *op. cit.,* p. 508.
94. O'Byrnes, *op. cit.,* pp. 158-9.
95. *ibid.,* p. 161.
96. FitzGerald, *op. cit.,* p. 405.
97. O'Byrnes, *op. cit.,* p. 170.
98. Farrell, *op. cit.,* p. 18.
99. O'Byrnes, *op. cit.,* pp. 172-9.
100. *ibid.,* p. 194.
101. *ibid.,* p. 196.
102. O'Malley, *op. cit.,* p. 46.
103. *ibid.*
104. *ibid.,* p. 48.
105. Bowman, *op. cit.,* pp. 185-6.
106. O'Malley, *op. cit.,* p. 54.
107. O'Byrnes, *op. cit.,* p. 217.
108. *ibid.,* p. 220.

109. O'Byrnes, *Face,* pp. 225-6.
110. *ibid.,* p. 228.
111. *ibid.,* p. 234.
112. *ibid.,* p. 235.
113. *ibid.,* p. 237.
114. FitzGerald, *Life,* pp. 436-7.
115. *ibid.,* pp. 434-5.
116. O'Byrnes, *op. cit.,* pp. 238-43.
117. Fitzgerald, *op. cit.,* p. 457.
118. *ibid.,* p. 609.
119. O'Byrnes, *op. cit.,* pp. 245-6.
120. Lee, *Irl. 1912-85,* p. 520.
121. O'Byrnes, *op. cit.,* p. 244.
122. FitzGerald, *op. cit.,* p. 606.
123. O'Byrnes, *op. cit.,* p. 312.
124. FitzGerald, *op. cit.,* p. 416.
125. O'Byrnes, *op. cit.,* p. 255.
126. FitzGerald, *op. cit.,* p. 417.
127. *ibid.,* p. 441.
128. *ibid.,* p. 445-6.
129. O'Byrnes, *op. cit.,* pp. 297-9.
130. FitzGerald, *op. cit.,* p. 629.
131. O'Byrnes, *op. cit.,* p. 323.
132. *ibid.,* p. 325.
133. FitzGerald, *op. cit.,* p. 626.
134. *ibid.,* p. 477.
135. *ibid.,* p. 491.
136. O'Byrnes, *op. cit.,* p. 306.
137. FitzGerald, *op. cit.,* pp. 497-515.
138. Lee, *op. cit.,* pp. 679-80.
139. FitzGerald, *op. cit.,* pp. 525-55.
140. O'Byrnes, *op. cit.,* p. 308.
141. Lee, *op. cit.,* p. 687.
142. O'Byrnes, *op. cit.,* p. 278.
143. *ibid.,* p. 280.
144. *ibid.,* p. 288.
145. *ibid.,* p. 312.
146. *ibid.,* p. 315.
147. FitzGerald, *op. cit.,* p. 621.
148. O'Byrnes, *op. cit.,* pp. 326-7.
149. Lee, *op. cit.,* p. 556.
150. *ibid.*

151. Lee, *Irl. 1912-85,* p. 556.

152. O'Byrnes, *Face,* p. 327.

Conclusion

1. Richard Sinnott, 'The electorate', in Penniman (ed.), *Ireland at the Polls 1977,* p. 41.

2. Gallagher, *Political Parties,* p. 58.

3. *ibid.,* p. 61.

4. *ibid.,* p. 64.

5. *ibid.,* p. 65.

6. *ibid.,* p. 66.

7. *ibid.*

Biographical Sketches

1. *Irish Times,* 12 April 1990.

2. *Dáil Eireann: Private Sessions 1921-22*, p. 95.

3. Ulick O'Connor, *Oliver St John Gogarty* (London, 1964), pp. 201-2.

4. Brian Farrell, *Chairman or Chief? The Role of the Taoiseach in Irish Government*, (Dublin, 1971), p. 22.

5. *ibid.,* p. 25.

6. Supplement to *Irish Times*, 21 April 1976.

7. Lee, *op. cit.*, p. 174.

8. Lyons, *Famine*, p. 447.

9. Terence deVere White, *Kevin O'Higgins* (Dublin, 1948), p. 150.

10. Lyons, *op. cit.,* p. 486.

11. *Irish Times*, 19 April 1990.

12. 'Mr. John A. Costello remembers', *Irish Times*, 4-8 September 1967.

13. *Irish Times*, 7 October 1985.

14. Lee, *op. cit.,* pp. 152-3.

15. *ibid.,* pp. 153-4.

16. Lyons, *op. cit.,* p. 498.

17. Nollaig Ó Gadhra, 'Earnán de Blaghd', in *Éire-Ireland,* 11, 3 (1976), p. 98.

18. Most of the foregoing is based on Ó Gadhra, *op. cit.,* pp. 93-105.

19. FitzGerald, *Life,* p. 6.

20. *ibid.,* p. 37.

21. Lyons, *op. cit.,* pp. 476, 606.

22. George O'Brien, 'Patrick Hogan', *Studies,* 25, September 1936.

23. Lee, *op. cit.,* p. 113.

24. Cited in Manning, *Blueshirts*, p. 171.

25. M.G. Valiulis, *Portrait of a Revoluntionary: General Richard Mulcahy* (Cork, 1992), p. 4.

26. *ibid.,* p. 35.

27. *ibid.,* p. 74.

28. *ibid.,* p. 123.

29. Valiulis, *Mulcahy,* chapter VIII *passim.*

30. *ibid.,* p. 216.

31. *ibid.,* p. 234.

32. *ibid.,* p. 235.

33. 'Mr John A. Costello remembers', *Irish Times,* 4-8 Sept. 1967

34. *ibid.*

35. *ibid.*

36. *ibid.*

37. *ibid.*

38. Lyons, *Famine*, p. 562.

39. Fanning, *Independent Ireland*, p. 185.

40. Farrell, *Chairman or Chief?*, p. 53.

41. Vincent Browne (ed.), *The Magill Book of Irish Politics* (Dublin, 1981), pp. 108-9.

42. 'Mr John A. Costello remembers', *op. cit.*

43. O'Leary, *Elections*, p. 74.

44. All of the foregoing is based on a series of articles by Garret FitzGerald in *Irish Times*, 12-14 April 1989, on the occasion of the centenary of the birth of Patrick McGilligan.

45. Cited in Manning, *Blueshirts*, p. 139.

46. Whyte, *Church and State*, pp. 193, 325-6.

47. 'A life with politics in the blood', *Irish Times*, 7 October, 1991.

48. *ibid.*

49. FitzGerald, *Life*, pp. 76, 326.

50. Browne, *op. cit.*, p. 230.

51. *ibid.*

52. Lee, *Irl. 1912-85*, p. 326; FitzGerald, *Life,* p.75.

53. Browne, *op. cit.*

54. FitzGerald, *Life,* pp. 76-7.

55. Lindsay, *Memories*, pp. 9-10.

56. *ibid.,* p.32.

57. *ibid.,* pp. 39-40.

58. *ibid.,* p. 53.

59. *ibid.,* p. 141.

60. *ibid.,* p. 152.

61. *ibid.,* p. 164.

62. *ibid.,* p. 188.

63. Gallagher, *Political Parties*, p. 52.

64. *The Word*, August 1966.

65. *ibid.*

66. Manning, 'The political parties', in Penniman (ed.), *Ireland at the Polls 1977*, p. 89.

67. Browne (ed.), *Magill,* p. 118.
68. Harvey, *Coalition*, p. 40.
69. Manning, 'The political parties', in Penniman (ed.), *Ireland at the Polls 1977,* p. 89.
70. Browne, *op. cit.,* p. 118.
71. *Irish Times*, 7 October, 1991.
72. Harvey, *op. cit.,* p. 40.
73. Lee, *Irl. 1912-85,* pp. 485-6.
74. Harvey, *op. cit.,* p. 41.
75. Lee, *op. cit.,* p. 486.
76. Harvey, *op. cit.,* p. 41.
77. Manning, *op. cit.,* p. 89.
78. Browne, *op. cit.*, p. 118.
79. *ibid.,* p. 188.
80. Cited *ibid.*
81. *ibid.*
82. *ibid.,* p. 266.
83. Lee, *op. cit.*, p. 90.
84. Cited in Michael Farrell (ed.), *The Magill Book of Irish Politics* (Dublin, 1984), p. 74.
85. Browne, *op. cit.,* p. 90.
86. O'Byrnes, *Face*, p. 225.
87. Brian Trench (ed.), *The Magill Book of Irish Politics* (Dublin, 1983), p. 32.
88. O'Byrnes, *op. cit.,* p. 325.
89. Browne, *op. cit.,* p. 194.
90. *ibid.,* p. 255.
91. *ibid.,* p. 242.
92. *ibid.*
93. J.J. Lee, 'Continuity and change in Ireland, 1945-70', in Lee (ed,), *Irl 1945-70,* p. 172.
94. FitzGerald, *Life,* pp. 45-6.
95. Whyte, *Church and State*, P. 334.
96. Tobin, *Decades,* p. 137.
97. Fitzgerald, *op. cit.,* pp 76-7.
98. *ibid.,* pp. 105-6.
99. Browne, *op. cit.,* p. 184.
100. Fitzgerald, *op. cit.,* p.109.
101. *ibid.,* p. 116.
102. *ibid.,* pp. 198-222; 225-243.
103. *ibid.,* p. 243.
104. Browne, *op. cit.,* p. 181.
105. FitzGerald, *op. cit.,* p. 341.

106. FitzGerald, *Life,* p. 357.

107. Browne (ed.), *Magill,* p. 185.

108. FitzGerald, *op. cit.*, p. 361.

109. *Irish Independent,* 9 October 1991.

110. Whyte, *Church and State*, pp. 288, 418.

111. Browne, *op. cit.,* p. 175.

112. *Sunday Tribune,* 17 May 1992.

113. Browne, *op. cit.,* p. 373.

114. FitzGerald, *op. cit.,* pp. 435-6.

115. *ibid.,* pp. 621-2.

116. O'Byrnes, *Face,* p. 70.

117. *ibid.,* p. 106.

118. FitzGerald, *op. cit.,* p. 362.

119. *ibid.,* p. 367.

120. O'Byrnes, *op. cit.,* p. 129.

121. *ibid.,* p. 194.

122. *ibid.,* p. 243.

123. FitzGerald, *op. cit.,* p. 430.

124. *ibid.,* pp. 429-30.

125. *ibid.,* pp. 454, 581, 583, 586.

126. O'Byrnes, *op. cit.,* p. 227.

127. FitzGerald, *op. cit.,* p. 622.

128. *ibid.,* p. 430.

129. FitzGerald, *op. cit.,* p. 362.

130. Lee, *Irl. 1912-85,* p. 507.

131. FitzGerald, *op. cit.,* p. 406.

132. *ibid.,* pp. 430.

133. *ibid.,* pp.323-4.

134. *ibid.,* p. 362.

135. *ibid.,* p. 430.

136. *Sunday Tribune,* 21 July 1985.

137. Lee, *op. cit.,* p. 556.

138. *ibid.*

139. *ibid.*

140. *ibid.,* p. 558.

141. *ibid.*

142. FitzGerald, *op. cit.,* p. 622.

143. *ibid.,* pp. 362, 429.

Afterword

Since the 1920s the capacity of the three original parties - Fine Gael, Fianna Fáil and Labour - to evolve to meet new needs has been striking - as, indeed, has been the failure of political observers to identify and describe this process. Thus Fianna Fáil was initially a radical and at least partly anti-clerical party - a consequence of episcopal denunciations of the anti-Treaty side in the Civil War - and drew much of its support from small farmers and also from some urban workers. By contrast Cumann na nGaedheal was more Church orientated, and by virtue of its support for the Treaty, it drew much of its support from those most concerned for stability and order: larger farmers and the urban middle class.

But the introduction of industrial protection on a large scale by Fianna Fáil after it came to power in 1932 brought it fresh support, both electoral and financial, from the new industrialists who owed their existence to this new policy, and also from workers who secured employment in these new industries. This pushed Fianna Fáil towards the centre. At the same time, unconscious of the counter-productive effects of an anti-clerical image, de Valera set out to woo the institutional Catholic Church. In these ways, and by an astute use of rhetorical nationalism, which in the post-revolutionary period had great attraction for many Irish people, Fianna Fáil secured the high ground, and the middle ground, in Irish politics.

Fianna Fáil had another great advantage: it was a party built up in opposition upon a firm foundation of grass roots support at local level. The Cumann na nGaedheal party, by contrast, had to be established from the top down, by members of a government struggling during and after a Civil War to re-establish order, to reconstruct a physically shattered economy, and to cut public spending from an imperial level to what an independent Irish State could afford from its own resources.

Against this background, it is not surprising that Fianna Fáil emerged as the stronger of the two main parties in the 1930s, while Fine Gael, which had started life as a party of government, experienced prolonged difficulty in adjusting to the role of what, for a period, seemed to be one of almost permanent opposition. As a result, between the early 1930s and the later 1940s it experienced a drop in its support from over one-third to less than one-fifth of the electorate.

In particular, Fine Gael's loyalty to the Treaty prevented it from casting off the invidious and increasingly anachronistic role of being the 'pro-commonwealth' party - until in 1949 it espoused the declaration of the Republic so suddenly as to leave some of its supporters (myself included), disconcerted.

Nevertheless, after 1948, Fine Gael found a new pragmatic role as the leader of several coalitions involving the multiplicity of parties that were a feature of that period; as a result it rapidly recovered the one-third share of the vote that it had secured in the 1930s. It also recognised during the late 1950s the need to attract new ideas and new blood - both through its Research and Information Council which encouraged public debate of political issues and through Alexis Fitzgerald's and Declan Costello's *National Observer* - by far the most intelligent political journal ever published by an Irish Party.

Moreover, in 1956 John A. Costello challenged the conventional economic wisdom imposed by Fianna Fáil, proposing a move towards a more open economy, thus foreshadowing the Whitaker Report *Economic Development*, and Fianna Fáil's economic policy reversal of two years later. And in the 1961 election, the new Fine Gael leader, James Dillon, tackled another Fianna Fáil sacred cow, proposing an end to compulsory Irish - the refusal of Leaving Certificates to students who did not achieve a pass in Irish, which Fianna Fáil had introduced in 1934.

It was in 1964-5 however, that Fine Gael finally established itself as an innovating party with a new and highly relevant role, in tune with the mood of the period. In April 1964, Declan Costello, who for long had been frustrated with the economic and social conservatism of Irish politics, proposed to the party a - by Irish standards - radical social democratic policy, involving a more active process of economic planning on the contemporary French model. When Seán Lemass called an election in spring 1965 a summary of the new policy was published as the Fine Gael manifesto, under the title *Towards a Just Society*.

The conversion of the party to social democratic policies was too sudden to be convincing to the electorate, however, and in that election a small gain in seats by Fianna Fáil from Independents, who had maintained it in power as a minority government during the preceding fours years, enabled it to return to office. James Dillon, having lost two elections, resigned and was replaced as leader by Liam Cosgrave.

Shortly afterwards, Declan Costello withdrew from the Fine Gael front bench, partly for health reasons and partly, perhaps, because he was unconvinced that his colleagues in the leadership were committed emotionally as well as tactically to his new policies. The momentum of change in the party was, nevertheless, maintained. As a new Senator I was able to ensure during the late 1960s a continuing flow of new policy documents under the *Just Society* rubric, covering a wide range of economic and social issues.

A negative factor influencing the 1969 election result was the refusal of Labour, which had increased its votes and seats at each of the previous two elections, to contemplate the formation of a government with Fine Gael after the election. Deluding themselves that the 'Seventies will be Socialist', they took up an isolationist left-wing stance, which received a severe rebuff from the electorate. Fianna Fáil's gains from Labour in this 1969 election, enabled it to secure its first overall majority since 1957.

It was in these circumstances that the three historic Irish parties faced into the Northern Ireland crisis of 1969-70. None of the three was ready for this challenge, but in both Fine Gael and Labour, there were elements prepared to withstand the dangerous wave of extreme nationalism that swept the state, encouraging elements in the Fianna Fáil government of Jack Lynch to arm groups in Northern Ireland which soon emerged as the Provisional IRA.

While the Cumann na nGaedheal government had accepted in 1925 the reality of Northern Ireland within its 1920 boundaries, the party had been disinclined in the 1930s and 1940s to challenge the popular Fianna Fáil irredentist claim to this area, especially after that claim had found its reflection in Articles 2 and 3 of the 1937 Constitution. And when the British Government had reacted to the declaration of the Republic in 1949, by incorporating in its related Ireland Act a guarantee that Northern Ireland would remain part of the United Kingdom until and unless its parliament decided otherwise, Fine Gael had joined with Fianna Fáil and Labour in an anti-partition propaganda campaign that expounded this traditional Fianna Fáil irredentist attitude.

Against this background none of the three parties was initially well equipped to handle the wave of nationalist feeling evoked in this state by the violent events of August 1969. Fine Gael, however, found it easier to adjust positively to the new situation than did Fianna Fáil. Within five weeks of these events it adopted a policy statement that I had drafted, which proposed among other things, establishing a joint Unionist/nationalist government in Northern Ireland - power-sharing as it later came to be known - as well as making reunification conditional on the support of a majority in Northern Ireland. This was a direct rejection of the Fianna Fáil thesis that Northern Ireland had no right to exist and that Britain should hand the area over to the Irish state regardless of the views of a majority of its inhabitants.

Several years were to pass before this reversion to the earlier Cumann na nGaedheal/Fine Gael stance on Northern Ireland secured the emotional as well as intellectual assent of some senior party members, who, over the years had come unconsciously to accept the Fianna Fáil position on the North. But, this move by Fine Gael quickly followed by Labour - which was strongly influenced at that period by Conor Cruise O'Brien - gradually shifted public opinion towards a more constructive attitude to the Northern Ireland problem.

During the 1960s, Fine Gael had been strongly supportive of Irish membership of the European Community which Seán Lemass had espoused in 1961, without evoking much enthusiasm from the more traditional wing of his party. Here again, as in the case of Northern Ireland, Fine Gael had much greater freedom of action than Fianna Fáil, encumbered as it was by its tradition of rhetorical nationalism. Thus in the 1972 referendum on EC membership, Fine Gael in opposition played a quite disproportionate role and the party confirmed its commitment by joining the powerful Christian Democratic Group in the European Parliament - while Fianna Fáil effectively marginalised itself in that assembly by affiliating itself with the isolated French Gaullist Group.

Meanwhile, as part of the process of party renewal, elements within Fine Gael had been developing more liberal policies on a range of domestic issues. This led to quite severe tensions within the parliamentary party in 1971-2, which were partly, however, a reflection of the frustrations of too long a period in opposition. The unexpected electoral victory of 1973, when a Fine Gael gain of four seats put Fianna Fáil into a minority and Labour joined with Fine Gael to form a national coalition, effectively eliminated these tensions within the party.

Under Liam Cosgrave's firm leadership that government introduced a wide range of social reforms and successfully overcame the economic difficulties created for Ireland, as for the rest of the world, by the first oil crisis. By mid-1977 the inflation generated by the sudden quintupling of the price of oil at the end of 1973 had been effectively mastered and a growth rate of 7% has been secured. Despite this remarkable achievement, the national coalition was defeated in June 1977 when Fianna Fáil won an unexpectedly large majority as a result of fatally extravagant promises of tax reductions and ill-timed expansionary policies which within a couple of years created an economic crisis without parallel in the history of the Irish state.

In the face of the disappointing 1977 election result Liam Cosgrave resigned the leadership and I was elected in his place. I set myself two objectives: building on the *Just Society* policies that had been Declan Costello's enduring legacy to the party, to give Fine Gael a leading role in the long overdue liberalisation of Irish society, and at the same time endowing it for the first time with an efficient organisational structure that would match that of Fianna Fáil.

In this latter task, I was aided by the knowledge that before the next election, the size of the Dáil would be substantially increased to reflect the remarkable increase in population that occurred between the censuses of 1971 and 1979. The availability of what turned out to be 18 additional seats made it possible without threatening the seats of existing TDs to impose a new selection process that would ensure a range of new, strong candidates in 1981. In conjunction with a shift in organisational control from the TDs to the party activists, this gave Fine Gael, for the first time in its history, a structure that more than matched the Fianna Fáil machine in the three crucial elections of 1981-2.

This process of party reorganisation achieved much greater political participation by women, (in the 1981 election Fine Gael increased its female parliamentary representation from one to 11), and by younger people, (in the government formed after that election four members of the cabinet as well as the Attorney General were in their mid-30s). Simultaneously the party's political centre of gravity was shifted in a liberal direction, thus reflecting the evolving aspirations of a large part of the population and in particular the younger age groups. This move was also relevant to the development of a pluralist, inclusive sense of identity that could embrace the two Irish traditions - Unionist as well as nationalist.

During the 1980s, a decade of conservatism and reaction worldwide, the party's more liberal stance in domestic policies suffered a setback, most notably in the divorce referendum of 1986. Nevertheless Fine Gael's open, pluralist approach to the Northern Ireland problem secured widespread support, and in 1990 the election of Mary Robinson as President, with the aid of transfers from the Fine Gael candidate, Austin Currie, reflected the extent to which, despite the setback of the 1980s, domestic opinion at a fundamental level had moved in a liberal direction in line with Fine Gael's evolution in the years after 1977.

From the time when in the late 1950s Fine Gael began, somewhat belatedly, to redefine its role in Irish politics, it has thus played the leading role in the readjustment of Irish society to the rapidly changing world of the second half of the 20th century. Starting with the tentative moves in 1956 to reverse the inward looking economic policies of the post-1932 years and with the 1961 challenge to the counter-productive 'compulsory Irish' policy, it moved in the mid-1960s to develop social democracy in Ireland, and from the end of that decade onwards successfully challenged the rhetorical nationalism of Fianna Fáil which in 1970 threatened to plunge the country into chaos. In the 1970s it played the leading role in a dual intellectual reorientation of Irish nationalism towards a pluralist approach to Northern Unionism and a positive and integrationist approach to our involvement in the European Community. And in the late-1970s Fine Gael took the lead in an overdue liberalisation of Irish society and the opening up of politics to women and to young people.

In thus adapting itself to the changing needs of modern Irish society Fine Gael had certain advantages vis-a-vis the two other established Irish parties. As against Labour it had the advantage of not being ideologically committed to a particular political doctrine as well as being free from the links which tied Labour to one of the basically conservative sectoral forces - the trade union movement. And vis-a-vis Fianna Fáil it had the advantage of not being ideologically committed to a narrow and backward-looking rhetorical nationalism. During the past third of a century it made constructive use of these advantages for the benefit of Irish society.

Finally, its commitment throughout its existence to the public interest and its avoidance of too close involvement with particular vested interests, has enabled it to play a crucial role in maintaining high standards in Irish politics where the temptation to take advantage of public office for private advantage at local and national level has not always been successfully resisted by others.

These characteristics of integrity, an inclusive rather than exclusive nationalism, adaptability and openness to change and to the outside world remain as important in Irish life today as at any time in the past. For these reasons Fine Gael continues to have a vital role to play in Irish life.

Garret FitzGerald. October, 1993

Name Index

プロフェッショナル進化論
「個人シンクタンク」の時代が始まる

Hiroshi Tasaka

田坂 広志